3'

Raymond E. Morton

The Chaos of Cults

Books by J. K. van Baalen

THE CHAOS OF CULTS
CHRISTIANITY VERSUS THE CULTS
THE GIST OF THE CULTS
IF THOU SHALT CONFESS
THE COMPENDIUM WITH OUTLINES
WHEN HEARTS GROW FAINT

THE CHAOS OF
CULTS

A STUDY IN PRESENT-DAY ISMS

BY

JAN KAREL VAN BAALEN

Fourth Revised and Enlarged Edition

WM. B. EERDMANS PUBLISHING COMPANY
GRAND RAPIDS, MICHIGAN

THE CHAOS OF CULTS
by J. K. VAN BAALEN, TH.M.

Copyright 1938, 1951, 1956, 1960, 1962 by
Wm. B. Eerdmans Publishing Co.

All rights in this book are reserved. No part may be reproduced in any manner without permission in writing from the publisher, except brief quotations used in connection with a review in a magazine or newspaper.

LIBRARY OF CONGRESS NUMBER LC 56-58880

Set up and printed, 1938

Twenty-second printing, July 1965

(First revised and enlarged edition, July 1951)

(Second revised and enlarged edition, July 1956)

(Third revised and enlarged edition, September 1960)

(Fourth revised and enlarged edition, February 1962)

PRINTED IN THE UNITED STATES OF AMERICA

PREFACE TO THE FOURTH REVISED AND ENLARGED EDITION

In this new edition this book continues to focus upon the major cults. It would not be feasible to give a record of all the minor cults, for many of them center around a personality rather than around ideas and beliefs, and all of them are likely to disappear soon. Thus, among others, *Psychiana* and *I Am Movement* have waxed and waned during the lifetime of the present book. The cult of *Father Divine* has always been too personally centered to merit a place in this book that has, for thirty years now, limited itself to a discussion of cults that promise to stay on the scene for some time.

The writer has been asked repeatedly why Roman Catholicism has not been included as one of the major cults. The answer is that the Roman Catholic Church is a stone with many facets. It is a corrupt and exceedingly dangerous political machine, and it is a religious body full of doctrinal error and superstition.

But it is also a church that stands upon the solid foundation of the Apostles' Creed. It holds and defends such cardinal Christian doctrines as that of the Trinity, the Deity of our Lord, His resurrection, His second coming to judge the world, and the atonement by His substitutionary blood. Some of the outstanding apologetic work in our day is done by Roman Catholic scholars. Such a body does not come under the heading of unchristian cults as described in the present volume.

However, to the question whether it is not time to eliminate Theosophy as a moribund cult, the reply is, No, for recent literature and announcements by Theosophists of Sunday worship and public reading rooms would indicate that this cult still lives on.

PREFACE

The changes in this fourth edition of the book are chiefly the following:

(1) A simplified and more up-to-date chapter has been substituted on *The Jehovah's Witnesses*.

(2) The chapter on *Faith Healing* which appeared in the third edition has been eliminated since this brief discussion proved unsatisfactory and extended discussion is precluded by the nature of the present volume.

Today we are facing a remarkable and somewhat contradictory situation. On the one hand, there is a vast increase in the study and disapproval of the anti-Christian cults. On the other hand, there is simultaneously an increase in tolerance toward them. For example, Mormonism, Christian Science, Unity, and similar non-Christian cults are allowed to list their services and hours of worship on the same bulletin boards at the entrance of cities and towns, and in hotel lobbies, with evangelical churches whose every tenet these cults not merely deny but combat. The writer believes that it would be well to stop this practice.

Grateful to publishers and public alike, the author invokes the divine blessing upon this renewed attempt to acquaint God's people with the devious and multiform devices of Satan to tear down the Church of Christ in the Saviour's own Name.

Lynden Washington J. K. VAN BAALEN

CONTENTS

PREFACE TO THE THIRD REVISED AND
    ENLARGED EDITION   5

1. THE ISSUE DEFINED   11
2. ASTROLOGY   18
3. SPIRITISM   31
4. THEOSOPHY (AND THE LIBERAL CATHOLIC CHURCH)   62
5. CHRISTIAN SCIENCE   85
6. ROSICRUCIANISM   104
7. THE UNITY SCHOOL OF CHRISTIANITY   128
8. BAHA'ISM   146
9. DESTINY OF AMERICA (ANGLO-ISRAELISM)   162
10. SWEDENBORGIANISM   177
11. MORMONISM   188
12. SEVENTH-DAY ADVENTISM   228
13. JEHOVAH'S WITNESSES   257
14. MORAL RE-ARMAMENT   277
15. UNITARIANISM — MODERNISM   292
16. THE BOOK AND THE FAITH   348
17. APPROACHING ADHERENTS OF THE CULTS   359
18. THE CHRISTIAN RELIGION   379
19. THE UNPAID BILLS OF THE CHURCH   390

BIBLIOGRAPHY   401

The Chaos of Cults

1

THE ISSUE DEFINED

In a recent study of "Bavinck as a Dogmatician" the noted Dutch scholar Dr. G. C. Berkouwer remarks that Bavinck's great work on Dogmatics (1918) is by no means antiquated, and that not only because the truth according to Scripture remains unaltered, but even more so because Bavinck's *magnum opus* contains much that is of an apologetic and polemic nature. And, says Berkouwer, in reading Bavinck one is again and again impressed with the fact that many of the problems that engaged the mind of the great Dutch theologian have returned in our own day with but slight variations. Thus the demythologizing of which Bultmann now speaks in Germany differs but very little from the antipathy of the older "higher critics" to miracles in the Bible.

This also holds for the cults. There is little that is new under the sun. Or, how could there be when Spiritists boldly claim their religion to be the oldest and most fundamental of human cults, when Theosophists call their system now Esoteric Buddhism and at another time Esoteric Christianity?

There is, however, at once an amount of progress and of historical development. And that calls for new and revised editions. The founders of the more popular cults are by no means all finished scholars; too often they are bunglers who stumble upon an idea, and afterward bolster it with pickings from many fields.

In the case of some religious systems later changes are mostly a slightly different emphasis. Such is the case with

Modernism, which now lays more stress upon sin, but loathes the Scriptural doctrine of justification by faith as much as ever. Here, therefore, a few citations from more modern works should suffice to show that "liberal theology" has altered but little in its opposition to the Biblical doctrine of an alien and forensic righteousness imputed to man. What is new in a chapter like that will therefore be found in the second part, which gives quotations from various authors.

Quite to the contrary the change from the old Buchmanism to the new MRA has been so great that the chapter had to be largely rewritten, although much of the material on the early history has been retained.

I have deemed it necessary to add but one more cult — where is the end? — namely, Swedenborgianism, perhaps because in Edmonton, Alberta, where I lived from 1950 to 1955, much house-to-house canvassing was done during my stay.

More and more I have come to the conclusion that we can learn from cultists, not only noting what not to believe, but also bearing in mind that "the cults are the unpaid bills of the church."

In general it may be stated that the cults are gradually dropping some of the old belligerency: even Jehovah's Witnesses are more sparing of vehement invectives. Having obtained a hearing and a following, they no longer go about carrying a chip on their shoulder. George Channing, CSB, writes, "The Christian Scientist does not feel superior to the adherents of any denomination. Every man is free to demonstrate the efficacy of his own faith; each is entitled to encouragement in his pursuit of spiritual objectives. Mrs. Eddy said: 'A genuine Christian Scientist loves Protestant and Catholic, D. D. and M. D. . . . loves God, good; and he loves his enemies.' "[1]

---

1. "What Is a Christian Scientist?" in *Guide to the Religions of America*.

THE ISSUE DEFINED

The newer spirit of ecumenicity, world-wide unity, finds an eloquent expression in such books as *Radhakrishnan. Comparative Studies in Philosophy*, Presented in Honour of His Sixtieth Birthday (Harper and Brothers, 1950). Here a group of twenty scholars from Asia, England, and America openly suggest a philosophical synthesis of East and West which will, in its own way, contribute to the growth of a world community. To these men religion is not a creed or a code, but "an insight into reality." If only the West will give up its age-old prejudice against reincarnation, it would be discovered that East and West are not so far apart.

And Professor Toynbee states that the Western world must produce a new religion, a universal cult, and it must be made up of Christianity, Buddhism, Hinduism, and Islam. A contributor to the Letterbox of the *Edmonton Journal* (Jan. 25, 1955) wrote: "Christianity expresses belief in one God, in life everlasting for each individual soul, and in the status of women as 'persons.' By contrast, Hinduism expresses belief in many gods; Buddhism in the eventual absorption of one's soul into Nirvana; and Islam holds for the predominance of the male sex, among other things. Yet with terrifying calm the Professor announces that there must be a synthesis of these religions which have divergent fundamental beliefs. Truly, his universal religion would belong to a composite order of architecture, a nightmare edifice looking like a combination of the Mosque of St. Sophia, Bombay Temple, and Rheims Cathedral, with probably a gigantic image of Buddha dominating the interior."

This is of a piece with the words of the late Dean Inge, who wrote of Buddhism and Christianity: "There is a cardinal affinity between the two religions in their attitude toward their divinized founders. There are differences due to the historical circumstances in which the two religions have grown up, and of the different demands of the peoples they were intended to lead; but the religious foundation of both is the same."

14   THE CHAOS OF CULTS

But in the words of John A. Mackay, President of Princeton Theological Seminary: "In the interest of world-loyalty mutuality should be promoted between East and West, each sharing with the other its ideals. But how utterly unreal is such a proposal at a moment in history when the traditional ideals of both East and West are passing away, and when a tremendous force, that of Marxist Communism, proclaims around the world that what matters is not the mutuality of ideals but the common recognition of realities."[2]

The Bible-believing Christian may easily detect that to which all this is bound to lead. The true Christians will be hated of all men for their aloofness, their refusal to recognize others as equally good; they will be accused of holding back unity and progress, world-peace, and similar desirable goods. Probably it will all end in renewed persecution. Already the unbalanced genius of Hitler has accused Christianity of standing in the way of the *Pax Germana* that was to bless the world through the race with the *Weltgeist*.

Paganism or Christianity?

There is a sufficient number of books on the market today that cater to this conciliatory spirit. Among these Braden's *These Also Believe* and Bach's *They Have Found a Faith* and *Faith and My Friends* occupy a prominent place. According to such books faith is of value because of its psychological effect rather than through its object. Writes Chester E. Tulga: "A world-religion is on the way, but it will be religious rather than Christian: it will be human rather than divine, it will be natural rather than supernatural. Its God will be its servant not its sovereign, its Christ will be its leader not its king, its political economy will be a democracy not a theocracy: its saints will be its socialists not its seers, its goal will be a human utopia not the Kingdom of the coming King. The coming world-

---

2. *God's Order*. The Ephesian Letter and This Present Time (New York: Macmillan, 1953), page 46. One of the truly great books of the decade.

religion is envisioned by liberals as the harbinger of the 'Kingdom' but by the biblical writers as the forerunner of the anti-Christ (II Thess. 2:3-12)" (*The Case Against Modernism*, 1950, p. 58). With this agree, from the opposite camp, such items as one reads from time to time, for example, a January 5, 1951, AP report, quoting Abdel Rahman Azzam Pasha, secretary-general of the Arab League, saying that "a spiritual alliance of the Moslem and Christian world would group more than one half of the men of the earth together against a common enemy." "The two religions," said the Arab leader in Rome, "are founded upon an exquisite high spirituality and are menaced by the same enemy, atheistic materialism."

Besides these we have the books that, like Frank S. Mead's *Handbook of Denominations in the United States*, 1951, write "with malice toward none, but in justice to all," yet do not only describe all cults as "churches," but dedicate their writings to "Those in the Church who see that the great truths we hold on common ground are of more importance to God and man than the little fences and barriers which divide us."

Among these must now also be numbered President Eisenhower's favorite Elton Trueblood, whose final chapter, "The Ground of Hope" in *Declaration of Freedom*, 1955, ends with these words, "This faith is so strengthening that it ought to be uniting. The chasm between a merely secular conception of the world and any conception in which the Personal Basis of the moral order is recognized is so great and so crucial that those who believe in the latter are foolish to let their particular differences divide them. Moslems and Christians and Jews and many more need to know that they have the greatest things in common. The question of the particular banner is secondary."

Over against all such lowering of the Christian standard the present volume maintains with H. Bavinck and B. B. Warfield that there are but two religions in the world. The one is autosoterism, that salvation is from man. The other ascribes the entire work of salvation from the world's ills to God. Christianity is the name of the latter. It matters not under what flag the former sails: it stands in opposition to the Christian, that is, the true religion.

Even the most cursory examination of the ethnic religions should convince one of this truth. The ancient Egyptians taught, "Prepare for the judgments of Osiris by observing the rules of right conduct." The Norsemen dictated, "Fight a good fight." Confucious prescribed, "Walk in the trodden paths; be a good citizen of the celestial empire." While in India the Buddha advised, "Walk the Noble Eightfold Path." Islam enjoins, "Stand by the Five Pillars of Conduct." All these religions instruct men to work out their own salvation.

Nor is this all. The ethnic religions not only teach men to save themselves; they also promise a salvation which is quite naturalistic in its concept. It is the life of this earth lived again, minus its disappointing features. To the Mohammedan, it means "places of innumerable sensuous joys — shadowy groves, fountains, fruits hanging low so as to be easily gathered, and wives *ad libidum*." To the old Norse king, heaven means, "Quickly, quickly, seated in the splendid habitation of the gods I shall be drinking beer out of a curved horn." Buddha not only said with dying lips, "Henceforth be ye to yourselves your own light, your own refuge, seek no other refuge. Look not to any one but yourselves as a refuge," but the salvation thus to be obtained by human effort is that "night of hopelessness," "to break through the prison walls, not of life only, but of being."

Even Zoroastrianism, the highest of the non-Christian religions except Judaism in its unadulterated form (and that was rare), taught that there is no saviour. Man must suffer the penalty of whatsoever evil he has done. The only saviour, so it asserted, is a virtuous life.

Aim of this Book

1. A study of cults will convince evangelical Christians of the necessity of studying more carefully *the faith which*

was once for all delivered unto the saints. Mormons, Jehovah's Witnesses, and Seventh-Day Adventists have their "prooftexts" at their finger tips, often carrying Bibles with passages marked in red and blue. Adherents of the sound doctrine, on the contrary, quite frequently are unable to match these texts with convincing and final arguments from Scripture.

2. In proportion as we study false creeds, we shall learn to appreciate the doctrine that is unto godliness.

3. As we mark the fundamental difference between autosoterism and the "Just as I am, without one plea" note of all true Christianity, we shall learn to think less severely of the many subordinate, and racial and national tenets that too often keep Christ's disciples apart. There still is too much of the spirit of "We forbade him because he followeth not with us" (Luke 9:49).

4. At the same time, a study of the cults may well humble us because most of them are the result of an insufficient emphasis by Christians upon some valuable point of Biblical teaching: the boast that we preach "the full counsel of God" is all too often vain, untrue, and the fruit of a narrowed view which is due to a refusal to look beyond one's own small group. The true Biblical doctrine would envisage not only doctrine but also ethics, economics, and sociology as much as a personal code of conduct, art in music, sobriety in public prayer, and beauty in church architecture. Few, if any, are capable of such all-embracing views.

Questions

1. Why is the study of cults useful?

2. What is the cardinal difference between Christianity and non-Christian religions?

3. Is certainty in religion obtainable? Where and how may it be found?

2

ASTROLOGY

Many years ago one of my neighbors one day rebuked my youthful conceit which had laughed at the zodiac on his wall, with the remark, "Why, Elder, the stars are the messengers of God!" He also drew my horoscope and regaled me with a character description that bade fair to rival the performance of today's psychologists. Some time later when my literary work was indeed progressing quite nicely, he stopped me in the street with the observation, "Well, Elder, your work ought to be coming along in pretty good shape these days, the conjunction of the planets is all in your favor."

I lost interest in astrology for many years afterward, but now, with the vast increase in its impact upon society, a brief discussion of the subject may well head the growing list of cults dealt with on the following pages.

Through the Ages

Astrology vies with Spiritism for the honor of being the most ancient cult. Perhaps it was first practiced by the Chaldeans in Babylon where, after being held in high esteem, it was at last despised as mere trickery.

From the Medo-Persian empire it traveled to Greece, under the influence of the efforts of Alexander the Great to amalgamate the East and the West; and here, in Greece, it is said to have been first developed into a science by Ptolemy. Some astrologers are of the opinion that the entire Greek-Roman mythology was based upon astrology.

Influenced by the native idolatry of Palestine and Syria, in turn affected by Babylon and Persia, and later by the Greco-Roman civilization, Israel at various times harbored convinced devotees of astrology, although the Old Testament frowned upon it. Judaea, it must be remembered, was at one time a Persian and a Roman province.

In ancient China astrology was in vogue prior to 2154 B.C., when the astrologers Hi and Ho were deposed for their failure to predict a sun eclipse. Among the Hindus, the classical writers on astrology were Garga, Parashara, and Mihina. They had legions of commentators.

In India astrology always has had and still has a strangle hold upon all of life. "The astrologer is perhaps the most important functionary in the social and religious life of the people. No marriage can be performed unless the horoscope of the bride and bridegroom harmonize. No social or domestic event of importance, and especially no religious ceremony of any consequence, can be carried on save during what are called auspicious days and moments. . . . Astrology is the right hand of Hinduism, and it has supreme authority in the direction of most of its affairs."[1]

In the middle ages astrology was much practiced in Mohammedan lands. Perhaps because astrology and astronomy were originally closely interwoven, and even identified, there has been a difference of opinion even among Christians as to its value. Thus we are told that Melanchthon taught astrology at the University of Wittenberg, for which he appealed to Genesis 1:14 and Jeremiah 10:2, and that Calvin wrote against it (*"Contre l'Astrologie"*).

The great Kepler, 1571-1630, strongly believed in it, and so did Dryden, Archbishop Usher, Dr. John Butler, and many others.

Present-Day Popularity

Today astrologers are increasingly consulted. Paperbound magazines containing horoscopes and astrological

---

1. John A. Jones, *India, Its Life and Thought*, pp. 217, 299.

advice, cozily nestled between Western stories and murder mysteries, are to be found on many newsstands. It is confidently asserted that scores of hardheaded businessmen and women would not dare to engage in any important enterprise without first consulting the stars (more accurately the planets), just as of old the German matrons warned Ariovistus that he could not win a war with Caesar if he engaged in it before the new moon.

Among the most noted advocates, priests, and priestesses of this revived interest in America are listed Evangeline Adams; Myrna Kingsley, "whose New York office is lined with photographs of stage people and café socialites she has advised"; "Hollywood's favorite astrologer Blanca Holmes, who operates from a home as lush as a movie setting"; Keye Lloyd of Chicago, President of the American Federation of Astrologers, "whose organization has about five hundred members, a code of ethics, and nothing but contempt for astrological 'charlatans' "; ex-follies dancer Nella Webb, who "has read horoscopes during tea hour at New York's Waldorf-Astoria hotel"; and last but not least, Lester Belt, "a Glendale, California, barber to whom astrology and dogs have been a dual lifetime hobby — he has prepared individual horoscopes for such famous dogs as Lassie and Fala and has written a generalized pamphlet of advice called *Your Dog's Astrological Horoscope.*"[2]

Its devotees have been currently estimated to number five million in the U.S.A., and Charles S. Braden says it is "probably the major divination technique in current use in the Western world."

The question therefore arises whether astrology is a science and a legitimate pastime, or a religious cult and a superstition.[3]

---

2. *Life* Magazine.
3. All dictionaries give a definition of the word "superstition" that stresses both its quasi-religious and irrational elements.

The "Science" That Is Astrology

"The man who holds to the principia of Newton," wrote Sepharial, "regarding the solidarity of the solar system, the interaction of the planetary bodies and their consequent electrostatic effects upon the Earth, cannot, while subject to the air he breathes, deny the foundation principles of astrology."

In order to understand even a little of this "science" and its principles, one must first master the meaning of certain of its leading terms.

"The *Zodiac* is an imaginary belt of the Heavens through which the sun and planets move in the apparent revolutions round the Earth."

The *Ecliptic* is a circle transecting this belt at an angle of 23° 27′ to the plane of the Equator. The points where it cuts the equator are called the *Equinoxes*.

The Ecliptic is divided into twelve equal sections, counting from the Vernal Equinox. These are called the *Signs of the Zodiac*. Each sign occupies 30° of the circle. A person is said to be "under" a sign, i.e., under its influence, when the sign is rising in the east at the moment of his birth.

Moreover, each sign has a *Ruler*, that is, a planet which has the strongest influence upon the section of the Zodiac. Thus the planet Saturn is said to govern Aquarius and Capricornus; Jupiter governs Pisces and Sagittarius; Mars governs Taurus and Libra; Mercury is ruler of Gemini and Virgo; the Moon, of Cancer; and the Sun governs Leo.

"Astronomical *aspects* are certain angular distances measured on the Ecliptic and they form a fundamental part of astrological science. Any planet may be good or bad in its effects on the character and destiny, according to the aspect that it throws to the chief points of the *Horoscope*. These aspects are: The *semisquare* aspect of 45°, the *sextile* of 60°, the *square* of 90°, the *trine* of 120°, the *sesquiquadrate* of 135°, and the *opposition* of 180°."[4] The

---

4. *Sepharial's Astrology.*

good aspects are the trine and sextile, the evil being the semisquare, square, sesquiquadrate, and opposition.

There is also the *conjunction,* when bodies are in the same degree or part of a sign. Planets in conjunction act according to their simple natures, but when in aspect, according to the nature of the aspect.

Then we have the term *Houses.* The imaginary circle which passes immediately over your head as you face south, is called the *Prime Vertical.* This is divided for astrological purposes into twelve equal divisions called *Houses,* six of which are above the horizon and six below it.

Finally, we have the term *horoscope* (from Greek *hora,* hour, and *skopos,* watcher). A horoscope is a chart of the position of the planets with relation to one another at a given time, especially at the time of a person's birth, regarded as determining, or at least apt to influence, his destiny.

To cast a horoscope is to draw such a chart so as to calculate the influence of the stars and planets on a person's life.[5]

The instructions given in books on astrology whereby the beginner may draw his own horoscope are — or so this writer has found them — mystifying and difficult to understand. Warnings are repeated that it takes many years of diligent study of trigonometry and kindred sciences to enable one to draw and read horoscopes accurately, and therefore it is small wonder that the average American prefers to buy one of the numerous magazines that, without further ado, warn against or encourage various activities for months ahead.

---

5. The Oxford Dictionary defines the casting of a horoscope as the calculation of "the degree of the ecliptic which is on the eastern horizon at a given moment, e.g., at the birth of a child, and thence to erect an astrological figure of the heavens, so as to discover the influence of planets upon his life and fortunes."

Astrological Claims

The claims of astrologers are truly astounding. One reads about planets whose nature is evil, and of others whose fundamental influence is salutary. But as each planet is given two Houses which modify its influence while it is in them, the bad influence of a bad planet may, under certain astronomical conditions, be neutralized or lessened.

One wonders whether this evil influence (*Uranus* is said to cause death by sudden catastrophies, *Neptune* by assassination, *Saturn* by blows and falls, *Mars* by cuts, burns, loss of blood) is founded upon facts when one remembers that God made all things good, the planets included.

One reads further that the "benefic" planets, Jupiter, Venus, Sun, and Moon "produce good effects when in good disposition with another planet or in a congenial sign"; but that even these good planets are "uniformly evil" when "in square aspect!"

The matter becomes more bewildering when one reads about the influence that certain conditions among the planets are said to be exerting. Thus, to a person's birth under a given sign of the zodiac is attributed his height, the shape of his face, nose, mouth, the color of his hair, etc. "When the fourth House contains benefic planets, there will be peace and comfort in old age, or in the end of life whensoever it may be determined.

From all these interactions of planets and stars astrologists claim the ability to predict how human characters will develop, when certain events are likely to occur, what human reactions are apt to follow, etc.

With such occult knowledge at their disposal, they do not hesitate to offer council as to the advisability of marriage with given individuals. "Let those who are unhappily mated compare their horoscopes, and they will find the signs of discord to which reference has been made above."

"Jupiter in good aspect to the Moon from the eleventh House will show gain by friends, advisers, and co-operative measures, because the eleventh House would show gain by the marriage partner if in good aspect to the Moon, or loss thereby if in evil aspect."[6]

There is almost nothing concerning which astrologers are not able to impart helpful advice. Journeys by land or sea, danger of drowning, are indicated by the position of the planets.

Certain persons are to be avoided as likely to bring mischief into life because the Sun is in the same longitude as their malefic planets. On the other hand, by finding the places of the benefic planets and also the place of the Moon, and their corresponding solar dates, one may find the birth dates of those persons whose friendship should be cultivated and with whom one should associate for mutual benefit.

Astrologers claim the ability to predict from the place of the planets in the various Houses not only that the end of a given person is near, but also whether death will come peacefully and in congenial surroundings or not. Even the cause of death may be predicted.

Periods of good or bad fortune are determined by relating the rising, setting, and meridian passage of the planets after birth. Thus the planets are brought to their places or aspects in the Radix, or horoscope of birth. This admittedly intricate method is said to have been discovered by Ptolemy and confirmed by Kepler.

Besides all this, there are "the effects of the transit," i.e., of the planets over the places of the *Significator* (the planet that rules the House) at birth. Thus Sun or Moon eclipses are said to affect health seriously when they fall upon the place of any Significator in the horoscope of birth.

Finally, each division or House carries its own significance for the human body. The first House governs the personal appearance, but chiefly the face and head; the

6. *Sepharial's Astrology.*

second House rules over neck and throat as well as over finance, movable goods, and commerce; the third House not only governs short journeys, letters, and other means of communication, but also, in the body, the arms and legs. And so down to the twelfth House, which rules ambushes, restraints, privations and, in the body, ankles and feet.

Astrology and Scripture

Specific references to astrology are comparatively few in Scripture because the matter falls under the general head of divination, which is forbidden throughout as a form of idolatry.[7]

Reference to astrology may, however, be found in Amos 5:21-26 and Acts 7:41-45. In Amos, Chiun (A.V., and Rephan meaning Saturn), or Moloch, the idol of the Ammonites and Phoenicians, was intimately connected with both the solar bull and the planet Saturn.

II Kings 23:5 contains a reference to the Zodiac. Isaiah 47:13 denounces the astrologers as "stargazers and monthly prognosticators."

The word Magi occurs but once in the Old Testament, namely in Jeremiah 39:8, 13 (Rab-mag) and twice in the New Testament, where the Magi came to Bethlehem (Matt. 2:1, 7, 16), and the name of Elymas is translated "Magus" (Acts 13:6, 8).

In Isaiah 14:12, Lucifer, i.e., light-bearer, or "the shining one," refers to Venus, and hence metaphorically to the king of Babylon. Nebuchadnezzar's magicians were presumably astrologers as were the Egyptian magicians before them.

Josiah removed the astrologers as part of his reformatory work (II Kings 23:5). Besides these, there are references in Scripture to those that "divide the heavens" and to "stargazers."

---

[7]. On the various forms of divination, consult a Bible dictionary, or M. F. Unger's excellent book, *Biblical Demonology*.

The Magi in Matthew 2

Numerous articles and essays have been written on the wise men or Magi who came from the East to find and worship the newborn Messiah. The problem from a Christian standpoint is, of course, how God could approve of their being astrologers, or at the least overlook that fact, when Scripture otherwise assumes a negative attitude toward astrology. When the matter is summed up, we have next to nothing to go by. It is, however, universally admitted that these wise men were astrologers.

As to their origin, opinions have varied greatly. Persia, Parthia, Babylon, and even Egypt have been suggested as the land from which they came. Tertullian suggested Arabia, for which he appealed to Psalm 72:10, 15 and Isaiah 60:6.

Thus we are left in the dark as to whether they were priests of Zoroastrianism, and consequently monotheists, or Babylonians, or not a race at all but a priestly caste inclined toward magic.

Again, whether the word "Magi" in Matthew 2 is used in the original favorable sense which the word had in antiquity, or in its later unfavorable sense, we cannot determine.

Whether the wise men's anticipation of the imminent birth of a Jewish king traces back to the prophecy of Balaam (Num. 24:17), or whether it derives from the Messianic expectation current in Israel at the time, we cannot say.

Regarding the nature of the sidereal phenomenon that prompted the wise men to travel to Palestine, and regarding the disappearing and reappearing star, numerous theories have been suggested, but all are hypothethical. How a "star" could stand over a house is a mystery.[8]

Perhaps we shall do best to conclude with Bendecke in Hastings' *Dictionary of the Bible*: "We must suppose that

---

8. But cf. "Star of the Magi" in the *International Standard Bible Encyclopedia*.

ASTROLOGY 27

the Magi, to whatever nationality they themselves belonged, derived their inference that a king of the Jews was born, from Jewish sources. The coming of Messiah seems certainly to have been expected among the Jews at this time (Luke 2:25); and though the widespread feeling in the East that a Jewish Messiah would conquer the world is only attested for a later period (Edersheim, *The Life and Times of Jesus the Messiah*, I, 203), Jewish authorities, if consulted on the appearance of an exceptional astronomical phenomenon, might well have explained it of Messiah."

The same author adds, "The newly-born king of the Jews receives homage from Eastern sages; their views (beyond the reference to the star, which does not imply any opinion on astrology in general) are not touched upon, and therefore neither praised nor blamed."

To this statement may be added this word from Smith's *Dictionary of the Bible*: The Magi of Matthew 2 seem to have been "at once astronomers and astrologers, but not mingling any conscious fraud with their efforts after a higher knowledge."

Perhaps we may here quote Peter's conclusion in Acts 10:35, "In every nation he that feareth him, and worketh righteousness, is acceptable to him," of which Dr. Charles R. Erdman wrote: "His opening sentence has been strangely misunderstood. Peter did not mean that Cornelius was already saved and that in all nations men like Cornelius are saved with no knowledge of Christ, but that through Christ men of all nations can be saved even though they are not Jews. Peter had learned that men like Cornelius were acceptable to God in the sense that they could be saved when the gospel was presented; Peter had yet to learn that a depraved Gentile could likewise be saved, and not merely the pious, godly, and devout." In other words, those who live in accordance with the light of nature at their disposal are not "given up to a reprobate mind" (Romans 1), but are apt to receive greater light.

Thus we conclude with the theme and division of a sermon by the late Dr. K. Schilder of Kampen, "The Wise Men and the Word of God." "The wise men were, first, drawn by the word of God in nature; second, led on by the word of God in Scripture; third, caused to worship the Word of God Incarnate."

Conclusion

1. The popular magazines that give advice for months ahead, regardless of individual dates and localities of birth, are worthless even from the standpoint of serious astrology. Fundamental to the latter is the conviction that we are permanently "charged" according to the sign under which we were individually born.

2. Astrology is of a quasi-religious, pagan, idolatrous origin. The Babylonians divided the Zodiac into three sections, which were controlled by their three chief gods. What happened on earth was a counterpart of that which occurred in heaven.

The Greeks knew of a larger number of planets and placed these under the controlling power of their idols, Neptune, Venus, Mars, etc. Each of these gods was supposed to manipulate his planet to further his own interests.

3. Maunder quotes "one of the chief living astrologers" as follows: "The true astrologer believes that the Sun is the body of the Logos of his solar system. 'In Him we live and move and have our being.' The planets are his angels, being modifications in the consciousness of the Logos" (*Knowledge*, XXIII, 228).

The American writer of a textbook on astrology openly confessed that he went to the roof of his house every noon to worship the sun.

4. It deserves mention that the covers of today's paperbound books on astrology advertise simultaneously books on palmistry and other superstitions, and quote such Scripture texts as, "He that prophesieth speaketh unto men to edification, and exhortation, and comfort" (I Cor. 14:3).

5. The division into twelve Houses is, as Rogers has remarked, "entirely arbitrary."

6. Since a "prophecy" can only turn out to be either correct or false, there is, of course, always a fifty-percent chance that the guesses of astrologers may turn out in their favor.

7. Twins, born under the identical planetary conditions, often turn out as two entirely different personalities.

8. Carroll Richter's *Astrology and You* may head each one of its six parts with the quotation, "The stars impel, they do not compel! What you make of your life is largely up to you!" But this does not do away with the fact that reliance upon the findings of astrology makes man dependent upon a *fate* rather than upon God. Obedience to the guiding influence of the Holy Spirit is replaced by abject submission to mute forces in nature.

"Find out," cries the front cover of Richter's book, "how to be more successful and enjoy greater happiness! Discover what the stars hold for you! Discover how the stars affect your future!" A child comes by his bad temper, not by sun, moon, and planets, but clearly by way of inheritance and example; and Christianity points him to the renewing power and sanctifying grace of the Holy Spirit.

Not the stars, but God is our ruler and guide. "God is faithful, who will not suffer you to be tempted above that ye are able; but will with the temptation make also the way of escape, that ye may be able to endure it" (I Cor. 10:13). These words were written to put us into living contact with our Lord Jesus Christ. Significantly, they are followed by the warning, "Wherefore, my beloved, flee from idolatry" (I Cor. 10:14). Astrology is idolatry.

9. The return of the East upon the West, illustrated by such books as Radhakrishnan's *Comparative Studies in Philosophy* and by the growth of astrology, spiritism, theosophy, and similar cults, is made possible by the apostasy of large sections of a onetime nominally Christian Western world. "For my people have committed two evils:

they have forsaken me, the fountain of living waters, and hewed them out cisterns, broken cisterns, that can hold no water" (Jer. 2:17).

For Discussion

1. Do you think all people who buy astrological magazines are aware of the fact that they are dealing with the results of divination? How would you approach those who consult these alleged helps to right behavior?

2. Do you think astrology is a science, a cult, a superstition, or a return to paganism?

3. Does the Christian need sources other than the Bible to tell him about the future?

4. Does reliance upon astrology take the place of faith in divine providential guidance?

3

SPIRITISM

The word "Spiritism" deserves preference over the more popular "Spiritualism," first, because it emphasizes the admitted fact that this system claims to deal with spirits, and also because it is rather difficult to see where its alleged spirituality enters.

Historical

The beginnings of Spiritism are lost in antiquity. We are probably dealing with the oldest religious delusion in existence. It results, first, from the desire to obtain information concerning the life beyond. Will the next life be as full of sorrow as the present is? Shall we be happy? Are we to have bodies? Next, Spiritism is the fruit of the wish to be still in touch with departed loved ones.

This will explain why this cult is the first one to be taken up. One could hardly look for Christian Science or modern Theosophy among the ancients, although these cults may have absorbed and assimilated ideas which also prevailed among the ancients. But we do find traces of Spiritism among ancient Chinese, Hindus, Babylonians, and Egyptians; Spiritism can be traced through the Roman Empire and the Europe of medieval times. Of the present-day religious delusions it is therefore the only one which existed in Biblical times, and the Scriptures are anything but silent on it.

There have, of course, been periodic revivals of Spiritism. The last three revivals are those caused by the Fox sisters and by the bereavements resulting from the two world wars.

In its modern form, Spiritism goes back to two American girls. Mr. John D. Fox, his wife and six children in December, 1847, entered a house in the village of Hydeville, N. Y. The two youngest children, Margaret and Kate, respectively twelve and nine years old, soon afterward heard knockings in different parts of the house, which at first were accounted for as coming from rats and mice. However, when bedclothes were pulled off the bed by invisible hands, chairs and tables removed from their places, and a cold hand was felt on the youngest daughter's face, and when no effort to explain these phenomena in a natural manner succeeded, Kate hit upon the idea of getting in touch with "Old Splitfoot." Snapping her fingers, she said, "Here, old splitfoot, do as I do." Instantly the knocking responded. As this was repeated several times, it was concluded that something supernatural was at work. The two girls devised a means of intelligent communication with the author of the noises, who would reply to questions by a number of raps. He revealed himself as Charles Rosma, a married man and a peddler, who, at the age of thirty-one had been murdered by one John Bell, a blacksmith and former tenant of the Fox home. The body was said to lie ten feet under ground in the cellar; the murderer had remained unpunished. Portions of a human skeleton were actually found in the cellar.

From this widely advertised event spiritistic séances spread all over the United States. In England, "table-turning" was already popular among the social elite. Hence the American mediums found a fertile soil there also, when in 1852 the "spirits" announced to American devotees that they were going to invade England, and would be "very religious and very scientific" over there. Other European lands also were successfully visited by American Spiritists.

From 1850 to 1872, according to an official report, local organizations sprang up throughout the U. S., but no attempt was made to organize a national association until 1863. In 1863 the *National Spiritualist Association of the*

U. S. of A., was organized as now constituted. Its members were officially reported as 126,000, its churches 682, and its ministers as 600 for the year 1923. The 1945 Yearbook of American Churches gives a total of 228,000 "spiritualists" in the U. S. scattered over four organizations. The *British Spiritualists Union's* 18,000 members meet in 500 "churches" — usually hired rooms, garages, or private drawing rooms, but sometimes in rooms equipped with pews, harmonium, and lectern.[1]

The Claims of Spiritists

Spiritists teach the following *doctrines*:

They emphasize right living here on earth, believing that their condition in the spirit world depends entirely upon what they do while in mortal form. "They believe in Infinite Intelligence, and that the phenomena of nature, physical and spiritual, are the expressions of Infinite Intelligence; that the existence and personal identity of the individual continue after the change called 'death,' and that communication with the so-called 'dead' is a fact scientifically proven by the phenomena of Spiritualism." They believe in the "Golden Rule" and that man makes his own happiness or unhappiness as he obeys or disobeys "Nature's psychic laws." The doorway to reformation is never closed against any human soul, here or hereafter.

The spirit world is said to be the counterpart of the visible world, only more beautiful and perfect. Those who enter it must be free from the impress of evil wrought while in the body. There is final restoration to happiness for all souls. But they who have lived on earth contrary to the laws of Intelligence will suffer in the hereafter the punishment of desiring to continue their evil course without the ability to do so. This will lead to remorse, and remorse to purification. Some Spiritists hold that life in the hereafter will be spent in seven different circles or spheres, which

---

1. *Newsweek*, Apr. 12, 1948.

surround the earth, each succeeding circle being around the former one, as the skin of a fruit surrounds the fruit, or the bark covers the trunk of a tree. Some hold that the lowest spirits are in a low, "earthbound" sphere, where they are taught by spirits in a higher sphere. The spirits of those who have died recently are quite near the earth; they can hear us, and they know of us. As the spirit becomes more perfect, it passes into a higher sphere and gradually loses its interest in the life we live in the flesh. Spirits are believed to have a body, although one that differs from the one we now have on earth.

Spiritists are opposed to war, to capital punishment, and to every form of tyranny. They do not believe in forgiveness of sin, but each person has to work out his own destiny through moral or spiritual evolution.

Spiritistic phenomena (the events whence such information reaches our Spiritists) are numerous. All men, so it is said, have *psychic force* (*psychic,* from the Greek *psyche,* soul, hence soul-force). While physical force resides in the muscles, psychic force rests in the minds of men. They who possess this force in greater measure than others are likely to become mediums. A *medium* is a go-between, the instrument through which spirits transmit supernatural knowledge to the *sitters* at a *séance,* the usual term for a spiritistic *session* or meeting.

Since psychic force is supposed to be enhanced when several people concentrate on it, and when they strengthen one another by physical contact, the simplest spiritistic phenomenon is perhaps that of *table tilting,* or *rapping.* The sitters spread their hands on the surface of a table around which they are seated. There is to be an unbroken circle, each sitter's two thumbs are to touch each other, while his little fingers touch those of the sitters next to him. The table begins to lift two or more legs off the floor, and bounds back. The sitters agree with the "spirit" that one thud will mean the letter "A," two thuds "B," and so on; and the message is conveyed through the number of thumps. Or, the sitters suggest a name, or a noun, and the "spirit" voices its assent when the right word is spoken.

A more advanced phenomenon occurs when the medium goes into *trance*. This is an unconscious or insensible condition, a state in which bodily consciousness and sensation are suspended for a time. The medium reports what he, more often she, hears and sees in this condition. At times the medium answers questions which the sitters ask the spirit.

Again the spirit, called the *control* of the medium, makes the latter *write*. When the medium comes out of the trance, she seldom remembers what she has said or done, but is much fatigued.

There are numerous other phenomena, some of which do not impart any information concerning the beloved dead or the hereafter but seem to aim only at impressing the sitters with the supernatural power of the spirit. Examples are the *floating* of objects through a room, the apparition of visible spirits, hands, and arms. This is called *materialization*. In a typical materialization séance ectoplasm is said to emanate from the mouth and body of the medium, which foggy, smokelike substance is then shaped into forms by the chemist in the spirit world. (Ectoplasm is defined as exteriorized protoplasm, which latter is described by Webster as "the physical basis of life," "ordinarily a thick viscous semi-fluid of almost jelly-like, colorless, translucent material containing a large percentage of water, and holding fine granules in suspension.")

Great Britain and the United States alike in World War II witnessed a revival of interest in Spiritism, and even before that, "Books for the Occult, Psychic and Mystical Library" advertised on the jacket of Stewart Edward White's *The Betty Book* numbered more than fifty. The chief difference between the later and the earlier spiritistic literature lies in the fact that the later books are written in a more gentle tone. Instead of deriding or vehemently accusing the doctrines of the universal Church, they conveniently ignore them. The main thesis, however, remains unaltered: Death itself need not be feared, for it is only a gentle passing into a life very similar to the one just left behind.

Many soldiers who died on the battlefield awoke as out of sleep and inquired in a somewhat bewildered way what had happened to them and where they were: those who had gone before were "kept busy" assuring them that all was well and they were still in the same world from which they had arrived.

Of Stewart Edward White's *The Betty Book* (1937), *Across the Unknown* (1939), and *The Unobstructed Universe* (1940), the second volume is introduced as "A Formula for Living," and of the third the publishers state, "In answer to the desperate need of a stricken world, this book offers a new pattern for individual and social living—based on recapture of faith, not in the *thereness* of immortality, but in its *hereness*."

In these more than 900 pages God is not mentioned; only in the concluding pages some references occur to the Bible as "full of stepladders" to spiritistic truth.

Yet of *The Betty Book* John Haynes Holmes, minister of the Community Church at New York, could only state that he found "an honest report of firsthand and unquestionably genuine experience, had by sincere and intelligent persons, moved by sober scientific interest, embodying a system of spiritual truth as sane as it is sublime. The important thing is to recognize the reality of what is here set down."

Thus Modernism, which itself has discarded the authority of Scripture in matters of faith, welcomes books which indeed contain sane advice concerning control of temper, worry and other faults, but which lead one far afield from all that Christendom has ever held dear, whether in its Eastern or Western branch.

SPIRITISM

When the devil comes in velvet slippers, is he less dangerous than he once was when he decreed through Spirittists, "We abrogate the idea of a personal God"? Are the thousands who have read the sixteen printings of *The Unobstructed Universe* which came off the presses between September, 1940, and October, 1941, on the right track? Did Mr. White himself, when he passed into the beyond on September 1, 1946, find what he expected to find? Or did he, together with the thousands who followed his guidance, meet with disastrous disillusion, having bypassed God's own revelation?

These questions will not down; too much depends upon their answer.

Mr. White (1873-1946) is known as the talented author of many books of adventure and travel. During the last twenty years of his life he added to his travels through Africa and Alaska an itinerary far into another land, a territory more unknown, yet close around us.

It began in 1919, when Mrs. White—the "Betty" in the three books—was summoned by "Invisibles" (spirits in the beyond) to take psychic matters seriously and to develop her natural gift for communication with the dead.

For many years Mr. White and others took down a vast mass of what was revealed to "Betty," and when in 1939 the wife died, the husband continued his wife's explorations, got in touch with her, and at the age of sixty-seven completed the message for the guidance of seekers after truth and comfort.

Fundamental in the White trilogy is the thought that "there is only one universe." Both "heaven" and "hell" are right here, hell being only suffering from frustrated urge, "since in the hereafter all are bound to desire the progress of evolution."

Betty states, "I am right here. There is only one universe. There is no other 'heaven.' It is only that you cannot see me. Your eyes are not attuned to the color, your ears to the sound. I am in the unobstructed phase of the one and only universe. That is all. It is only that my I-Am is separated from the obstruction that was my body. My world is your world *plus*."

Man is "a bit of individualized consciousness," and "the only rock" is "recognition of the creator as greater than the thing created," "acceptance of the Oneness of Consciousness as a whole."

Thoroughly pantheistic is the new Spiritism as was also the old.

When asked how she could formerly pray the Lord's Prayer while yet "always beyond the anthropomorphic idea," Betty replied from the beyond that she was wont to address her prayer "to consciousness." "Did you think of consciousness with personality, warmth, such warmth as comes with personality, I mean?" "As though I were drowning in a great sea, and there was a shipful of people, any or all of whom could help me."

While in his earth-life, man has two bodies, the Alpha and the Beta body. The Beta is "the actual invisible substance which you have for long termed soul or spirit." It has weight and if a man had scales he might weigh the medium before the cold goes into the room and after: the difference would be the weight of the cold which is the Beta going out in response to a magnetic call of another consciousness to his own. When this going out is done under proper conditions and in the right mood, great good may result, for one can get in touch with "the oversoul" only through the subconscious, which is in the Beta, while the conscious mind is in the Alpha body.

Spiritism, then, is the very opposite of Russellism with its rationalistic praise of "the intellect." White belittles the intellect, "the brain." It is "a marvelous mechanism," but effective only "in combination with the inner self." It is "a machine which must be worked by the other, wiser guiding consciousness."

Thus the man—the "person" is said to be in the Beta—is left a prey to all sorts of suggestions from the "spiritual world."

SPIRITISM 39

Mr. White did not receive vulgar, obscene, irreverent, silly information, as have countless other Spiritists before him. And there are beautiful literary touches, fine illustrations in the White books. The mysteries of spiritistic phenomena become quite plausible events when he speaks on "Orthos and the Essences": Time, Space, Motion, Frequency, Conductivity.

Take a few samples.

Time has three aspects. The first is *sidereal time* (from Latin *sidera,* the stars). The term stands for our ordinary time, determined by the stars and ticked off by the clock. Already here, however, we know that there is a different aspect of time, which may be called *psychological time.* An hour is not always the same: five minutes may seem like sixty when we wait for a pot to boil. Fifteen minutes may seem endless when we nervously wait for a train to arrive; let the same fifteen minutes be spent in intent survey of beautiful surroundings, and the train arrives before we realize we have waited any time at all. Thus time is elastic, not fixed at all.

There is also a third time, *orthic time* (*orthos* being the Greek word for right, correct, as most people know from the word orthodox [right in opinion]). This orthic time, in which those live who have graduated from our life, is also "malleable"; it expands and contracts; it is a timeless present, of which we have a slight experience when we pace about oblivious to past and future moments. The "dead," therefore, are far from dead: they are like the Old Testament Jehovah who said "I Am," not I was or will be, but just *am.* Just plain being is the time condition of the hereafter.

There are also three aspects of *space.*

The first is determined by the *geometrical distance* between two points. *Psychologically,* however, that distance varies: long if we walk it, footsore and weary; short if we ride over a concrete road in a modern car geared to do 70, 80, 100 miles an hour. When we sleep in a Pullman compartment, we may awake at a distance of many miles, but all that space has vanished. What obstructs us is not the number of miles but "our inexpertness in telescoping them, or, if you will, telescoping through them."

In the third, or *orthic space*, those who have gone on before live in the same universe in which we dwell, but are minus the obstructions of the dense Alpha body, and they know that space itself is not solid. They pass right through it at will.

There is also an *orthic motion*. In the universe in which we live, the obstructed universe, motion is real: the train may move faster and faster, though only up to a certain point. It may also stand still and yet be in motion, because it moves through space with the earth on which it stands. But in Betty's universe motion is obstructed neither by time nor space: "In orthos, motion is instant."

No wonder the wise Spiritist does not fear death. He gladly anticipates it. It will be a permanent laying aside of all obstructions, something he has done quite frequently for a while, if, namely, he has developed the psychic aptitude of leaving the Alpha body and stepping out in the Beta. It is "a pleasurable releasing, quite different from the death-agony idea."

Nor can those "stepladders" to which Mr. White referred fail to lead some poorly instructed souls astray. For many other Spiritists freely and with gusto point to the facts that Abraham, Moses, Saul, Samuel, Isaiah, Daniel, and Paul all were psychics and had definitely spiritistic experiences, while Jesus was the greatest medium of all. He was clairvoyant, Matthew 21:2; clairvoyant and clairaudient, Matthew 3:17; telepathic, John 4:17-19; and He was a materializing medium, Luke 9:28-30.[2]

Besides, all the information from the other side points to the happy existence of the Invisibles. As the older Spiritists spoke of seven spheres all around the earth as the layers of an onion around its core, so White speaks of different "levels" of existence hereafter. Those on the first

---

2. See Marcus Bach, *They Have Found a Faith*, Ch. 4.

SPIRITISM

level are guided on toward the next and more felicitous by those already inhabiting them.[3]

To the Christian, however, this fast-and-loose play with the Bible is self-condemnatory. For if all the information by so-called visiting spirits from the beyond says that "there is nothing in death to fear," that "life goes on exactly as it did here," then Jesus must have been a poor medium. For Moses and Elijah discussed with Him His *exodus* at Jerusalem, that is, His death, resurrection, and ascension; yet the same gospel from which the Spiritists endeavor to prove Jesus a materializing medium, continues to describe His anguish in Gethsemane at the approach of death. Do we have "the greatest medium" so out of harmony with the unanimous testimony of the spirits; or shall we scrap the comparatively large sections of the four Gospels describing His death-agony?

Yes, it is all very attractive and quite scientific. It is as Darby concludes in *The Unobstructed Universe*: ". . . so inclusive a philosophical structure, so closely knit, so airtight logically: one that proceeds through so wide a range of subjects and interlocks them all so perfectly that not a seam shows; and, with all that, expresses it so simply and so clearly." And there is a gradual development from the first book through the second and the third, beginning with the demonstration that psychic phenomena are possible; continuing to show how it should be tried and what pitfalls to avoid; and working up toward a climax which leaves little to be asked.

Explanation of Phenomena

There is so much counterfeit Spiritism that the appraisal of the phenomena becomes a complicated task. We have:

(1) *Fraudulent Spiritism*

Under the cover of darkness (spirits are said to be sensitive to light) and with the aid of electricity, phonographs,

---

3. For a somewhat detailed description of existence in the "seven spheres," cf. Charles S. Braden, *These Also Believe*, pp. 344-346.

and numerous other modern inventions, there is not a genuine spiritistic phenomenon that cannot be reproduced a hundredfold for commercial reasons. There is a host of well-organized crooks who gather information concerning prospective dupes in the most systematic manner, who carefully file such information for future reference, or sell it to other mediums. With the information obtained beforehand, the sitter is duly impressed with the knowledge of the medium, the voice of the "spirit" is produced seemingly from the "ether," and the dupe is gradually enslaved by the medium, until he is advised where to invest his capital. When the victim at last awakes to the fact that he has been misled, the medium goes scot-free; she has only plied her "religion." Thus a gang of crooks discovered that a sitter was a musician whose favorite master was Brahms. A supposed medium, an able pianist, herself actually memorized the chief works of Brahms. The sitter was then asked to summon his favorite musician through the medium, who sat at the piano in a supposed trance, and was guided by the "spirit of Brahms" to play the master's works called for by the sitter. Struck with awe, our musical dupe surrendered to the medium, lost his fortune, and committed suicide. The extent of this fraudulent Spiritism is so large that it is difficult to know where it begins and where it ends.[4]

---

4. This side of the matter is well described by E. H. Smith in an article "Crooks of Ghostland" in *Saturday Evening* Post, April 24, 1920; *Behind the Scenes with the Medium* by D. P. Abbott; *Houdini's Spirit Exposés and Dunninger's Psychical Investigations*, New York, 1928. In "I've Unmasked a Thousand Frauds" by Mackenberg and Fishman in *Saturday Evening Post*, March 3, 1951, Miss Mackenberg asserts that she has never found a genuine medium. Julien J. Proskauer, *Spook Crooks*, 1932, and *The Dead Do Not Talk*, 1946, discusses "some of the new rackets . . . sprung up because of the deaths in the armed forces, and the boys who were 'Missing in Action.' " He states that he has never seen "a true believer in spiritism give advice in what stocks to buy, how to invest money, how to cure an ill, prescribe medicine, or in any single way do anything that a priest, minister, or rabbi would not do." Among the new rackets are skotography, futurescopes, spirit motors, etc. Proskauer estimates from police records that a 250-million-dollar income for charlatans is a modest figure for 1946.

But our difficulties increase when we consider the fact that even genuine psychics have been caught in fraud time and again. This is supposedly due to the fact that psychic force does not always work when the medium wants it. Consequently, when the scene has been set for a séance and the sitter expects results, the medium often resorts to trickery. Thus the Fox girls admitted that their early raps were achieved by the snapping of the joints of their toes. Eusapia Paladino, most famous medium in her day, was caught deceiving at least twice. In short, the original P(sychical) R(esearch) S(ociety), which consists of eminent scholars and has investigated spiritistic phenomena since 1882, has found only two or three mediums above suspicion during a period of forty years. To this one may add that such prominent advocates of Spiritism as Sir Wm. Crookes in 1874, *Light* in 1909, and Sir Conan Doyle in 1919 have admitted that there is no test known whereby we may determine whether information which does come from departed spirits, comes to us bona fide or from a "naughty spirit" or *Poltergeist* bent upon deceiving.

Besides all this, good spirits may attempt to convey a message through a medium's *control*, the spirit who communicates with her in her trance condition. But the control itself at times seems to take a wicked pleasure in twisting the information of the good spirit. Thus we have a confused mass of information by so-called Shakespeares and Carlyles who cannot spell their own names; and upon such dubious sources we depend for our information concerning the hereafter.

However, let us give our Spiritist friends the benefit of the doubt. Let us rule out of court the fact that undoubtedly the bulk of spiritistic phenomena is deceptive, and likewise the consideration that it is very difficult for the average man to know whether he deals with a fake or with a genuine medium, and she in turn with a true or a fraudulent source of information. In other words, let us consider

(2) *Bona Fide Spiritism*

Here we have the following opinions:

1. Spiritists themselves assert that such *information* as they believe has reached them through honest channels *has come from the spirits of departed human beings* who live in the spheres close to our own world. Since this is known to be contrary to the teachings of Christianity, prominent Spiritists do not hesitate to denounce Christian leaders as incompetent judges. Sir Oliver Lodge may be thought to speak the mind of modern Spiritism when he informs us that "the clergy can hardly form a good court of enquiry" since they "look at the matter from the Christian standpoint." He wants us to lay aside all "prejudice" and to "proceed hypothetically." At the same time, however, Sir Oliver admits that his own conviction remains a hypothesis, although he states, "It is not an unreasonable hypothesis. It is the hypothesis to which I have been impelled after thirty years of study." In itself this would not be so bad, since the doctrines of Christianity are as much a "hypothesis" from the standpoint of the exact sciences as the doctrines of Spiritism or any other metaphysical opinions and convictions. After all, we all walk by faith. We maintain, however, that the Christian faith is based upon such well-established historic facts that we should not discard them for something so unproven and so diametrically at variance with the doctrines of Christianity itself. It is not concerning the *facts* of genuine Spiritism that we contend; it is the interpretation, the *alleged source* of these facts, which we dispute. That information reaches the medium, we have no doubt. But why must Sir Oliver Lodge inform us with passion that the hypothesis that such information comes from our departed dear ones is superior to any other hypothesis? This hypothesis leads Sir Oliver himself to discard all the "terribly depressing doctrines, about repose in graves and fleshly resurrection at some long distant day," and similar "mediaeval absurdity." If it remains a matter of one hypothesis versus another, we Christians have a full right, it

would seem, to refuse to surrender the heritage which the Church has so painstakingly and universally derived from the Bible. And when we add that, in general, the findings of Spiritism are in direct opposition to all that Bible and Church teach, can we be rightly blamed for refusing the "hypothesis" of Spiritism?

2. A second *account* is that *all communications come from medium and audience.* In Spiritism we are dealing with physical phenomena (moving of heavy bodies without contact, alteration in weight, the appearance of hands and other limbs), and with psychical phenomena (knowledge in the medium in trance condition which cannot be traced to any known source). It is alleged that all men have *physical, electric, and psychic* force; that the physical phenomena of Spiritism are due to exceptional physical force, or, to unusual power of mind over matter; that the psychic features are the result of phenomenal psychic force. Under this head come *telepathy* (thought-transference from sitters, or others, to the medium); *mind-reading* (in some cases the subconscious mind of the medium is even asserted to read the subconscious mind of the sitter, and to read long-forgotten data from his memory); *clairvoyance* and *clairaudience* (ability to see and to hear below or beyond the ordinary amount of ether thrillings seen and heard by human beings); and similar attributes of the soul that are only partially known quantities. The book of Dr. A. T. Schofield, an English physician and psychologist, contains much of interest in this connection. It remains noteworthy that so little of even that which is *known* of these forces is really *understood,* that prominent Spiritists themselves have admitted that many so-called spirit-manifestations may be due to these mysterious qualities of the soul.

The writer heard Dr. C. Eaton state that he had demonstrated the truth of this theory time and again by the following challenge. He would open a book in the presence of a medium in trance, read the number of the page, turn the book upside down, and ask the medium to mention the number of the page. This she could invariably do, since she read the number from his mind. He would then close the book and reopen it while it was upside down. In this way "no one on earth knew the number of the page at which the book had been opened, and the same medium would invariably guess the page wrongly."

This is indeed a remarkable test. Moreover, in the light of the fact that telepathy and mind reading occur in almost every human life some time or other, we do not wonder that psychics are said to have this mysterious power in a great measure, especially when in trance, that is to say, when their conscious mind has surrendered to the play of their unconscious mind. The well-known novel *Jane Eyre* presents a case of mental telepathy which might be duplicated today. One of the present writer's professors told him that two days after he had spent a night celebrating with fellow students, a letter arrived from his mother in a distant city inquiring why he had not been in bed that night, as it had worried her until the early morning hours. In support of the thesis that at least some of the phenomena of spiritualism are due to telepathy and clairvoyance, J. Stafford Wright in his book, *Man in the Process of Time* (p. 110), points to the fact that upon occasion a "medium has received messages and descriptions from some friend of the sitter, believed to be dead, and later found to be alive. The most famous instance is the Gordon Davis case reported by Dr. S. G. Soal in *The Proceedings of the S.P.R.*, Vol. XXXV."

We are not surprised, therefore, to discover that men who, like the Sadducees, say that there is no resurrection, neither angel, nor spirit, attribute all spiritistic phenomena to these natural forces. This means, of course, genuine phenomena, since throughout we should bear in mind that there is much deception. Thus table-tilting is produced by means of a hook and chain connecting the table with the medium's clothing, or through a hollow table-leg which is being moved by an accomplice in a room below the sitters, and so forth. For those who deny the spiritual world, the

SPIRITISM 47

above is the logical interpretation of all Spiritism that is genuine.

3. There remain, however, two difficulties in the way of accepting this theory as explanatory of all spiritistic phenomena.

a. Spiritists who have gone into the matter deeply have occasionally confessed to obsession by vile and evil spirits. E. F. Hanson's excellent book contains several pages filled with quotations from such spiritistic authorities as the magazine *Mind and Matter* in which it is admitted that mediums are at times subject to the control of evil spirits. He mentions a medium who was in such poor physical condition that a "spirit doctor" commanded an evil spirit to leave the body of the medium-victim, after which he invited, equally successfully, a gentler spirit to take control of the mediumistic patient.

In support of this is the testimony of mediumistic or psychic people who, after a few experiments, discarded Spiritism entirely because the information they received was so unspeakably vile, obscene, and blasphemous that they were fairly shocked out of Spiritism. It will not do to blame all of this on the medium's or sitter's subliminal self, as honest Spiritists have admitted, for, as Mr. Wallace the Spiritist states, "then that second self is almost always a deceiving and a lying self, no matter how moral and truthful the first self may be." This, he calls a "stupendous difficulty."

To this we may add that the physical effects upon the medium are often of such painful or violent character "as have been," to quote a Spiritist, "in all ages imputed to possession by evil spirits." They are, in point of fact, the same as they were in Jesus' day, the symptoms of the demon-possessed, to wit, prostration, foaming, and similar phenomena.

b. This leads us inevitably to the second obstacle in the way of attributing all spiritistic phenomena to psychic force. The Bible, in both the Old and the New Testaments, apparently warns severely against Spiritism as demonology. In this connection we take issue with the assertion of Canon Barnes and Jane T. Stoddart, "that the worst way of attacking spiritualism is to admit its fundamental claim that communication with 'spirits' can be set up, and then to assert that the 'spirits' with whom intercourse is established are evil."

Contrary to this, we maintain that there is a marked difference between the "fundamental claim" that contact can be established with departed mortals, and the Christian view that it cannot be done. We also assert that those seeking after such contact fall an unknowing prey to evil spirits, that is, to demons, whose very existence they deny. We can see no yielding of ground to Spiritism in this view.

In defending this latter position as explanatory of at least part of the spiritistic phenomena, we present the following cumulative argument.

1. Spiritism has always existed, and its history may be traced through the centuries. It has ever revealed the same characteristics, according to the spiritist Colville as well as the ex-Spiritist Hanson. Accordingly the *International Psychic Gazette* for September, 1916, contained the interesting information that an English medium, Mr. W. W. Love, held a spiritist séance in a Chinese temple in the presence of Chinese priests who considered him "a brother spiritist" and who expressed their surprise that he, a European, should know so much about spirit manifestation.

2. But to these priests in their Chinese temple their Spiritism was undoubtedly religion. Is it, then, so far amiss to remind ourselves of the fact that Scripture warns against heathen idolatry as against the worship of demons?

3. Certainly Scripture teaches that demons can influence human beings. Read Genesis 3:1; Revelation 12:9; I Kings 22:19-23; Ezekiel 28:11-19 (observe that here the king of Tyre is addressed in language partly fitting him, and partly only his satanic master, the inference being that they must have worked much together); John 8:44; Ephesians 6:11, 12.

4. In perfect harmony with this, Scripture teaches that men may worship demons under semblance of worshiping "god" (Deut. 32:17; I Cor. 10:20).

5. To this it may be added that demon-possession was of frequent occurrence in Bible times, especially when the devil ("God's ape" according to Luther) imitated the incarnation of the Son of God by taking possession of the bodies of human victims. It is preposterous to assert that evil spirits cannot do in "these last days" what they did in the first century of our era.

We may state in this connection that, in our own opinion, a combination of views two and three is the most satisfactory. We hold that many spiritistic phenomena are the natural result of little-studied soul force, but that in some cases demons are at work. Nor do we consider it at all strange that a medium who has surrendered his mind to the dictation of outside influences, should at times become the willing instrument of a strong human will and mind, and at other times the unsuspecting tool of superhuman spirits who have equal access to him in his trance condition.[5] And this view, it would appear, accounts fully for the notorious fruit of Spiritism, namely, The Three Black I's: *Infidelity, Insanity, Immorality*. However, in making this statement we must bear in mind that, like other "liberal" cults and currents of thought, modern Spiritism has absorbed something of the spirit of the times, that is to say, the newer writers and practitioners of Spiritism, instead of decrying Christianity as absurd, false, and

---

5. This is, of course, widely different from attributing insanity to direct influence of evil spirits. Dr. Mulder shows conclusively that many symptoms formerly ascribed to demonic influence have only a disturbed physical background, such as hysteria. Dr. Mulder seems to incline toward the view that at Endor the presence of an evil spirit may be suspected. Cf. *Essays on Mental Disturbance and Demon Possession* by Jacob D. Mulder, M.D., Grand Rapids, Michigan. The present writer, in view of the *energeia tou satana* predicted of "the lawless one" in II Thess. 2:9, would not wonder if toward the end of time demon-possession, as manifest in Jesus' days, occurred on a limited scale.

the like, maintain that it is essentially in agreement with its own teachings.

There remains the task of examining briefly, first, Scripture's attitude toward Spiritism; and secondly, Spiritism's attitude toward Scripture and Scriptural truth.

The Bible on Spiritism

The Scriptures contain many references. For an intelligent understanding of these the following definitions from the International Standard Bible Encyclopaedia may serve.

Consulter with a familiar spirit: one who was possessed of a python or soothsaying demon (I Sam. 28; Acts 16: 16-18).

Divination: the art of obtaining secret knowledge, especially that which related to the future, by means almost exclusively within the reach of special classes of men.

Familiar spirits: spirits which were supposed to come at the call of one who had power over them. They were probably called "familiar" because it was a servant (*famulus*), belonging to the family (*familiaris*) who might be summoned to do the commands of the owner. The Hebrew word means *hollow,* because the voice of the spirit might have been supposed to come from the one possessed, as from a bottle, or because of the hollow sound which characterized the utterance, as out of the ground (Isa. 29:4).

Necromancy: consultation with the dead. The attempt was condemned though the end could not be attained.

Sorcerer: one who muttered incantations or spoke in ventriloquial whispers, as if under the influence of the spirits of the dead.

Witch: "one who knows." The Hebrew word means "a woman that hath a familiar spirit."

Wizard: "a knowing one." The word in the Old Testament always denotes a man who can interpret the ravings of the medium.

Among the Scriptural passages are Leviticus 19:26, 31; Deuteronomy 18:9-14; I Samuel 28; II Kings 21:2, 6; I Chronicles 10:13, 14; Isaiah 8:19-22; 19:3; Acts 16:16-18.

SPIRITISM

There are likely to be many more, though some of the divinations mentioned were of a different character. These are certain, and they teach:

1. That all seeking of the dead was forbidden (Ex. 22: 18; Lev. 20:6).
2. That Spiritism caused the destruction of seven nations; and, together with other sins, the death of Saul (I Chron. 10:13).
3. That Israel was as much in danger of resorting to this sin as are "Christians" today.
4. That Egypt, in punishment for its sins, was abandoned by God to Spiritism (Isa. 19:3).
5. That its sinful character consists of finding out things hidden, apart from the divine revelation (Deut. 18:11, 14, 15, 20; Isa. 8:19, 20).
6. That Spiritism is the rejection of Christ (Deut. 18: 14, 15).
7. In the light of the foregoing texts the modern revival of Spiritism seems to be clearly predicted in I Timothy 4:1, and perhaps in Revelation 16:13, 14 (as frogs live in water or on the earth, so demons live in the air or in human beings).

The Seance at Endor

That Spiritists cannot appeal to I Samuel 28 to support the view that the Old Testament sanctions communication with the dead, forbidding only iniquitous practices attending Spiritism in its decadent form, is evident from I Chronicles 10:13, 14. Even if Samuel did appear, this passage would only mean that God upset the séance and intervened.

That this is what happened is held by Keil, Haldeman, Pink, Gray, Panton, Schofield, and many others. Their arguments are:

1. The medium was terrified when the *unexpected* happened.

2. Scripture speaks five times of *Samuel*.

3. The prophecy was fulfilled: Saul died the next day and his army was routed.

Yet the only apparent indication of Samuel's return is verse 15, "And Samuel said to Saul." If, however, other considerations prove that Samuel did not appear, these words must be explained:

a. As a rendering of what the woman said to Saul.

b. Or, as calling Samuel what looked like Samuel, just as angels appearing like men are called men (Gen. 18:1, 2; Dan. 9:21); and men called *gods* because they resemble or represent God in certain aspects or positions (Ps. 82: 6).

That Samuel did not appear is held by Hanson, Bavinck, Orr (*Intern'l Stand. Bible Enc.*) and Honig.[6] Their arguments seem clinching, although they differ as to what did happen. We advance:

1. Neither the woman nor her familiar spirit ("control") had power over Samuel. God had. But He refused to answer Saul (v. 6); surely, He would not answer him now that Saul took refuge to forbidden means, least of all by doing a thing He has never been known to duplicate.[7]

2. After Samuel informed Saul that God had rejected him, the prophet had no more dealings with the king.

---

6. *Handboek v. d. Geref. Dogmatiek*, Kampen, 1938, p. 796, quoting extensively from the 18th century Dutch theologian P. van Mastricht.

7. Houdini, lifelong antagonist of spiritism, promised his wife that, if at all possible, he would visit her after his death. For years Mrs. Houdini waited in accordance with her late husband's instructions. At last she extinguished the light she had left burning to guide the spirit in his search for her.

Clarence Darrow, the agnostic, promised Claude Noble, Detroit businessman and musician, "that if he found an after life he would manifest it on the anniversary of his death." On March 13, 1942, Mr. Noble made his fourth annual attempt in Jackson Park, Chicago, to contact Darrow. It was in vain as in previous years. Even recital of the Lord's Prayer could not aid in producing the promised "violent vibration of Noble's arm." And no wonder: the Lord's Prayer cannot avail in an attempt to run afoul of the Lord's written Word.

SPIRITISM

3. The true Samuel would not have lied, by saying that Saul had disturbed his rest, if not Saul but God had ordered him; nor by saying that Saul would be with him the next day (cf. Luke 16:26).

4. After rejecting Saul for the sin of disobedience and subsequently ignoring him for years, God would not at the last moment

a. have catered to Saul's desire to receive another revelation;

b. have acted contrary to the conviction He has always impressed upon His people, namely, that there is no contact between the living and the dead (Job 7:10; Eccl. 9:6; Isa. 63:16; Luke 16:31);

c. have created the impression that seeking information from the dead is not so bad, since elsewhere He has commanded this sin to be punished with death (all Spiritists appeal to this passage);

d. have stated that Saul had to die because of this thing in which God yielded to his request (I Chron. 10:13).

5. Saul told the medium whom to call up. In accordance with our explanation of psychic phenomena the *sensitive* (medium) would thereupon read from Saul's mind what Samuel looked like, and describe him *as Saul had been wont to see him* (not as he was after death).

6. The woman was afraid:

a. Because in her trance she recognized Saul (v. 12), who was known as a mighty enemy of the medium (mind reading); see verse 3; or

b. Because she saw *elohim, spirits*, hover above the apparition, who, with "lying wonders" (II Thess. 2:9), impersonated Samuel.

7. Saul never saw Samuel; he *perceived* from the woman's description what *she* saw in her trance.

8. As to the prophecy, here are several possibilities:

a. The woman read Saul's dread that his end was coming. This she predicted.

b. The woman read the prophecy by Samuel (I Sam. 15:16, 18) which had haunted Saul (I Sam. 16:2; 20:31, etc.) in his frightened mind, and told him what he expected to hear.
c. If a demon, impersonating Samuel, spoke through the medium, it would remember Samuel's prophecy and make use of it.

Spiritism on the Bible

Lest we repeat ourselves in Chapters 3 and 16, we shall merely present statements by prominent cultists on various important and generally accepted Christian points of doctrine. In Chapter 18 we shall briefly recall that these doctrines are indeed contained in Scripture and believed by "the holy catholic church" of the ages. It will be observed, we trust, that the various antichristian "isms" reveal their true character when they denounce the revealed truth of the Word of God.

As to Spiritism, it teaches — which means sundry Spiritists teach, there being no official creed of Spiritism — as follows:

God

"We abrogate the idea of a personal God."[8]

"It should be understood that there are as many Gods as there are minds needing Gods to worship; not only one, two, or three, but many . . . . The noble forest trees, sun, moon, and stars, all things are Gods to you, for they minister unto the needs of your soul. It is vain to suppose you can all bow down to, and truly serve one God."[9]

Q. (by Mrs. Connant, medium). "Do you know of any such spirit as a person we call Devil?"

A. (through the controlling spirit at séance) : "We certainly do, and yet this same Devil is our God, our Father.[10]

---
8. Wilkins, *The Physical Phenomena in Spiritualism Revealed* quoting "one of the presidents at a national camp of Spiritualism.'
9. *The Banner of Light*, Feb. 3, 1866.
10. *Ibid.*, Nov. 4, 1865.

Jesus Christ

"What's the meaning of the word Christ? Is it not, as is generally supposed, the Son of the Creator of all things? Any just and perfect being is Christ."[11]

"It seems nevertheless that all the testimony received from advanced spirits only shows that Christ was a medium and a reformer in Judea; that he now is an advanced spirit in the sixth sphere." — DR. WEISSE.[12]

"High above all these is the greatest spirit of whom they (the spirits) have cognizance — not God, since God is so infinite that He is not within their ken — but one who is nearer God and to that extent represents God. This is the Christ Spirit. His special care is the earth. He came down upon it at a time of great earthly depravity — a time when the world was almost as wicked as it is now, in order to give the people the lesson of an ideal life. Then he returned to his own high station, having left an example which is still occasionally followed. That is the story of Christ as spirits have described it."[13]

"Christ was a good man, but He could not have been divine except in the sense perhaps that we are all divine." —MESSAGE BY A "SPIRIT."[14]

"I do not find that Christ claimed for Himself more than he held out as possible for others. When He identifies Himself with the Father, it was in the oneness of mediumship. He was the great Medium or Mediator." — GERALD MASSEY.[15]

"As God is Spirit, that is the Infinite Spirit's presence acting by the law of mediation, the Apostle with a singular clearness of perception pronounced the Nazarene a Medi-

---

11. *Spiritual Telegraph*, No. 37.
12. Dr. Weisse, as quoted by Hanson, *Demonology or Spiritualism*, p. 147.
13. A. Conan Doyle, *The New Revelation*, p. 57.
14. Quoted by Raupert, *Spiritistic Phenomena and Their Interpretation*, p. 47.
15. Quoted by Pollock, *Modern Spiritualism Briefly Tested by Scripture*, p. 13.

ator — i.e., a Medium — between God and man." — Dr. J. M. Peebles.[16]

"In the Spiritualist hymn-book the name of Jesus is deleted — for example, 'angels of Jesus' reads 'angels of wisdom.' At their services His name is carefully omitted in the prayers." — Rev. F. Fielding-Ould.[17]

"The miraculous conception of Christ is merely a fabulous tale.[18]

"Christ arose in spirit. It was the spirit that appeared to the disciples so constantly after the crucifixion. It was a spirit that ascended into heaven, and it is a glorious spirit that appears and has appeared during the long centuries to thousands of wearied Christians on earth." — Colville.[19]

"I, Jesus, appeared in spirit in 1861, and do say and declare unto the world that the new era or dispensation has commenced, called the coming of Christ. It commenced about the year 1847, and as represented and spoken of by the prophet Daniel and others, by my coming as a cloud in the heavens, with tens of thousands of angels, to overshadow the earth with my glory."[20]

"This is the second coming — a coming in power and glory — a coming of ministering angels and spirits — a coming to morally and spiritually enlighten all conscious intelligences. It is the overshadowing return of the living Christ. There will be no such personal return as theologians have taught. This will be, and is, the spiritual return to his people, by the voice of his messengers speaking

---

16. *Ibid.*, p. 14.
17. In *Light*, July 12, 1919.
18. *Spiritual Telegraph*, No. 37.
19. *Universal Spiritualism*, p. 234. It deserves attention that these are the words of a modernist preacher (F. Phillips) which the spiritist Mr. Colville quotes "without addition of our own to make their salutary influence felt upon every attentive reader's mind." That also other Modernists are in perfect agreement with the spiritist idea of Christ's appearance as materializations, see *Princeton Theol. Review*, July, 1922, p. 487.
20. Opening words of the book *New Dispensations*, quoted by Hanson, *op. cit.*, p. 212.

to those whose ears are open; even as he said . . . ." — STAINTON MOSES (Imperator).[21]

The Atonement

"Your atonement is the very climax of a deranged imagination, and one that is of the most unrighteous and immoral tendency." — A. J. DAVIS.[22]

"The orthodox doctrine of Atonement was a survival of the greatest abuses of earliest time, and it was immoral to the core. . . . The reason for this doctrine is that you are born into this world a lost, ruined, hell-deserving sinner. But what an outrageous lie! . . . Does not your blood boil with indignation at such a doctrine?"[23]

"One can see no justice in a vicarious sacrifice, nor in the God who could be placated by such means." — A. CONAN DOYLE.[24]

Man

"Never was there any evidence of a fall." — A. CONAN DOYLE.[25]

"We must reject the conception of fallen creatures. By the Fall we understand the descent of spirit into matter."— G. G. ANDRE.[26]

Bible

"We must have no desire to hide the plain fact that there is much in some parts of the Bible which does not amalgamate with our teaching."[27]

"To assert that it is a Holy and Divine Book, that God inspired the writers to make known His Divine will, is a gross outrage on and misleading to the public."[28]

---

21. Colville, *op. cit.*, pp. 322, 323.
22. *Nat. Div. Rev.*, p. 576.
23. R. B. Jones, *Spiritism in Bible Light*, p. 172, quoting the spiritist paper *Medium and Daybreak*.
24. *Op. cit.*, p. 55.
25. *Loc. cit.*
26. *The True Light*, p. 162.
27. *Spirit Teachings*, p. 74.
28. *Outlines of Spiritualism*, p. 13.

Hell

"Hell, I may say, drops out altogether, as it has long dropped out of the thoughts of every reasonable man. This odious conception, so blasphemous in its view of the Creator, arose from the exaggeration of Oriental phrases, and may perhaps have been of service in a coarse age when men were frightened by fires, as wild beasts are scared by the travelers. Hell as a permanent place does not exist. But the idea of punishment, of purifying chastisement, in fact of Purgatory, is justified by the reports from the other side." — A. CONAN DOYLE.[29]

"It [the ancient Egyptian view of transmigration] is immeasurably superior to any view of endless, useless torment such as many benighted Christian theologians have proclaimed ... a conception for which there is neither rational explanation nor apology." —COLVILLE.[30]

"There is nothing that can properly be called Hell in the mediaeval sense of eternal hopelessness; but yet Hell in very truth in so far as they suffer the pangs of remorse when their rebellious spirit is broken, and when in their felt poverty of soul they begin to long to return to the Father." — SIR OLIVER LODGE.[31]

"Hell is a great remedial agency. The punishment of sin is remedial. No great gulf is fixed between Heaven and Hell." — "JULIA," a supposed spirit speaking through W. T. STEAD.[32]

Spirits

"All spirits in the other world are nothing else but the souls of those who have lived here."—LANSLOTS.[33]

"If for convenience we designate the high ranks (of the departed) Angels, and the lower as Evil Spirits, let us be

---

29. *Op. cit.*, p. 68.
30. *Op. cit.*, p. 82.
31. *Raymond; or Life and Death with Examples of the Evidence for the Survival of Memory and Affection After Death.*
32. Quoted by A. T. Schofield, *Modern Spiritism, Its Science and Religion*, p. 65.
33. *Spiritism Unveiled*, p. 36.

careful not to lose sight of the fact that they differ only as elder and younger."—G. G. ANDRE.[34]

The Church

"Step by step the Christian Church advanced, and as it did so, step by step the torch of Spiritualism receded, until hardly a flickering ray from it could be perceived amid the deep darkness. . . . For more than 1800 years has the so-called Christian Church stood between mortals and spirits, barring all chance for progress and growth. It stands today as complete a barrier to human progress, as it did 1800 years ago."[35]

"It [Spiritualism] is vastly more firmly fixed than the rock on which it has been falsely said, Jesus Christ founded his church. . . . It is for that reason that we have felt it our duty, as a sincere friend of Spiritualism, to show what Christianity is. . . . If the latter lives, Spiritualism must die; and if Spiritualism is to live, Christianity must die. They are the antithesis of each other. . . . Modern Spiritualism has come to give it its *coup de grâce;* and those who would hold back that flow are the enemies of spiritual truth."[36]

"Resolved: (1) That Sunday Schools should be discontinued; (2) That all Christian ordinances and worship should be abandoned; (3) That sexual tyranny should be denounced; (4) That abstinence from animal food should be affirmed." — Spiritist Conference held in Providence, Rhode Island (1920?) [37]

"I will exercise that dearest of all rights. . . the right of maternity — in the way which to me seemeth right; and no man, nor set of men, no church, no State, shall withhold me from the realization of that purest of all inspirations inherent in every true woman, the right to re-beget myself when, and by whom, and under such circumstances as to me seem fit and best." — J. M. SPEAR, a medium.[38]

---

34. *Op. cit.*, p. 76.
35. *Mind and Matter*, May 8, 1880.
36. *Ibid.*, June, 1880.
37. Cited by Vine and Pollock.
38. Waggoner, *Modern Spiritualism*, p. 147.

Conclusions

That Spiritism has again called attention to the existence of a spiritual world, to life hereafter, to future retribution in a time of gross materialism, we can appreciate. But when we see that this spiritual conception is accompanied by such hatred of Biblical truth, and leads to such disastrous physical and mental results, we can only condemn it from the Christian standpoint. Christianity and Spiritism cannot go together. We think Rudyard Kipling was warranted in saying,

> Oh, the road to En-dor is the oldest road.
> And the craziest road of all.
> Straight it runs to the witch's abode,
> As it did in the days of Saul.
> And nothing has changed of the sorrow in store
> For such as go down on the road to En-dor.

For You to Answer

1. Why is Spiritism the first cult we consider?
2. What tends to revive interest in Spiritism?
3. Would you call Spiritism a cult that stresses clearly defined doctrines? In this respect is it similar to, say, Mormonism, Russellism?
4. What do Spiritists mean by the terms: séance, trance, a psychic, materialization, Invisibles?
5. Has the new Spiritism a different attitude toward the Church than had the older type? Is this spirit characteristic of our time?
6. What is a fundamental thought in White's exposition of Spiritism?
7. Do Spiritists believe in a personal God? Do they believe man is soul and body?
8. What does Mr. White understand by the terms orthic time, orthic space, orthic motion; and why does he consider our universe to be obstructed?
9. If the modern philosophy of Spiritists is logically airtight, why can it still be wrong?

SPIRITISM

10. Is there much fraudulent Spiritism? Why are there no proven methods whereby genuine Spiritism may be differentiated from spurious Spiritism?

11. How many differing interpretations are there of spiritistic phenomena? Why can we not accept the explanation of Spiritists themselves? What do you think of the second one? Can you give any reasons for thinking that at least some phenomena are caused by evil spirits?

12. Do the Old and New Testaments indeed refer to Spiritism? Does the Bible express itself as to the source of spiritistic phenomena? Why does it forbid all Spiritism?

13. Do you think Samuel appeared to Saul at Endor?

14. Mention some cardinal doctrines that are taught in Scripture and denied by Spiritism. Why does Spiritism deny these?

15. A student asked, "Would it be wrong for me to attend a séance in a 'Spiritualist Church' merely to see what goes on?" What would you reply? Give your reasons.

4

THEOSOPHY

Theosophy, or Divine Wisdom, is the apostate child of Spiritism mixed with Buddhism. It is far more complicated and more intricate than Spiritism; at the same time its world-and-life view is more complete and fascinating.

History

Helena Petrovna, a Russian girl, at the age of seventeen married N. B. Blavatsky in 1848. She deserted him after two months and led a wandering life for twenty-five years. She flitted between Paris, London, Russia, Greece, the United States, Mexico, and India. She became a spiritistic medium early in life, and for ten years was under the "control" of a spirit calling himself John King. In 1857 "Madame" Blavatsky tried to found at Cairo a spiritistic society, but failed. Coming to New York in 1873, she sought co-operation with mediums; but just then so much fraud was exposed that she wearied of the Spiritism of the day.

In 1875 she founded the Theosophical Society in New York, aided by Colonel Olcott, a colonel in the Civil War. She said of it, "It is the same Spiritualism, but under another name." In 1882 Blavatsky and Olcott visited India together and rounded out their system by adding Hindu and Buddhist elements. Blavatsky died in 1891, aged sixty years.[1]

Her greatest successor was Mrs. Annie Besant (1847-1933), daughter of an English minister, later wife of one. She left her husband in 1873, and, after challenging the

---

1. Braden shows conclusively, not only that "H. P. B." was personally interested in Spiritism, but also that she wrote in defense of it repeatedly (*op. cit.*, p. 225). Proskauer also lists Blavatsky among the earliest spiritists (*The Dead Do Not Talk*, p. 36).

doctrine of the Church of England, she identified herself with Free Thought and radical political movements. Then suddenly Mrs. Besant was converted to Theosophy. She became a scholar, public speaker, and voluminous writer. She died on September 20, 1933, in her eighty-sixth year. Her outstanding claim was that her adopted son Krishnamurti (also called Krishnaji) was the new Messiah, or the reincarnation of the World Teacher (see below). This she discovered on December 28, 1925. In 1926, Baron Philip Van Pallandt gave his large estate at Ommen, Netherlands, to be the headquarters of the new Messiah. Here annual conferences were held with, at first, as many as two thousand attendant disciples, while in 1928 there were seventeen hundred fifty women and eight hundred men. Some of these ladies slept with the picture of Krishnamurti under their pillows. At Krotona, California, the American headquarters of Theosophy, Krishnaji announced on November 20, 1931, that he had become convinced that he was not the Messiah, and refused to receive further adoration. "I am not an actor; I refuse to wear the robes of a Messiah; so I am again free of all possessions. I have nothing except my creed." Since then he has lived in retirement, giving lectures occasionally. Mrs. Besant died in 1933, and was succeeded by George S. Arundale, who upon his departure was followed by C. Jinarajadasa, the president of the Society since 1945. He is a prolific writer; among his works is *The Golden Book of the Theosophical Society*, published upon the fiftieth anniversary of the Society at Adyar, 1925.

Teachings

Theosophy, called by L. W. Rogers "a religion, a philosophy, a science and yet, accurately speaking, none of these, for it is truly all of them, and yet something beyond them," can here be described only in briefest outline. Since the doctrine of God is always determinative for an entire system, we shall first inquire into Theosophy's very complex ideas concerning God.

God

Theosophy, like its prototype, Buddhism — which was originally a reaction against the polytheism of India — is on the whole remarkably silent or evasive in its statements concerning God. It is pantheistic and teaches an impersonal God. "God is all, and all is God." Over and over again theosophic writers speak of *the unity of all life*. From this principle, considered fundamental, follow many doctrines. If "everything that is, is God," and this God is thought of as "Universal Life, the Limitless Consciousness, the Eternal Love, the very source and heart of all that is," it follows that every form of activity is conceived of as "wave after wave of this Life pushing its way up through matter."

Given this, we do not marvel that all religions are esteemed fundamentally one. There may be a different emphasis, but "the Brotherhood of Religions" is the first plank in the platform of the Theosophical Society. "Every religion has a note of its own, a color of its own, that it gives for the helping of the world . . . blended together they give the whiteness of truth, blended together they give a mighty chord of perfection" (Besant).

To be sure, this impersonal God, from which all religions emanate, when occasionally described, is spoken of as a Trinity. But this is a Trinity in name only, for it is "a threefold manifestation of Power or Will, Wisdom, and Activity," to quote Mrs. Besant. Elsewhere she expresses this thought as follows, "Trinity of Divine Beings [sic], one as God, three as manifested Powers." Worse than this, we are told there is "a fourth Person or in some religions, a second Trinity, feminine, the Mother. This is That which makes manifestation possible, That which eternally [!] in the One is the root of limitation and division, and which, when manifested, is called Matter. This is the divine Not-Self, the divine Matter, the manifested Nature. Regarded as One [later on 'She' is regarded as triple], She is the Fourth, making possible [!] the activity of the Three, the

Field of Their operations by virtue of her infinite divisibility, at once the 'handmaid of the Lord' (S. Luke 1, 38) and also His Mother, yielding of her substance to form His Body, the Universe, when overshadowed by His power."

Let us give one more taste of this. The Second Person is revealed by interaction between "Her"—divine Matter—and the Third Person of the Trinity, and thus becomes the mediator; hence "the Second Person of the Trinity of Spirit is ever dual; He is the One who clothes Himself in Matter, in Whom the twin-halves [!] of Deity appear in union, not as One."

We shall not vex the reader with more of a similar nature; the above may suffice to show that the theosophic conception of the Godhead is widely different from that held in "the holy Catholic Christian Church." *It* is impersonal; *It* lies at the root of all existence; *It* manifests itself as Power, as Wisdom, and as Activity when considered as a spiritual entity. Besides, *It* also manifests itself as Divine Matter which is the necessary condition for *Its* manifestation. The second Person, Wisdom, is dual in nature, spiritual as Reason, material as Love.

Cosmogony

Theosophy, considering matter eternal, reckons the cycles of the universe by the millions. We are at present in the fifth subrace of the third human rootrace, and even a subrace goes on for millennia without any visible changes preparing for a new subrace. The present subrace, called the *Teutonic,* is a subrace of the Aryan rootrace; the latter has been preceded by the Atlantean, and this in turn by the Lemurian race; this was the first that can be truly called human, as it was preceded by semi-animal races. The proper history of man, according to Blavatsky, began no less than 18,000,000 years ago. As a result of "clairvoyant investigation" (getting in contact with *devas* and *mahatmas,* see below), Theosophists publish maps of the world as it was 800,000 years ago, and again as it appeared 11,500 years ago. We are told of the Atlantean race, living on the Atantean Continent 800,000 years ago. This continent formed a belt around the earth, stretching almost uninterruptedly from Mexico, right across the (present) Atlantic Ocean, on to Egypt and Asia. An older continent, the Lemurian, once stretched from the Indian Ocean to Australia. From the same "occult" source of information Theosophists know that during the Atlantean period very early immigrations resulted in the grand civilization of Egypt, which was in progress long before the time assumed by modern historians. Of this early civilization little is left beyond the pyramids because of the great convulsion which is said to have taken place 11,500 years ago. At the time, of the Atlantean Continent only an island was left, about as large as all modern Europe minus Russia. Owing to a cataclysm this island subsided with terrific suddenness, "and the sea, which then covered what is now the desert of Sahara, was driven eastward so as to completely deluge Egypt." In support of this clairvoyant assertion a Mexican document is proudly pointed to, which was translated in 1893. It "is in itself an ancient manuscript of immense antiquity, and it says that the catastrophe took place '8060 years before the writing of this book.' Ten countries, it says, were torn asunder in the convulsion, and sank with their 64,000,000 inhabitants."

"Man, Whence? What? Whither?"

This conception of the world makes room for the countless reincarnations of millions of human souls as taught by Theosophy. Man is said to be a "Divine Fragment, the Divinity becoming patent"; and his ultimate destiny is to return to God (the impersonal *It*). He attains to this goal, the Buddhist nirvana, only through a process of evolution, calling for many incarnations. The idea of reincarnation, itself of ancient Hindu origin, has been civilized in so far as Theosophists do not teach that a man may be reborn as an animal, as was the teaching of the East. Nevertheless, it was not introduced by the authors of Theosophy (Madame H. P. Blavatsky and Colonel H. S. Olcott) until after their journey to India. At first they considered reincarnation exceptional. Since 1882, however, this purged Hindu idea has become the "pearl doctrine" of theosophy. "The actual number of incarnations for each monad is not far short of eight hundred," says A. P. Sinnett, an Englishman to whom Madame Blavatsky wrote many letters, and an author of theosophical literature.

In speaking of man's *bodies*, Theosophy becomes bewildering. "Man has a 'natural body,' which is made up of four different and separable portions, and is subject to death." "Man has further a 'spiritual body.' This is made up of three separable portions, each portion belonging to one of, and separating off, the three Persons in the Trinity of the human Spirit." Let us consider the "natural body."

The natural body of theosophic speculation consists of a *physical body* with its *etheric double*, and an *astral body*, and a *mental body*. These bodies occupy the same space, just as "the space in a bowl can be occupied by a sponge and by water that fills it, because the latter grade of matter interpenetrates the former." The physical is the body of activity; the astral the body of emotions, the "desire-body"; the mental body is the body of thought.

In sleep and in trance-condition man leaves his physical body and, in his astral and mental bodies, dwells in the astral world. Here Theosophy reveals its kinship to Spiritism. We have seen that, according to Spiritists, a medium's subconscious mind gets into contact with the spirit-world through telepathy and clairvoyance. According to theosophists it is the man himself who leaves the physical body and visits the astral plane. The latter is thought of as "an envelope, surrounding the earth," at the same time penetrating it, "just as water penetrates the pores of a wet sponge. It is infused in all matter as a salt dissolved in water exists in association with all of its molecules."

The astral world, thickly populated with all sorts of people formerly in the flesh, is described much after the manner of Spiritism's lower spheres beyond the veil. While man in his astral body visits the astral world, the etheric double (of the dual physical body) may be "abused" by "a disembodied entity living in the astral world, to re-establish his connection with the physical." This is mediumship, which is dangerous. Thus Theosophy, a true apostate, at once acknowledges and discourages the phenomena of modern Spiritism.[2] What does it propose instead? That man should learn both to remember his "dreams," and to dwell on the astral plane even in his waking condition, that he may learn from the astral beings. He should reach a point where he can dwell with equal ease in the physical or in the astral world.

Man's third body is the mental body. It requires a still higher stage of evolution to withdraw from both the physical and the astral bodies, and in the mental body to dwell in the corresponding mental world, or the world of thought. Here again Theosophy reveals its spiritistic origin. The mental world, also called *Devachan,* is the abode of *devas,* or angels. They are the spirits of those who have graduated from the astral world. Few people "at this stage of human evolution" are able to withdraw into the mental world.

---

2. The kinship between Spiritism and Theosophy reveals itself in various other ways; for instance, in the fact that the *Catalog of Theosophical Publications and Importations* advertises books by Sir A. Conan Doyle, the Spiritist; and that Colville, the Spiritist, in describing *The Spirit World,* inserts a chapter by C. W. Leadbeater, prominent theosophist, afterward bishop for Australia of the *Liberal Catholic Church,* which is an offshoot of the Theosophical Society.

It seems, moreover, that Spiritism is moving more in the direction of Theosophy. Consider the following from White's *The Betty Book,* p. 108: "Apparently some part of Betty, call it whatever you like, has left the body lying on the couch and has visited and reported back from other states of being. That some part of her has left the body has been sufficiently proved to us by her reports of distant actual physical things of this world. I say, some part of her; and you can call it her clairvoyant sense; or her acute consciousness; or herself; or whatever you please."

For the close relationship of Freemasonry to Theosophy, consult William J. Whalen, *Christianity and American Freemasonry* (1958); also J. S. M. Ward, *Freemasonry and the Ancient Gods* (1926).

W. Q. Judge, theosophist, gives seven reasons why the phenomena of "Spiritualism" cannot be the voice of the dead, and seven more arguments for interpreting them upon theosophic grounds (*The Ocean of Theosophy,* pp. 167-173).

Those who, through the practice of yoga, have learned to do so (advanced Theosophists), receive "inspirational thought forms" from the devas.

"The Path"

To man, who does not reach his final goal in a few incarnations, "each life on earth is like a day in school." "The normal interval between one life and another varies from a few score years in the case of an undeveloped soul to twenty centuries or even more in the case of a far advanced type." Meanwhile he first pays the price of every uncontrolled passion and appetite of the ignoble sort in the astral world. He does so by literally starving those passions to death, which means keen suffering. In this respect theosophic teachings run parallel with those of Spiritism. Afterward man dwells in Devachan (heaven). Sooner or later he returns to earth, being born anew in an infant body, to work out his *Karma*.

This Karma — a Buddhist idea — is described as "the law of Action and Re-action," or "the Law of Causation"; or in the Scriptural phrase, "As a man soweth so shall he also reap" (Besant). It means "actions pursuing the soul through successive births and compelling it to reveal by its conditions and reflect by its experiences in each birth the experiences of the previous birth." Karma might also be called the divine law of retribution. "When a man has created a vice by evil desire, evil thought, and evil act, he, its creator, can also be its destroyer by good desire, good thought and good act." "We can build our character as surely as a mason can build a wall, working with and through the law. As by law we suffer, so by law we triumph." This then, must be largely done in future lives.

Thus Theosophy reveals its kinship to Buddhism in the autosoterism it proposes. Buddhism teaches salvation through *The Noble Eightfold Path*. Besant and Krishnamurti speak of a *Fourfold Pathway* which man must tread in order to become an *Initiate*.

For advanced Theosophists, however, the system has a shortcut to perfection in the practice of *yoga*, that is meditation, holding the breath, and similar exercises.

The Mahatmas

Even the merest outline of Theosophy should not fail to refer to the Mahatmas, beings of the greatest importance to the system. They parade also under the names of Masters, Adepts, Initiates, the Great White Lodge, the Occult Hierarchy, Brotherhood of Teachers. Mrs. Besant is credited with the saying, "If there are no Masters, then the Theosophic Society is an absurdity." They are "the finished products of human evolution," "divine men made perfect." Sinnett says they are as far above ordinary mankind as man is above the insects of the fields. Their habitat is Tibet.[3] They are ready to reach Nirvana, but they remain in order to supervise human evolution. According to Annie Besant, "They have many ways of working in the world; through their own subtle, spiritual bodies they work, sending out floods of blessing over the whole world." They become incarnate in the body of a Theosophist who has reached that stage of inspiration "at which the mind and emotions of the man no longer sway his body, but the body is wholly taken possession of and used by One greater than himself." To their information and inspiration Theosophy owes its complete knowledge of occult matters. Most of their inspiring work is done on the astral and the mental planes. When a human being has traveled the path of evolution to the end, he becomes an Initiate; he is welcomed by the Great Brotherhood of Teachers.

Above all these teachers there is *One Supreme Teacher*. When *he* becomes incarnated, we have a Christ among us. Yet — for such is Theosophy's faith in the divinity of man — Mrs. Besant states, "Every man is a potential Christ."

---

3. A question directed by the author to the Theosophic Society concerning the present whereabouts of the Mahatmas, now that Tibet is no longer the isolated refuge it formerly was, remained unanswered.

William Q. Judge, in *The Ocean of Theosophy* (1958), lists Abraham, Melchizedek, Moses, and Solomon among the Adepts.

What Is Coming?

There have been three human races thus far: the Lemurian the Atlantean, and the Aryan. Each one of these has developed several subraces. The present, or Aryan, "rootrace" has now its fifth subrace, the Teutonic. It is soon to be followed by a sixth subrace. Each subrace makes a distinct contribution to the race. The present subrace is that of the *intellectual* man. This, at first sight, looks rather flattering. But hear the end of the tale! The sixth subrace will be that of the — *spiritual* man. The present brotherhood-feeling and unity-efforts are a direct preparing for the sixth Aryan subrace. Now at the beginning of each subrace the "Supreme Teacher of the World" becomes incarnate to contribute to the evolution of that race. He does so by entering into the body of a disciple who is ready for initiation; in this body he dwells among men. He has been among us five times in the Aryan race: first as Buddha (rather, in the Buddha's body) in India (first subrace); next as Hermes (Egypt, second subrace); then as Zoroaster (Persia, third subrace); again as Orpheus (Greece, fourth subrace); finally as Christ, when the disciple Jesus surrendered his body to the World Teacher upon the occasion of his baptism. He is shortly to appear again, since the sixth subrace is in the making.

Each time the Supreme Teacher becomes incarnate, he contributes to the human race, not the totality of his divine knowledge (which would be "crushing") but as much as the race can bear at that state of its evolution. It follows at once that Theosophists can speak dearly of Christ Jesus as the greatest revelation of God the world has witnessed thus far; and, that the next Christ will be a greater one than the Christ in Jesus' body, because the *spiritual man* will be superior to the *intellectual man*. The particular task of the coming Messiah will be "again to strike the keynote of a new civilization, gathering all the religions of the world under that supreme teaching of His own."

Theosophy in its modern form, claiming to be "nothing less than the bedrock upon which all phases of the world's thought and activity are founded" (Cooper), lays itself open to criticism as a philosophy and as a religion.

Philosophy

1. Theosophy has endeavored to swallow too large a lump. It tries to be philosophy and theology at once. And this creates a dualism which affects its views of God and of man. Trying to prove to the mind that which can only be known by faith, it has called for proof and it loudly denounces those who doubt its evidence. Such assertions as the insistence upon a revelation from the masters of Karma are simply to be accepted upon the word of Theosophists, and although this, in the abstract, may not be a larger *tour de force* than any other religious axiom or dogma, it certainly is not a sufficiently clear intellectual premise to serve as a foundation for a philosophy of life.

2. Theosophy suffers from a mixture between monism and dualism. While avowedly pantheistic in its concept of God, and while considering God a spiritual being, Theosophy at the same time speaks of the material side of God and this material is thought of as ethereal, *geistleiblich,* a sort of dream-entity, the existence of which again must be accepted merely upon theosophical authority.

3. It is difficult to understand whence arrives the human will, the intellect, and the personality of man since man is a spark of divinity encased in matter. Since the creation, or rather the evolution, of man is the result of divine interaction between the Self and the Not-self in the impersonal God, and since it is the purpose of man to be again absorbed into the impersonal Godhead, whence comes the personality of man, his distinct knowledge and will? Pantheism and the polytheism of the Hindus are mixed in Theosophy.

4. Again, we object to the reincarnation theory from a

philosophic standpoint. It is beyond comprehension that
the human soul, after having escaped through evolution,
first into the astral world, and hence into the higher spiritual world of *Devachan* or heaven, should long for the
lower life in the grossly material body. Why should man,
who is on the way to escape from earthly sorrowful experience, "thirst for more experience . . . such as may only
be gained on earth"? It is, say Theosophists, because the
man in the higher worlds, not quite perfected, is not fully
attuned to the prevailing vibrations there, hence cannot
be fully conscious. He must therefore return to taking on
the coarser bodies in which he can feel fully at home. But
the constant boast of evolution upon which the entire system rests would rather suggest that the man, having dwelt
in the mental world, should return to the astral, than all the
way back to the physical; while the inability to receive all
the impact of the higher worlds, the semi-consciousness that
is due to incomplete perfection, appears to contradict the
claim of man's great felicity in "Devachan."

5. The Karma doctrine we hold to be untenable. Experience teaches that it is not correct to ascribe all suffering
to evil done in a former period of existence. We suffer
much as a result of the misdeeds of others.

6. There can be no merit in suffering for sins done in a
former existence since the sufferer has no knowledge of his
former life, cannot trace cause and effect. The assertion
that the soul remembers, although it cannot communicate
through the brain, is a mere subterfuge.

7. The Karma doctrine is unjust. Why should one after
death suffer the penalty of evildoers in the astral world,
and later on another penalty for evil deeds in lives to come?
Here the Spiritism of Blavatsky's first period and the Buddhism of her second period have been joined together in a
fruitless effort to arrive at unity.

8. Dr. Gaius Glenn Atkins has suggested in his book
Modern Religious Cults and Movements that the hold of
Theosophy upon the West is due to two factors: (1) "It
offers a coherent explanation of the problem of pain and

sorrow." (2) "The speculative aspects of Theosophy also appeal to tempers which love to dream without accepting the laborious discipline of a truly reasoned speculation" (p. 270).

At the same time he grants that "a little book called *At the Feet of the Master* by a young Indian student (Krishnamurti) has in it a wealth of insight and an understanding of the balanced conduct of life which is wanting in a good many of the Western interpretations of life, but none the less, things must be judged by their massed outcome and the massed outcome of Eastern Pantheism does not commend itself" (p. 281).

Religion

1. As a religion, Theosophy is *gnosticism*. Knowledge is enthroned, and the ignorant are to be pitied.

    a. It is a religion for the initiate, not for the masses. Consider the following announcement of an expensive publication: *Theosophic Glossary. Gives information on the principal Sanskrit, Pahlavi, Tibetan Pali, Chaldean, Persian, Scandinavian, Hebrew, Greek, Latin, Kabalistic and Gnostic words and Occult Terms Generally Used in Theosophic Literature. Shows Elaborate and Extraordinary Scholarship.* Does the "Path" to God require that much "scholarship"?

    b. Its gnosticism fosters pride. Sinnett derisively calls those who deny the existence of astral faculties *deafmutes, O. P.'s* (ordinary persons).

    c. The gnostic character of Theosophy makes the system look suspicious, to say the least. Besant, calling one of her books *The Lesser Mysteries,* states, "The Greater will never be published through the printing-press; they can only be given by Teacher to pupil, 'from mouth to ear'." Blavatsky wrote, "Being obliged to start an esoteric section, to teach those things which it was impossible to impart to the students except under the bond of an oath between the teacher and pupil, I carefully prepared those whom I could trust, so that they would not drift back into the worldly methods. I sought in this way to impart magnetic and sexual truths which could be imparted only from ear to ear."

2. Theosophy on the one hand declares the seat of evil to be in matter, and on the other hand speaks of matter as emanating from God. Thus it actually blames God for evil, something Manicheism dared not do: it declared matter, the seat of evil, to be eternally existent beside God. Here lies also another inconsistency. Why speak of matter as an emanation of the divine Logos, while at the same time speaking of man's "physical bondage"? Annie Besant said, "Each successive body is a fresh limitation, or an increased dimming of our vision."

3. Theosophists parade as mystics who live in continual fellowship with God. So do all pantheists. At the same time, however, one finds very scanty reference to God in theosophical writings. God, to them, is a great unknown quantity. But what good is a fellowship with a God who either is unknown and not understood, or who is one with us because we are sparks of God? It is at best a mystic feeling of unity with an impersonal something which pervades us as well as other things.

Theosophy, then, notwithstanding its high-sounding phrases, does not rank more highly as a religion than it does as a philosophy.

Theosophy and Christianity

1. Occultism, as exemplified by Theosophy, not only fosters unbelief in regard to other religions; it is likely to lead to superstition and spirit-worship, since the spirits with whom we are supposed to come into contact are conceived of as more or less omniscient. It is exactly in this attitude of mind that we are in danger of being influenced by supernatural spirits from below. M. E. Sloan informs us that "in explanation of Blavatsky's constant inconsistencies, Olcott advanced the theory that she was subject to the influence of 'incarnating entities,' resulting in 'double personality,' and producing the 'second self' in place of the

'Normal self.' " "He was correct," adds Mr. Sloan, "but failed to recognize the real import of the situation." In this we are inclined to follow this able critic of Theosophy. Very insufficient attention is paid today to the Biblical warning against "doctrines of demons."

2. The Karma doctrine is the sworn enemy of forgiveness. The proud Theosophist needs no forgiveness. He is willing to work out his own destiny.

3. Notwithstanding Krishnamurti's "path of *Desirelessness*," Theosophy is selfish to the core. Its aim is self-improvement, evolution as an end in itself. It lacks the Bible's "unto Him are all things."

4. Like Mormonism, Theosophy is anti-scriptural in teaching the pre-existence of the human soul. Scripture teaches that God first formed the body of man, then gave him the breath of life, making him a living soul.

The Liberal Catholic Church

Numerically, the Liberal Catholic Church is so small that we might ignore it. Yet the tendency that "all faiths and no faith can dwell together in harmony" appears so clearly here that it merits attention.[4]

The Liberal Catholic Church (hereafter L.C.C.) pretends to be a Christian Church, and one catering to the needs of those cultured and mystical souls who feel the need of concerted worship in a beautifully appointed building, and with a great deal of ritual and "atmosphere." Among such there is, quite naturally, a group that refuses to be held down by

---

4. Under date March 1, 1951, Miss Marion M. Matthews, Provincial Secretary-Registrar, wrote as follows from the Provincial Headquarters of the Liberal Catholic Church, 2041 North Argyle Avenue, Los Angeles 28, California:

There are now twenty-three Centers of the Liberal Catholic Church now functioning.

Both Bishop Leadbeater and Bishop Cooper have passed on. There are two Liberal Catholic groups in this country. One is headed by Bishop Newton Dahl in Minneapolis. The other by Bishop Matthews who is the Regionary Bishop for the Liberal Catholic Church in the Province of the United States and the Province of Canada. As you will note above, his office is located here, above address, the Provincial Headquarters for the United States.

any creedal commitments. They want to "feel" Christianity rather than think it through.

Here the L.C.C. offers an ideal scheme. Its "Statement of Principles" begins as follows: "The L.C.C. exists to forward the work of her Master — Christ — in the world, and to feed His flock. It is an independent and autonomous body, in no way dependent upon the See of Rome, or upon any other see or authority outside its own administration. It is neither Roman Catholic nor Protestant — but Catholic."

Here then we have a sort of original World Council, the "twin-half" to the goddess "Ecumenicity."

"The apostolic succession of the L.C.C. is derived from the ancient Church of Holland, sometimes called 'Jansenist.' With characteristic hospitality the Dutch people had given sanctuary to many unfortunate Jansenist refugees who had fled from France and Belgium to escape Jesuit persecution." There was some subsequent friction between the Jansenists and the holy see at Rome, which culminated in the organization of the Old Catholic Church when the former refused to bow to the 1870 dogma of the infallibility of the pope. The Dutch bishops consecrated some English bishops, one of whom, James I. Wedgwood, in turn consecrated Charles W. Leadbeater, Mrs. Besant's co-discoverer of Krishnamurti, as bishop for Australia of the L.C.C. Bishop Wedgwood one year later (1917) consecrated as bishop for the U.S.A. Irving Steiger Cooper.

Aided by Wedgwood, Leadbeater set to work on the liturgy of the L.C.C., and wrote the volume, *The Science of the Sacraments*. Thus the new liturgy, to borrow Mr. Ferguson's spicy speech, "was modeled after that of Rome and has since been filled with the ghosts of Theosophy, so that not so much as an article remains without a spooky and cryptic reference of one sort or another."[5]

If this should sound irreverent, consider a few samples.

The L.C.C. has all the features of a regular Church. It has a summary of doctrine — but no dogma ("The L.C.C.

---

5. Charles W. Ferguson, *The Confusion of Tongues*, p. 282.

permits to its members entire freedom in the interpretation of Creeds, Scriptures and Tradition, and of its Liturgy and Summary of Doctrine"). It uses the Holy Scriptures, creeds, and other traditions of the Church as the vehicle in which the teaching of Christ has been handed down to His followers. "It deduces from them certain principles of belief and conduct . . . ." Thus baptism "is a sacrament by which the recipient is solemnly admitted to membership of Christ's holy Church and 'grafted into his mystical body' " — the mystical body interpreted theosophical fashion. For: "The Sacrament of Baptism takes on a new significance when we realize *that man is essentially an unfolding spiritual intelligence* who expresses himself through a physical body. Thus in an infant the body only is new; the soul standing behind and animating it is old — with a long past behind him."

"The Holy Eucharist is the central act of Christian worship." But how does it work? "Each time it is celebrated, there passes forth into the world a wave of peace and strength, the effect of which can hardly be overrated. . . . This flood of spiritual force affects the spiritual body of the recipient . . . to unfold his latent powers . . . ."

There are healing services, and sermons; and the vesper service "ends with prayers, asking God's help and protection"; but when the beautiful benediction of the Church of England is used the Trinitarian formula is understood in the sense of the Summary of Doctrine: "The manifestation of God in the universe under a triplicity — Father, Son and Holy Ghost."

And the return of Christ is expected after the theosophical manner: "We look for the Lord Christ, the Great Teacher of Angels and of men, to walk once more as a Man among men in the not far distant future, so that He may give this new, yet old teaching, which will place religion on a basis of science as well as revelation."

To these samples I add only that Leadbeater's book on the sacraments is said to be "scientific, because it is the testimony of a great physicist of the spiritual worlds to the things which he has observed, and with which in all reverence he has experimented."

For all this, the writer is convinced that many mystically inclined folk might walk into one of these "churches" and follow its worship without sensing the serious deviation from the age-old tenets of the Christian Church. Is it not time, then, for us to teach the youth of our churches not only *what to confess*, but also *how to understand their confession?*

The Bible and Theosophy

Such Scriptural passages as plainly teach the fundamentals of the Christian faith may be used, of course, with equal force against any system denying those doctrines. It remains remarkable, however, that certain passages seem to have a distinct bearing upon theosophical errors. We submit the following:

1. Against the claim, *ex oriente lux*, Isaiah 2:6, "For thou hast forsaken thy people, the house of Jacob, because they are filled from the east."

2. Against the universal brotherhood of men, Matt. 12:50; John 1:12, 13.

3. Against brotherhood of all religions, Gal. 1:8; II John 10, 11.

4. Against the gnostic distinction between the disciple Jesus and the Christ making use of his body, I John 2:22.

5. Against new revelation beyond that in Christ Jesus, John 1:14; 14:9; II Cor. 4:3, 4; Col. 1:19, 20, 25, 26; Heb. 1 and 2; I John 5:20; II John 10, 11; Jude 3; Rev. 22:18, 19.

6. Against disembodied state in an astral world: II Cor. 5:1-4; Phil. 3:21.

7. Against reincarnation (a) of Jesus, Heb. 9:26; (b) of the rest of us, Heb. 9:27.

8. Against Mahatmas and Christs in the caves of Tibet, Matt. 24:24-26.

9. Against Karma, Isa. 1:18; I John 1:9.

Theosophy and the Bible
Angels
"We regard those mighty archangels and angels as the product of the evolution of older worlds than this, as those who have won beyond the point towards which we now are climbing . . . their younger brothers who are treading the Path that they have trod so long ago in the days of their struggle, ere their victory was won."—A. BESANT.[6]

Blood Atonement
"For what is the doctrine of Atonement as seen from the Theosophical standpoint? It is the declaration that the Atonement wrought by Christ lies not in the substitution of one individual for another, but in the identity of nature between the divine man and men who are becoming divine." —A. BESANT.[7]

"Karma takes no account of custom; and the Karma of cruelty is the most terrible of all. . . . Superstition is another mighty evil, and has caused much terrible cruelty. . . . Think of the awful slaughter produced by the superstition that animals should be sacrificed, and by the still more cruel superstition that man needs flesh for food. Many crimes have men committed in the name of the God of love, moved by this nightmare of superstition."—KRISHNAMURTI.[8]

Brotherhood of Believers
"Objects of the Theosophical Society:
"1. To form a nucleus of the Universal Brotherhood of Humanity, without distinction of race, creed, sex, caste, or color."[9]

"The stately figure of the Ancient Wisdom named Theosophy,' after the Greek 'divine Wisdom,' enters the field as a unifier and peacemaker in religion. 'Sirs, ye are brethren,

---
6. *Is Theosophy Anti-Christian?* p. 11.
7. *Ibid.*, p. 15.
8. *At the Feet of the Master*, pp. 64, 67.
9. I. C. Cooper, *Theosophy Simplified*, p. 1.

why do ye wrong one another?' is the expostulation that falls from her lips."[10]

Christ

"This word, 'the Christ,' means to us more than the name of one, however lofty, or however holy, and to us the Christ is less an external Savior than a living Presence in the human Spirit, a Presence by which the human Spirit unfolds its innate divinity, so that in time all men become Christ."—A. BESANT.[11]

Man

"When your body wishes something, stop and think whether *you* really wish it. For *you* are God, and you will only what God wills; but you must dig deep down into yourself to find the God within you, and listen to His voice which is *your voice*."—KRISHNAMURTI.[12]

"Man is a Spiritual Intelligence, a fragment of Divinity clothed in matter."—A. BESANT.[13]

"Lastly we come to the true man, the soul, of whom it is said in an ancient scripture: 'He is not born, nor does he die, nor having been ceaseth he any more to be.' Unborn, perpetual, eternal and ancient, he is not slain when the body is slaughtered."—I. S. COOPER.[14]

"The popular conception is that God created the world and mankind as a mechanic creates a complicated machine — a thing apart from himself. . . . On this great central problem of life Theosophy is, as on all other matters, in perfect agreement with science, showing that creation is the act of God, but that his process of creation is an evolutionary one; that the life of the supreme Being, permeating every atom of the universe . . . is slowly evolving into high-

---

10. *The Brotherhood of Religions*, p. 8.
11. *Op. cit.*, p. 16.
12. *Op. cit.*, p. 10.
13. *Man's Life in Three Worlds*, p. 3.
14. *Theosophy Simplified*, p. 30.

er and higher powers of consciousness through gradually increasing complexities of form."—L. W. ROGERS.[15]

Inspiration of the Bible

"I confined myself to the Hindu scriptures, and in all cases I stated that I regarded these scriptures and the Hindu religion as the origin of all the scriptures and all the religions."—MRS. BESANT.[16]

"The doctrines of the Gospels, and even of the Old Testament, have been taken bodily from the book of Enoch.

"In its hidden meaning, from Genesis to the last word of Deuteronomy, the Pentateuch is the symbolical narrative of the sexes, and is an apotheosis of Phallicism, under astronomical and physiological personifications."—BLAVATSKY.[17]

Forgiveness of Sins

"The word Karma simply means action.... Hence Karma may be called Causation, or the Law of causation. Its scientific statement is: 'Action and Reaction are equal and opposite'.... This sane and true teaching bids man... surrender all the fallacious ideas of 'forgiveness,' 'vicarious atonement,' 'divine mercy,' and the rest of the opiates which superstition offers to the sinner."—BESANT.[18]

Hell

"If this (Luke 13:23, 24) be applied in the ordinary protestant way to salvation from everlasting hell-fire, the statement becomes incredible, shocking. No Savior of the world can be supposed to assert that many will seek to avoid hell and enter heaven, but will not be able to do so. But as applied to the narrow gateway of Initiation and to salvation from rebirth, it is perfectly true and natural."—BESANT.[19]

---

15. *What Theosophy Is*, p. 8.
16. *The Daily Chronicle*, April 9, 1894.
17. *The Secret Doctrine*, III, 87, 172.
18. Leaflet *Karma*.
19. *Esoteric Christianity*, p. 42.

THEOSOPHY

Mediator

"It is the event of the Baptism which marks the coming of the Christ ... and it is *then*, from the occult point of view, that the *Jesus* became the *Christ*.... Jesus the Hebrew, the individual, the spiritual man, stepped out of the body that he had been dwelling in through all those years and preparing for the coming of his Lord, giving it over as a holy temple for the incoming of the supreme Teacher, so that the body became the habitation of the supreme Teacher, for the three years of his ministry."—A. BESANT.[20]

Prayer

"Whether the person pray to Buddha, to Vishnu, to Christ, to the Father, it matters not at all."—A. BESANT.[21]

"The action of prayer—which is concentrated thought."—A. BESANT.[22]

"Then he learns that Divinity lies hidden within himself, and that nothing that is fleeting can satisfy that God within; that only union with the One, the Perfect, can still his cravings. Then there arises within him the will to set himself at one with the Divine; ... he has risen above all prayer, save that which is meditation and worship; he has nothing to ask for, in this world or in any other."—A. BESANT.[23]

Providence

"Man, an immortal soul, is the moulder and master of his own destiny, because he has started and will start all the forces which mould the circumstances in which he lives.... No one is to blame except ourselves for our birth conditions, our character, our opportunities, our abilities, for all these things are due to the working out of forces we have set going either in this life or in former lives.... From the seed of good and bad actions spring the harvests of pleasant and

---

20. *The Changing World*, p. 306.
21. *The Seven Principles of Man*, p. 58.
22. *The Changing World*, p. 68.
23. *Esoteric Christianity*, p. 257.

unpleasant physical circumstances; . . . from the seeds of good and evil thoughts and desires spring the harvests of good and bad character."—I. S. COOPER.[24]

For Discussion

1. What is the difference between the Christian and the theosophical conception of the divine Trinity?

2. Point out the affinity between Spiritism and Theosophy as to clairvoyance. What does Theosophy substitute for contacting disembodied spirits?

3. Describe the "astral world" and the human "astral body."

4. What is the resemblance and what the difference between the spiritistic and the theosophical conception of "hell," or rather, "purgatory"?

5. What is meant by "Karma"; what by "Mahatmas"?

6. Describe the difference between the theosophical and the Christian idea of incarnation.

7. State your objections to Theosophy as a philosophy; also as a religious system of thought.

8. Do certain passages of Scripture indeed apply directly to certain theosophical ideas?

9. Trace evidences of pantheism in quotations from spiritistic and theosophical writers; see pp. 54-59 and 79-83.

10. Point out similarities and differences between the Christian and the theosophical understanding of Jesus Christ as Mediator.

11. Can you agree with the late Dr. Francis L. Patton of Princeton: "The strongest argument against theosophy is that there is no argument in its favor"? (Machen, *What Is Christianity?* p. 70).

24. *Op. cit.*, p. 55.

5

CHRISTIAN SCIENCE

There is an abundance of incontestable evidence that the author of the religio-medico cult known as Christian Science was to the end of her eighty-nine-year life beset with maladies of both mind and body; that she was in her concluding years "through fear of death subject to bondage"; and that throughout she remained as self-centered as the cult which she had propagated.

She claimed for herself, however, such divine inspiration and God-likeness as to make her assertions appear utterly incompatible with the impression she made upon the majority of her contemporaries. And since her followers have deified both her personality and her teachings, it is almost necessary for them to erase the picture of Mrs. Eddy left behind by those who lived in her own time.

In this assiduous effort, time, as might be expected, has proved to be on the side of the Committees on Publication that have been organized in every state and province where Christian Science has gained a footing. The earlier works, written by contemporaries of the founder, are now mostly out of print; large quantities of "obnoxious literature" have been collected and destroyed; the life of Mrs. Eddy has been rewritten, and whatever has been considered unfriendly has promptly been set aside as "not authentic."

In an effort to practice their claim that Christian Science is a religion that strictly adheres to the Golden Rule, Christian Scientists send, free of charge, approved literature to those who have written adversely on Eddyism, and they courteously request such writers to change their appraisal in consonance with said literature. This has been the experience of Charles S. Braden, F. E. Mayer, Lloyd M. Wallick, and lately of the present writer.[1]

But none of these writers have changed their estimate of Christian Science or its author as a result of such correspondence. Miss Milmine's *The Life of Mary Baker G. Eddy and the History of Christian Science* (1909) remains the fruit of such painstaking efforts and so much traveling through cities in which Mrs. Eddy lived, and contains so many sworn affidavits, that it is impossible to set all this aside as negligible. And Mr. Dakin's biography, *Mrs. Eddy, the Biography of a Virginal Mind* (Scribner's, 1929), is so well documented that it cannot be ignored. Of this best-seller such outstanding and unbiased reviewers as R. L. Duffus (*The New York Times*), Heywood Broun (*Book of the Month Club News*), H. L. Mencken (*American Mercury*) spoke with the highest regard. Gilbert Seldes in *The New York Herald Tribune* wrote: "The decency of the author's attitude, his fine judgment, his poise, and his common sense make his work entirely praiseworthy." And Lewis Mumford stated in *The New Republic*: "Mr. Dakin has committed an unforgivable offense against Mrs. Eddy: he has done her justice."

Christian Science statements that this scholarly standard work "has been written without dependable data," official efforts to boycott and to suppress the sale of the book,[2] and later assertions that these efforts were only those of a few hypersensitive enthusiasts are therefore not very convincing. Moreover, because the officially recommended biographies of Mrs. Eddy present a palpably one-sided

---

1. Braden, *These Also Believe*, pp. 180, 181; Mayer, *The Religious Bodies of America*, p. 524; Wallick, in *The Lutheran Quarterly*, October, 1954; van Baalen, private correspondence with Will B. Davis, Manager, Committee on Publication, Boston, 1958.
2. See "The Blight that Failed," a pamphlet that tells the story of attempts by Christian Scientists to suppress Dakin's book.

CHRISTIAN SCIENCE

portrayal in the interests of glorifying the founder, they cannot be relied upon as historical material.³

Perhaps it will be most charitable to conclude this painful introduction to our subject with the following two remarks.

First, it is, no doubt, difficult to take a totally unbiased view of a person by whose teachings one has greatly benefited; and few, if any, will deny that Mrs. Eddy's teachings have been beneficial to some who take "the grain of truth" in "the bushel of error" which is the system of Eddyism.

And, secondly, when Mrs. Eddy's own experience so violently contradicted her teachings, is it any wonder that the truth is sometimes stretched or even distorted in order to make the facts tally with the firmly believed theory?

Stubborn Facts

When all the evidence is in, this much is beyond dispute. Mrs. Eddy, born July 16, 1821, at Bow, New Hampshire, suffered much from a spinal weakness which affected her physically as well as mentally. This lasted well into her earlier womanhood and marred her first and second marriages. Her troubles caused her to visit the then famous P. P. Quimby at Portland, Maine, who followed in the footsteps of the Frenchman Charles Poyen, a noted mesmerist.

Twice Mrs. Eddy, then known as Mrs. Patterson, visited Quimby. She spent considerable time with him in private and discussed his teachings and methods. After her visit she would sit for hours to write down her conclusions. This has given rise to many confusing reports. Some

---

3. Dr. James H. Snowden states as his conclusion in *The Truth About Christian Science* that in the official biography by Miss Wilbur, "even the most desperate cases are made the best of, though the ugly truth cannot always be denied or explained away. The personal adulation of Mrs. Eddy, approaching divine worship, is nauseating" (p. 10). Lyman Powell's *Mary Baker Eddy, A Life Size Portrait*, written in reaction to Dakin's book, does not even contain the name of Augusta Stetson, although the Stetson episode is undoubtedly one of the blackest marks upon the character and methods of Mrs. Eddy.

hold that Mrs. Eddy's "Bible," *Science and Health,* first published in 1875, contains many of these notes and/or embodies material taken home from Quimby. But Mrs. Eddy maintained that her book was the result of direct, divine inspiration and that it differed radically from Quimby's findings.

Christian Scientists, of course, believe Mrs. Eddy. Miss Wilbur has gone so far as to state that there never were any Quimby manuscripts. But reprints of official documents and affidavits disprove this theory.[4]

It remains an undeniable fact that Mrs. Eddy was at first eloquent in her praise of Dr. Quimby (he "heals the sick as Jesus did)"; that she continually dinned into the ears of people, "I learned this from Dr. Quimby"; and that, as time went on, she gradually denounced not merely this source of her theories but pronounced the man she had at first eulogized a mere mesmerist whereas she advocated healing through the mind.

We may pass by in silence such questions as: In how far was Mrs. Eddy prompted by selfish motives? Was she herself ever healed of any organic trouble? Why was it that she, the divinely inspired prophetess of a new Bible, kept on revising her book throughout the years? What plausible explanation may be given for the fact that the later, revised editions contain a far purer and grammatically more correct English than the earlier ones? Certainly we cannot take seriously her own explanation that she was so inspired with Divine Science when she wrote the first edition that "grammar was eclipsed." And why do even the later editions of *Science and Health with Key to the Scriptures* leave the impression of terrible confusion upon intelligent readers, both as to the arrangement and re-

---

4. The case for Mrs. Eddy's dependence upon Quimby and her later denial of it, and also for her dependence upon the Rev. J. H. Wiggins, her literary editor and ghost writer ("I often feel as if the Lord spoke to me through you"), has recently been argued from unimpeachable sources by W. Martin and N. Klann, *The Christian Science Myth,* 1954.

arrangement of chapters and their failure to limit themselves to their subjects?

Christian Scientists have always indignantly objected to the fact that New York newsmen attempted to obtain an interview with Mrs. Eddy during her declining years at Chestnut Hill. They have boldly denied the almost identical assertions by nine of the newsmen that, after heroic attempts to get near her, they found the aging woman in a tottering condition, both physically and mentally.

Christian Scientists should, however, remember that Mrs. Eddy had for many years denied the reality of sickness and death. Her entire system depended utterly upon the "demonstration" of the correctness of these denials. Consequently, rumors that Mrs. Eddy herself was making frantic but fruitless efforts to prove that correctness in the face of increasing weakness and approaching death more than warranted an honest attempt to inform the public at large of what was going on in and around Chestnut Hill. Was it true that Mrs. Sargeant doubled for Mrs. Eddy during her daily rides in her brougham because Mrs. Eddy was camouflaging her own deteriorating physical condition?

True it is that Mrs. Eddy, on December 2, 1910, at the age of eighty-nine and a half years, died as all have done before her, in spite of her teaching that "God is All, God is Life, and therefore Sickness and Death are non-existent."

Therapeutic Fruits of Christian Science

The Powell biography of Mrs. Eddy contains a chapter "By Their Fruits," and we are willing that Eddyism be judged by its fruits.

These fruits are not wholly evil. If they were, the system could not have survived as it has. The good that is to the credit of Eddyism lies in the many cures it has effected. These demonstrate the power of mind over matter. And it is all to the good that Mrs. Eddy, together with numerous other faith healers and mental healers,[5] has called attention to this power. Medical science is, perhaps more than it likes to admit, indebted to Mrs. Eddy for the rediscovery of the all-important interaction between the physical and the spiritual in man. "Psychosomatic" troubles have been recognized mostly in the wake of Christian Science.[6]

However, alongside of the little good that Eddyism has accomplished we must place the great evil it has wrought.

1. Mrs. Eddy as well as her numerous followers have repeatedly made claims that could not be substantiated. Not only have they refused to be guided by competent diagnosis, as do all faith healers, but they have claimed the ability to heal when such ability was totally lacking. In brief, Christian Science cannot remove organic troubles. Mrs. Eddy herself reluctantly granted the feasibility of calling in surgical help.[7]

One of the unsubstantiated claims made by Mrs. Eddy was: "I healed the malignant tubercular diphtheria and carious bones that could be dented by the finger, saving them when the surgeon's instruments were lying on the table ready for their amputation. I healed at one visit a cancer that had so eaten the flesh of the neck as to expose the jugular vein so that it stood out like a cord."[8] The official Christian Science literature would have us believe that Mrs. Eddy repeatedly raised those who had been held in the clutches of death.[9] Such preposterous claims can be multiplied many times from Mrs. Eddy's own writings.

---

5. The difference between the two categories, in general, is that the former direct the mind to an outside, supposedly divine, power which heals in answer to prayer, whereas the latter hold that the human mind itself is capable of reasoning away sickness. Both, however, presuppose receptivity of mind.

6. W. W. Sweet in his admirable study *The Story of Religion in America* similarly suggests: "And perhaps the growing interest in psychiatry as a new technique is not unrelated to Christian Science" (3rd edition, p. 377).

7. *Science and Health*, last chapter.

8. *New York Sun*, Dec. 19, 1898, as quoted by Martin and Klann.

9. Clifford P. Smith, *Historical Sketches*, p. 80.

CHRISTIAN SCIENCE

2. There is a large amount of literature dealing with authentic cases in which Christian Science practitioners were condemned by the United States courts for needlessly causing deaths by their refusal to call in medical and surgical aid. Reports of these cases may be found in books available in public libraries, if not in Christian Science Reading Rooms.[10]

3. Whether Mr. Eddy died of ordinary physical ailments or of "arsenic poison mentally administered," as Mrs. Eddy asserted, the fact remains that Mrs. Eddy was not able to cope with the results of the evil forces the reality of which she denied. The same is true of the practitioners who have followed after her. At best they have attributed the results of evil forces to "error of Mortal Mind," which apparently proved too strong for "Omnipotent Good" to remove it. In spite of her denial of the existence of the devil, Mrs. Eddy was in her old age to an unusual degree driven to mortal fear by that real devil of her system which she was pleased to call "Malicious Animal Magnetism." M.A.M. stands for unkind and hostile thoughts directed against one. M.A.M. has become the nightmare of Christian Science and is the real devil of this devil-denying philosophy.

Philosophy of Christian Science

Eddyism is first of all the result of Mrs. Eddy's quest for physical health. When she thought she had found this for herself through P. P. Quimby, she thought to find it for others through influencing their minds against the existence of their physical troubles. Over a period of years, she developed the system that has spread over parts of the United States and Canada and many other lands.

---

10. Cf. Peabody, *The Religio-Medical Masquerade;* Paget, *The Faith and Works of Christian Science,* pp. 151-180 (sixty-eight cases cited); W. A. Purrington, *Christian Science, an Exposition of Mrs. Eddy's Wonderful Discovery, Including the Legal Aspects: A plea for Children and Other Helpless Sick.*

(Christian Science's influence has remained limited largely to urban communities and to the prosperous middle class. This can be seen in Seattle, for instance, where the eighteenth Church of Christ, Scientist was officially dedicated on the Sunday after Easter, April 5, 1959).

It matters not whether this system originated with Quimby or with Mrs. Eddy, whether it goes back to 1862 or to 1866. Mrs. Eddy certainly went beyond Mesmer, Poyen, and Quimby, although the finished product contains elements found in their systems and elements strongly reminiscent of Shakerism, hypnotism, philosophical idealism, and perhaps of other systems of thought that were popular in her day and environment. The final product, however, went beyond any and all of these in that it became, and is now, what has been called "precisely acosmic pantheism, that, all that, and nothing but that."[11]

Since Mrs. Eddy was essentially a poorly educated and self-made woman who dealt with problems far beyond her ken, her book, the now notorious *Science and Health,* is hopelessly confused. From the first to the last edition, it contains a mass of confused ideas. Its popularity is to no small degree due to the fact that the confused and endlessly repetitious statements leave, with certain readers, the impression of great profundity. Intelligent readers, of course, detect her rare taste for illogical rambling and harping upon one single thought.

Mrs. Eddy did, however, face grave difficulties in maintaining her one single idea in the face of the facts of a largely material universe. Few pantheists would go the length Mrs. Eddy went to: she held that since God is All, and God is Omnipotent Good, therefore all that is not God simply has no objective reality. And since she could not deny that evil in its many spiritual and physical forms surrounds us on every hand, Mrs. Eddy found herself forced to postulate something she called "Mortal Mind" which

---

11. B. B. Warfield, *Miracles Yesterday and Today,* p. 217.

exists, she maintained, in opposition to God and Good. This mind is filled with error, and to it must be attributed all apparent evil. Since evil is mental, it must be reasoned away; it must be silenced by Divine Mind. That there is actually no room for such an erroneous Mortal Mind in a theory that postulates the existence of a good and omnipotent God to the exclusion of all evil is the one stubborn fact that destroys the entire philosophy of Christian Science.

The practical difficulty Christian Science encounters here lies in the fact that even Mrs. Eddy herself was not so filled with "Science" as to be able to demonstrate the nonexistence of evil, sorrow, pain, and death. Man in his present condition is able to reason away only certain diseases and evils; to the end of his earthly career he remains subject to "the tyranny of Mortal Mind"; only ultimately will mankind be able to "demonstrate" the truthfulness of Mrs. Eddy's one fundamental thought that God and Truth and Health and Opulence are the one, only reality.

It is this grudgingly acknowledged fact that (1) makes all Christian Science literature so difficult to understand by non-initiated; that (2) plagued Mrs. Eddy grievously with her lifelong mortal fear of M.A.M.; and that (3) prompted a well-known doctor of philosophy of a generation ago to accuse Mrs. Eddy of "the trick of two languages," stating that the key to Christian Science and the understanding of its textbook lies in the recognition of the fact that the same words are used with two different meanings, the one that of "Science" and the other that of "Mortal Mind."[12]

Dr. Snowden has summed up the popular appeal of Christian Science in a concluding chapter under the following headings: 1. The Appeal of Health; 2. The Appeal of Comfort; 3. The Appeal of Idealism; 4. The Appeal of Liberal Revolt. He adds:

---

12. Richard L. Swain, *The Real Key to Christian Science.*

Though Christian Science is a pretentious and fallacious system of philosophy that has no standing or respect in the schools, yet this very aspect of it has been an attraction for a certain type of unschooled and superficial mind. The vague mystic ideas, the strange doctrines, the claim and appearance of being a new "revelation," the peculiar catch-words and phrases of its jargon, and especially the great, swelling, sonorous polysyllables, even such uncouth words as "allness" and "somethingness," and the rolling, reverberating sentences have a kind of hypnotic effect, fascinating and attracting minds not given to careful attention and reflective thought, as bright electric lights attract swarms of summer flies and moths.[13]

Christian Science as a Religion

Mrs. Eddy at first thought only of healing. It was not until 1879 that she organized her "Church." The first edition of her book contained no "Key to the Scriptures," and the latter never went beyond a few comments on the opening chapters of Genesis.

Here Mrs. Eddy is not at her best. She accuses Scripture of falsehood where she cannot make it agree with her own findings (e.g., "It must be a lie" — note on Gen. 2:7); and she claims for her book, which is replete with contradictory statements, a verbal inspiration. That, however, is ruled out by her numerous alterations and emendations in each new edition, and by her pronouncement that each new edition is the one and only authoritative edition. Nevertheless, her claim to inspiration caused her to state that she was the woman of Revelation 12; to forbid her followers to call any one on earth "mother" except their own mother in the flesh and the founder of the "First Church of Christ, Scientist"; and to change the address of the Lord's Prayer to "Our Father-Mother God."

---

13. Snowden, *The Truth about Christian Science*, p. 269.

As a religion, Christian Science lulls men to sleep by denying the reality of all the evils which Scripture asserts exist and by remaining silent about the retribution to be meted out hereafter to those who "deny that Jesus Christ has come into the flesh" and has given His life a ransom for many on the accursed tree.

Conclusion

Christian Scientists place the textbook of Mrs. Eddy above the Bible when the First Reader in their worship services reads from *Science and Health* and is followed by the Second Reader, who selects a portion of Scripture which is supposed to corroborate Mrs. Eddy's theory.

Christian Scientists therefore have a strong ally in the modern mind that has been weaned away from faith in the Scriptures. For an entire century now men have been taught to regard the Bible as a book that contains both truth and error. That Christ accepted the Old Testament as fully inspired, and was herein followed by His apostles, who regarded each other's writings as inspired, is ignored. Are not all men children of their own day, erring and knowing but in part? And were not the Master and His apostles woven of the same cloth, though they far surpassed those of their own day in inspirational and intuitive insight into truth? Furthermore, the laborious, conscientious, and painstaking efforts of the Early Church to formulate the teachings of Scripture are set aside as having been "the best available in their day."

As a result many Biblical doctrines that are offensive to the unregenerate are totally ruled out of court, and even those within the churches are at sea, groping for authority and truth. Every "lo, here" and "lo, there" receives a hearing, and such preposterous works as *Science and Health* and *The Book of Mormon* obtain a ready allegiance, for they claim to speak with divine authority.

Moreover, in a country of which Henry Van Dyke said long ago, "There are Americans who have too little respect for special training, and too much confidence in their power to solve the problems of philosophy and statesmanship extemporaneously," any misinterpretation of Scriptural truth, whether by Charles Taze Russell, Mrs. Ellen G. White, Joseph Smith, Jr., the Seer, or Mrs. Mary B. G. P. Eddy, is bound to receive a hearing and a following. As long as the teaching sounds faintly reminiscent of Scriptural phraseology and of the historic Christian faith and, above all, if it only be broad-minded and appreciative of other interpretations that give satisfaction to others who claim to hold Christ in high esteem, it will probably receive a hearing, whatever kind of fictitious Christ it presents.

Over against all this the Church today needs an intelligent return to the objective truth presented in Scripture, and a clear perception of the fact that two mutually exclusive interpretations cannot be equally acceptable to God. Christian Science Committees on Publication may state, "We, too, hold Jesus Christ in high esteem; therefore we are brethren," but we must say with the apostle Paul, even weeping, that they are enemies of the cross of Christ. "For many deceivers are gone forth into the world, even they that confess not that Jesus Christ cometh in the flesh. This is the deceiver and the antichrist" (II John: 7).

Summing Up

Thirty years ago, when the first edition of the present work was published, there was still a great deal of the "believe as I tell you or else" spirit abroad. Even at ministerial meetings the Baptist sat with the Baptist, and the Presbyterian kept aloof from the Methodist. But now all this has changed. The spirit of tolerance is in the air. And the cults have benefited from this change.

Of course, politeness, tolerance, and amiability are Christian virtues. And we all know in part. This apostolic admission is true for denominations as well as for the individuals who constitute the denominations. There is, however, great danger in an unbiblical tolerance. Scripture does not teach that we all shall get to heaven. Scripture does not teach that a "religion" that is interested only in good results for this mundane life is just one more form of Christianity.

Of all the anti-Christian cults, none, perhaps, produces more gentlemanly, soft-spoken, and suave defenders than does Eddyism. That is nice. That is pleasant. Let its devotees, however, bear in mind that the Scriptures which they honor with their lips state, "Even Satan himself fashioneth himself into an angel of light." And let them note the words that follow: "It is no great thing therefore if his ministers also fashion themselves as ministers of righteousness; whose end shall be according to their works (II Cor. 11:15). And did not the same apostle warn against satanic "lying wonders"?

Most assuredly, the apostles would not have approved, and the Early Church would not have tolerated, a "religion" that, in veiled language and much double talk, teaches that Jesus was laid down, as a result of an apparent death, into a fictitious tomb, in an unreal body, to make an unnecessary atonement for sins that had never been a reality and had been committed in an imaginary body, and that He saves from non-existing evil those headed toward an imaginary hell, the false fancy of erroneous Mortal Mind.

The Bible and Christian Science

Angels

"Angels are pure thoughts from God, winged with Truth and Love, no matter what their individualism may be . . . . My angels are exalted thoughts."—MRS. EDDY.[14]

---
14. *Science and Health*, ed. 1910, p. 298.

Atonement

"One sacrifice, however great, is insufficient to pay for the debt of sin. The atonement requires constant self-immolation on the sinner's part. That God's wrath should be vented upon His beloved Son, is divinely unnatural. Such a theory is man-made. The atonement is a hard problem in theology, but its scientific explanation is, that suffering is an error of sinful sense which Truth destroys."

"The efficacy of Jesus' spiritual offering is infinitely greater than can be expressed by our sense of human blood. The material blood of Jesus was no more efficacious to cleanse from sin when it was shed upon 'the accursed tree,' than when it was flowing in his veins as he went daily about his Father's business. His true flesh and blood were his Life; and they truly eat his flesh and drink his blood who partake of that divine Life."—MRS. EDDY.[15]

Death

"What appears to the sense to be death is but a mortal illusion, for to the real man and the real universe there is no death-process."

"Death.—An illusion, the lie of life in matter; the unreal and untrue."

"His disciples believed Jesus to be dead while he was hidden in the sepulchre, whereas he was alive, demonstrating within the narrow tomb the power of Spirit to overrule mortal material sense."—MRS. EDDY.[16]

Devil

"Christian Science teaches us that 'the evil one,' or one evil, is but another name for the first lie and all liars."

"DEVIL, evil, a lie, error, neither corporeality nor mind."—MRS. EDDY.[17]

---

15. *Ibid.*, pp. 23, 25.
16. *Ibid.*, pp. 289, 584, 44.
17. *Ibid.*, pp. 331, 256.

Evil

"If God, or good, is real, then evil, the unlikeness of God, is unreal."

"All sin is insanity in different degrees."

"Man is incapable of sin, sickness, and death."—MRS. EDDY.[18]

Fall of Man

"If man was once perfect but has now lost his perfection, then mortals have never beheld in man the reflex image of God. The *lost* image is no image. The true likeness cannot be lost in divine reflection [that is, man]. Understanding this, Jesus said: 'Be ye therefore perfect even as your Father which is in heaven is perfect.'"—MRS. EDDY.[19]

God

"God is All-in-All."

"God is incorporeal, divine, supreme, infinite Mind, Spirit, Soul, Principle, Life, Truth, Love."

"Life, Truth, and Love constitute the triune Person called God, that is, the triply divine Principle, Love ... the same in essence, though multiform in office; God the Father-Mother; Christ the spiritual idea of sonship; divine Science or the Holy Comforter."

"The theory of three persons in one God (that is, a personal Trinity or Tri-unity) suggests polytheism, rather than the one ever-present I Am."—MRS. EDDY.[20]

Inspiration of Scripture

"The Bible has been my only authority. I have had no other guide in 'the straight and narrow way' of Truth."

"Genesis 2:7. Is this addition to His creation real or unreal? Is it the truth, or is it a lie concerning man and God? It must be a lie, for God presently curses the ground."—MRS. EDDY.[21]

---

18. *Ibid.*, pp. 470, 407, 475.
19. *Ibid.*, p. 259.
20. *Ibid.*, pp. 113, 465, 331, 256.
21. *Ibid.*, pp. 126, 524.

Jesus Christ

"God is indivisible. A portion of God could not enter man; neither could God's fulness be reflected by a single man, else God would be manifestly finite, lose the deific character, and become less than God."

"Jesus is the human man, and Christ is the divine idea; hence the duality of Jesus the Christ."

"The Christ dwelt forever an idea in the bosom of God, the divine Principle of the man Jesus, and woman perceived this spiritual idea, though at first faintly developed."

"Christ, Truth, was demonstrated through Jesus to prove the power of Spirit over the flesh. . . . Jesus represented Christ, the true idea of God."

"The Virgin-mother conceived this idea of God, and gave to her ideal the name of Jesus."

"Jesus was the offspring of Mary's self-conscious communion with God."

"Mary's conception of him was spiritual, for only purity could reflect Truth and Love."

"Jesus bore our sins in his body. He knew the mortal errors which constitute the material body, and could destroy those errors; but at the time when Jesus felt our infirmities, he had not conquered all the beliefs of the flesh or his sense of material life, nor had he risen to final demonstration of spiritual power."

"Our Master fully and finally demonstrated divine Science in his victory over death and the grave. . . . The persecutors had failed to hide immortal Truth and Love in a sepulchre."—MRS. EDDY.[22]

Justification by Faith

"Final deliverance from error, whereby we rejoice in immortality, boundless freedom, and sinless sense, is not reached through paths of flowers nor by pinning one's faith without works to another's vicarious effort."—MRS. EDDY.[23]

---

22. *Ibid.*, pp. 336, 473, 29, 316, 29, 332, 53, 45.
23. *Ibid.*, p. 22.

Marriage

"Until time matures, human growth, marriages, and progeny will continue unprohibited in Christian science."—Mrs. Eddy.[24]

"Until the spiritual creation is discerned and the union of male and female apprehended in its soul sense, this rite should continue."[25]—Mrs. Eddy.

"Until it is learned that generation rests on no sexual basis, let marriage continue."[26]—Mrs. Eddy.

"Until it is learned that God is the Father of all, marriage will continue."[27]—Mrs. Eddy.

Prayer

"Desire is prayer. Such a desire has little need of audible expression. It is best expressed in thought and life."

"Shall we ask the divine Principle of all goodness to do His own work? His work is done."

"God is not influenced by man."

"The mere habit of pleading with the divine mind, as one pleads with a human being, perpetuates the belief in God as humanly circumscribed—an error which impedes spiritual growth."

"Here let me give what I understand to be the spiritual sense of the Lord's Prayer:

> Our Father which art in heaven,
> *Our Father-Mother God, all-harmonious,*
> Hallowed be Thy name.
> *Adorable One.*
> Thy kingdom come.
> *Thy kingdom is come; Thou art ever-present.*
> Thy will be done in earth, as it is in heaven.
> *Enable us to know — as in heaven, so on earth, —*
> *God is omnipotent, supreme.*
> Give us this day our daily bread;
> *Give us grace for today; feed the famished affections;*

---

24. *Miscellaneous Writings*, p. 289.
25. *Science and Health*, ed. 1881, p. 152.
26. *Ibid.*, ed. 1889, p. 274.
27. *Ibid.*, ed. 1910, p. 64.

And forgive us our debts, as we forgive our debtors.
And Love is reflected in love;
And lead us not into temptation, but deliver us from evil;
And God leadeth us not into temptation, but delivereth us from sin, disease, and death.
For thine is the kingdom, and the power, and the glory, forever.
For God is infinite, all-power, all Life, Truth, Love, over all, and All."—MRS. EDDY.[28]

Sacraments

"Our baptism is a purification from all error." "Baptism: Purification by Spirit; submergence in Spirit." [Note: Baptism is not a sign and seal; baptism itself is spiritualized away.—V. B.]

"The true sense is spiritually lost, if the sacrament is confined to the use of bread and wine. . . . Jesus prayed; he withdrew from the material senses to refresh his heart with brighter, with spiritual views . . . and this supper closed forever Jesus' ritualism or concessions to matter. His followers partook of the heavenly manna, which of old had fed in the wilderness the persecuted followers of Truth. Their bread indeed came down from heaven. It was the great truth of spiritual being, healing the sick and casting out error . . . they had borne this bread from house to house, *breaking* (explaining to others), and now it comforted themselves.

"For this truth of spiritual being, their Master was about to suffer violence and drain to the dregs his cup of sorrow . . . . Christians, are you drinking his cup? Have you shared the blood of the New Covenant, the persecutions which attend a new and higher understanding of God? If not, can you then say that you have commemorated Jesus in his cup? Are all who eat bread and drink wine in memory of Jesus willing truly to drink his cup, take his cross, and leave all for the Christ-principle? Then why ascribe this inspiration to a dead rite . . . ?

---

28. *Ibid.,* pp. 1, 11, 3, 7, 2, 27.

"What a contrast between our Lord's last supper and his last spiritual breakfast with his disciples in the bright morning hours at the joyful meeting on the shore of the Galilean Sea! . . .

"This spiritual meeting with our Lord in the dawn of a new light is the morning meal which Christian Scientists commemorate. They bow before Christ, Truth, to receive more of his reappearing and silently to commune with the divine Principle, Love. They celebrate their Lord's victory over death, . . . and his spiritual ascension above matter, or the flesh, when he rose out of material sight."—MRS. EDDY.[29]

Consider

1. Is "Christian Science" among the more profound substitutes for Christianity, or is it one of the most superficial?
2. Is it possible to be an intelligent "Christian Scientist" and an intelligent Christian at the same time?
3. What is the great inconsistency in Eddyism?
4. How do you account for Mrs. Eddy's popularity?
5. Mention some cardinal Christian doctrines and show how "Christian Science" denies and perverts them.
6. Is "Christian Science" only unchristian, or is it also unscientific? Would you prefer a "practitioner" to a physician?
7. What is "the grain of truth in the bushel of Christian Science"?

---
29. *Ibid.*, pp. 32-35, 581.

6

ROSICRUCIANISM

Rosicrucianism is powerful in California, headquarters of so many false cults. From Oceanside the widow of Max Heindel, late apostle of modern Rosicrucianism, sends forth the copyrighted reprints of her husband's profound and voluminous tomes, *The Rosicrucian Cosmo-Conception or Mystic Christianity* (606 pp.), *The Rosicrucian Philosophy in Questions and Answers* (426 pp.), *The Rosicrucian Christianity Lectures* (347 pp.), and numerous pamphlets and correspondence courses.

There may be some small comfort in the knowledge that the Rosicrucians, too, are divided against one another. The lady who sold me the books informed me that the "AMORC" (see Bibliography at the end of this volume) have lost their title to the name Rosicrucians because "they commercialize religion, whereas *we* only charge for the books."[1]

She also informed me that she had been "a member of the Mother Church for twenty-five years prior to joining the Rosicrucian Fellowship, but made the change because here truth is taught so much more clearly." This at once suggests that Rosicrucianism and Christian Science are related; and they are, as all forms of pantheism are related.

Approaching Rosicrucianism more closely, however, we soon discover that it far more intimately resembles Theosophy. In fact Rosicrucianism admits being "the Western

---

1. On the third floor of the Arcade Building in Seattle the average Christian worker may receive an eye opener. Rosicrucians, Baha'is, the Unity School of Religion, Astrologists, Spiritists, all have their studios; and each studio has not only a rack or a bookcase with literature, but there are chairs which are arranged in classroom fashion: the cultists are evidently of the opinion that religion can be taught. Had the evangelical churches done more doctrinal teaching, there would today be fewer victims of all these strange cults.

teaching given to the Western people at this time for their advancement." "If we take Theosophy as meaning *Theo Sophia* (Divine Wisdom), then, of course, the Rosicrucian Philosophy is only part of that Divine Wisdom, like all other religious systems. But if we take theosophy to mean the philosophy promulgated by the Theosophical Society, or Societies, for there are several brands, then we may say that the Rosicrucian teaching is much more comprehensive and complete." Besides, Rosicrucianism is opposed to the arrogant attitude of Theosophy in regard to other systems that also have the idea of universal brotherhood at heart. "It is not necessary to be a theosophist in order to follow that object, but it is necessary to be an occultist in order to follow the third object of the Theosophical Society, namely, the study of the unexplained laws of nature and the powers latent in man." "The Theosophical Society is simply an exoteric organization [I wonder how the Theosophists like that "exoteric"!] for the dissemination of a certain philosophy, mostly derived from the Eastern religions, while the Rosicrucian Fellowship aims to promulgate the teachings of the Western Mystery School, the Order of Rosicrucians, which is secret and not accessible to anyone except upon direct invitation."[2]

I believe, if I were to choose between the two, I'd choose Rosicrucianism. From a purely philosophical viewpoint it seems to me the more acceptable of the two. It does not believe in Karma, but holds that, though every Ego is reincarnated many times, each individual birth brings one into the world innocent because the evil has been purged away; yet one is born with certain tendencies which may develop into vices, therefore we must be tried to see whether we will develop virtue.

And I would prefer Rosicrucianism to Christian Science from a medico-religious viewpoint because, all according to the nature of the malady and the bias of the patient, I should be allowed to choose between employing a Christian

---
2. *The Rosicrucian Philosophy*, pp. 358-360.

Science practitioner, a Faith Healer of some other brand "materia medica used in conjunction with astrology," or even be permitted to "attempt to cure the ills from which we suffer in any other way possible that appeals to us."

However, as a Christian I need not choose between Theosophy and Rosicrucianism, but may have the clear and sufficient teachings of the Scriptures which leave enough unexplained as to the manner of Christ's return and the hereafter for *faith* to be satisfied for the time being without *sight;* and so there is no need of the ill-founded vagaries of the occult.

And here, perhaps, we touch upon the fundamental fruit of the "Rosicrucian Philosophy." There is literally nothing these people cannot and do not explain. One marvels at the patient digging and the interminable babbling that produces a never ending stream of facts and subjects, all fitting neatly within the confines of this all-absorbing system. And, of course, there is no argument against information that obtains from an "occult" source. If you do not believe it, you simply are on the outside.

The Rose Cross

The name of the cult itself is an apt illustration of this uncanny ability to interpret all things and make them fit. It happens that in the thirteenth century a man named Christian Rosenkreuz began to bring out into the open teachings which hitherto had been promulgated only in secret. Christian Rosenkreuz, what a name to conjure with! He founded the mysterious order of Rosicrucians with the object of throwing occult light upon the misunderstood Christian Religion and to explain the mystery of Life and Being from the scientific standpoint in harmony with Religion.

All of which, it will be seen, might have been written by a theosophical Rogers or Sinnett; all except for the "symbolical name Christian Rosenkreuz."

The Rosicrucians have taken the offense out of the Cross (and they call that esoteric Christianity!). The Cross should not be interpreted as an emblem of suffering and shame, so reads the amazing account of this "mystic Christianity."

What then did and does it stand for? Ask Plato, who was an initiate, and wrote, "The world-soul is crucified." With these words, we are informed, the Greek philosopher gave out occult truth. And what is that truth? That "the Cross is symbolical of the life currents vitalizing the bodies of plants, animal and man"; it is "symbolical of man's past evolution, present constitution, and future development."

"The mineral kingdom ensouls all chemical substance of whatever kind, so that the Cross, of whatever material it is made, is first symbol of that kingdom.

"The upright lower limb of the Cross is a symbol of the plant kingdom because the currents of the group spirits which give life to the plants come from the center of the earth where these group spirits are located and reach out toward the periphery of our plant and into space.

"The upper limb of the Cross is the symbol of man, because the life currents of the human kingdom pass downward from the sun through the vertical spine. Thus man is the inverted plant, for as the plant takes its food through the root, passing it *upward,* so does the man take his nourishment by way of the head, passing it *downward.* The plant is chaste, pure and passionless, and stretches its creative organ, the flower, chastely and unshamed *toward the sun,* a thing of beauty and delight. Man turns his passion-filled generative organ *toward the earth.* Man inhales the life-giving oxygen and exhales the poisonous carbon dioxide. The plant takes the poison exhaled by man, building its body therefrom, and returning to us the elixir of life, the cleansed oxygen.

"Between the plant and the human kingdom stands the animal with the horizontal spine, and in the horizontal spine the life currents of the animal group spirit play as they circle around the globe. Therefore the horizontal limb of the Cross is the symbol of the animal kingdom."[3]

---
3. *Ibid.,* p. 202.

"The animal, which is symbolized by the horizontal limb of the Cross, is between plant and man. Its spine is in horizontal position and through it play the currents of animal group-spirit which encircle the Earth. . . .

"To keep him steadfast and true through adversity, the Rose Cross holds aloft, as an inspiration, the glorious consummation in store for him that overcometh, and points to Christ as the Star of Hope, the 'first fruits,' who wrought that choicest of all gems, the Philosopher's Stone while inhabiting the body of Jesus."[4]

This, then, interprets the Rosicrucian emblem: the Cross as well as the Star against which it stands; while the garland of roses around the center of the Cross points to yet another symbolism. "In the form where it is represented with a single rose in the center it symbolizes the spirit radiating from itself the four vehicles: the dense, vital, and desire bodies plus the mind; where the spirit has drawn into its instruments and become the *indwelling* human spirit." But there was a time when that condition did not obtain, a time when the threefold spirit hovered above its vehicles and was unable to enter. Then the Cross stood alone without the rose, symbolizing the condition which prevailed in the early third of Atlantis. There was even a time when the upper limb of the Cross was lacking and man's constitution was represented by the Tau (T). That was in the Lemurion Epoch when he had only the dense, vital, and desire bodies, but lacked the mind. Then the animal nature was paramount. Man followed desire without reserve. At a still earlier time, in the Hyperborian Epoch, he was also minus the desire body and possessed only the dense and vital bodies. Then man-in-the-making was like the plants: chaste and devoid of desire. At that time his constitution could not have been represented by a Cross. It was symbolized by a straight shaft, a pillar (I).

Thought and voice, we are told further, are both creative but the selfish, dominating creative faculty (symbolized

---
4. *Cosmo-conception*, pp. 86, 519.

by the larynx, at the crossing of head and body) must give way to a less selfish creative force. It is here that the roses enter; for "the rose, like any other flower, is the generative organ of the plant. Its green stem carries the colorless, passionless plant blood. The blood-red rose shows the passion-filled blood of the human race, but in the rose the vital fluid is not sensuous; it is chaste and pure. Thus it is an excellent symbol of the generative organ in the pure and holy state to which man will attain when he has cleansed and purified his blood of desire, when he has become chaste, pure and Christ-like."

Thus we get the Cross, the long limb representing the body, the two horizontals the two arms, and the short upper limb the head, with the circle of roses around the center instead of the larynx. "Therefore the Rosicrucians look ardently forward to the day when the roses shall bloom upon the cross of humanity, therefore the Elder Brothers greet the aspiring soul with the words of the Rosicrucian Greeting: 'May the Roses bloom upon your Cross,' and therefore the greeting is given in the meetings of the Fellowship Centers by the leader to the assembled students, probationers and disciples who respond to the greeting by saying, 'And on yours, also.' "[5]

It is all very profound, quite esoteric, and eminently fitting the name of Christian Rosenkreuz of the thirteenth century. Perhaps, though, the name was not quite as accidental as an outsider might surmise: we are told that this Mr. Rosenkreuz, or rather the Ego dwelling in him, was already then "a high spiritual teacher." His birth as Christian Rosenkreuz merely marked the beginning of a new epoch in spiritual life in the Western world. And he has since that day "taken a new body when his successive vehicles have outlived their usefulness, or circumstances rendered it expedient that he change the scene of his activities. He inspired Bacon's works (altho through an

---
5. *Ibid.*, pp. 534ff.

intermediary), and he enlightened the mystic Jacob Boehme. He is also embodied today, an Initiate of high degree, an active and potent factor in all affairs of the West—although unknown to the World" (1909, but still printed in the 1944 edition of the *Cosmo-conception*).

In accordance with such symbolism Christian emblems of long standing are made to fit in. "In esotericism the Cross was never looked upon as an instrument of torture, and it was not until the sixth century that the crucified Christ was shown in pictures. Previous to that time the symbol of the Christ was a Cross and a lamb resting on its foot, to convey the idea that at the time when Christ was born the sun at the vernal equinox crossed the equator in the sign of Aries the Lamb.... Some claimed that the vernal equinox at His birth was really in the sign of Pisces, the Fishes, and that the symbol of our Savior should have been a fish. It is in memory of that dispute that the Bishop's mitre still takes the form of the head of a fish."[6]

The apostle John evidently lacked this occult information, and in his ignorance interpreted the Lamb in Old Testament style as a sacrifice that takes away the sin of the world. And the early Christians, who for fear of being betrayed to the enemy, drew a fish in the sand to see if there were an understanding response, interpreted the symbol of the fish as follows: ICHTHUS (Greek for "fish"): *I(esous) CH(ristos) TH(eou) U(ios) S(oter)*, i.e., Jesus Christ, God's Son, Savior.

The Worlds

The explanation of the Cross, however, contains sufficient hints at other Rosicrucian doctrines to launch us upon a more complete, though ever so brief, exposition of this complicated system of thought. For we have heard of the various bodies of man, of many spirits, of evolution through reincarnation, and of many races.

---

6. *Rosicrucian Philosophy*, p. 203.

There are seven Worlds which together form the Universe. Each one is amenable to laws which are practically inoperative in the other. For instance, the laws of gravitation, and of contraction and expansion to which matter is subject in the Physical (the lowest) World, do not exist in the next higher or the Desire World. Neither is there heat or cold there.

Each World is subdivided into seven Regions or subdivisions of matter. In the Physical World we have denser forms, namely, solids, liquids, and gases; and also four ethers of varying densities. But ether still remains a physical matter. The four etherics together form the Etheric Region. Above all this is the Universal Spirit, expressing itself in the visible world as four great streams of Life, at varying stages of development. This fourfold spiritual impulse molds the chemical matter of the Earth into variegated forms of the four kingdoms—mineral, plant, animal, and man.

The Etheric Region of the Physical World is as tangible to the clairvoyant as are the solids, liquids, and gases of the Chemical Region to ordinary people. The clairvoyant sees four ethers: Chemical Ether, Life Ether, Light Ether, Reflecting Ether. Rather than invent instruments to learn the secrets of nature (as does the scientist), the occultist would develop the investigator himself.

Thus we may find that our senses or faculties may become the "open sesame" in searching for truth. The trained senses of the clairvoyant see clearly the interaction between the physical and the etheric body of man.

For example, the Chemical Ether expels from the physical body of man the materials in food which are unfit for use (negative pole) and also assimilates that which can be incorporated into the body (positive pole).

The Life Ether, also working through a positive and a negative pole, takes care of the forces of propagation, the positive working in the female during the period of gestation, and the negative pole of life enabling the male to produce semen.

Light Ether negatively operates through the senses, manifesting the passive functions of sight, hearing, feeling, tasting, smelling; it also builds and nourishes the eye; positively, it is the avenue of the forces that circulate the blood. In plants and animals Light Ether is responsible for color.

Reflecting Ether has in it the reflections of the memory of nature (as the giant ferns of the childhood of the Earth have left their picture in the coal beds). But no clairvoyant likes to read in this book of memory, as the pictures are blurred. Spiritist mediums and psychometers may be forced to do that sort of thing: the Rosicrucian clairvoyant rises to greater heights, knowing that in higher Worlds nature has better memories.

The Desire World, like the Physical World, and like every other realm of nature, has the seven subdivisions called Regions, but it does not have the four great etheric divisions. "Desire stuff" in the Desire World persists through its seven subdivisions or regions as material for the embodiment of desire.

The desires, wishes, passions, and feelings of man express themselves through these seven regions of "desire matter," which is only one degree less dense than the matter of the Physical World. It is not a *finer* physical matter: rather it is in unceasing *motion*, whereas the matter of the Physical World is *inert*. The Desire World is ever-changing light and color, in which forces of animal and man intermingle with the forces of innumerable Hierarchies of spiritual beings which mold our desires. Our desires in turn create *interest*. Interest, once it is thoroughly aroused, starts the forces of *attraction* and *repulsion*.

Observe now the following verbatim citation, to point out the close resemblance of the "western" occultism to the "oriental" "esoteric" Christianity.

"The Physical and the Desire Worlds are not separated from each other by space. They are 'closer than hands and feet.' It is not necessary to move to get from one to the other, nor from one Region to the next. Just as solids, liquids, and gases are all together in our bodies, interpenetrating one another, so are the different Regions of the Desire World within us also."

The World of Thought also consists of seven Regions of varying qualities and densities, and, like the Physical World, the World of Thought is divided into two main divisions: the Region of Concrete Thought, composing the four densest Regions, and the Region of Abstract Thought, comprising the three Regions of finest substance. All of this is also thought of as consisting, if not of material, at least of "mind-stuff." The *thought-forms* are acting "as regulators and balance wheels upon the impulses engendered in the Desire World by impacts from the phenomenal World."

The Evolution of Man

As to the evolution of man and the growth of the soul, we find a more sensible account here of the character of dreams than we met in Theosophy. When during sleep the desire body does not fully withdraw from the vital body, but remains connected with it, the vehicle for sense perception and memory has its "axis askew," and the memory becomes confused. For sleep is just that: a withdrawal of the higher vehicles from the dense body which then gets a rest and a chance to rebuild itself.

Death is something else again. Here the higher vehicles leave the dense body more completely, though for a while remaining connected by "the silver cord." One end of the silver cord is fastened to the heart by means of the *seed-atom,* and it is the rupture of the seed-atom which causes the heart to stop. The cord itself is not snapped until the panorama of the past life, contained in the vital body, has been reviewed. At death the dense body at once loses weight because *not the soul* but the vital body has left.

In his vital body the man still has all his desires, but he lacks the organ to satisfy them. This causes the sufferings of *purgatory*; for example, a miser may hover over his bonds and stocks in his invisible desire body, trying to hang on to them, but his relatives go right through him and take them away. He may even hear them mock "the old tightwad." A drunkard may penetrate the dense body of a drinker in a tavern, but he lacks a stomach and the organs of taste, therefore can but very slightly satisfy his craving for drink.

Thus, through suffering, the departed person finally learns to despise and relinquish the vices of his former days on earth, and he becomes ready to go to heaven.

However, there are three heavens, just as there were three regions of the Desire World (purgatory). In the *first heaven*, located in the three highest regions of the Desire World, the results of the soul's sufferings are "incorporated in the seed-atom of the desire body, thus imparting to it the quality of right feelings, which acts as an impulse to good and a deterrent from evil in the future."

"At last the man, the Ego, the threefold spirit enters *the second heaven*. He is clad in the sheath of Mind, which contains the three seed-atoms, the quintessence of the three discarded vehicles." Upon arrival in the second heaven follows "the great Silence," and after this period of wonder the awakening. The spirit is now in its home-World. Here it hears "the music of the spheres" and learns to do many-sided work. It prepares for the next life. Before reincarnation, however, the spirit must first dwell in the third heaven, the higher Region of the World of Thought.

But why should the human spirit experience another "dip into matter" at all? Because the purpose of life is not pleasure but experience, which is knowledge of the effects which follow acts. If I did not feel pain when I put my hand on a hot stove, my hand might burn off without my knowing it; but now my experience teaches me to be more careful next time.

It would take us too long to speak of the "preparations for re-birth." Suffice it to say that each re-birth (about every one thousand years) begins with a birth of the *dense* body; that the *vital* body is formed within this in the seventh year; that the *desire* body is formed at the time of puberty; and the mind is not completed until the twenty-first year.

As the Etheric Region extends beyond the atmosphere of our dense Earth, the Desire World extends out into space further than the Etheric Region, and the World of Thought further into interplanetary space than either of the others, so also the seven Worlds and Cosmic Planes are not one above another in space, but the seven Cosmic Planes interpenetrate each other and all the seven Worlds. They are states of spirit-matter, permeating one another, so that God and the other Great Beings are not far away in space. They pervade every part of their own realms and realms of greater density than their own. (Here the apostle Paul is quoted, "In Him we live, and move, and have our being.")[7]

The Great Being called God "proceeds from the Root of Existence." He is the Absolute, but "positively not Christ." This threefold Supreme Being exists as *Power*, the *Word*, and *Motion*; and from this threefold Supreme Being proceed the seven Great Logoi. In the Highest World of the seventh Cosmic Plane dwell the God of our Solar System and the Gods of all other Solar Systems in the Universe. These great beings are also threefold in manifestation. Their three aspects are *Will, Wisdom,* and *Activity.*

With the aid of diagrams (pictures of things seen in clairvoyant state), we are told of the evolution of the earth and its inhabitants, and with all of this agrees an "Occult analysis of Genesis."

In every Period of evolution there are those who "fall behind," the *stragglers*. Thus "the lower monkeys, instead of being the progenitors of the higher species, are stragglers occupying the most degenerate specimens of what was once the human form." Instead of man having ascended from the anthropoids the reverse is true: these have degenerated from man. The mosses likewise are the lowest degeneration of the plant kingdom. "Material science, deal-

---

7. Ask your teacher to explain to you the difference between the doctrines of pantheistic immanence, deistic transcendence of God, and theistic teaching of the Trinity which includes both these elements. Or, see my volume *Our Christian Heritage,* on the subject.

ing only with the Form, has thus misled itself and drawn erroneous conclusions in this matter."

Apart from these stragglers, then, there is a continuous upward movement. Thus we also have *newcomers,* which we might call converted stragglers. And here a remarkable feature enters. Most human beings are not in need of salvation. For "progression with our present wave of evolution is what is meant when 'salvation' is spoken of in the Christian religion, and it is something to be earnestly sought, for though the 'eternal damnation' of those who are not 'saved' does not mean destruction nor endless torture, it is nevertheless a very serious matter to be held in a state of inertia for inconceivable milliards of years, before a new evolution shall have progressed to such a stage that those who fail here can have an opportunity to proceed. The spirit is not conscious of the lapse of time, but it is none the less a serious loss, and there must be also a feeling of unhomelikeness when at last such spirits find themselves in a new evolution."[8] The atonement was wrought by Christ for such as these. For Christ, who is the highest initiate of the Sun Period, became the Regent of Earth at Golgotha, his mission being the salvation of those who had bogged down in matter. These "lost ones" he saved "by raising them to the necessary point of spirituality, causing a change in their desire bodies which will make the influence of the life spirit in the heart more potent."[9]

This theory of "vicarious atonement" is not to be objected to on the ground that each must be willing to take the consequences of his own act; for it is perfectly just: it is like a man placing a rope above the cataract at Niagara: this he does that others, in danger of falling down, may have something to hold to even though he knows that in doing so he must go down himself: should or would that prevent any one else in danger from taking hold of the rope?

---

8. *Cosmo-conception,* p. 230.
9. *Ibid.,* p. 403

Universal Evolution

The axiom for the understanding of all this ceaseless activity of evolution is the Hermetic axiom, "As above, so below," and vice versa. There is a constant flaming out and dying down of activity in every department of nature.

In the beginning of a *Day of Manifestation* a certain *Great Being* (called a *God* only in the Western World) limits himself to a certain portion of space, in which he elects to create a Solar System for the evolution of added sense consciousness. It all begins with the *Cosmic Root Substance* which is an expression of the negative pole of the Universal Spirit, while the great Creative Being we call God (of whom we, as spirits, are part) is an expression of the positive energy of the same Universal Absolute Spirit. From the work of one upon the other, all that we see about us has resulted.

Now there are seven Worlds, not separated by space or distance (as is the earth from the other planets) but by their rate of vibration. The highest Worlds are the first to be created, the densest World last. But every World, as well as man, passes through seven Periods of Rebirths. The names of the seven Periods are as follows:

1. The Saturn Period
2. The Sun Period
3. The Moon Period
4. The Earth Period
5. The Jupiter Period
6. The Venus Period
7. The Vulcan Period

These names have nothing to do with our planets, but they are the Rosicrucian names for the successive rebirths of our Earth.

We know nothing of the six Cosmic Planes above our own except that God, "the Architect of our Solar System, is found in the highest division of the seventh Cosmic Plane, which is his World." But we do know that our own Plane during its Saturn Period (the first or lowest Period of its existence) traveled in its evolutionary impulse seven times around seven Globes, and when that laborious process ended, there followed the first Cosmic Night after the First Day of Creation, after which the Sun Period dawned. Here the same process of the life-wave circling seven times around the seven Globes was repeated, and the Moon Period was entered. From here on, we are told, the evolution of the Universe cannot be understood except by students of Arithmetic and the "Fourth Dimension."

It is interesting to learn, however, that even during the Saturn Period "great creative Hierarchies," far more perfectly evolved spirits, helped man in his evolution. These Hierarchies called "Thrones" in the Bible, worked on man of their own free will.

Among these the *Lords of Flame,* emitting a strong light, "by repeated efforts during the first Revolution, succeeded in implanting in the evolving life the germ which has developed our present dense body."

During this Saturn Period the Lords of Flame also labored on other spirits, namely, the *Lords of Wisdom,* spirits not as highly evolved as themselves. But during the second, or Sun Period, the Lords of Wisdom aided man "by radiating from their own bodies the germ of the vital body, making it capable of interpenetrating the dense body and giving to the germ the capability of furthering growth and propagation and of exciting the sense centers of the dense body and causing it to move. This work occupied the second, third, fourth, and fifth Revolution of the Sun Period."

And so it continues and will continue. Spiral evolution for the ordinary people, with spirals within spirals, and the "straight and narrow path" of access to divinity for the initiate. The *Conscious soul* of man will be absorbed by the divine spirit in the seventh Revolution of the Jupiter Period; the *Intellectual soul* will be absorbed by the life spirit in the sixth Revolution of the Venus Period; the *Emotional soul* will be absorbed by the human spirit in the fifth Revolution of the Vulcan Period.

Since the mind is the most important instrument possessed by the spirit, and its special instrument in the work of creation, at this stage of human development "the spiritualized and perfected larynx will speak the creative Word, but the perfected mind will decide as to the particular form and the volume of vibration, and will thus be the determining factor. Imagination will be the spiritualized faculty directing the work of creation."

In the Jupiter Period the human mind will imagine forms which will *live* and grow, like plants. In the Venus Period of that distant stage he can create living, growing, and *feeling* things. And when at the end of the Vulcan Period man reaches perfection, he will be able to "imagine" into existence creatures that will live, grow, feel, and *think*.

He will, in other words, do for plants and animals, and even for minerals, what the *Lords of Mind*, those ancient Hierarchies, did for him in the ages of long ago; he will help them acquire dense bodies, desire bodies, mind bodies, and other equipment.

Finally the divine Spirit, God, will absorb man. His spirit will be merged into God from whom it came, to reemerge at the dawn of another Great Day, as One of His glorious helpers. "During its past evolution its latent possibilities have been transmuted to dynamic powers. It has acquired *Soul power* and a *Creative Mind* as the fruitage of its pilgrimage through matter. It has advanced from *impotence to Omnipotence, from nescience to Omniscience.*"

The question remains how man in his present average stage of evolution may acquire firsthand knowledge of the truth of all the foregoing.

The answer is that as a mechanic is a better worker in proportion to the precision of his tools, so man must develop his various bodies. The dense body must be trained by means of the proper food (pages and lists of minerals and vitamins in the right combinations are given). The diet must, of course, be vegetarian. The sex impulse must be trained to produce spiritual rather than material creative force.

Moreover, man must learn to use the pituitary body and the pineal gland, two small organs in the brain. He must thus become a clairvoyant, which is far more difficult than becoming a medium. The latter is merely a revival of the mirror-like function possessed by man in the far past, by which the outside world was involuntarily reflected in him.

The clairvoyant cannot live to eat and drink and gratify the sex-passion in an unrestrained manner. Because he lives a life that causes less confusion in the dense body, he need not spend his entire period of sleep in repairing the damage done in the daytime by means of the desire and vital bodies, leaving no time for outside work of any kind. Thus it becomes possible to leave the dense body for long periods during sleeping hours, and function in the inner worlds in the higher vehicles. (*Tout comme chez nous*, the Theosophist might well say.)

Next it is necessary to reach a state in which the spirit is within the bodies and in full control of the faculties, as it is in the waking state, and yet able to work inwardly and properly sensitize the spirit's vehicles.

Concentration in such a state (not *yoga*, because the vehicles of the Caucasian are so very differently constituted than those of the Hindu that the methods of *yoga* — union with the Higher Self—would not benefit us), *Meditation, Observation, Discrimination, Contemplation, Adoration*, these are the words used in the description of how to become an initiate; but it would lead us too far afield for our purpose to inquire into the how of all these things.

Evaluation

1. Max Heindel's textbook *The Rosicrucian Cosmo-conception or Mystic Christianity* begins as follows:

"The founder of the Christian Religion stated an occult maxim when He said: 'Whosoever shall not receive the kingdom of God as a little child shall not enter therein' (Mark 10:15). All occultists recognize the far-reaching importance of this teaching of Christ and endeavor to 'live' it day by day."

Thus a system that denies and perverts everything taught by Christ and concerning Christ appeals to the authority of His name in order to make us see the necessity of coming to the Rosicrucian occultism with minds that are completely blank, divested of all opinion, and shorn of any and all "preference" and "prejudice." In all occult schools the pupil is first taught to forget all else when a new teaching is being given, allow neither preference nor prejudice to govern but to keep the mind in a state of calm, dignified waiting.

This is impossible for any one who knows that he is twice-born as a result of the regenerating power of the Holy Spirit. Once a Christian by the saving and renewing grace of Christ, a man cannot possibly start with a blank mind, but is inwardly and outwardly bound to compare a new teaching with what he has found to be the universally and age-old accepted teachings of the Scriptures.

2. We readily grant that the Rosicrucian philosophy has many fine points, such as its inexorable logic. It gives a more plausible reason for rebirth than does Theosophy. It appears to present a better case for a clean and lofty life than do the "ear-to-ear and mouth-to-mouth" secrets of a Blavatsky. But all this logic and all this loftiness cannot annul the fact that the entire structure is built upon a false foundation, namely, another than the Christ of the Scriptures.

3. Many points of criticism that have been advanced against the kindred systems of Spiritism and Theosophy hold true also against Rosicrucianism: when the mind and heart are left blank to be played upon by outward forces, it may, according to Scripture, be expected that "doctrines of demons" will be infused from without. It is no wonder that astrology and spiritism and necromancy are so consistently forbidden in the Old Testament. Attention should be given, therefore, to the great similarity among these various cults.

4. The crowning test of a religious or philosophical system of thought from the viewpoint of the present volume

must always be: How do its statements compare with what has been held to be in harmony with Scripture by the entire Christian Church? When we do this, we reach the conclusion that the apostle Paul would say of the followers of the Rose Cross that they are "enemies of the cross of Christ."

Rosicrucians and Biblical Doctrine
Christ

(a) *His Person*

"In the Christian creed occurs this sentence: 'Jesus Christ, the only begotten Son of God.' This is generally understood to mean that a certain person Who appeared in Palestine about 2000 years ago, Who is spoken of as Jesus Christ—one separate individual—was the only begotten Son of God. This is a great mistake. There are three distinct and widely different Beings characterized in this sentence. It is of the greatest importance that the student should clearly understand the exact nature of these Three Great and Exalted Beings—differing vastly in glory, yet each entitled to our deepest and most devout adoration.

"The student is requested to turn to diagram 6 and note that 'The only begotten' ('The Word' of Whom John speaks) is the second aspect of the Supreme Being.

"This 'Word,' and It alone, is 'begotten of His Father [the first aspect] before all Worlds.' . . . Therefore the 'only begotten' is the exalted Being which ranks above all else in the Universe save only the Power-aspect which created It."—M. HEINDEL.[10]

(b) *His Sacrifice*

"We are now approaching the winter solstice, the darkest days of the year, the time when the light of the sun has almost faded, when our Northern Hemisphere is cold and drear. But on the longest and darkest night the sun turns on its upward path, the Christ light is born on the earth

---
10. *Ibid.*, p. 374.

ROSICRUCIANISM

again, and all the world rejoices. By the terms of our analogy, however, when the Christ is born on earth He dies to heaven. As the free spirit is at the time of birth finally and firmly encased in the veil of flesh which fetters it all through life, so also the Christ Spirit is fettered and hampered each time He is born into the earth. This great Annual Sacrifice begins when our Christmas bells are ringing, when our joyful sounds of praise and thanksgiving are ascending to heaven. Christ is imprisoned in the most literal sense of the word from Christmas to Easter."—M. HEINDEL.[11]

(c) *Second Coming*

"'The law and the prophets were until Christ,' it is said, but we know that even today law is, and is necessary. Therefore, it is evident that law was not abolished at the physical coming of Christ. It is the coming of Christ into 'the within,' the inner nature of man, that is to abolish law. Paul speaks of this advent as the 'Christ being formed in you,' and until Christ has been formed in us we are not ready for the Second Coming . . . The Second Coming of Christ depends upon how soon a sufficient number of people have become Christ-like and attuned to the Christ principle, so that, as tuning forks of the same pitch sing together when one is struck, they will be able to respond to the Christ vibrations that will be set up at the return of the Savior. Every time we endeavor to imitate Christ and fulfil His teachings, we are hastening His Coming; so let us thus strive."—M. HEINDEL.[12]

Jesus

"*I understand you to say that the Christ has been incarnated only once in Jesus; was he not previously incarnated in Gautama Buddha and still earlier in Krishna?*

"*Answer*: No. Jesus Himself was a spirit belonging to our human evolution, and so was Gautama Buddha. The

---
11. *The Mystical Interpretation of Christmas*, p. 21.
12. *The Rosicrucian Philosophy*, p. 206.

writer has no information concerning Krishna, but is inclined to believe that he was also a spirit belonging to the human race, because the Indian stories concerning him tell of how he entered heaven and what took place there. The Christ spirit which entered the body of Jesus when Jesus himself vacated it, was a ray from the cosmic Christ. We may follow Jesus back in his previous incarnations, and we can trace his growth to the present day. The Christ spirit, on the contrary, is not to be found among our human spirits at all."—M. HEINDEL.[13]

God

(a) *Trinity*

" 'The Father' is the highest Initiate among the humanity of the Saturn Period. The ordinary humanity of that Period are now the Lords of Minds.

" 'The Son' (Christ) is the highest Initiate of the Sun Period. The ordinary humanity of that Period are now the Archangels.

" 'The Holy Spirit' (Jehovah) is the highest Initiate of the Moon Period. The ordinary humanity of that Period are now the Angels."—M. HEINDEL.[14]

(b) *The Holy Spirit* (Rev. 1:4)

"It is necessary for all beings high or low in the scale of existence, to possess vehicles for expression in any particular world in which they may wish to manifest. Even the Seven Spirits before The Throne must possess these necessary vehicles, which of course are differently conditioned for each of Them. Collectively, They are God, and make up the Triune Godhead, and He manifests in a different way through each of Them."—HEINDEL.[15]

---

13. *Ibid.*, p. 181.
14. *Cosmo-conception*, p. 376.
15. *Ibid.*, p. 252.

Man

(a) *Races of man*

"The Bible does not state anywhere that the negroes are the descendants of Ham; besides it is well known that the Biblical ethnology as commonly understood among orthodox people is an utter impossibility in view of the facts of geology and ethnological research... The Biblical ethnology also has the exact year of the flood and similar events fixed, but from the occult point of view, which is derived from a direct reading in the picture gallery of the past, which we call *the memory of nature*, the case is very different... We find there that there have been various epochs or great stages of unfoldment in the earth's history, and that the negro was the humanity of the third of these epochs, the Lemurian. The whole human race of that time was black-skinned. Then came a time, called the Atlantean Epoch, when humanity was red, yellow, except one race which was white. These people were original Semites, the fifth of the Atlantean Races. These Atlanteans are called Niebelungen, or *children of the mist*, in the old folk stories, for at that time the atmosphere of the earth was a very dense fog. In the latter half of the Atlantean Epoch this atmosphere condensed, floods resulted, and gradually the sea covered the larger part of the globe. Then the atmosphere became clear above the earth. This point in evolution is described in the Bible where Noah, the leader of the Semites, came out from the drowning Atlantis and first saw the rainbow, a phenomenon impossible in the foggy atmosphere of early Atlantis. We also hear of that emigration in the story of Moses and the Israelites coming out from Egypt while the Egyptian king and his men drown in the waters of the Red Sea. These people had been chosen to become the progenitors of our present Aryan races, but not all of them were true to the command of their leader. There were some of them who 'went after strange flesh,' and that is the greatest crime possible at such a time, for when a leader is aiming to instill new faculties into a new race, the admixture of strange blood has a tendency to frustrate his plans. Therefore, some of these chosen people were lost, that is to say, they were abandoned by their leaders and did not become the forebearers of the new humanity. *Those who were thus lost or left behind are, strange to say, the present day Jews*, who at one time married into the families of their Atlantean brethren, contrary to the commands of their divine leader, and yet today think themselves the 'chosen people' of God."—M. HEINDEL.[16]

(b) *Divinity of man*

"There is endless progress, for we are divine as our Father in heaven, and limitations are impossible."—M. HEINDEL.

Pantheism

"We would ask, what do you mean by nature? Bacon says that nature and God differ only as the print and the seal. Nature is the visible symbol of God, and we are too apt to think of nature nowadays in a materialistic sense. Back of every manifestation in nature are forces, *not blind forces, but intelligences* .... What we speak of as electricity, as magnetism, as expansion in steam, etc., are intelligences which work unseen to us when certain conditions are brought about. Nature spirits build the plants, form the crystals of the rock, and with numerous other hierarchies are working around and about us unseen, but nevertheless busy in making that which we call nature."—M. HEINDEL.[17]

Parenthood

"Unless there is an Ego seeking embodiment through a married couple, their efforts will be fruitless.... We know that if we mix hydrogen and oxygen in proper proportions we always get water; we know that water will always flow downhill; and thus all the laws of nature are invariable, so that unless there were another factor than the chemical mixture of semen and ova there would always be issue.

---

16. *Rosicrucian Philosophy*, p. 54.
17. *Ibid.*, p. 85.

ROSICRUCIANISM

And this unknown and unseen factor is the reincarnating Ego which goes where it pleases and without which there can be no issue. If the inquirer will pray earnestly to the angel Gabriel, who is the ambassador of the Regent of the Moon to the Earth, and therefore a prime factor in the generation of bodies (*vide* the Bible), it may possibly avail to bring the desired result. The best time is Monday at sunrise, and from the new Moon to the full."[18]

Prayer

"*Hallowed be Thy Name*: prayer of the Human spirit to the Holy Spirit for the desire body.
Thy kingdom come: prayer of the Life Spirit to the Son for the vital body."—M. HEINDEL.[19]

Hints

1. In what particulars does this system resemble Spiritism; Theosophy?
2. In which points do these cults differ?
3. What is the meaning of the Cross, and what that of the Roses in Rosicrucianism?
4. What is the place of God in this philosophy?
5. How many Worlds are there said to be, and through how many periods of evolution is each World said to pass?
6. Is Christ a Person or an impersonal spirit according to this ism?
7. Do you find any elements of superstition in this boastfully superior system of thought?

---

18. *Ibid.*, p 64.
19. *Cosmo-conception*. Diagram 16.

7

THE UNITY SCHOOL OF CHRISTIANITY

Charles W. Ferguson has, in his inimitable style, defined Unity as "an enormous mail order concern dispensing health and happiness on the large scale of modern business enterprise. It is mass production in religion and its work is carried on shrewdly and systematically.... It has transformed the United States Mail into a missionary machine.... It is the work of a retired realtor and his inspired wife, and with its tedious array of tabular facts and its insufferable efficiency, it suggests pretty well what Americans want in the realm of the spirit."[1]

Side by side with this we submit Dr. Atkins' opinion on New Thought: "It is the apotheosis of what James called, 'The Religion of Healthy Mindedness'; it all fits easily into the dominant temper of our times and seems to reconcile that serving of two masters, God and Getting On, which a lonely teacher long ago thought quite impossible."

These two opinions of two writers on two religious cults coincide thus remarkably because the two cults are almost one, being as two branches on the same tree. There is a third branch, and we have come to know it as Christian Science.

Origin

To understand the interrelationship of these three cults we should go back to Franz Anton Mesmer, the great German physician who, from 1774 to 1814, wrestled with the problem of psychotherapy, as we call it today. Mesmer, however, incidentally discovered the power of one man over another; but his discovery was too great for his genius. He

---

1. *The Confusion of Tongues*, passim.

did not understand his own remarkable find, so unorthodox in his day, and attributed the powers of the subconscious mind to magnetism, later on to a fluid supposed to emanate from the healer and to affect the patient. Mesmer, though by turns worshipped and despised, adored and hated, never commercialized his find, never lost faith in his discovery, and never used his great power to take advantage of others.

But what Mesmer would not have thought of doing, his disciples, the one hundred percent and the forty percent disciples and the ten percent followers of this remarkable man, have not hesitated to do. Just as the bona fide evangelism of America's earlier days has degenerated into a loudly screaming, money-making scheme which has destroyed its own usefulness, so the hypnotists and the mesmerists and the spiritists and theosophists, together with the host of faith healers and mind curers, have misused the newly discovered fact of the power of mind over matter for the sake of filthy lucre. They have amassed large fortunes. And they have helped suffering humanity to forget its nervous troubles and its organic diseases just as many have found relief and "healing" from the use of the Owens Electric Belt, the Oxypathor and the Oxygenor, the Electro-Chemical Ring, the Rice Rupture Cure, and Swoboda's Conscious Evolution which "has made possible for everyone the possession of super-health, super-vitality, super-courage, super-aggressiveness, super-mental power, and super every power." And as these officially condemned and exposed quacks could nevertheless produce testimonies of physicians as well as of those who had benefited by being fleeced by them, so Unity and New Thought and Christian Science can boast of swarms of people who would lay down their lives in gratitude for the obtained salvation. For in one respect the Mardens and Eddys and Fillmores have outwitted the ordinary quacks: they have turned their healing recipes into the conundrums of a deeply mystic religion, thereby adding a fervor and a flavor which the common garden variety of healer has missed.

To Count Maxime de Puységur belongs the honor of having discovered in 1784 that Mesmer's alleged magnetic fluid is indeed a power of the human mind, and he opened up the large field of hypnotism and somnambulism. Charles Poyen, a French hypnotist, introduced the revived mesmerism to the gullible American public of the New England states in 1836. Phineas Park Quimby heard Poyen lecture at Belfast, Maine. Poyen told "Park" that he had vast psychic power. Quimby, the clockmaker, began to experiment with sick folk, used his rare hypnotic power upon suffering New England, and in his own right discovered the power of mind over matter.

Quimby became the pioneer mental healer of his day and country. It was not medicine but faith in medicine which healed people, according to Quimby. He wrote his philosophy in ten volumes of longhand. These manuscripts he generously lent to his disciples and patients, being of the old style which did not think of healing in terms of self-aggrandizement. He disclaimed divine inspiration when his admirers tried to force it onto him, and he was glad to have others spread his knowledge.

Among those who benefited by Quimby's manuscripts and methods of healing were Mrs. Eddy, who, as Mrs. Patterson, came to him in 1862 (when he was 60 and she 41), and Julius Dresser. Mrs. Eddy plagiarized the Quimby manuscripts after Quimby's death and denounced the man to whom she had earlier written poetry, "To P. P. Quimby, Who Heals the Sick as Jesus Did." Meanwhile, Dresser became one of the early propagandists of "New Thought."

Observe then the following dates: *Science and Health* was first printed in 1875; the name *New Thought* first appeared as the title of a small magazine devoted to mental healing in 1894; Mrs. Fillmore and her husband decided in 1889 to devote themselves to propagating their "discovery" of health and harmony through "practical Christianity" which is the very name that was in use for New Thought in the West. No wonder there is a great family likeness among these three.

Charles Fillmore was a cripple from infancy. He suffered from a hip disease. Besides, he had curvature of the spine, and was deaf in his right ear. When his wife contracted tuberculosis, they lived for six years in Texas and Arizona, hoping to find health in the arid climate. During a boom Mr. Fillmore amassed a fortune of $150,000 in real estate, but he lost it all during a depression. Penniless and sick, they saw little ahead that was hope-inspiring. It was then that Myrtle Fillmore, so the Unity literature has it, heard a lecture "by a now all-but-forgotten metaphysical lecturer that marked the turning of the tide in Mrs. Fillmore's life, and through her, in that of others. From that lecture one idea stood out in her mind, 'I am a child of God, and therefore I do not inherit sickness.' " "This idea," so the pamphlet continues, "was far reaching." And indeed it was. The good lady's tuberculosis vanished, "and she began healing her children and neighbors." "Gradually the influence of Mrs. Fillmore began to take on the aspects of a religious movement." The husband also became interested in the work of his wife. He, too, regained his health. By 1889 they decided not to take any more risks in real estate, but to make others share in their religio-medico find.

A letter from "The Society of Silent Unity" ("Unity School of Christianity") dated March 17, 1942, states: "Myrtle Fillmore passed on in October of 1951. The present Mrs. Fillmore was formerly Cora Dedrick, Charles Fillmore's secretary, and she is of invaluable help to him in his work."

That the aged gentleman continued long to "prove" his theories appears from the following citation from his article on "The Atomic Prayer" in *Unity*, November, 1945.

"Our modern scientists say that a single drop of water contains enough latent energy to blow up a ten-story building. This energy, existence of which has been discovered by modern scientists, is the same kind of spiritual energy that was known to Elijah, Elisha, and Jesus, and used by them to perform miracles.

"By the power of his thought Elijah penetrated the atoms of hydrogen and oxygen and precipitated an abundance of rain. By the same law he increased the widow's oil and meal. This was not a miracle — that is, it was not a divine intervention supplanting natural law — but the exploitation of a law not ordinarily understood. Jesus used the same dynamic power of thought to break the bonds of the atoms composing the few loaves and fishes of a little lad's lunch — and five thousand people were fed."

The article continues as follows:

"The foregoing extract is from our *Health and Prosperity Column* in *Unity* for May, 1927, some eighteen years ago. Comparison with our class words for this month shows that those comments are peculiarly applicable to the present and also to a subject that has been agitating the public mind for some time, the atomic bomb.

"Of all the comments on or discussion of the indescribable power of the invisible forces released by the atomic bomb none that we have seen mentioned its spiritual or mental character. All commentators have written about it as a force external to man to be controlled by mechanical means, with no hint that it is the primal life that animates and interrelates man's mind and body.

"The next great achievement of science will be the understanding of the mental and spiritual abilities latent in man through which to develop and release these tremendous electrons, protons, and neutrons secreted in the trillions of cells in the physical organism. Here is involved the secret, as Paul says, 'hid for the ages and generations . . . which is Christ [superman] in you, the hope of glory.' It is through release of these hidden life forces in his organism that man is to achieve immortal life, and in no other way. When we finally understand the facts of life and rid our mind of the delusion that we shall find immortal life after we die, then we shall seek more diligently to awaken the spiritual man within us and strengthen and build up the spiritual domain of our being until, like Jesus, we shall be able to control the atomic energy in our body and perform so-called miracles."

UNITY SCHOOL OF CHRISTIANITY 133

However, on July 5, 1948 Charles Fillmore, too, "passed on" and joined the ranks of the immortals.

In 1956 the work was carried on by his two sons, Lowell, who was 74, and Richard, who was 71. But, according to *Coronet* magazine (March 1956), "the spirit of Charles Fillmore still dominates Unity. Every morning at 11 o'clock all work stops at Unity School. 750 workers stand in a moment of quiet while Charles' recorded voice recites the Lord's prayer."

Today the Unity School of Christianity, with headquarters at Kansas City, Missouri, has its own broadcasting station, an efficient and large office force, the "best vegetarian café in the world," its own oil wells; and it sends by telegram or telephone, prayers and healing thoughts to those in need of them. The Unity Training School Prospectus each year offers a summer schedule with an elaborate course in Healing, Prayer, Bible Interpretation, with a regular Teaching Staff and Great Teachers, with large and well-equipped classrooms and dormitories, various Conferences for Leaders and for Youth, an attractive picture of what "Unity City" will look like in the future, and the general encouraging information, "Rooms are nearly always used to capacity."

The literature of this amazing religious fungus, apart from textbooks and pamphlets carried by "national lecturers," comprises six magazines, *Unity, Unity Daily Word, Weekly Unity, Progress, Wee Wisdom,* and *Good Business.*

System

Unity is so much like Christian Science and like New Thought that a few comparisons must be drawn. These three systems—although New Thought was from the start almost too evasive, too unorganized to merit the name of system — all believe in healing through the mind. Mrs. Eddy, to be sure, repudiated the term "mental healing." She preferred to say that Mind, with a capital *M*, demonstrates that there is no such thing as sickness. But the effect is the same. Patterson, New Thoughter, said "Christian Science and the New Thought agree that all life is one; that all intelligence is one; that God is all in all. And they disagree on the following points: Christian Science says that the visible world is mortal mind [that is, an illusion]; the New Thought declares the visible world to be an expression of God's handiwork. Christian Science asserts that sin, sickness, and death have no existence. The New Thought affirms that they have an existence; but that their existence is only limited and their destruction comes through right thinking and hence right living."

And the Unity literature warns that "many of those not acquainted with the distinctions of metaphysical thought class Unity with Christian Science because of a common emphasis on healing; nevertheless Unity, in nearly all its expositions of Truth, is quite distinct from Christian Science. To class them together, except in the fundamental concepttion of the being of God, common to all religions, is a mistake. It has also been said that Mr. and Mrs. Fillmore were at one time associated with the Christian Science church. This is also a mistake. While the Fillmores were not students of Mary Baker Eddy, nor connected with the Christian Science church in any way, a friendly feeling is always expressed by Unity and its workers toward Christian Science and all other religions. 'God is no respecter of persons' or of sects."

We shall have to be quite careful, then, lest we fall into Error and Delusion in identifying these various "religions." We maintain, however, that they are as much alike as triplets. In Unity we find the same vagueness we meet with in the New Thought literature; also the same key-words, such as *harmony, prosperity, affirmation, health, poise, affluence*. Unity recommends that its disciples shall go into silence, there to repeat "Unity Class Words," "Unity Daily Words," and to meditate upon its "Suggestions for Daily Meditation." The truth of the matter is that at first, owing to the founders' own physical troubles, the emphasis in the Unity movement was mostly upon physical healing, while later on a greater stress was laid upon prosperity and happiness. We offer the following samples, taken at random from its magazines.

"God in the midst of me is mighty to quicken and to illumine. Through the power of God in Christ Jesus I am saved from sin, sickness, and death. Through the power of God in Christ I am saved from the thought of lack, and I am made rich in all my affairs."

"No longer looking to any external place or to any future time for heaven, I find the kingdom of God — the kingdom of peace, joy, health, and plenty — within me."

"I have faith in God to supply all men's needs everywhere."

"I always think of substance as being abundant and sufficient for all needs. Therefore my material needs are always bountifully supplied."

"Prosperity follows prosperous thinking. For this reason I am thinking prosperous thoughts, wasting no time worrying about what I am to lack."

Marden's chapters on "Power of the Mind, The Law of Opulence," "Imagination and Health," "Why Grow Old?" "How Mind Rules the Body," "Thinking Brings Success," simply abound with almost identical statements, as every student of New Thought knows.

As to Mrs. Eddy, one only needs to glance at the chapter on "Physiology" in *Science and Health* to find the parallel words, "Science can heal the sick, who are absent from their healers, as well as those present, since space is no obstacle to Mind."

Of death Mrs. Eddy wrote, "Sin, disease and death have no foundation in Truth." And again, "DEATH — An illusion." Charles Fillmore has this to say of death, "God is not dead; he does not recognize or countenance death; neither does man when freed from its delusion. . . . The first step in demonstrating over death is to get the belief entirely out of the mind that it is God ordained, or that it is of force or effect anywhere in the realm of Pure Being. The next step is to live so harmoniously that the whole consciousness shall be not only resurrected from its belief in death, but also so vivified and energized with the idea of undying life that it cannot dissolve or separate."

From such quotations it is easily seen that the common pantheistic paternity of these systems has bequeathed to them many fundamental points of similarity. Could pantheism express itself more alike than in Mrs. Eddy's "What is God? God is incorporeal, divine, supreme, infinite Mind, Spirit, Soul, Principle"; and Mr. Fillmore's, "The truth is, then: That God is Principle, Law, Being, Mind, Spirit, All-Good"? Furthermore, he continues as a good brother to Mrs. Eddy: "That God is individually formed in consciousness in each of us, and is known to us as 'Father,' when we recognize him within us as our Creator, as our mind, as our life, as our very being."

On the other hand, Unity has some ideas that are found neither in Christian Science nor in New Thought. Among these the doctrines of reincarnation and of the "regeneration of the body" are noteworthy. Death is but a temporary laying down of the body. Man is a complex being. At death "the spiritual ego reverts to its original essence in the bosom of the Father; soul falls asleep until the next incarnation. Body and sense consciousness are earthbound and in due season they disintegrate." It is not necessary to die. If one believes faithfully in the Christ life he will never die, but continue to live in one's last and final body. "Here," wrote Dr. Braden, "is a daring doctrine." Indeed, it is. But not only is it contrary to Scripture, but with it goes what Paul undoubtedly would have called a doctrine "forbidding to marry." "Through the sins of the sex-life the body is robbed of its essential fluids and disintegrates. The result is called death, which is the last great enemy to be overcome by man. Immortality in the body is possible to man only when he has overcome the weakness of sensation and conserves his life substance. . . . So long as your eyes see sex and the indulgence thereof on any of its planes, you are not pure. You must become mentally so translucent that you see men and women as sexless beings — which they are in the spiritual consciousness."[2]

Our Estimate of Unity

1. It may be well for us to remind ourselves once more that it would be neither wise nor in the interest of truth to deny whatever good elements an Ism may contain. Truth is never helped by untruth. Hence we admit that Unity, for all its antichristian elements, emphasizes certain elements of truth which would be well for Christians to bear in mind more generally. Thus the Sermon on the Mount certainly forbids worry as a sin of the Gentiles. The child of God should not be anxious for the morrow, but should know himself to be safe in the Father's loving care. Thousands of orthodox Christians, however, will admit, at times even boast, that they are "the worrying kind." New Thought and Unity deserve a vote of thanks for reminding such Christians that fear is our worst enemy and that no good whatever can result from worry.

For all that, is it not possible to insist upon Jesus' teaching against worry, so deeply religious in Matthew 6, without turning this antiworry principle into the grossest parody upon the choicest parts of Scripture? Or, what else is it but blasphemous parody when the Twenty-Third Psalm is paraphrased as follows — and here it is remarkable how the pantheistic ignoring of a personal God leads to the most brutal materialism:

> "The Lord is my banker; my credit is good.
> He maketh me to lie down in the consciousness of omnipotent abundance; He giveth me the key to His strong-box.
> He restoreth my faith in His riches,
> He guideth me in the paths of prosperity for His name's sake.
> Yea, though I walk through the very shadow of debt, I shall fear no evil, for Thou art with me; Thy silver and gold, they secure me.

---

2. Charles Fillmore in *Twelve Powers of Man*, as quoted by Charles S. Braden, *These Also Believe*.

Thou preparest a way for me in the presence of the collector;
Thou fillest my wallet with plenty; my measure runneth over.
Surely, goodness and plenty will follow me all the days of my life;
And I shall do business in the name of the Lord forever."[3]

It is also true that the reading of such literature as these cults produce may be an aid to the discouraged by directing their attention to the recuperative powers laid by God within the human mind and body. However, here, too, though a Christian may find sentiments which he may well utilize against his own believing background, such sentiments and elements of truth cannot atone for the violently antichristian teaching which underlies the entire cult of the Unity School. Nor should it be forgotten that when Dr. Braden visited the Kansas City institution in 1945, he was frankly informed that in order to be healed the Unity way, it was neither required to have a physician's diagnosis of one's trouble nor even desirable that the healing should be attested to by medical authority. "The whole operation is based," said a leader of the cult, "on faith — not upon proof, and the intromission of an intent to prove might even be counter-productive and lessen men's faith rather than increase it."[4]

2. It is not necessary for Unity to spiritualize story after story from the Bible, until there is nothing left of the story, as is done continually in its Sunday School lessons. Thus the parable of Dives and Lazarus is reconstructed as being a parable which speaks of one man, and not of two. The rich man is said to be the outer personality. Dives is self-indulgent. Lazarus, on the other hand, is the undeveloped psychic or spiritual body, which Dives neglects and allows to suffer and starve. The two characters represent each one of us. Each person is double. The fight of the dual man results either in Dives becoming Lazarus, as Saul

3. Fillmore, *Prosperity*, p. 60.
4. *Op. cit.*, p. 150.

became Paul, or in Dives gaining the upper hand as Mr. Hyde defeated Dr. Jekyll.

In a similar manner we are informed in the discussion of the International Lessons: "King Herod represents the ego in the outer or sense consciousness. The Herod man is temporal because he does not understand his origin or the law of his being. He is narrow, jealous, and destructive. His destructive thoughts react upon his body, making it full of pain and misery. Such a man does not fulfill the divine idea of a man, and another ego must supplant him. Jesus represents God's idea of man in expression: Christ is that idea in the absolute [again: compare Mrs. Eddy on Jesus Christ].... The Wise-men from the east are the inner planes of consciousness, which, like books of life, have kept the records of past lives and held them in reserve against the great day in which the soul should receive the supreme ego, Jesus.

"When the Jesus ego first appears in the subconsciousness, it is a mere speck of light, a 'star in the east.' The East is the mystical and occult realm where great wisdom and rich presents await the one who is born 'King of the Jews.'"

And so it goes *ad infinitum*. In the same lesson-notes from which the above is taken (*Unity*, Vol. 72, No. 1) we find such gross teaching as, "Galilee represents the life activity or soul energy of man acting in conjunction with substance. Nazareth, a city of Galilee, means a *sprout*, a small thing held of slight significance, hence a term of reproach. It typifies the commonplace mind of man; but it is in the commonplace mind actuated by the soul energy of true substance that the Christ idea takes root and grows up in consciousness."

Or, take this example of pantheistic spiritualizing of truth: "'And there shall come forth a shoot out of the stock of Jesse, and a branch out of his roots shall bear fruit.' The meaning is 'Jah, Jehovah, or I AM,' representing eternal existence. The shoot or *sprout* out of Jesse therefore, would typify the dawning realization by men of the eternal existence of I AM . . . ."

And this is Sunday School instruction! And thousands are said to swallow this teaching as though it were Christian doctrine. Poor America! How we agree with the conclusion of Dr. Atkins, "There is need of a vast deal more of sheer teaching in all the churches. The necessity for congregations and the traditions of preaching conspire to make the message of the Church far less vital than it ought to be. Preaching is too much declamation and far too much a following of narrow and deeply worn paths."

3. Like Christian Science and New Thought, Unity overemphasizes the importance of intellectual considerations. It will meet with no objections on our part if anyone teaches the primacy of the intellect. But these cults stress the intellect at the expense of the totality of human experience. Thus it is good to be an optimist, but to deny the very possibility of evil is as dangerous as pessimism itself.

4. In the light of Unity's travesty upon the cardinal doctrines of Scripture we wonder why this school should call itself a School of Christianity, why its prospectus should present a well-known portrait of Jesus.

Here are a few excerpts from the literature of Unity:

God

"The author of Genesis was evidently a great metaphysician. He described Being as God, Lord God and Adam. We would express the same truth in the terms Mind, Idea, and Manifestation . . . . But Mind, Idea, and Manifestation are one. Manifestation rests upon, and is sustained by the Idea, and the Idea is encompassed by the Mind that conceives it; therefore the Real of Adam is the Lord God, and the Omnipresent Fount of the Lord God is the One God.

"Man is by nature an organizer. It is his function in the God-head to formulate the potentialities of the Principles."[5]

"God is not loving . . . . God does not love anybody or any-

---

5. Charles Fillmore, *Christian Healing*, pp. 133, 217.

thing. God is the love *in* everybody and everything. God is love.... God exercises none of His attributes except through the inner consciousness of the universe and man."[6]

"Never be formal with God. He cares no more for forms and ceremonies than do the principles of mathematics for fine figures or elaborate blackboards.... You cannot use God too often. He loves to be used, and the more you use Him, the more easily you use Him and the more pleasant His help becomes.... He will do you a favor just as quickly if you ask in a jolly, laughing way as He would if you made your request in a long, melancholy prayer. God is natural and He loves the freedom of the little child."[7]

Trinity

"The Father is Principle, the Son is that Principle revealed in a creative plan. The Holy Spirit is the executive power of both Father and Son carrying out the creative plan."[8]

Jesus Christ

"The Bible says that God so loved the world that he gave his only begotten Son, but the Bible does not here refer to Jesus of Nazareth, the outer man; it refers to the Christ, the spiritual identity of Jesus, whom he acknowledged in all his ways, and brought forth into his outer, until even the flesh of his body was lifted up, purified, spiritualized, and redeemed. Thus he became Jesus Christ, the Word made flesh. And we are to follow him into this perfect state and become like him for in each of us is the Christ, the only begotten Son. We can, through Jesus Christ, our Redeemer and Example, bring forth the Christ within us, the true self of all men, and be made perfect even as our Father in heaven is perfect, as Jesus Christ commanded his followers to be. Paul wrote to the Galatians, 'It was the good pleasure of God . . . to reveal his Son in me.' We do most certainly

---

6. *Jesus Christ Heals*, Unity School of Christianity, Kansas City. Missouri, 1944, pp. 31-32.
7. *Ibid.*, p. 15.
8. *Metaphysical Bible Dictionary*, Unity School, p. 692.

accept the divinity of Christ and of Jesus Christ, and we believe most thoroughly in the work which he did for mankind."[9]

Man

"In his true estate man is the Christ, the head of the body .... The I *am*, or Christ, goes through the body to each center, quickening, cleansing, purifying the consciousness with the Word of Truth."[10]

"Statements for the Realization of the Son of God:

"I am the Son of God, and the Spirit of the Most High dwells in me."

"I am the only begotten Son, dwelling in the bosom of the Father."

"I am the Lord of my mentality and the ruler of all its Thought-People."

"I am the Christ of God."

"Through Christ I have dominion over every thought and word."

"I am the Beloved Son in whom the Father is well pleased."

"Of a truth I am the Son of God."

"All that the Father hath is mine."

"He who hath seen me hath seen the Father." "I and my Father are one."[11]

"As the oak is in the acorn, so God is in man."[12]

Sin

"There is no sin, sickness or death."[13]

"As we explore the mental realm, ... we find it filled with a whole legion of narrow beliefs, foolish, ignorant beliefs, selfish beliefs, and discordant beliefs. These we have lumped together and denominated 'mortal mind' or 'carnal

---

9. *Unity*, Vol. 57, No. 5, p. 464; also *Unity*, Vol. 72, No. 2, p. 8.
10. *Unity*, Vol. 48, No. 2, p. 128.
11. Fillmore, *Christian Healing*, p. 26.
12. *What Practical Christianity Stands For*, Unity School, p. 3.
13. *Unity*, Vol. 47, No. 5, p. 403.

mind.' It is here we first do our 'raising of the dead.' Each of these beliefs of mortality is a sin."[14]

Atonement

"The atonement is the union of man with God the Father, in Christ. Stating it in terms of mind, we should say that the atonement is the at-one-ment or agreement or reconciliation of man's mind with Divine Mind through the superconsciousness of Christ mind. The very foundation of the Christian religion is the atonement of Jesus Christ; but the results of the past teachings show that there has been a misconception of the nature and scope and object of this atonement, else the race would not now still be suffering from the results of the fall. Jesus came to redeem men from sin, and salvation through Him is complete.... So long as the belief is held that man must worry along somehow with all the afflictions of sin and be taken to a heaven somewhere after death, just so long will the blessings of the atonement be delayed. A living faith in the atoning grace of Jesus Christ will prepare the way to an understanding of His mission and will open the consciousness to the saving Christ power, which alone can, here and now, make the transformation of the soul and body that is called redemption."[15]

Heaven

"It is often assumed that Jesus went away into the skies to prepare a material heaven with golden streets, but the Spirit of truth reveals that the place that Jesus went to prepare is here. 'Lo, I am with you always.' That place is in the mind. 'The kingdom of God is within you.' By his redeeming work Jesus Christ is forming and establishing a new consciousness, into which all may enter. He went first into the interior spiritual realm of consciousness,

---

14. Fillmore, *Christian Healing*, p. 164.
15. *What Practical Christianity Stands For*, p. 5.

and thus opened and prepared the way for all to follow Him and enter with Him into the realization of a perfect union with the Father-Mind."[16]

Resurrection (rejected for Reincarnation)

"We believe that the dissolution of spirit, soul and body, caused by death, is annulled by rebirth of the same spirit and soul in another body here on earth. We believe the repeated incarnations of man to be a merciful provision of our loving Father to the end that all may have opportunity to attain immortality through regeneration, as did Jesus. 'This corruptible must put on incorruption.' "[17]

Prayer

"We believe that creative Mind, God, is masculine and feminine, and that these attributes of Being are fundamental in both natural and spiritual man.... Almighty Father-Mother, we thank Thee for this vision of Thine omnipotence, omniscience, and omnipresence, in us and in all that we think and do, in the name of Jesus Christ. Amen."[18]

"*Society of Silent Unity*: It is with joy and gratitude that I report to you that I am entirely healed of the trouble about which I wrote to you — varicose veins and an ulcer on my ankle. When I first wrote to you asking for your prayers I was in bed in a rather serious condition. My recovery has been slow and at times I seemed to lose ground. But the months have been a season of renewing, of rebuilding." —Mrs. B. G. T., Chattanooga, Tenn.[19]

"*Society of Silent Unity*: About a month ago I wrote to you asking for prayers for my skin. I had boils on my face. I had tried creams, salves, and many other things without obtaining relief. Your wonderful prayers did the work of healing." —Mrs. C. H. C., Los Angeles, Calif.[20]

---

16. *Ibid.*, p. 11.
17. *Unity's Statement of Faith*, Art. 22.
18. *Ibid.*, Arts. 16, 32.
19. *Unity*, Vol. 72, No. 3, p. 72.
20. *Unity*, Vol. 72, No. 1, p. 71.

UNITY SCHOOL OF CHRISTIANITY 145

To Aid Digestion (metaphysically conceived)

1. What is the common source of New Thought, Christian Science, and Unity?
2. How were "miracles" performed by Elijah, Jesus, and others, according to Unity?
3. Explain the use of atomic energy according to Unity leaders.
4. What is the difference in understanding of "sin" in the three above-named systems?
5. Is death a reality to Unity minds?
6. Give some samples of spiritualizing truth as found in Unity literature.
7. What is wrong with the Unity concepts of God, Jesus Christ, Atonement, Heaven, Resurrection, Prayer?

8

BAHA'ISM

"There is a snag," wrote Dr. E. Stanley Jones, "in the statement of the Theosophists and the Baha'is that all religions are basically one and the same, and are equally good, therefore join the Theosophical Society or the Baha'is on that basis. If they are all the same, why another?" It would indeed seem superfluous. Yet Baha'is report "a much stronger response from the public during recent years than ever before." Perhaps Ferguson was right when he stated that "no cult bears a gospel better suited to the temper of our times than the Bahai."[1]

A movement which claims something over one million adherents "in nearly every country of the world" is worth studying. Dr. Atkins was right in observing that there is among all the cults "nothing more curious than that the old controversy as to the true successor of Mohammed the prophet should at last have issued in a universal religion with a temple of unity on the shores of Lake Michigan."

History

Baha'ism is of Persian Mohammedan origin, tracing its beginning to the Mohammedan belief "that the last true successor of Mohammed who disappeared in the tenth century never died, but is still living in a mysterious city, surrounded by a band of faithful disciples and 'that at the end of time he will issue forth and fill the earth with justice after it has been filled with iniquity.'" This hidden successor is said to have revealed himself from time to time through those to whom he has made known his will, and who are known as *Babs* or *gates*, "the gate, that is, where-

---

1. *The Confusion of Tongues*, p. 231.

BAHA'ISM 147

by communication was reopened between the hidden one and his faithful followers."

The last one of these Babs was a young Persian merchant, named Mirza 'Ali Muhammed who took the title of Bab in 1844 and who "had much the same relation to Baha'u'llah as John the Baptist had to Christ." The Bab's career was short lived; he died a martyr's death at the hand of Persian Mohammedans at the age of thirty years, A.D. 1850. He had constantly pointed to a divine prophet who was shortly to succeed him. Before his death he sent his signet rings and writings to one of his friends and foremost supporters, one Mirza Husayn 'Ali, his senior by two years. The two had never met, and were not related. 'Ali at first continued the teachings of the Bab; but soon afterwards announced himself as the divine manifestation predicted by him. He is known as *Baha'-u'llah*, that is, *Glory of God*. The followers of the cult then changed their name from Babs to Bahais and proceeded to ascribe to Baha'u'llah divine honor and worship. Like the Bab, Baha'u'llah and his disciples suffered much from persecution and exile, which, of course, only proved once more that "the blood of the martyrs is the seed of the church."[2]

Baha'u'llah passed away in May, 1892, at the age of seventy-five, after forty years of hardship, imprisonment, and exile, in his villa of Behje near Akka (Palestine, "the Holy Land"). He was succeeded by his son Abbas Effendi, born in Teheran, Persia, May 23, 1844, "on the very day upon which the Bab made his declaration to the disciples in Shiraz." Abbas, who had shared his father's hardships as well as his greater ease in his declining years, is known among Bahais as *'Abdu'l-Baha*, that is, *The Servant of God*. He became "the authoritative interpreter" of the teachings

---

2. The matter is so stated in J. E. Esslemont, *Baha'u'llah and His Message;* also in S. G. Wilson, *Baha'ism and Its Claims*, p. 22. W. E. Miller, however, identifies Baha'u'llah with Baha, half-brother to Mirza Yahya, which latter reigned undisputed from 1852-1863, when Baha gained the ascendency. In his earlier work Miller states that "the more the Baha'i doctrine spreads . . . the more the true history and nature of the original Babi Movement is obscured and distorted." *Baha'ism: Its Origin, History and Teachings*, p. 90.

of "The Master," Baha'u'llah. He, too, has known adversities and persecutions, although not as severe or numerous as those of his predecessors in the Cause. In 1912 he visited the United States, where the first disciples were won in Chicago and where the Cause has since grown more rapidly than in any other country except Persia. 'Abdu'l-Baha died on November 28, 1921, aged seventy-seven years. The leadership of the movement, after some wranglings, fell to his eldest grandson, Shoghi Effendi, the head of a Committee of Nineteen, and known by the title of *Guardian of the Cause.*

Teaching

Baha'ism is the unifying cult *par excellence.* "It has," in the words of Mrs. Chandler, "accepted all the religions of the world, found them fundamentally and essentially alike, and reveres equally as divine all nine of the prophets. So it may appeal equally to Hindus, Moslems, Christians, and Jews; it admits the divinity of the prophet or Messiah of each. It does not even claim any greater divinity for its own particular prophet, Baha'u'llah. It merely claims that the Great Beauty of Blessed Perfection, coming later, has brought the latest message from the Divine Source to the peoples of the world, and that the message doesn't differ fundamentally, or in essence, from the message of his predecessor, but is, one might say, brought up to date in dealing with certain specific matters that didn't concern the people whom Christ or Mohammed addressed."

In the words of another Baha'i writer, "Jesus could not speak of international problems; his people did not know of the existence of Japan." A new revelation for our modern day must therefore complete that brought by Jesus. When Jesus warned to "watch and pray" for the coming of the Lord He meant, "Receive Baha'u'llah." This prophet, therefore, referred to Jesus as "the Son of God," or "a Manifestation of God," but claimed to be, himself, "a later Manifestation."

In accordance with these fundamental ideas, and to attain to their unifying ideal, Baha'is present the following "principles" for which they strive:

"The Oneness of God and Oneness of Religion;
The Oneness of Mankind;
Independent Search After Truth;
All Prejudices must be Abandoned (to wit, religious, color, national, class, sexual, and personal prejudices);
International Peace;
International Auxiliary Language;
Education for All;
Equality for the Sexes;
Abolition of Industrial Slavery (Abolition of Wealth and Poverty);
Personal Holiness (Work in the Spirit of Service is Worship)."

Baha'ism claims that unity and brotherhood are the only important things and not doctrine. "Love" is the ever recurring word in its literature. But its conception of love is neither correct, nor consistently carried out. In the first place, Baha'ism itself proves that "love" without certain definite teachings is untenable. When in New York in 1912, 'Abdu'l-Baha was approached by two Baha'is who, arguing a point of Baha'i teaching, asked him to decide who was right. The answer of 'Abdu'l-Baha was: "Neither is right. To be a Baha'i there must never be any discord; all must agree. Unity is the aim." And yet this same system now insists "that nothing whatever should be given to the public by any individual among the friends, unless fully considered and approved by the Spiritual Assembly in his locality."[3] The implication is that it is not safe to let individuals air their views on Baha'i teaching except after official approval of their views. The *Star of the West* is the official organ of the movement in America. And, in the next place, if a member of the Baha'is leaves the movement because of changed views, he — or, generally *she*, for this is a ladies' cult like Christian Science — has good reason

---

3. Shoghi Effendi in a letter addressed from Haifa, March 12, 1922, to "Dear Fellow Workers in the Cause of Baha'u'llah."

to hide as far as possible out of reach of the leaders of this loving cult. The last statement can, in the nature of the case, not be backed up by references; but the author vouches for its truth. There is no salvation for apostate Baha'is according to the system.

The Wilmette Temple

One would think that the frightfully outlandish names in use among Baha'is tend to make the movement unpopular. The Baha'is, however, do not shrink from pointing to their great temple as *Mashriqu'l-Adhkar*.[4] And with this temple they conjure. It has cost more money and time to complete this temple than seems to have been originally expected, and the dream of building similar structures in every State of the Union has, for the time being at least, been abandoned.

The temple at Wilmette, near Chicago, embodies in visible form many of the ideals of the cult, and is its chief means of propaganda. In an illustrated pamphlet on "The Baha'i House of Worship, An Institution of the World Order of Baha'u'llah," Genevieve L. Coy informs us that, as musicians, artists, poets receive their inspiration from another realm, so the late Louis Bourgeois, architect of the Temple, "through all his years of labor was ever conscious that Baha'u'llah was the creator of this building to be erected to his glory.... When the man-made creeds are stripped away from all the religions we find nothing left but harmony. Today, however, religion is so entangled in the superstitions and hypotheses of men that it must needs be stated in a new form to be once again pure and undefiled. Likewise in architecture those fundamental structural lines which originated in the faith of all religions are the same, but so covered over are they with the decorations picturing creed upon creed and superstition upon superstition that we must needs lay them aside and create a new form or ornamentation. Into this new design, then, of the Temple, is

---

4. Also spelled Mashrak-ul-Azkar, and meaning "The Dawning-place of Praises."

woven, in symbolic form, the great Baha'i teaching of unity — the unity of all religions and of mankind. There are combinations of mathematical lines, symbolizing those of the universe, and in their intricate merging of circle into circle, of circle within circle, we visualize the merging of. all the religions into one."

We shall not weary the reader with a detailed account of the cost ($895,000 has been spent, and the end is not yet). "When the *Mashriqu'l-Adhkar* at Wilmette is completed, it will include a hospital and dispensary, a school for orphan children, a hospice, and a college for higher scientific education. In these institutions the principle of the oneness of mankind will be put into concrete practice. Their services will be dispensed irrespective of color, race, or nationality." The scientific college, we are told, is included because "religion and science are the two wings upon which man's intelligence can soar into the heights, with which the human soul can progress."

There are nine entrances into the "nonagon Temple," each one representing one of Nine Great Religions, and all together leading into the inner sanctuary of Truth. From the headquarters of the "National Spiritual Assembly of Baha'is of the U.S. and Canada" we are also informed that "when the interior decoration is completed, the central hall of the Wilmette Temple will be open for daily prayer and meditation and for meetings consisting only of reading from the words of Baha'u'llah and 'Abdu'l-Baha."

The work on the great temple appears to proceed but slowly. In a letter dated February 21, 1942, Mr. Horace Halley, secretary of the National Spiritual Assembly of the Baha'is, of Wilmette, Illinois, informs me thus: "Since the pamphlet by Genevieve L. Coy was published, the work of external decoration has been carried forward to a point very near completion. The enclosed photograph, taken December 18, shows the progress on the main story, which is now nearly completed, except for two of the nine sides. We hope that this work can be done before the fall of 1942 and at the same time construct the circular steps which are to surround the building.

"When this construction work is finished, the exterior of the building will be complete, but the work of the interior is still to be done. We do not plan any immediate work on the interior, but assume that after a few years a definite scheme of interior decoration and arrangement will be undertaken."

Compare with this slow financial sacrifice for the movement's chief enterprise the remark of W. M. Miller: "It is startling to read in the census statistics as given by the Bahais of America that whereas the property of the Baha'i Temple in Chicago is worth more than a million dollars, the amount given in 1936 by the members of the Cause to charity was only $281. Even if this figure is incorrect, we wish that the Bahais would show their 'love' more in deed than in word, if they would win our confidence. How much more convincing a great medical mission in India or Tibet than a million-dollar Temple in Chicago, beautiful as the Mashriq-ul-Azkar may be!"

To this may be added that *The Baha'i Centenary,* 1844-1944, published in 1944 by the Baha'i Publishing Co., Wilmette, Illinois, states that the superstructure was finished in 1931 and the exterior ornamentation was completed between 1932-1943. From the same source we learn that four Baha'i schools have been established in the United States, some of which, judging from the photographs, are quite elaborate. Of the Temple this source states: "Records of daily visitors kept since July 1, 1932 show that the total number who went through the building with Baha'i guides up to October 1, 1943, was 164,360. To deal with this throng of inquirers a body of Temple guides has been rendering service, its members prepared by a special course of instructions based upon long experience with the types of question asked and the information desired."

The year 1953 marked a Holy Year for Baha'is, it being the one hundredth anniversary of the call of the founder Baha'u'llah, to his mission. Pioneers went as far north as Yellowknife, Alberta, Whitehorse, Baker Lake, and Arctic

Bay. This was the opening of a ten-year crusade by Ruhiyyih Khanum, the former Mary Maxwell of Montreal, and the wife of Shoghi Effendi, the present guardian and international head of the faith. Baha'is consider it encouraging that during these one hundred years Baha'ism from its native land, Iran, has spread to 124 countries. "Its followers are of diversified cultures, races and nations. Its teachings are based upon the principles of the oneness of mankind, the unity of religions, and justice without principles."

Meanwhile, as Baha'ism obtains a firmer footing, the lines of membership are being drawn more tightly. A recent Baha'i work, *All Things Made New* by John Ferraby (1958), states: "For a Baha'i to belong to an organization, religious or secular, membership of which implies holding beliefs or approving aims out of harmony with the teachings of Bah'u'llah, would amount either to a denial of faith in those teachings or to open insincerity. Anyone applying for membership of the Baha'i Community who is unwilling to relinquish membership in such an organization proves by his unwillingness that he has not fully understood the Baha'i teachings, and consequently he is unacceptable. For the same reason, a Baha'i who insists on joining such an organization after his Assembly has warned him not to is liable to be deprived of his voting right in the Baha'i Community.

"There are very few organizations whose beliefs and aims are wholly consistent with the Baha'i teachings. Virtually all religious organizations, except perhaps a few concerned with comparative religion, require some sort of belief to which a Baha'i cannot subscribe . . ." (p. 285).

Appraisal

It is evident that a movement which so strongly stresses the unity of all religious forces in the world should be somewhat vague and general. There are not many points of Christian doctrine upon which the cult teaches. It rather ignores them one and all. Perhaps it is exactly here that we should start.

1. It should be clear that Baha'ism has some very fine points which, from the Christian standpoint, make it all the more dangerous *as a religion*. The last three words are underscored with a purpose. Who would not praise it in the Baha'is when they advocate world peace? Who has not grasped by this time the terribleness of a universal war fought with modern means of wholesale destruction, and in the interest of international investments of large capital? Who does not realize that modern warfare comes as close to hell as anything on earth can come? Or, who does not realize that it is more than a noble gesture for a white man from the South (conceivably) to lay a sick Negro child in the bed next to his own in the same ward, and tend to both with equal tenderness? For all that, there are great gifts of what Calvin called God's common grace. But all such nobility of character does not atone for sin. It is not religion. Least of all is it a religion superior to Christianity.

2. With its plainly implied pantheism Baha'ism is one more example of what Dr. Abraham Kuyper called many years ago "the irresistible tendency of our age to change along every line the God-man into the Man-god." As pantheism, Baha'ism stands condemned from the standpoint of Christianity. Not man's reaching up to ever higher manifestations of the divine, but the transcendent God descending to man in divine revelation, is the way out of human ills.

3. Baha'ism has much in common with Theosophy. Both emphasize the idea that one more divine spokesman must add to Jesus' words. But, whereas Theosophists are looking for this man to appear since Krishnamurti stepped down from "the throne that was Christ's" Baha'is assert that this man has appeared in Baha'u'llah.

With Theosophists the Baha'is also agree that all religions are one. We remember Annie Besant's words, "Blended together they give the whiteness of truth, blended together they give a mighty chord of perfection." This is due, of course, to their common pantheism.

4. Baha'ism has much in common with Spiritism and Free Masonry.

Of Spiritism Sir Arthur Conan Doyle wrote, "To me it *is* religion — the very essence of it." He called it "the great unifying force, the one probable thing connected with every religion, Christian or non-Christian, forming the common solid basis upon which each raises if it must needs raise, that separate system which appeals to the varied types of mind." How greatly like Baha'ism that sounds!

The discussion of Free Masonry in a separate chapter has been omitted from this volume. It had been inserted in *Our Birthright and the Mess of Meat.*[5] The writer realizes that Free Masonry is not a cult like the other isms here discussed. To a great many Free Masons the lodge is the badge of sociability, mutual helpfulness. They laugh at the idea that the Masonic lodge or the Independent Order of Odd Fellows should be considered a competitor, let alone a substitute, for the Christian religion.

Nevertheless, many leaders of the Masonic movement, the officially recommended literature of the movement, its signs and emblems which are all borrowed from oriental pagan religions, all these and other things show Free Masonry to be such that Dr. Torrey was right in saying, "A man can be a Christian and a Free Mason, but he cannot be an intelligent Christian and an intelligent Mason at the same time."

Without wanting to give offense, therefore, to Christian Masons we would ask of them to study such works as *An Encyclopedia of Freemasonry and Its Kindred Sciences,* 1914; *Lexicon of Freemasonry; Masonic Ritualist;* all by Albert G. Mackey, M.D. 33. *Freemasonry and the Ancient Gods* by J. S. M. Ward, 1926; *New Odd-Fellows' Manual,* by Rev. A. B. Grosh, 1882. We would ask Freemasons to

---

5. The first edition of the present work. An up-to-date appraisal of Lodgism may be found in *A Handbook of Organizations* by Theodore Graebner (St. Louis: Concordia Publishing House, 1948).

consider why there is a *Co-masonic Order* in the Theosophical Society. We would ask why the assertion that all religions are one, should be tolerated in Free Masonry, but condemned in Theosophy and Baha'ism. Said Baha'u'llah in his "Last Will and Testament":

"O ye people of the world! The religion of God is for the sake of love and union; make it not the cause of enmity and conflict.... The hope is cherished that the people of Baha shall ever turn to the Blessed Word: LO: ALL ARE OF GOD:—"

Said the Supreme Council of the 33rd Degree, F. A. A. M., Southern Jurisdiction of the U.S. in 1874, "Freemasonry is a worship, but one in which all civilized men can unite; for it does not undertake to explain or dogmatically to settle those great mysteries that are above the feeble comprehension of our human intellect."[6]

And Mackey wrote, "If Free Masonry were simply a Christian institution, the Jew and the Moslem, the Brahman and the Buddhist, could not conscientiously partake of its illumination. But its universality is its boast. In its language citizens of every nation may converse; at its altar men of all religions may kneel; to its creed disciples of every faith may subscribe."[7]

5. Whereas Baha'is claim for their religion a later emphasis upon the same truth taught also, among others, by Christianity, we maintain that it is, at least in its manifestation in Christian lands, a sad imitation of the Christian religion. Baha'u'llah as final manifestation of God in the flesh we believe to be an imitation of the incarnation as seen in Jesus Christ; Baha'i "inspired tablets" we consider fake scriptures. Their "spiritual baptism," "Holy Land," "Beatitudes," "Unity Feast" (for the Lord's Supper), their

---

6. *Morals and Dogmas of the Ancient and Accepted Scottish Rite of Freemasons*. Prepared for the Supreme Council of the 33rd Degree for the Southern Jurisdiction of the U. S. and published by its authority, New York, 1874, p. 526.

7. *An Encyclopedia of Freemasonry and Its Kindred Sciences*. Subtitle: *Christianization of Freemasonry*. Two volumes. (New York and London: the Masonic History Co., 1914).

imitation Pentecost (a surprising peace is said to fill the souls of those who repeat ninety-five times daily the words *Alla hu Abha*)— these would-be Christian touches, apparently calculated to catch Christians, do not increase our respect for Baha'ism.

Editorially, the *Christian Century* of September 25, 1946, informs us that the Baha'is have decided to begin to advertise their cause in a twofold manner: for the rank and file, through *Newsweek* and similar periodicals, while others will be reached through trade journals of the publishing and broadcasting industries. This is interesting, first, because we are now prepared to look for a more open method of propaganda by this cult that teaches the unity of any and all religions. Secondly, however, we get an interesting glimpse of the mentality of Modernism, when we see the (at that time) editor of this prominent journal of religion go so far in his vehement antagonism against "denominationalism" as to write: "The plan is all right. *The Baha'is have something to sell* . . . . It is interesting, and may be helpfully suggestive to other religious bodies, to see how *this worthy group*, which had its origins among the Mohammedans of Persia about a century ago, makes use of the most modern techniques for making friends and influencing people" (italics mine).

Baha'ism and Scripture Doctrine

God

"Further than this [Baha'u'llah] man has no other point for concentration. He is God."[8]

Sin

"The only difference between members of the human family is that of degree. Some are like children who are ignorant and must be educated until they arrive at maturity. Some are like the sick and must be treated with tenderness and care. None are bad or evil. We must not

---

8. *The Star of the West* (official organ of the movement in America), Feb. 7, 1914.

feel repelled by these poor children. We must treat them with great kindness, teaching the ignorant and tenderly nursing the sick."

"Evil is imperfection. Sin is the state of man in the world of the baser nature, for in nature exist defects such as injustice, tyranny, hatred, hostility, strife: these are characteristics of the lower plane of nature. These are the sins of the world, the fruits of the tree from which Adam did eat. Through education we must free ourselves from these imperfections."—'ABDU'L-BAHA.[9]

Jesus the Only Name

"Christ was the Prophet of the Christians, Moses of the Jews — why should not the followers of each prophet recognize and honor the other prophets also? If men could only learn the lesson of mutual tolerance, understanding, and brotherly love, the Unity of the world would soon be an established fact."—'ABDU'L-BAHA.[10]

"The revelation of Jesus was for His own dispensation —that of 'the Son.' Now it is no longer the point of guidance to the world. We are in total darkness if we are refusing the revelation of the present dispensation. Bahais must be severed from all and everything that is past — things both good and bad — everything. Now all is changed. All the teachings of the past are past. 'Abdu'l-Baha is now supplying all the world."—C. M. REMEY.[11]

The Resurrection

"'Abdu'l-Baha explains the meaning of the resurrection as follows: 'The disciples were troubled and agitated after the martyrdom of Christ. The Reality of Christ, which signifies His teachings, His bounties, His perfections and His spiritual power, was hidden and concealed for two or three days after His martyrdom, and was not resplen-

---

9. *The Wisdom of 'Abdu'l-Baha*, pp. 128, 155.
10. *Ibid.*, p. 43.
11. *Star of the West*, Dec. 31, 1913.

dent and manifest. No, rather it was lost; for the believers were few in number and were troubled and agitated. The Cause of Christ was like a lifeless body, and, when after three days the disciples became assured and steadfast, and began to serve the Cause of Christ, and resolved to spread the divine teachings, putting His counsels into practice, and arising to serve Him, the Reality of Christ became resplendent, and His bounty appeared; His religion found life, His teachings and admonitions became evident and visible. In other words, the Cause of Christ was like a lifeless body, until the life and the bounty of the Holy Spirit surrounded it.' "[12]

Faith Versus Reason

"There are two kinds of light. There is the visible light of the sun by whose aid we can discern the beauties of the world around us — without this we could see nothing.

"Nevertheless, though it is the function of this light to make things visible to us, it cannot give us the *power* to see them or to understand what their various charms may be, for this light has no intelligence, no consciousness. It is the light of the *intellect* which gives us knowledge and understanding, and without this light the physical eyes would be useless.

"This light of the intellect is the highest light that exists, for it is born of the *Light Divine*.

"The light of the intellect enables us to understand and realize all that exists, but it is only the Divine Light that can give us sight for the invisible things, and which enables us to see Truths that will only be visible to the world thousands of years hence."—'ABDU'L-BAHA.[13]

"We must not accept traditional dogmas that are contrary to reason, nor pretend to believe doctrines which we cannot understand. To do so is superstition and not true religion."—J. E. ESSLEMONT.[14]

12. Ferraby, *op. cit.*, p. 178.
13. *Op. cit.*, p. 62.
14. *Baha'u'llah and His Message*, p. 11.

Sufferings of Christ

"Why did Christ Jesus suffer the fearful death on the Cross? Why did Mohammed bear persecutions? Why did the Bab make the supreme sacrifice and why did Baha'u'llah pass the years of his life in prison?

"Why should all this suffering have been, if not to prove the everlasting life of the Spirit?

"Christ suffered, He accepted all His trials because of the immortality of His spirit. If a man reflects he will understand the spiritual significance of the law of progress; how all moves from the inferior to the superior degree."—'ABDU'L-BAHA.[15]

We hold that Baha'ism stands condemned by the following statements of Scripture:

Matthew 24:24, 26: "For there shall arise false Christs, and false prophets, and shall show great signs and wonders; so as to lead astray, if possible, even the elect.... If therefore they shall say unto you, Behold, he is in the wilderness; go not forth: Behold, he is in the inner chambers; believe it not."

Colossians 1:19-20: "For it was the good pleasure of the Father that in him should all the fulness dwell; and through him to reconcile all things unto himself, having made peace through the blood of his cross; through him, I say, whether things upon the earth, or things in the heavens."[16]

---

15. *Op. cit.*, p. 85.

16. We have purposely presented Baha'ism as it reveals itself in its Western cloak. It will be noted that even this is, more or less openly, antichristian. And this is an adaptation of Persian Baha'ism for consumption in the West. A close student and adherent spoke of "Persian Baha'ism and not that American fantasy which bears its name." The original Baha'ism is far more hateful toward its opponents; it advocates bigamy rather than equality of sexes; its literature is replete with historical and religious falsehoods. For that matter, the statement that the Bab pointed to an early successor of his, is itself untrue, although now believed by Baha'ists both in the East and the West. In Persia the movement is now boosted with the legend that half America is Bahai. Cf. the well-documented works by S. G. Wilson and W. Miller, previously cited.

BAHA'ISM

Pointers

1. Why is Baha'ism suited to our times?
2. What is the relation between Bab, Baha'u'llah, 'Abdu'l-Baha, Shoghi Effendi?
3. Can you mention some cardinal teachings of this system?
4. Is Baha'ism as tolerant as it pretends to be?
5. Why have Baha'is made but little financial sacrifice for their views?
6. What do you think of the stand of the Christian Reformed and other churches who maintain that lodge membership and church membership are inconsistent and incompatible?

9

DESTINY OF AMERICA

Destiny of America! This cult is more generally known as British-Israelism, or Anglo-Israelism; but why not use the more fascinating of its names, Destiny of America. That name holds for the entire North American continent; and the program can appropriately close its broadcasts with the one tune that to Canadians means, "God save the King," and to Americans, "My country, 'tis of thee." One program, and one melody for Dominion Day on July 1, and for Independence Day on July 4, one glorious, world-saving destiny indeed for all who have at one time or another emigrated to the North American continent; for Britain is Ephraim and the United States is Manasseh, and the throne of David is now the British throne.

With Mormonism, Anglo-Israelism has in common some wild speculations concerning the early inhabitants of America.

With Seventh-Day Adventism it has in common that it has some earnest Christians among its ranks, while both systems are vicious.

With the early Russellism it shares the intricate mathematical measurings of the Great Pyramid of Egypt from which "Pastor" Russell determined the date of Christ's return (afterward condemned by Rutherford) and Prof. G. P. Smith wrote *Our Inheritance in the Great Pyramid*.

On page 1 of the First Book of Nephi — (which also opens the Book of Mormon) we read: "I Nephi . . . make a record in the language of my father, which consists of the learning of the Jews, and the language of the Egyptians."

Not only were the "reformed Egyptian *caractors*" the product of a deceptive brain, but there never existed such a language.

On page 549 of the Book of Mormon we read: "And it came to pass that I Mormon, being eleven years old, was carried by my father into the land Zarahemla, the whole face of the land having become covered with buildings, and the people were as numerous almost, as it were the sand of the sea."

Now this boy Mormon was one of the last descendants of the godly Nephi who had left Jerusalem in the days of Zedekiah. These Nephites had built a godly civilization during four hundred years. But they backslid, and were utterly destroyed in A.D. 384 by the descendants of Ishmael who had come from Jerusalem with Nephi. Israel's descendants, the black-skinned Lamanites, destroyed all vestiges of civilization in Central America. Mormon and his son Moroni fortunately recorded the entire story on golden plates, which were afterward hidden in the hill Cumorah in New York, until in 1827 they were revealed by Moroni, now an angel, to Joseph Smith Jr., the Prophet.

The Book of Mormon also tells of an earlier settlement in America, by the Jaredites, who had come in cigar-shaped boats to America after the Confusion of Tongues at Babylon. The Book of Mormon insists that between the Jaredites and the Nephites, Central America and Mexico lay idle for six hundred years, and the land was so desolate that it was named Zarahemla, the Land of Desolation.

According to such famous anthropologists and historians as Bancroft, Baldwin, and others, however, these lands have always had a dense population; and the inhabitants have always been copper-colored, that is, neither white Nephites nor black Lamanites; and they have ever been a gentle people.

Now when Christians refuse upon scientific grounds to accept these grotesque Mormon ethnological vagaries and fantasies, why should they accept the equally unattested Anglo-Israel fiction which traces America's white population to the Israelites of Zedekiah's time because "Saxon" is said to be really *Isaacson,* or son of Isaac; and "British" is alleged to be really a Hebrew word, derived from Hebrew *berith,* covenant, and *ish,* man, meaning therefore "the men of the covenant"?

At best, writes Dr. M. Wyngaarden, emeritus Professor of the Old Testament in Calvin Seminary, if the word "British" had aught to do with *berith* and *ish,* it could not mean "men of the covenant," but only "covenant of man"; but besides, all scholars are agreed, and every seminary student discovers to his grief, that the Semitic and Anglo-Saxon tongues have nothing in common.[1] And so it is; and this is in keeping with the elaborate History of the English Language at the beginning of Webster's Dictionary, and also with the findings of the Oxford Dictionary. The only resemblance between Hebrew and English is to be found in a few words that have been taken over from the Old Testament.

Dr. Albertus Pieters, late professor in the Western Theological Seminary, Holland, Michigan, reminds us that the Anglo-Israelites have gone to such ridiculous lengths in this matter as to draw even the Japanese within the pale of ancient Israel; for, so they say, there is a remarkable similarity between the Japanese word *Samurai,* the name for the old Japanese military caste, and *Samaria,* the capital of the kingdom of Israel.

Not only so; they have even ventured to conclude that since the Hebrew word for a young bullock was *engle,* therefore the land of the Anglo-Saxons was called "England," and since these Isaac's sons no doubt, as good Israelites, sacrificed plenty of young bullocks or Hebrew *engles,* therefore England's inhabitants were called John Bull.[2]

---

1. "The British-Israel Movement" in The *Calvin Forum,* Dec., 1947.
2. *The Seed of Abraham.* (Grand Rapids: Eerdmans, 1950), p. 159. The author concludes "after careful study," "that it is one of the most baseless and absurd varieties of Bible study that the human mind has yet produced — which is saying a great deal!"

DESTINY OF AMERICA

For all such palpable nonsense the movement keeps growing until it now claims some two million adherents scattered through many denominations.

In an article "Religion and Race" in *The Christian Century*, April 22, 1953, Ralph L. Roy writes: "Of the scores of Anglo-Israelite leaders in the United States a few are worthy of special note. Howard B. Rand of Haverhill, Massachusetts, 'dean' of the movement, led in the organization of the Anglo-Saxon Federation in 1930. Rand operates Destiny Publishers, the cult's central publishing house, and edits an expensive monthly magazine with 15,000 subscribers. James A. Lovell of Fort Worth, Texas, intermittently sponsors weekly broadcasts over 50 radio stations throughout North America. He edits a 70-page monthly, *Kingdom Digest*, and claims to distribute 300,000 pieces of literature annually. Wesley Swift of Lancaster, California, a loyal devotee of Gerald L. K. Smith, is regarded as the leading racist chieftain on the west coast. William L. Blessing, a lone-wolf Anglo-Israelite leader of Denver, Colorado, operates the House of Prayer for All People and publishes a monthly, *Showers of Blessing*. One of his novel fancies is that when Negroes become Christian, "God begins to remove the caste of color and to restore them into the White Israel race!" Interested parties will do well to order Mr. Roy's book on Protestant fringe groups, *Apostles of Discord* (Boston: Beacon Press, 1953).

What, then, exactly, are the teachings of this bizarre system; and what, briefly, is the answer to its claims?

The theory is set forth clearly in the 52-page brochure *The Lost Tribes of Israel* by the late Reader Harris.[3]

This booklet opens with the incredible claim that when in Leviticus 26 God says that disobedient Israel will be punished "seven times more fiercely for your sins" (v. 18), and, "I will bring seven times more plagues upon you according to your sins" (v. 21), and, "I will also walk contrary unto you, and I will smite you, even I, seven times for your sins"

---

3. 10th ed., (Haverhill, Mass.: Destiny Publishers, 1941).

(v. 28), these words "seven times more fiercely" and "seven times more plagues" do not refer to the intensity of the punishment but must be understood as referring to time. "A time," Mr. Harris informs us, "is generally taken to mean 360 years"; seven times would therefore mean 2,500 years, "which if calculated from the captivity of Israel, would reach to about the beginning of the nineteenth century."

From this strange substitution of chronology for multiplication we are to infer that about the beginning of the nineteenth century we may look for the beginning of the end of Israel's afflictions; and, so we are told, with this agrees that just about that time some of God's people are awakened to "a spirit of enquiry as to the fate of the tribes with regard to their destiny."

The next link in the chain of reasoning is that until about a hundred years ago the great fault of Christians has been their refusal to distinguish and separate Judah and Israel. "The Bible, however, is perfectly plain. When it speaks of Israel in ninety-nine cases out of a hundred the ten tribes are meant." Judah and Israel always remained distinct after the latter had been carried captive in 721 B.C. and the former in 588 B.C.

Upon this distinction, of course, rest all of those modern theories which have identified the Lost Tribes with the Mormons, or which placed them in Arabia, or identified them with the Nestorians, or again rediscovered them in the Anglo-Saxons.[4]

Before we view the alleged results of these "facts," therefore, let us examine the Scriptural data. And when we do, this is what we find.

The Scriptures teach that all twelve tribes were under Babylonian and Persian dominion; and that the restoration was not a restoration of two tribes but of all twelve; and so indeed it had been predicted. Jeremiah (7th century B.C.) 3:18, "In those days the house of Judah shall walk with the house of Israel, and they shall come together out of the

---

4. A. Pieters, *op. cit.*, ch. IX.

land of the north to the land that I gave for an inheritance unto your fathers."

For Jeremiah had also stated definitely that Judah and Israel were together in Babylon as its fall drew near; and there was no hint at the tribes being lost: Jeremiah 50:33-34, "Thus saith Jehovah of hosts: The children of Israel and the children of Judah are oppressed together . . . . Their Redeemer is strong. . . ."

Similarly Isaiah (8th century) had predicted, 11:12, "And he will set up an ensign for the nations, and will assemble the outcasts of Israel, and gather together the dispersed of Judah from the four corners of the earth. (For the return of the ten tribes, see Isa. 10:20-23; 14:1.)

Two other eighth-century prophets were Hosea and Micah. Said Hosea, "And the children of Judah and the children of Israel shall be gathered together, and they shall appoint themselves one head, and shall go up from the land; for great shall be the day of Jezreel (1:11).

And Micah's famous advent message, 5:2, stated that out of Bethlehem in the land of *Judah* the ruler of *Israel* would come forth.

Nowhere appears the arbitrary distinction between post-exilic Judah and Israel which has given rise to Mormon and British-Israel fancies.

In harmony with the above, the prophet Daniel prayed for the restoration of all the tribes (Dan. 9:1, 7, 11, 15, 18).

Consequently, Ezra mentions among those who returned men from Bethel and Ai, centers of the idolatrous worship of the northern kingdom: Ezra 2:28, "The men of Beth-el and Ai, two hundred twenty and three."

And Ezra goes on to say (2:70), "So the priests and the Levites, and some of the people . . . dwelt in their cities, and all Israel in their cities."

Furthermore, Ezra offered a sacrifice for all Israel: ". . . and for a sin offering for all Israel, twelve he-goats, according to the number of the tribes of Israel. . . . And the children of Israel that were come again out of the captivity, and all such as had separated themselves unto them from all the filthiness of the nations of the land, to seek Jehovah, the God of Israel, did eat . . ." (6:17, 21).

The New Testament, following in the wake of the Old, knows of no lost tribes. Paul said, ". . . unto which promise our twelve tribes, earnestly seeking God night and day, hope to attain (Acts 26:7). Anna, the prophetess, was of the tribe of Asher (Luke 2:36).

Robert Moyer[5] states that the expression "house of Israel" is used fourteen times in the Old Testament before the nation was divided into two kingdoms, while the phrase "house of Judah" also occurs four times before the division. But the British-Israelites claim that after the division these two terms are strictly confined to the two kingdoms respectively. Why, then, if according to this theory only decendants of the two tribes returned, did Jesus say that His disciples should enter neither into homes of gentiles nor of Samaritans "but rather to the lost house of Israel" (Matt. 10:6)?

At the time when Jesus spoke, according to our opponents, the house of Israel was dwelling in Ireland and Scotland.

The above-quoted passages of Scripture, then, are in themselves sufficient to knock the foundation from under the entire Mormon as well as Anglo-Israel deductions concerning remote descendants of so-called Lost Tribes upon whom the Lord God should still look as upon His ancient Israel. It should be borne in mind that the group that returned from Judah and Benjamin was a small minority as well as those who returned from among the ten tribes; but these minorities are called Israel and the Jews; those that remained dropped out of the ranks, intermarried, and were amalgamated among the nations. It would then be as logical and Scriptural to speak of the lost tribes of Judah and Benjamin as it is to refer to the lost ten tribes, but not more so.

---

5. *The British-Israel Delusion*, p. 10.

Having thus rejected the foundation upon which this structure rests, let us trace to what fictitious and fantastic ideas this ill-based theory has given birth. Let us consider the things of which Reader Harris wrote, "The objection may again be raised that this is all very wonderful but that it rests to a large extent upon tradition. Tradition, however, is the basis of all earlier history."

Among these "wonderful" traditions, then, we meet with the following. British-Israelism does not abandon Scripture for tradition, but it takes such Scriptural passages as refer to pre- or post-exilic conditions of Israel and applies them, without further ado, to where they fit in with tradition.

Israel was to become "a company of nations," God said to Jacob; Joseph was to become "a fruitful bough; his branches run over the wall," Jacob added upon his deathbed. Israel was to be a maritime nation: "I will set his hand also on the sea" (Ps. 89); he was to possess the isles of the sea" (Isa. 24:15; 11:11; Jer. 31:10).

So, with the fiction of the Lost Tribes roaming the earth and with the centuries to work with, the British-Israelites move the descendants of the Ten Tribes over the map as the men upon a chessboard are moved. "His seed shall become a multitude of nations," said Jacob of Ephraim (Gen. 48:19). It will at once be seen that this eminently fits that modern melting pot, the United States.

The principle of British-Israel exegesis is to follow "the pattern of history." When certain features are predicted concerning Israel, look for the nation exhibiting those features, and, presto, you have found the Lost Tribes.

For instance, Israel was to be a Sabbath-keeping nation: that was to be "a sign between me and you throughout your generations," (Ex. 31:13). Great Britain and the United States "alone have observed the Christian sabbath" as over against the so-called Continental sabbath: Great Britain and the U. S. A. are Israel.

It was also said of Israel, "Thou shalt lend unto many nations, and thou shalt not borrow" (Deut. 28:12); Great

Britain and the United States have become the greatest money-lenders among the nations.

Similarly, Isaiah predicted that Israel would be an undefeated people (Isa. 54:17; 41:10).

But what of the United States? Isaiah prophesied that part of Israel was to split off from the mother country (49: 19, 20). Besides, already Jacob had predicted that while Ephraim was to be the greater, Manasseh also was to become a great people. "Where," exclaim British-Israelites rhetorically, "are the descendants of Manasseh?" And the answer is, "In Isaiah 49:20 we find these words, 'The place is too strait for me; give me place that I may dwell.'" Therefore, the descendants of Manasseh must be a great people, and "Many students of Scripture believe that in the U. S. A. we find the branch of Joseph that was to run over the wall. Manasseh was to be the thirteenth tribe, and the number thirteen plays an important part in much that pertains to the U. S. A. The original flag had thirteen stars for the thirteen states; 13 letters make up the American slogan E Pluribus Unum; the American dollar contains 13 stars and 13 letters on the scroll; the eagle on the reversed side has 13 wing feathers, 13 tail feathers, 13 arrow heads, 13 horizontal stripes, and 13 parallel lines."

The original white population of the United States came from England — but the Destiny Shapers of America fail to advise us how in the process of crossing the Atlantic these Ephraimites changed into children of Manasseh.

There is, of course, a great deal more, and it makes interesting reading; but it is all founded upon the same arbitrary method. And all of this pseudo-exegesis is backed up by equally precarious tradition.

Thus, beginning with Esdras in his second book in the Apocrypha, we know that "the ten tribes took this counsel among themselves that they should leave the multitude of the heathen and go forth into a further country, that there they might keep their law which they had never kept in their own land, and they passed by the way of the Euphrates." This is confirmed by Josephus who wrote A. D. 70:

"The ten tribes are now beyond the Euphrates and are an immense multitude." What became of them?

British Israelites have the answer. Past old gravestones in the Crimea and a town on the Danube near the Black Sea called Isacha — "evidently an Israelitish name" — they trace these tribes to Scandinavia and to western Europe. The Saxons, having come from the Black Sea, captured England from the original Britons, and divided the country into sections whose names all remind us of God's promise "In Isaac shall thy seed be called" (Gen. 21:12), for they are Sussex or South Saxon, Essex or East Saxon, Middlesex, and the like.

There is an Irish tradition that the prophet Jeremiah escaped from Egypt with a daughter of Zedekiah, the last (and, by the way, illegally appointed) king of Judah. These two first reached Spain, and later Ireland. Here this female descendant of David — entitled to David's throne only by favor of Nebuchadnezzar — married an Irish tribal chief or king between 580 and 565 B.C. From then on the line of David has continued, first in Ireland, then in Scotland and England.

This feat, however, was by no means the only accomplishment of the aged prophet Jeremiah. He also succeeded in taking with him "the stone of destiny." It should be borne in mind, namely, that Jacob, when departing from Bethel, had taken with him the stone which he used for a pillow as a token of the Divine Presence, and on his deathbed had referred to it when according to Genesis 49:24 he said concerning Joseph, "From thence is the shepherd, the stone of Israel." This same stone went with the Israelites into the wilderness; Paul referred to it in I Corinthians 10:4, "the rock followed them" (just look that up in its context!).

Jeremiah, then, took this stone with him and it became the coronation stone of the kings of Argyle, then of the kings of Scotland, and until recently of the kings of England, resting as it did in Westminster Abbey. Small wonder the removal of this Stone of Scone, December 25, 1950, caused much consternation. The writer fears, however, that there is about as much historic evidence for all this as there is for the alleged story which claims that there is among Roman Catholic relics the stone upon which the rooster stood when he crowed at Peter's denial of his Lord; or, for that matter, for the feather that dropped from the wing of the angel Gabriel when he announced the Saviour's birth to Mary.[6]

Much after the same fashion great things were expected some years ago from the Prince of Wales, one of whose names was David, and who, reaching the age of 30 years in 1924, would duplicate his ancestor, the original King David. But Prince David, having become King Edward VIII, abdicated from the throne of Judah and Israel in favor of "the woman I love"; and the Duchess of Windsor proved a spoke in the wheels of Anglo-Israelitish exegesis.

It is impossible to look from the narrow confines of this brief chapter into various other angles of the strange theory which, as said before, is reported to have two million adherents; such as the fact that anthropological and racial studies and comparisons have refuted the British-Israel assertions concerning the racial peculiarities of the English and British as thoroughly as those of the Mormons that the American Indians are the Lamanite seed of Jacob. We refer the reader to the work of Dr. William Henry Smith for a knowledge of this and other features of the movement.

But, having given a brief description of the teachings and method of Destiny of America, let us ask in conclusion, Why should we concern ourselves about this cult? Why not let it alone. What is the harm it may do, the danger it may harbor?

The answer lies close to hand. Anglo-Israelites themselves reply to the question, "What's the good of it?" by saying, first, it will make believers out of unbelievers.

---

6. Prof. A. C. Ramsey of the Dept. of Geology in London University submitted the stone to a chemical and to a microscopic examination, and pronounced it "calcareous sandstone of a reddish or purplish color with heterogeneous pebbles, and of Scottish origin." W. H. Smith, *The Ten Tribes of Israel Never Lost*, p. 91.

More men have remained unbelievers because in reading the Bible and studying history they reached the conclusion that God has failed to fulfill His promises in regard to Israel. But now, by studying the history of Britain and North America, they see these promises taking shape and being fulfilled.

And secondly, all these numerous material, national and international, racial and economic blessings that have been held out to the true Israel should be of great encouragement to us in these days of dire distress of the nations and of great international fear.

It is all so very simple. "This is important to you, tremendously important. Be not hasty in your judgment. Let the overwhelming evidence *prove* to you that the Anglo-Saxon-Celtic people of today are Israelites — and that their nations form the nation of Israel. Then if *you* are of Anglo-Saxon-Celtic descent, you are an Israelite; or if *you* are not of Anglo-Saxon-Celtic descent, but are a Christian, then you are an Israelite by adoption! You are one of God's chosen race: the Bible gives the story of your ancestors and, importantly, the Bible shows the present, predicts the future, and declares the coming greatness of the Israel Kingdom. The Bible is, in fact, *your pattern of history!*"[7]

Observe, then, that British-Israel literature does not bother with speaking of the deity of the Saviour or the atonement for the sins of unworthy ones in His blood. It speaks of the greatness of men, of some, nay, many men. Their greatness is to be sought in physical descent or adoption, as the Pharisees of old considered themselves God's chosen people, and despised all others except those drawn into their own circles as proselytes.

Surely, it is all very soothing, as long as it lasts. For the Bible thus read says of Great Britain, the Dominion, and the United States of America that they shall prosper; that they shall be invincible; that their foot shall be upon the neck of

---

7. *The Pattern of History* (Haverhill, Mass.: Destiny Publishers), p. 16.

their enemies: "Israel is to be mistress of the ends, sides, and uttermost parts of the earth."[8]

We are even now accused of imperialism. What would it be if the Anglo-Israel ideas should become the prevailing view of prophetic Scripture? What if a future dictator, himself neither Anglo-Saxon-Celtic nor Christian, should decide that, the Christians themselves being witness, the Bible, that horrible, racial, material book, does indeed teach that all nations are to be subject to a fancied Israel with its numerous satellites? Surely, here lurks a danger. A political, an international peril.

The greater danger, however, lies elsewhere. The fundamental error of this cult lies in its positing another source of divine authority besides the inspired Bible. What to Roman Catholics is the ecclesiastical tradition, and to Spiritists the voices from departed spirits, that to British-Israelites is the Great Pyramid. All are condemned, together with Astrology, the voice of the planets, by Deuteronomy 18:9-15. For all substitute other sources of religious information for the God-appointed Christ.

The easy, superficial optimism of the cult is amazing. Before me lies a 40-page "Shopping Guide for Tourists," the page being 17 by 11½ inches. It is the Easter, 1954, edition of the *International Consumers Magazine*, left on my doorstep. Its subtitles are, "The King of King's Gazette," "The Universal Educator of the Sound Money Economic System Association."

Its pages are chiefly filled with advertisements by hundreds of business and professional people in Manitoba, Saskatchewan, Alberta, British Columbia, Washington, Idaho, Montana, North Dakota. The centers of the pages, however, contain such articles as: "Resurrection Life Brings Abundance of All Things"; "The Altar-Pillar in Egypt Speaks"; "King David Destroys the Lord's Enemies"; "A Sound Solid Money System Value for Value." Also, incidentally, "World News in Advance," predictive articles

---

8. *Ibid.*, p. 15.

concerning the future of Trans Canada Airlines and other big businesses. We learn that "A Man, a Great Engineer and a Master Mechanic . . . has built this earth . . . . He has laid in it all materials needed for economic abundance. He has risen from the dead for this very purpose to make us understand that the Bible is 'God's lawbook of sound economics.' " Kingdoms that did not know this have been destroyed (Dan. 2). But now The Man proclaims abundance and prosperity to his own, "the fifth universal Stone Kingdom, made up of the British empire and the U. S. A. and Scandinavian people, who are all the same people of the Tribe of Judah, Christ's Kingdom now on earth." The Man now stands and proclaims, "I am the resurrection and the life." But "no one can get these but through me from the Father." And to bring to pass all this economic abundance He has made known in these latter days "the four great powers made by the Great Engineer: steam, electricity, gasoline and oil."

Apparently, it is quite safe to trade with the advertisers, for the magazine proclaims (to the few favored nations), "The eternal gospel of abundance, peace, security coming for all."

Yes, indeed. *"And as it came to pass in the days of Noah, even so shall it be also in the days of the Son of man . . . . Likewise even as it came to pass in the days of Lot they ate, they drank, they bought, they sold . . . but it rained fire and brimstone from heaven and destroyed them all. After the same manner shall it be in the day that the Son of man is revealed"* (Luke 17:26, 28-30).

Thus Heedless was slain in Bunyan's allegory, while one Take-heed escaped. But Mr. Greatheart commented, "You cannot imagine how many are killed hereabouts, and yet men are so foolishly venturous as to set out lightly on pilgrimage, and to come without a guide!"

How About It?

1. Mention some of your objections to the theory of British-Israelism, and give reasons.

2. Why is it that these strange ideas appeal especially in our day and age?

3. Why does Satan conjure up before our eyes theories which have a following both among evangelical believers and among those who care only for the material blessings of God's promises?

4. If all Christian people had been grounded in the fundamental doctrines of Scripture, do you think Destiny of America would be able to boast as large a following as it does?

10

SWEDENBORGIANISM

The cult of Swedenborgianism announces itself as "The New Church" or "The Church of the New Jerusalem." For all that, it is not nearly as new as the other cults described in this volume. Its founder lived in Sweden from 1688 and died in London in 1772. Consequently, one of our earliest great theologians, Dr. Charles Hodge of Princeton, took note of Swedenborg in his famed *Systematic Theology* in 1875.

As to the founder, he stands apart from, and intellectually miles above, founders of "new" religions as Joseph Smith, Mary Baker Eddy, Russell-Rutherford, the Fillmores, and others to whom the words of Henry Van Dyke apply: "There are many Americans who have too little respect for special training, and too much confidence in their power to solve the problems of philosophy and statesmanship extemporaneously."

Emanuel Swedenborg was a genius and a scholar of the first dimension who, as a confirmed bachelor, had more time than others to devote to his profound studies, and did so unstintedly. Recognized by his government, he was for thirty years the Royal Assessor of Mines, one of the body of men responsible to the government for the mineral wealth of Sweden. He wrote some thirty-three scientific works on metallurgy, mineralogy, physiology, geology, mathematics, cosmology, and the structure and functions of the human brain. He anticipated the airplane and the submarine. His name would have gone down in history as of one of mankind's greatest scientists, but at fifty-nine years of age he resigned from his government post, and began to spend another twenty-five years investigating the things of the spirit. He then wrote another thirty works (no small pamphlets either) on "theology," being firmly convinced that the Lord had called him to revive a dying Church. This conviction he had in common with his contemporary, John Wesley (1703-1791), but the results of the two convictions and inspirations differed widely indeed.

Swedenborg's works are chiefly the *Arcana Coelestia, Heaven and Hell, The True Christian Religion, The Four Doctrines, The Divine Providence, Conjugial Love, Miscellaneous Theological Works.*

A great intellect, however, together with a deep religious sense, does not make a man right. In Swedenborg we encounter one more man who, interpolating Scripture in accordance with "revelations" that came on top of the inspired Scriptures, drifted into rewriting the Scriptures to make them tally with his pantheistic and spiritistic intuitions. And this, for all his intellectual superiority, vast scholarship, and unquestionable integrity, he had in common with the untrained and unscrupulous founders of today's weird American religious cults.

It cannot be reiterated strongly enough that divine revelation has terminated with the final book of the New Testament. The Mormon excuse that the curse pronounced in Revelation 22:18 upon those who add to "the words of the prophecy of this book" merely warns that no chapters are to be added to *this* particular book, whereas new revelations remain to be expected, is to be rejected as a mere subterfuge. Whatever man must know of God in His saving activity is to be found within the covers of the Bible; and it will be found that all those who have come with additional "revelations" have added and/or subtracted, thus robbing us of the cardinal doctrines of Scripture. This holds of Swedenborg, too.

When Swedenborg said that he had frequent communication with numerous spirits of the departed, who gave him all sorts of information that was supposed to be firsthand, but in addition to the Scriptures; and when he stated that all the history, symbols, and parables of Scripture have a threefold sense, one for this life (the natural sense), one for the next life (the spiritual sense) and one for the life of angels (the celestial sense), he opened the floodgates to the most fanciful speculation.

Swedenborgianism, therefore, has become as much a type of gnosticism as, for example, Theosophy; and they who reject Swedenborgianism are written off as people who are unable "to struggle upward through the dogma of the past."[1]

To Swedenborg the Bible was fully inspired; but this inspiration is upon three levels: for the natural man (man seeking after God); for the spiritual man (men who, like Swedenborg, can live in two worlds at once, or alternatively) and for the celestial spirits (the angels in heaven).

By way of illustration, let us turn to one of the Ten Commandments. "Remember the sabbath day to keep it holy." What does it mean? According to the Swedish seer these words have a natural meaning. "With the children of Israel the Sabbath, because it represented the Lord, was the sanctity of sanctities, the six days representing His labors and conflicts with the hells, and the seventh His victory over them, and consequent rest; and as that day was a representative of the close of the whole of the Lord's work of redemption, it was holiness itself." But in the spiritual sense this command represents man's reformation and regeneration by the Lord. The six days of labor are his warfare against indwelling sin; the seventh day means victory in conjunction with the Lord. While in the highest, or celestial sense, the Sabbath means a state of peace that comes of perfect harmony with the Divine Will.

At times the natural sense is disregarded for the sake of the spiritual, as when Swedenborg said that the Mosaic account of creation, the story of the Flood, that of the

---
1. Bach, *Faith and My Friends*, p. 218.

Tower of Babel, are not literally true, but are the outer garments of imperishable truths.

Angels are in need of Scripture, not for the same reason sinners on earth are, but because they delight in the search of Truth, which is contained in the celestial sense of the words. And how did Swedenborg himself know of the spiritual and celestial meanings of Scripture? Because he lived in continuous rapport with spirits and angels who revealed to him many things. At times he would go without food for days when he was in trance condition. This man, who in truth was a psychic, would not read theology for fear of being misled; but he would let "spirits" guide his hand in writing.[2] He was also firmly convinced that God visited him as a man in order to divulge to him the spiritual sense of the Scriptures.[3]

Thus, although it is beyond doubt that our Swedish mystic was sincere and honest, he laid himself open to all sorts of suggestions from another world, in true spiritistic fashion; and the information he brought back from his journeys into the spiritual realm is often so contrary to the plain meaning of Scripture that it is impossible to receive it as a restoration of true Christian spirituality.

It may be true that Swedenborg wanted only Christ, and that he was afraid of being taken for a saint or seer, lest men might give to him the honor that is due only to Christ; but at the same time his *rationalism* which made him demand that Scripture should be in harmony with the human reason, led him astray. Rationalism, whether in its bold and unvarnished form like that of Russell-Rutherford-Knorr, or in its more refined cloak of mysticism, always ends in rejecting the cardinal doctrines of Scripture.

Thus Swedenborg, the son of a noted Lutheran bishop, rebelling against the cold intellectualism of his day, went so far as to identify the Reformation with the dragon of the Apocalypse. And he was quite convinced that he,

---

2. Cyriel O. Sigstedt, *The Swedenborg Epic*, pp. 207, 211.
3. *Ibid.*, p. 198.

Swedenborg himself, had succeeded after many efforts, to bring the spirit of Martin Luther to peace at last by causing that spirit to repent of Luther's nefarious doctrine of justification by faith!

For to Swedenborg sin is not something that needed expiation. God would not visit sin upon another than the sinner. Sin is something that has to be eradicated by repentance, which is the act of feeling sorry for sin and ceasing to sin. Here we deal with two errors: sin to Swedenborg was exclusively something that has to be wiped out ethically; and man, although a sinner, can repent at any time he feels like doing so. Regeneration is a process following upon man's initial repentance and faith. This, of course, implies a totally free will, unhampered by any sort of determinism. Sin is caused only by man's refusal to use his totally free will.

As to God, Swedenborg rejected the Trinity in the accepted sense. To him God is one Person, the Father. In order to reach and save man, this Father became incarnate, that He might thus unite Man with God by overcoming evil as a Man. The Holy Spirit is the energy that proceeds from God to man, as the human energy proceeds from man's body and soul.

Any man can attain to faith. This is done by living in accordance with the truth as one knows it. Unbelievers are impenitent sinners, who will go to hell, but not because God punishes them; for God knows no anger and is all compassion; but because they will choose to go to their own place. Heathen people who have not heard of Christ will receive an opportunity to learn of Him in the spirit world.

Swedenborg clung to the doctrines he had learned in his youth to such an extent as not to abandon, for example, such practices as baptism and the Lord's Supper. But he changed their meaning beyond recognition. The water in baptism to him meant the cleansing power of Truth; the bread in the Supper the Divine Goodness ("O, taste and see that the Lord is good"). What natural bread is to the body, that the goodness of the Divine Substance is to the soul. The wine represents the Lord's blood, the spiritual meaning of which is His Divine Truth.

The resurrection of Christ was, and that of believers will be, spiritual: the body decays and will not be resumed.

Such teachings naturally called only for a spiritual return of the Lord. This occurred about 1745, when Swedenborg had a revelation concerning the "New Church."

Numerically, this cult is not strong. Mead (*Handbook of Denominations in the U.S.*) listed, in 1951, 52 congregations with 4,621 members for the General Convention of the New Jerusalem in the U.S.A., plus 10 churches with a total membership of 1,496 for the General Church of the New Jerusalem. Yet these small groups maintain theological schools in Cambridge, Massachusetts and Bryn Athyn, Pennsylvania. The Swedenborg Foundation in New York City distributes Swedenborg's writings. The names of such stars as Galli Curci and Helen Keller (*My Religion*) have added luster to the movement.

We can perhaps best impress upon the reader the heterodox character of this cult by following the outline of previous chapters, giving a few authentic citations on the chief doctrines confessed through the ages by Christian churches of various names and antecedents.

A Few Samples from Thousands of Pages of Print

Revelation

"I went to my room, but that night the same man revealed himself to me again. I was not frightened then. He said that He was the Lord God, the Creator and Redeemer of the world, and that He had chosen me to declare to men the spiritual contents of Scripture; and that He Himself would declare to me what I should write on this subject.

"Then, on that same night, the world of spirits, hell, and heaven were opened to me with full conviction. I recognized there many acquaintances of every condition in life. And from that day on I gave up all practice of worldly letters and devoted my labor to spiritual things."[4]

"I have written entire pages, and the spirits did not dictate the words, but absolutely guided my hand, so that it was they who were doing the writing . . . it being allowed me only to tell such things as flowed from God Messiah mediately and immediately."[5]

"That men, therefore, may not continue to doubt whether the Word is Divine and most holy, the Lord has revealed to me its internal sense. . . . That sense is the spirit that gives life to the letter; consequently that sense can bear witness to the Divinity and holiness of the Word, and convince even the natural man, if he is willing to be convinced."[6]

"The essential reason why it is hurtful to confirm the appearances of truth that are in the Word, which thereby become fallacies and thus the Divine truth concealed within the appearances is destroyed, is that each thing and all things of the sense of the letter of the Word communicate with heaven. For it has been shown above that within each thing and all things of the sense of the letter there is a spiritual sense, and this sense is opened in passing from man to heaven. All things of the spiritual sense are genuine truths; so when man is in falsities and applies the sense of the letter to those falsities, the falsities enter into that sense, and when they enter truths are dissipated, which is done on the way from man to heaven."[7]

"When understood spiritually this does not mean that the sun and moon would be darkened, that the stars would fall from heaven, and that the sign of the Lord was to appear in the heavens, and that they were to see Him in the clouds, and also angels with trumpets; but by each particular word here something spiritual pertaining to the church is meant,

---
4. Quoted by Sigstedt, *op. cit.*, p. 198.
5. *Ibid.*, p. 211.
6. *The True Christian Religion*, Stand. Ed., I, 289.
7. *Ibid.*, p. 344.

the state of the church at its end here being treated of. For in the spiritual sense the sun that shall be darkened means love to the Lord; the moon that shall not give her light means faith in the Lord; the stars that shall fall from heaven mean knowledge of what is true and good; the sign of the Son of man in the clouds of heaven with power and glory means the Lord's presence in the Word and revelation; the clouds of heaven signify the sense of the letter of the Word, and glory signifies its spiritual sense; angels with the great sound of a trumpet mean heaven from whence comes Divine truth. . . ."[8]

Trinity
"From the Nicene Trinity and the Athanasian Trinity together a faith arose by which the whole Christian church has been perverted. That both the Nicene and Athanasian trinities are a trinity of Gods can be seen from the creeds above quoted."[9]

Forgiveness
"And I have heard from heaven that the Lord forgives to every man his sins, and never takes vengeance nor even imputes sin, because He is love itself and good itself; nevertheless sins are not thereby washed away, for this can be done only by repentance."[10]

Imputation
"That no faith imputative of Christ's merit is taught in the Word, is very clear from the fact that this faith was unknown in the church until after the Nicene Council had

---

8. *Ibid.,* p. 295.
9. *Ibid.,* p. 263. Note: This is essentially the same misrepresentation of the Christian creed of which Jehovah's Witnesses make themselves guilty. Such misrepresentations would not have made their sad inroad upon the churches had not the ministers in America abandoned the teaching of doctrine to God's youth, listening to the siren song of Modernism that "religion must be taught in the language of the man in the street." Neither Paul's Epistle to the Romans nor the adherents of modern cults teach religion in that way!
10. *Ibid.,* p. 531.

introduced the doctrine of three Divine persons from eternity. . . .

"In order to know that an imputation of the merit and righteousness of Jesus Christ is impossible, what His merit and righteousness are must be known."[11]

Mixture of Doctrine

"The Divine Energy and Operation, which are meant by the Holy Spirit, are, in general, reformation and regeneration; and in accordance with these, renovation, vivification, sanctification and justification; and in accordance with these latter, purification from evils, forgiveness of sins, and finally salvation."[12]

Death

"When the body is no longer able to perform the bodily functions in the natural world that correspond to the spirit's thoughts and affections . . . man is said to die. This takes place when the respiration of the lungs and the beating of the heart cease. But the man does not die; he is merely separated from the bodily part that was of use to him in the world, while the man himself continues to live. . . . Evidently, then, the death of man is merely his passing from one world into another."[13]

Second Coming

"Since the Lord cannot manifest Himself in Person . . . it follows that He will do this by means of a man, who is able not only to receive these doctrines in his understanding but also to publish them by the press. That the Lord manifested Himself before me, His servant, and sent me to this office. . . . I affirm in truth. . . ."[14]

"By the New Jerusalem coming down from God out of heaven a new church is meant for the reason that Jerusalem was the metropolis in the land of Canaan, and the tem-

---
11. *Ibid.*, II, 171, 172. Cf. Romans 5.
12. *Ibid.*, I, 219.
13. *Heaven and Hell*, p. 269.
14. *True Christian Religion*, II, 339.

ple and altar were there. . . . This is why 'Jerusalem' signifies the church. . . .

"It is in accordance with Divine order that a new heaven should be formed before a new Church is established on earth, for the church is both internal and external, and the internal church makes one with the church in heaven, thus with heaven itself. . . .

"That this church is to follow those that have existed since the beginning of the world and that it is to endure for ages and ages, and is thus the crown of all the churches that have preceded, was foretold by Daniel. . . .

"What this church is to be is fully described in the *Apocalypse,* where the end of the former church and the beginning of the new are treated of . . . .[15]

"The Second Coming of the Lord is a process already going on, changing the very environment . . . of all mankind. . . . It is not to be a bodily Coming. . . . That Second Coming is as the very spirit of truth. . . . We feel Swedenborg has been a chosen instrument . . . to make the truth concerning the Second Coming better known."[16]

Little Children in Heaven

"I have talked with angels about little children, whether they are free from evils, inasmuch as they have no actual evil as adults have; and I was told that they are equally in evil, and in fact are nothing but evil; but, like all angels, they are so withheld from evil and held in good by the Lord as to seem to themselves to be in good from themselves. For this reason when children have become adults in heaven, that they may not have the false idea about themselves that the good in them is from themselves and not from the Lord, they are now and then let down into their evils, which they inherited, and are left in them until they know, acknowledge, and believe the truth of the matter. . . .

---

15. *Ibid.,* II, 341-351, *passim.*
16. Franklin H. Blackmer, Pres. 131st General Convention, Church of the New Jerusalem, at Manhattan, June, 1954, quoted in *Time,* June 28, 1954.

"In the other life one never suffers punishment on account of his inherited evil, that is, it is not his fault that he is such. . . . When, therefore, the children that have become adults are let down into the state of their inherited evil it is not that they may suffer punishment for it, but that they may learn that of themselves they are nothing but evil, and that it is by the mercy of the Lord that they are taken up into heaven from the hell in which they are, and that it is from the Lord that they are in heaven and not from any merit of their own. . . ."[17]

Autosoterism

". . . and they fail to understand that the Lord from mercy leads every one who accepts Him, and that He accepts him who lives in accordance with the Laws of Divine order, which are the precepts of love and of faith, and that the mercy that is meant is to be thus led by the Lord from infancy to the last period of life in the world, and afterwards to eternity."[18]

Questions

1. Is it sufficient in religious matters, to be "sincere," "deeply spiritual," and the like? Or is it perhaps more dangerous to be spiritual, sincere, and zealous than to be apathetic?
2. Do the followers of Swedenborg have a right to deny that he was a Spiritist (or Spiritualist)?
3. Can you point out similarities between Swedenborgianism and other cults described in this textbook? If so, which are the cults, and on which points of teaching do they touch?
4. What is the root error in this system?

---

17. *Heaven and Hell,* Stand. Ed., p. 198.
18. *Ibid.,* p. 258.

11

MORMONISM

We are taking quite a leap. We are leaving the isms which have been more or less directly influenced from the East or from Europe. We are bidding farewell to the out-and-out pantheistic cults (although there are many more). And we are turning to isms of a simon-pure American make. Among these Mormonism, Seventh-Day Adventism, and Russellism are perhaps the most persistent propagandists; hence we intend to devote considerable attention to these three.

Mormonism is a marvelously composite faith. It has developed over a period of time, and as it went along it took over some of the most divergent elements from other sects and groups. They brewed, to speak with Mr. Ferguson, a synthetic religion in Utah.

A Charming People

There is an imposing story of Mormonism's accomplishments that makes not only good reading, but cannot fail to arouse admiration. It is the story of how, all before their first centennial, the Mormons have not only encircled the globe, with their missionaries donating a year or two of their youthful lives, but also of how the later Mormons have succeeded in blotting out the dark record of early Mormon antisocial doings in Illinois and Missouri. "These amazing Mormons" have indeed come near to approaching the ideal state. Their co-operatives in matters socio-religious have yielded astonishing fruit. In war or depression, no Mormon becomes a burden upon the state and no help from the national capital is accepted. By means of a strictly enforced sense of stewardship, which does not only involve money but also physical and mental faculties, an unemployed man may hold his head as high as the captain of industry; for does not his donated labor fill the warehouses and the granaries of "Zion" from which in time of distress all will receive the just rewards of their former labors? Enormous business enterprises such as the U and I (Utah and Idaho) sugar industry with its sugar-beet fields and refineries throughout western states are all under the control of the Church's hierarchy. For the Church, like the business organization that it really is, is headed by a "President" with a staff of numerous lesser officials with high-sounding titles, who not only watch over the moral but also over the business conduct of the citizen-members.

A high level of family life is maintained which is, compared with the rest of the nation, remarkably free of juvenile and adult delinquency. Not only religious exercises in the strict sense of the word, beginning with the celebrated first "testimony" of small youngsters in Sunday Schools, but also dances and other recreational enterprises are sanctioned with a bishop's prayer and made to redound to the increase of the Church of Latter-Day Saints. Mormons have indeed the right to ask proudly, "Can you point me to a better group of citizens, one that has resulted in greater willingness to lend support to education and removal of poverty and disgrace?" And Fundamentalists whose "uneasy conscience" may have occasion to rebuke them for letting Satan have his way with the world, and Calvinists who withdraw from all cooperation with other Christians because "we must be separate," may well stop to see the bold attack that is launched under their noses by such groups as Mormons and Jehovah's Witnesses, who go into all corners of the world to propagate without ever a fear that they might "lose their distinctiveness."

Only a vigilant and aggressive Christianity, one that has the promise of the life that now is and of the life that is to come, can successfully oppose the mushroom growth of these movements. And such a Christianity is all the more necessary today since Unitarianism-Modernism has so misplaced the emphasis as to make the average man think that the best Christianity is that society which, regardless of religious doctrine, improves the lot of man upon the earth and maintains a high standard of economic and personal ethics.

Since, however, Christianity is supposed to be a *salt* retarding corruption, a *leaven* that permeates, and a *light* that shines in darkness, and since only the Christ according to the Scriptures is the Light of the World, Mormonism must stand condemned. It is not only guilty of many crimes in its earlier history, but, for all its sociological improvements, it is guilty of the two cardinal sins of our time: first, it identifies the kingdom of God with a here-and-now social utopia; and secondly, it fosters the essentially pagan idea that salvation is by works rather than of grace.

History

The Mormon "prophet" Joseph Smith, Jr., was born on December 23, 1805, in Sharon, Vermont. He was reared in ignorance, poverty, and superstition. Moreover, he was indolent in his youth. However, quite in keeping with the superstitious atmosphere in which he breathed, he claimed to have visions and divine revelations as early as 1820 and 1823. In the latter year the angel Moroni revealed to him the spot where golden plates lay buried containing the history of ancient America in "reformed-Egyptian *caractors*." Smith undoubtedly meant *characters,* but, unlike Mother Eddy, he had never known enough grammar for it to be "eclipsed" by a divine revelation; hence he made occasional grammatical and spelling errors.

In 1830 "Joe," as he was known, organized the "Church of Jesus Christ of Latter-Day Saints" at Fayette, New York. This he accomplished after having convinced a few friends that his "translation" of the Golden Plates — afterward duly returned into the hands of the angel Moroni — had been done, not as was maliciously slandered, with the aid of "a peepstone in a hat," but with the assistance of the proper "Urim and Thummim" which the obliging angel had provided. The plates are stated to have been hidden in the earth from the year 420 of our era until September 22, 1823, when "Joe Smith" discovered them in the "Hill Cumorah"; and yet the Book of Mormon, being a faithful rendering of the said plates, gives extensive quotations from the Bible in — the King James Version (1611)! It contains modern phrases and ideas that could not have been known to its supposed author in A. D. 420. It puts the words of Jesus (though often twisted) into the mouths of men alleged to have lived centuries before Christ. It was not only written in a poor imitation of Biblical style; it also undermines the Bible by declaring it *insufficient,* by *adding to and changing many Biblical passages,* "by divine revelation." For such reasons as these it could hardly have been revealed by an angel. Its story of the ancient inhabitants of America, the supposed ancestors of the "Latter-Day Saints," contains twelve historical errors.

The Book of Mormon is officially recognized by both branches of Mormonism as of equal authority with the Bible, and practically receives honor far beyond the Bible. But there is an abundance of incontestable evidence that the origin of the Book of Mormon must be sought in Solomon Spaulding's unpublished and stolen novel, *The Manuscript Found*. The Mormons try to obliterate this evidence by referring to another manuscript, *The Manuscript Story*, by the same Spaulding; they prove that the Book of Mormon is not a copy of the latter manuscript. The unknowing are thus convinced that Joseph Smith did not copy from "*the* Spaulding manuscript"; but the real argument, that the "Golden Bible" is the work of copying and embellishing by Rigdon and Smith, remains unanswered.

In June, 1831, a "revelation" commanded the Saints to settle in Missouri, the "land of Zion." Kirtland, Ohio, and Zion, Missouri, now became headquarters of the movement. But, for some pagan reason or other, the "Gentile" neighbors did not trust the Mormons, and accused them of various crimes. The Saints did not hesitate to denounce the Gentiles as "enemies of the Lord." When the "Safety Bank" at Kirtland, a Mormon enterprise, failed in 1838, Smith and his friend, Sidney Rigdon, fled to Missouri. From Missouri they were driven away by order of Governor Boggs in 1839.

Finding a welcome in Illinois, they erected the city "Nauvoo." Here our prophet made his biggest display, announcing himself, among other feats, candidate for the presidency of the United States. Accused of gross immorality, counterfeiting, sheltering criminals in the act of fleeing from justice, and other misdeeds, Smith was arrested, but a mob stormed the jail and shot to death both prophet Joseph and his brother Hyrum.

This was rather unfortunate for the anti-Mormon cause, since the prophet now became a martyr. When his indictment was in sight and the movement might have died a natural death, hotheaded men with a just grievance killed their cause by immortalizing their opponent and giving his followers a supposed occasion for seeking revenge upon the wicked inhabitants of Gentile America and their descendants.

Brigham Young came from England, where he had been proselytizing, and by the force of his personality put several rivals out of commission. He became the recognized leader of the large majority of Mormons. Young was a strong man. With only eleven days of formal schooling he went far in this world and became a statesman and leader of no mean proportions. With the simple faith of an uneducated mind, Young believed in Joseph Smith, and remained true to the "prophet" all his life.

Brigham Young led the thousands of disciples amid untold sufferings until, in July 1847, they reached Utah, which was then unoccupied Mexican territory. Young did not know himself whither the long trek was. Now and then he would say, "I will know the place when I see it." When the outposts of the travelers reached Salt Lake, he announced his one and only "revelation," to wit, the Lord had revealed to him that here would be the place where the Saints would be free from Gentile American persecution.

The Mormons under Young's leadership became excellent pioneers. For many years they had things entirely their own way. The incident of the sea gulls that ate the grasshoppers which had settled upon their first crop, convinced them that the Lord was with them and approved their new venture. Hard pioneering conditions, frugal habits, tithing in the interest of their Church, made the early Mormons and their Church rich. Soon missionaries were sent to England and other European countries to fetch converts, especially women. Young, who had twenty-five wives, ruled with an iron hand in the colony. As to his rule in the Beehive and Lion's House, the opinions of his runaway wife, Ann Eliza, and his daughter, Susan, differ somewhat.

When in 1849, at the close of the Mexican War, Utah bebecame American territory, the Mormons refused to be ruled from Washington. Had they not fled from the U.S. because of "persecution"? There followed a long history of diplomatic and other blunders on both sides, until finally Young, the first governor of the State of Utah, had to admit another governor. Young, however, remained the First President of the Church. He was assisted by twelve apostles.

Notorious is the incident of the Mountain Meadow Massacre. In 1857 an entire group of immigrants on their way from Arkansas to California (during the gold rush) was murdered in Utah. For this the Mormon John D. Lee was executed by the U. S. government in 1877.[1]

Brigham Young lived to the age of 76 and died in 1877. After the United States obtained greater influence, the Mormons became known as good pioneers, although also as political intriguers. They continued to erect costly temples. Among these is the great ninth, or Mesa temple in Arizona,

---

1. *The Mountain Meadows Massacre* by Juanita Brooks (Palo Alto: Stanford University Press, 1950). The writer is a Mormon, who admits that the murder of the unarmed men by the armed Mormons who were supposed to protect them against the Indians, was a Mormon crime which she attributes to mob hysteria.

built in 1927. Here visitors from every state are shown mural paintings portraying the history of Mormonism as twisted by the Mormons. In 1937 two more temples, at Los Angeles and Idaho Falls, were on the program of the Church at a total cost of $2,600,000. On the hill Cumorah in New York, a tall monument now tries to convince large numbers of people of the truth of the Moroni Urim and Thummim legend.

In 1956 Utah announced the opening of "one of the biggest tourist attractions in California," to wit, their tenth temple, the Los Angeles Temple of the Church of Jesus Christ of Latter-Day Saints, erected at a cost of six million dollars, covering twenty-five acres, at a height of 257 feet, topped by a golden statue of the Angel Moroni. Besides an assembly room (capacity 2,600), a marriage "sealing" room, a room for the instruction of brides, a huge baptismal font, the second floor of the Temple contains "the Five Rooms" — "a series of class rooms explaining the purpose of life, where we come from, what we are doing, where we are going." These rooms are called successively the Creation Room — oval-shaped, with murals of the sun and moon. No. 2 is the Garden of Eden, "where," reads a sign, "Adam and Eve made their great decision." Next is the World Room, with murals inspired by Death Valley, which "represents the lone and dreary world, the testing ground." No. 4 is the Terrestrial Room, "fourth stage on the path to celestial glory, the step before entering the Celestial Kingdom." One of its walls opens onto the fifth room decorated as a luxurious sitting room, with well-upholstered chairs and settees, delicate murals and elaborate chandeliers. This represents the Celestial Kingdom itself, "where exalted man may dwell in the presence of God."

The other nine temples of the Utah Mormons are in Logan, Utah; Cardston, Alberta; St. George, Utah; Manti, Utah; Mesa, Arizona; Honolulu; Salt Lake City; Idaho Falls; Bern, Switzerland. In addition to the temples, the most extensive building program in Mormon history is going on of "stakes," centers of Mormon activity in many college towns, on or nearby the campuses.[2]

At the death of George Albert Smith, distant relative of Joseph and eighth "prophet, seer and revelator," in April, 1951, the Council of Twelve Apostles chose as his successor David O. McKay, who thus began his administration at the age of 77. He has paid less attention to business than did some of his predecessors and has emphasized making converts to the Mormon faith.

In 1948 the writer was treated to a lecture given at the end of a conducted tour through the Utah temple grounds. In this lecture the tremendous organization of the Mormon Church in the direction of social security was duly stressed. The lady who spoke said, "Not only do I and many others freely donate our time to conduct these tours; I have at the present two sons who are on a one-year missionary tour. For all Mormon young men are required to donate from one to two years of their time going forth preaching the gospel at no other pay than their room and board. These are supported as much as possible by parents and other relatives. In addition to that we live on two meals one Sunday a month, have a meatless day once a month, and the amount so saved is given to the church for distribution among the poor." This custom was begun during the great depression in the nineteen-thirties. The unemployed donated their time, working in charity houses where surplus grain and other staples are taken care of. For the work done these received their "keep"; and thus the central clearinghouse in Salt Lake City has provided, all by means of mutual aid and self-help, for all members of the Church, so as to cast no one at any time on public relief.

These and other laudable works of the Mormons are described in a booklet published by the Deseret Book Company in Salt Lake City, *These Amazing Mormons* by Joseph H. Weston.

---

2. *Life* magazine, Jan. 16, 1956.

Perhaps these means toward social security, together with the enormous zeal of six thousand Mormon "missionaries" touring the continent, are largely responsible for the growth of the Utah Mormons from 215,796 in 1906 to 870,346 in 1946. For almost any system that stresses, as does Mormonism, "temporal salvation" as well as "spiritual salvation," is bound to receive a hearing in these days when people ask for material results rather than for doctrinal foundation.[3]

The Two Factions

At the death of Joseph Smith, Jr., the Prophet, the Mormons broke up into numerous groups. Brigham Young succeeded in combining most of these under his leadership, with the exception of a small minority which, as "The Reorganized Church of Latter-Day Saints," or Josephites, set-

---

3. Canada has 25,000 Mormons, 15,000 in small towns of southern Alberta, the rest scattered throughout Canada. A $1,000,000 temple is in Cardston, headquarters for the Alberta Stake (diocese) with 6,100 members. There are two other Canadian stakes, Taylor with 3,800 and Lethbridge with 5,000 members. Cardston was founded by Charles Ora Card, who had three wives and trekked into Canada in 1886, four years before plural marriage was abandoned, because U. S. marshals were after him. —*MacLean's Magazine*, Jan. 15, 1951.

The Mormon Church claims 12,000 members in New Zealand, as of Dec., 1951. It has launched a $2.8 million building program. "Plans envision a coeducational agricultural boarding school in the north island, completion of a large church and administration center in Auckland, and extension of schools and church halls in other areas. To secure materials for their projects, the Mormons have bought a timber mill and erected a plant which is turning out 3,000 concrete blocks a day. Most of the converts to Mormonism in the commonwealth are Maoris." —*The Christian Century*, Jan. 9, 1952.

The Utah branch in April, 1953, reported at their 123rd annual conference, held in Salt Lake City, a membership of 1,189,053, at their 125th annual conference (Jan. 1, 1955), 1,302,240 members — an increase of 55,878 in one year, with 10,814 missionaries. The Utah branch now has two temples in Europe, the first in Switzerland (1953), the second (1958) in England. To "the serenely beautiful Mormon Temple at Laie," on the island of Oahu, there has been added a college with twenty buildings, for the opening of which the 85-year-old "President of the Church of Jesus Christ of Latter-Day Saints" came in December, 1958, from Utah. The school is boldly advertised as "The Church College of Hawaii for the Training of Hawaiian Youth."

tled in Missouri. They chose the leadership of a son of Joseph Smith. The reorganized group felt the restraint put upon them by their Christian environment in the East to the extent of their repudiating polygamy altogether. They have since put forth brave efforts to fasten the guilt of polygamy onto the sister-body which, under Young, went to Utah. At that time Utah was unoccupied Mexican territory, and the system could be practiced to the heart's content. But the facts are overwhelmingly against their contention. Not only did Smith undoubtedly write the *Revelation on Celestial Marriage,* but, of Joseph's followers, twenty thousand went with polygamous Young over against one thousand who went with the Josephites. In fact, polygamy was taught and practiced by all the original twelve Mormon apostles and by at least six factions of the Church as it became disrupted at Smith's death. Moreover, prominent leaders of the early Josephites have admitted the Josephite origin of the doctrine, whereas the denials by later Josephites prove to be flimsy upon closer scrutiny. They also "are often rather vague and uncertain in fixing the responsibility for polygamy and the time when it was introduced into the church." Fawn M. Brodie lists forty-eight wives of Joseph Smith himself.[4]

There are, then, certain differences between the teachings of the Brighamites and those of the Josephites. These center chiefly around prophetic succession and polygamy.

1. The Josephites claim that the President of the Church must be "of the seed of Joseph Smith." Charles A. Shook has wittily remarked, "It appears to me that if they would split the difference they would have about the truth, and that, as it now stands, the Josephites have the president and the Brighamites the church."[5] Another convert from the Reorganized Church, however, repudiates on good grounds the alleged hint of Joseph Smith that his son should succeed him, while the Josephites admittedly were without the President from 1852, the year of their organ-

---

4. *No Man Knows My History. The Life of Joseph Smith.*
5. *The True Origin of Mormon Polygamy.*

ization, until 1860, when Joseph's son joined their ranks. Where, then, was the "Church" from 1844-1860 if the Josephites are right?

2. Again, the Josephites reject polygamy. But this is just as illogical on their part as is the Utah rejection of the "Inspired Translation" of the Bible which the Josephites accept.

3. The Josephites reject *in toto* the Adam-god doctrine of the Brighamites. But they do believe in many gods, and gods with flesh and bones, as does the Utah group.

What Constitutes Mormonism

Thus the differences are few and, with the exception of the Josephite rejection of polygamy, insignificant. Both groups hold before the public misleading documents supposed to state their beliefs, but in reality concealing them. "But the real beliefs," to quote a lifelong student of Mormonism, "are essentially in common, as follows: Smith a prophet; continuous revelation through him and others; the *Book of Mormon* and *Doctrine and Covenants* as such revelations; the *Pearl of Great Price* as translated by Smith, parts of which are parts of the 'Inspired Translation' by him; more revelations yet to come — at least equal to the Bible; Melchizedec and Aaronic priesthoods; gathering; tithing; flesh-and-bones God; many gods logically involved in this (but not often advocated by Josephites); Christ and the Spirit (but not Bible conceptions); sin a necessity for man; hell a saving agency; salvation through works instead of by faith in Christ; baptism (immersion) essential to salvation; pre-existence of all men; apostasy of the Christian church; authority; organization of the church, on their style; punishment after death temporary and measured by sins; premillennialism; the Bible defective and practically superseded by their revelations; their President alone the mouthpiece of God, etc."

Quite a list of rarities, yet one that does not lay claim to completeness. As to that, the Rev. Van Dellen reminds us that their system contains elements reminiscent of such widely divergent sources as Christianity, Judaism, Mohammedanism, Fetishism, Communism, Manicheism, Campbellism, and other isms. To discuss and trace all these errors one by one, he adds, one ought to write a voluminous book on the doctrine of Mormonism alone, and in it discuss wellnigh all religious sects of earlier and later times. It is, indeed, next to impossible to give a concise view of its many heterogeneous elements. Its earlier advocates were anything but theologians.

The Reorganized Church launched a $500,000 campaign in November, 1951, toward the completion of their temple, construction of which was begun in 1926. The coppersheathed dome was finished during the summer of 1951. The main "auditorium" is to seat 6,700, and a basement section to give room for 3,000 temporary seats.

The Doctrine of Polygamy and Its Development

It is well known that many pagan religions have arrived at what Paul describes in Romans 1 as the logical outcome of heathenism, the deification of the sexual life. Thus many ancients deified the steer as an emblem of fertility. The refined Greeks had their temples for pederasty. Popular Hinduism of today has traveling temple cars with grossly sensual carvings, while dancing-girls, the professional prostitutes of India, are supposed to be married to the gods in whose temples they serve.

1. With Mormonism, polygamy was not an afterthought; it was one of the first thoughts that entered into the lustful brain of Joseph Smith when he perceived that certain people could be made to believe in him as a prophet. But the "doctrine" was at first communicated to a few select of the inner circle only; the surroundings in New York, Ohio, Missouri, and Illinois were too antagonistic to it. And to the very end of Joseph's career (April, 1830 to June, 1844) it was understood that this "strong meat" was not to be fed to "the Gentiles," who were to receive only the "first principles." The first public announcement of polygamy was in Utah, in 1852; and here it also became a popular

hobby. Nor was the practice officially abandoned till after a long legal battle. Even after President Wilford Woodruff published his manifesto against polygamy because of strong government opposition (1889), it was practiced in secret. At the present time it may not be widely practiced; it may be true that "the average young Mormon has no use for it." It is also true that Mormon missionaries, when pressed for an answer, will say, "We believe in it, but we do not practice it." And since the Mormon belief is that a polygamous priesthood is to rule the earth, it is justifiable to believe that the old Danish Mormon was correct when he stated that loud denunciations of polygamy from the Salt Lake City tabernacle are "yust to fool the Yentiles." Young Mormons still give an entire year, in their early twenties, to go forth as "missionaries" among "Gentiles," being supported entirely by their families; and these do propagate the old Mormon teachings. Yet their Conferences now deal more with purely ethical problems. Thus, for instance, an AP report from Salt Lake City, Oct. 7, 1946, states: "From comment on labor-capital relations to discussions on world peace, the 117th semiannual conference of the Latter Day Saints (Mormon Church) cut a wide swath through temporal affairs." We are reminded of Dr. James H. Snowden's comment in 1926: "It seems to me if they would give up their prophet and their Bible, they might be taken into the other churches."[6] This, of course, they will not do; but the emphasis seems to be more on general humanistic principles, as is the case in the modernist churches.

Early in 1944, however, a scandal filled our daily papers for several days. Moving simultaneously in Utah, Idaho, and Arizona, federal and state law-enforcement officers arrested forty-six members of the Fundamentalist sect. The charges against them — both by state and federal governments — were severe: Mann Act and Lindbergh kidnap law violations; mailing obscene literature; conspiracy; unlawful cohabitation. Nine young women "cheerfully" faced

---

6. *The Truth About Mormonism*, p. 46.

MORMONISM

charges of advocating polygamy and had their group picture published in *Newsweek* for March 20, 1944. Several indictments followed the court trials. It was found that the magazine *Truth,* of which the seventy-one-year-old sect leader was editor, was devoted chiefly to propagandizing polygamy. Mormons of the "orthodox Church" commended officials for making the arrests, but "doubted that the new drive would stamp it out entirely." "Of course we believe in what we are doing," said Mrs. Rhea A. Kunz in an interview with the Salt Lake *Telegram.* "This thing is far bigger than the individual, for it inevitably will encompass much more than the man-made laws by which the world lives and will become a fundamental component in the lives of all right-living people."[7]

Why is the practice hard to stamp out? A Baptist minister to whom the writer gave a copy of his booklet *The Gist of the Cults* at the time, said, "I was naturally interested in your treatment of Mormonism, for I have been a minister for many years in Salt Lake City, and have had frequent contacts with Mormons. Your view is entirely correct: Mormonism is a fleshly religion, and the Fundamentalists of whom we read so much of late, learned the theory from

---

7. On Nov. 18, 1946, the Supreme Court of the U. S. upheld the Salt Lake City convictions of the following six "Fundamentalists" who had practiced polygamy: Heber Kimball Cleveland, David Brigham Derger, Theral Ray Dockstader, L. R. Stubbs, Follis Gardner Petty and Vergel Y. Jessop. The majority of the Court, as represented by Justice Douglas, held that polygamy is not excluded from the Mann Act. The minority of the Court (Justices Hugo L. Black, Robert H. Jackson, and Frank Murphy) dissented. Said Justice Murphy: "Marriage, even when it occurs in a form of which we disapprove, is not to be compared with prostitution or debauchery or other immoralities of that character." He said that the Court's majority decision was but another consequence of its long-continued failure to recognize that the white slave traffic act is aimed solely at the diabolical interstate and international trade in white slaves. The argument of the defense that the six cult members were motivated by a religious belief, "claims too much," in the words of Justice Douglas. "If upheld, it would place beyond the law any act done under the claims of religious sanction."
After the U.S. Supreme Court refused to reconsider this verdict, the Utah Supreme Court on Dec. 16 confirmed the conviction of twenty Fundamentalist cult members on charges of conspiring to violate state laws prohibiting plural marriages.

the official Mormons. When the matter became public, they threw them out to save their own face."

2. The Mormon theory of polygamy may have followed in the wake of its practice, but it has become an integral part of the doctrine. Elder William Clayton, who was the confidential clerk of the Prophet, told in his affidavit what he learned of Joseph Smith concerning it in these words, "Of him I learned that the doctrine of plural and celestial marriage is the most holy and important doctrine ever revealed to man on the earth, and that without obedience to that principle no person can ever attain to the fulness of exaltation in celestial glory." This does not mean that "Joe" Smith desired or allowed people to live in promiscuity without due regard to the wishes of the Prophet. In his Diary he wrote (Oct. 5, 1843):

"Gave instructions to try those persons who were preaching, teaching, or practicing the doctrine of plurality of wives; for, according to the law, I hold the keys of this power in the last days, for there is never but one on earth at a time on whom the power and its keys are conferred; and I have constantly said no man shall have but one wife at a time unless the Lord directs otherwise."

This statement is in full harmony with the guarded language in which the Book of Mormon, as early as 1830, hinted at polygamy. After the statement (introduced by the usual "Behold" for which the book is noted) that "David and Solomon truly had many wives and concubines, which thing was abominable before me, saith the Lord," the people are admonished not to "do like unto them," but to "keep my commandments." But this passage is followed by words that leave a loophole: "For if I will, saith the Lord of Hosts, raise up seed unto me, I will command my people; otherwise they shall hearken unto these things." The Josephite exegesis that the word "otherwise" here means "in other words" is plainly born of embarrassment; the evident import of the clause is in full accord with the passage in Smith's Diary.

3. The *Doctrine and Covenants* which was written at a

later date by Smith, when opposition to the doctrine had sufficiently waned among the Saints, contains a "Revelation on the Eternity of the Marriage Covenant, including Plurality of Wives, Given through Joseph, the Seer, in Nauvoo, Hancock County, Illinois, July 12th, 1843." Here the plural wives of David and Solomon are stated to have been given by the Lord. Here also occurs this noted passage: "And again as pertaining to the law of the Priesthood: If any man espouse a virgin, and desire to espouse another, and the first give her consent; and if he espouse the second, and they are virgins, and have vowed to no other man, then he is justified; he cannot commit adultery, for they are given unto him; for he cannot commit adultery with that that belongeth unto him and to no one else. And if he have ten virgins given unto him by this law, he cannot commit adultery for they belong to him, and they are given unto him, therefore is he justified."

These references, although the last one has been removed from the *Doctrine and Covenants* by the Josephites, prove that the real Mormon doctrine on this point is taught in Utah; and they corroborate the evidence that the *Revelation on Celestial Marriage* came from Joseph.

The Theory Underlying Polygamy

That so much attention is paid to this feature of Mormonism is not because we consider it a bit of spicy gossip. Rather, we are convinced that polygamy is part and parcel of the system, and that true Mormons must long for the time when the practice of polygamy shall be restored. Young's daughter informs us, "The principle of plural marriage was adopted by my father as it was taught him by the Prophet Joseph Smith, after great inner struggle and earnest prayer. His strict puritanical training ill-fitted him to accept such a doctrine. He foresaw — as who would not? — the storm of abuse and opposition which such action would arouse. And it was as death to him.... But the fact remains that the men and women who entered into that relationship in early days, did so from purely religious motives. It was a high and sacred undertaking with them, involving much suffering and sacrifice on the part of both men and women."[8]

Perhaps the picture of the ideal home life in Young's family as presented by Mrs. Gates, with all the fifty-six children and the "aunties" living in perfect mutual love and understanding, is somewhat colored by the love for propaganda. Perhaps, also, Young was not quite the indifferent husband Ann Eliza makes him out to be. Whatever may be the truth of this, we gladly accept Mrs. Gates' statement on the principle that led to polygamy. We have no desire to speak of Mormon polygamy in the light vein of Mark Twain's *Roughing It*.

The fact that someone does something because of principle does not, however, make that principle right. The question remains why self-willed, headstrong Brigham Young yielded to the unwelcome doctrine. And why is this principle considered so highly important that it clings with tenacity even after its practice has been officially suspended?

1. Mormons proceed from the thought that a marriage that has been solemnized for this life amounts to but little. Husband and wife must be united for eternity. "Be fruitful and multiply" is the great commandment. Upon its keeping depends the future glory of the married. Woman cannot be saved apart from man; at any rate, she cannot attain to the highest glory possible for woman. It is therefore the man's duty to take pity upon woman, and to marry her. Better to be a plural wife than no wife at all. When, hereafter, the saved Mormon reigns, a king in a new world, his wives will be enthroned as queens at his side.

2. The doctrine as contained in Smith's *Revelation on Celestial Marriage* contains two elements. The first is termed *plurality of wives;* the second, *spiritual wifery.* Marriages are not valid for eternity except there be spiritual affinity, and such marriages can be solemnized only

---
8. Susan Young Gates, *The Life Story of Brigham Young*, p. 321.

in the Mormon secret temples which continue to appear. The element of secrecy and the high-sounding titles of almost every Mormon, be it said by the way, remind us that all the original Mormons were at one time Freemasons. What wonder then, if a man discovers, after some years of married life, that there exists spiritual affinity between himself and some other woman, that he betakes himself to the Temple in order to be "sealed for eternity," if not "for time *and* eternity," to his newly discovered attraction? Or, what wonder that women who have been taught since infancy that man is to be woman's savior defend the doctrine and would rather share eternity as polygamous wives in the highest glory than occupy the role of servants in the hereafter?

3. The gods of Mormonism are "big men, like Brigham Young," graduates, one might say, of the school of human life, and post-graduate students in the sacred science of procreation. One of the earliest conspirators with Rigdon and Smith was Parley P. Pratt, who was converted to Mormonism and became a missionary in August, 1830. This "Saint" wrote the following on our subject: "O candidates for celestial glory! Would your joys be full in the countless years of eternity without forming the connections, the relationship, the kindred ties which concentrate in the domestic circle, and branch forth, and bud and blossom, and bear fruits of eternal increase? Would that eternal emotion of charity and benevolence which swells your bosoms be satisfied to enjoy in 'single blessedness,' without an increase in posterity, those exhaustless stores of never ending riches and enjoyment? Or, would you, like your heavenly Father, prompted by eternal benevolence and charity, wish to fill countless millions of worlds with your begotten sons and daughters and to bring them all through all the gradations of progressive being, to inherit immortal bodies and eternal mansions in your several dominions?" And a little further, "The eternal union of the sexes, in and after the

resurrection, is mainly for the purpose of renewing and continuing the work of procreation."⁹

Endless, aimless procreation. If that is not the religion of phallicism, what is it? Meanwhile, the manner in which the saintly lords in Utah exercised "eternal benevolence and charity" from their "swelling bosoms," in anticipation of greater bliss to come, may be learned from the sober, but eloquent and heart-rending tale in Ann Eliza Young's *Wife No. 19*.¹⁰

Polygamy Influencing the Entire System

The hankering after sexual indulgence that characterized Smith, Young, Pratt, and other founders of the Mormon system, resulted in the doctrine of polygamy. This, in turn, became so basic to the theory that polygamous marriage was transferred from life on earth to that in heaven hereafter. And that influenced the entire view of heaven and God, whose dwelling-place is heaven. And since one's view of God naturally determines his conception of sin against God, of salvation, and of Christ the Saviour, it becomes evident that the phallicism of Mormonism is responsible for the strange mixture of doctrines that seem to be borrowed on every hand.

Since the highest conception of bliss is that of begetting sons and daughters, God Himself becomes a polygamist.

Men who attain to that blissful state hereafter have reached the pinnacle, and are gods themselves. Thus a gross polytheism is taught.

It follows that every god was a man on earth at one time.

---

9. Under date May 15, 1947, "Elder" H. Harris writes to me from Llano, New Mexico, concerning this telling quotation: "I think it is quite beautiful, easy to believe, and lots more logical than the theology of modern-day, so-called 'Christianity' (like playing harps forever!)"

10. This interesting book is difficult to obtain. I have been told that Mormon missionaries buy up copies and send them to Utah for confiscation. In the same category is the massive and well-documented account of the sordid early history of Mormonism and of the equally ungodly acts of some of their moblike antagonists in *Polygamy, or the Mysteries and Crimes of Mormonism* by J. H. Beadle, Editor of the *Salt Lake Reporter* and Clerk of the Supreme Court for Utah, and Hon. O. J. Hollister, U.S. Revenue Collector for Utah.

These gods and their wives beget children as spirits; these spirit-children are waiting for an opportunity to come to earth to receive bodies.

Hence it is the duty of every woman to be married, and of every man to beget as many bodies as possible. The doctrines of the pre-existence of the human soul and of the duty of polygamy are thus seen to be closely interwoven. Is it a strange thing that Mormon missionaries will state that "we hope for a better day when polygamy will again be practiced"?

The gods being conceived as such, Christ becomes the ordinary child of Adam-god and one of his wives. He cannot be a Saviour in any sense.

Nor is sin against a once earthly and still human god anything so very dreadful. Man becomes his own saviour. And, since salvation is only obtained in the Mormon pathway — it is a peculiarity of all the non-Christian sects that they condemn every doctrine but their own most severely — Mormons have an authoritative priesthood with a baptism that is absolutely necessary unto salvation.

And this, in turn, results in the doctrine of *baptism for the dead*. Mormons are kept busy looking up their genealogies, and some have been baptized "by proxy" fifty and more times for the benefit of their "Gentile" ancestors. This is always done in the secret temples, and by immersion.[11]

---

11. It is considered highly important to have lived and died a Mormon; and Mormon missionaries, even today when outsiders almost welcome this sect as one more Christian denomination, display charts teaching the following with graphs: At death all who have not accepted the doctrines of Joseph Smith go to a "Spirit Prison." Here they receive a chance to accept "the Truth" (as per the much-abused passage in I Peter 3:19, 20, Mormon version). All good Mormons go to the *celestial* degree of glory, where God the Father and the Son dwell. Non-Mormons who have led a fairly good life are assigned to the *terrestrial* degree of felicity, visited occasionally by Christ. The wicked go to the *telestial* abode, there to be ministered to by good spirits from the celestial sphere.

Another diagram shows the "revelation" that the steps leading to heaven are: Faith, Repentance, Baptism, Confirmation, and that there are degrees of glory in heaven parallel to one's services rendered the Church on earth as Deacon, Teacher, Priest, Elder, Bishop, Seventies, Apostles, President.

Other Groups

I have come into contact with a third group, perhaps the most subtle of all. It calls itself "The Church of Christ, Headquarters on the Temple Lot, Independence, Missouri." It publishes *Zion's Advocate,* a monthly journal, of which W. A. Sheldon, 11427 E. 16th St., Independence, Missouri, is Editor-in-Chief.

The subtlety of this group lies in the fact that they disclaim the name Mormons as well as that of Latter-Day Saints, and even refuse to admit that they are followers of Joseph Smith. "We are no more Mormons because we believe the Book of Mormon to be inspired than you would call yourself a Catholic because you believe the Bible to be inspired," one of their "elders" informed me. "We are just the Church of Christ; we only recognize the Bible and the Book of Mormon as authoritative. We only follow Joseph Smith in so far as he received a divine revelation in addition to the Bible."

All authentic books written by prominent Mormons are brushed aside with the words, "That was published in Utah, and we do not recognize it." Even "The Holy Scriptures Translated and Corrected by the Spirit of Revelation by Joseph Smith, Jr., the Seer," is ruled out of court with, "That was put out in Iowa by the Reorganized Church of Jesus Christ of Latter-Day Saints: we are not Latter-Day Saints, we are just the Church of Christ."

Meanwhile this group has all the earmarks of Reorganized Mormonism: their missionaries labor among church members, whom they endeavor to wrest away from evangelical churches; they teach them the doctrine of a flesh-and-bones God, at any rate a God who has a body as well as a spirit; the message of God's Word has been obscured until Smith found the Book of Mormon; salvation is by the blood of Christ, "which cannot be taken literally, but *typifies* his life and the power that sustained him, and supports and sustains *every* man who is saved to the uttermost. God is the Supreme Saving Power — He sent his Son to make the terms of Salvation known to man — The Son appointed the Holy Ghost as his successor to guide and to teach, and to help the obedient on to perfection. When the body of Christ, his Church, has the living blood, the real life of the body, in it as a spiritual force to develop and cleanse, then there is joy and hope of victory."[12] This means salvation by character, a truly Mormon teaching. They re-baptize their converts, and impart to them "the Holy Spirit" by the laying on of hands. They are ruled by twelve apostles, and have a bishop who receives "all tithes, offerings, consecrations and donations to the Temple Fund and Storehouse" (all Mormons and Seventh-Day Adventists are supposed to tithe their income for their Church).

This movement appears to be growing; the monthly paper contains news items from many quarters. Their faith in the fulfillment of predictions made in the Book of Mormon remains unshaken and accounts for the missionary zeal toward the Navajos and other American Indians. Thus we are told that the literal seed of Abraham, Isaac, and Jacob are the American Indians, whose seed, the Lamanites, are to be visited by a return of Jesus Christ. These American Indians therefore always refer to themselves as "the People," and the Hopi Indians of the Southwest have a legend of a "white brother" who is to come in the future and decipher the predictions found on a sacred prayer stone. This "white brother," according to these Mormons (with reference to I Nephi 3:192-237) is one of the white or Nephite Indians whose people have been preserved "somewhere deep in that jungle country of Central America or Mexico." Then the Father shall commence his work; then the Indians will build the Temple of the Lord upon the temple lot in Independence, Missouri, where Joseph Smith laid the cornerstone, and they will do so with the aid of the Gentiles converted in the meantime (III Nephi

---

12. *Zion's Advocate*, Jan., 1942, p. 15.

10:1-5), "and they shall build up a holy city unto the Lord like unto the Jerusalem of old."[13]

Meanwhile Clarence and Angela Wheaton report in a "Letter to the Church" that they have actually located these White Indian people "and that they live in a walled city secluded deep in the jungle country of southern Mexico." These White Indians have golden plates, bracelets, and legends predicting the time of their going north (to Missouri).[14]

Since the missionaries and "elders" of this group will admit faith in the Book of Mormon as divinely inspired, we here append a few remarks which, taken by themselves, ought to be sufficient to convince anyone that the Book of Mormon is a rank fake. We acknowledge our indebtedness to the thorough work of the Rev. M. T. Lamb, in which much more of a similar nature may be found.[15] However, we have carefully checked all references, and are quoting from the Seventh Independence Edition, printed at the Zion's Printing and Publishing Company, Independence, Missouri.

1. The book is written in a would-be imitation Bible style, a) pompous, verbose, and b) full of incorrect grammar and nonsense.

a) Take this: *Book of Alma,* Ch. 5, p. 249:

> 49. And now I say unto you, that this is the order after which I am called; yea, to preach unto my beloved brethren; yea, and every one that dwelleth in the land; yea, to preach unto all, both old and young, both bond and free; yea, I say unto you the aged, and also the middle aged, and the rising generation; yea, to cry unto them that they must repent and be born again;

---

13. "The Relationship of the American Indians to the Restoration," a sermon by Apostle Clarence L. Wheaton in *Zion's Advocate*, Dec., 1950.
14. *Zion's Advocate*, Jan., 1951. Frank S. Mead, *Handbook of Denominations in the United States*, also numbers these under Mormons; and besides this "Church of Christ (Temple Lot)" he gives three more shall Mormon bodies: Bickertonites, Cutlerites, and Strangites, all under the official name "Church of Jesus Christ."
15. *The Mormons and Their Bible.*

50. Yea, thus saith the Spirit, Repent, all ye ends of the earth, for the kingdom of heaven is soon at hand; yea, the Son of God cometh in his glory, in his might, majesty, power, and dominion. Yea, my beloved brethren, I say unto you, that the Spirit saith, Behold the glory of the King of all the earth; and also the King of heaven shall very soon shine forth among all the children of men;

51. And also the Spirit saith unto me, yea, crieth unto me with a mighty voice, saying, Go forth and say unto this people, Repent, for except ye repent ye can in nowise inherit the kingdom of heaven.

52. And again I say unto you, the Spirit saith, Behold the axe is laid at the root of the tree; therefore every tree that bringeth not forth good fruit, shall be hewn down and cast into the fire; yea, a fire which cannot be consumed; even an unquenchable fire. Behold, and remember, the Holy One hath spoken it.

Here, then, is but one of numerous passages, many of far greater length, which show the empty loquaciousness of the book, very contrary to the brevity of the Scriptures; and at the same time we have here a book that is supposed to have been written or spoken by "Alma the High Priest," centuries before the Christian era, but which contains passages obviously taken from the lips of John the Baptist as recorded in the Gospels!

b) How is the following for "inspired" writing?

And it came to pass that he rent his coat; and he took a piece thereof, and wrote upon it . . .; and he fastened it upon the end of a pole *thereof* (p. 370).

These our dearly beloved brethren, who have so dearly *beloved* us (p. 311).

Yea, if my days could have been *in them days* . . . . But behold, I am *consigned* that these are my days (p. 449).

I say Jew, because I mean *them,* from whence I came (p. 127).

And they *having been waxed strong* in battle, that they might not be destroyed (p. 260).

We did *arrive to* the promised land (p. 260).

Even until they had *arriven* to the land of Middoni (p. 297).

There were no robbers, nor murderers, neither were there Lamanites, nor any *manner of ites;* but they were *in one*, the children of Christ (p. 545).

Now immediately when the Judge had been murdered; he being *stabbed* by his brother *by a garb of secrecy;* and he fled, and the servants ran and told the people (p. 454).

Yet, a book containing such grammatical nonsense and rank crudities is prefaced by a "Testimony of Three Witnesses," who "through the grace of God the Father, and our Lord Jesus Christ, have seen the plates which contain this record ... and we also know that they have been translated by the gift and power of God, for his voice hath declared it unto us; wherefore we know of a surety that the work is true."

2. The book contains several so-called miracles, which are not miracles in any Biblical sense of the word, but stunts which God provides, often without any necessity, merely to favor his pets. Here are just a few samples:

a) Lehi has left Jerusalem upon command of the Lord, because the inhabitants, whom he has warned concerning their iniquity, seek his life. With him are his wife and four sons. Nephi, the youngest son, takes the others back to Jerusalem, to marry daughters of Ishmael. Afterward they travel again in the wilderness and suffer hardships. However, the Lord sees them through their difficulties as follows:

> And it came to pass that the voice of the Lord spake unto my father by night, and commanded him that on the morrow he should take his journey into the wilderness. And it came to pass that as my father arose in the morning and went forth to the tent door, to his great astonishment he beheld upon the ground a round ball of curious workmanship, and it was of fine brass. And within the ball were two spindles; and the one pointed the way whither we should go into the wilderness (p. 36).

b) This curious ball obviates much seeking and labor for food:

MORMONISM

And I said unto my father, whither shall I go to obtain food. And it came to pass that he did inquire of the Lord.... And it came to pass that the voice of the Lord said unto him, Look upon the ball, and behold the things which are written.... And it came to pass that I, Nephi, beheld the pointers which were in the ball, that they did work according to the faith, and diligence, and heed which we did give unto them. And there was also written upon them, a new writing, which was plain to be read, which did give us understanding concerning the ways of the Lord; and it was written and changed from time to time, according to the faith and diligence which we gave unto it: And thus we see that, by small means, the Lord can bring about great things. And it came to pass that I, Nephi, did go forth up into the top of the mountain, according to the directions which were given upon the ball. And it came to pass that I did slay wild beasts, insomuch that I did obtain food for our families (p. 38).

c) On the way to the Western continent, there was a mutiny against Nephi, which the "inspired" translation announces in the heading of the Book of Nephi as follows: "They come to the large waters. Nephi's brethren rebelleth against him [!]." Now God had prepared for them a compass, which refused to work when Nephi, the Lord's favorite, had been bound by his brothers. The result was a terrible storm. When Nephi had been released, he took the divinely wrought compass into his hands, and lo, it again pointed the way across the waters! (p. 46).

d) Jared's brother and his company have prepared eight barges, all "according to the instructions of the Lord"; but the opening for air and light has been forgotten. So the Lord bids him cut an opening in the roof for air, which he is to close when the waves go over the barges in a fierce storm. As to the lighting system, Jared's brother goes upon a very high mountain "and did moulten out of a rock sixteen small stones, and they were white and clear even as transparent glass." These sixteen stones he presents before the Lord, and says,

> Therefore touch these stones, O Lord, with thy finger, and prepare them that they may shine forth in the darkness; and they shall shine forth unto us in the vessels which we have prepared, that we may have light while we shall cross the sea.

And the Lord did so, and the light-giving stones were put two in each barge, one at each end. Incidently, Jared's brother fell down with fear because he saw the Lord's finger touch the stones. He is encouraged: he should not fear, for the fact that he has seen the finger shows that he has great faith. Wherefore, he is rewarded for this faith with the sight of the entire body of the Lord, called "the body of my spirit." And the Lord says to him:

> Behold, I am he who was prepared from the foundation of the world to redeem my people. Behold, I am Jesus Christ. I am the Father and the Son. In me shall all mankind have light, and that eternally, even they who shall believe on my name; and they shall become my sons and my daughters (p. 577).

e) Perhaps the silliest of all the "miracles" in this book is the story that, when some twenty or thirty years after Nephi has separated from his two brothers Laman and Lemuel, and these two groups within those few years have become two rival *nations* [!], God suddenly makes the entire group of Lamanites black lest they might become a temptation to the Nephites: "Wherefore, as they were white, and exceeding fair and delightsome, that they might not be enticing unto my people, the Lord God did cause a skin of blackness to come upon them" (p. 72).

Then, some five hundred years later, some of the descendants of these Lamanites united with the then Nephites, "And their curse was taken from them, and their skin became white like unto the Nephites; and their young men and their daughters became exceeding fair, and they were numbered among the Nephites, and were called Nephites" (p. 480).

This, according to Mormons, explains the origin of Black and "White" Indians!

3. To this must be added that the whole fantastic story of the Book of Mormon is contradicted on every point by careful scientific investigation of early American anthropology. According to the Mormon story there were two entirely different early American people, the first being the Jaredites, who came from the tower of Babel under Jared and his brother, crossing the Atlantic Ocean in 344 days in the above-named eight cigar-shaped barges and locating in Central America. They came to an end, after some 1600 years, about 600 B. C., as a result of dissensions and revolts. The second history described in the book is that of Lehi's four sons, Laman, Lemuel, Sam, and Nephi, which Nephi left Jerusalem in the time of Zedekiah and arrived "on the coast of Chili, not far from the thirtieth degree, south latitude." Nephi at once began to record the history of his people upon metal plates. His descendant Moroni, a prince of royal blood, finished the plates and hid them in the hill Cumorah in New York in A.D. 420. That this entire fabrication, in its description of the American aborigines, their language and writing, and their names, contradicts in every detail what has become known of early American civilizations may be read in Charles A. Shook's *Cumorah Revisited*, and in M. T. Lamb's *The Mormons and Their Bible*.

4. The final test of the fraudulent character of the Book of Mormon may well be found in the fact that it postulates the necessity of further revelation in addition to the Bible, because the Bible is said to have been greatly marred by an apostate church, and was only meant for a certain generation anyhow. Consider this: An angel informs Nephi that the Bible has come out of the hands of the Jews and gone forth to the Gentiles pure and "according to the truth which is in God": but "a great and abominable church" of the Gentiles has so corrupted the Bible that further revelations and corrections through the golden plates have become necessary:

"And after they go forth by the hand of the twelve apostles of the Lamb, from the Jews unto the Gentiles, thou seest the foundation of a great and abominable church, which is most abominable above all churches; for behold, they have taken away from the gospel of the Lamb, many parts which are plain and most precious; and also many covenants of the Lord have they taken away; And all this have they done, that they might pervert the right ways of the Lord; that they might blind the eyes and harden the hearts of the children of men; Wherefore thou seest that after the book hath gone forth through the hands of the great and abominable church, that there are many plain and precious things taken away from the book, which is the book of the Lamb of God" (p. 27).

To this may be added the brazen statement by "Apostle" Pratt, "Indeed, no one, without further revelation, knows whether even one-hundredth part of the doctrines and ordinances of salvation are contained in the few books of Scripture which have descended to our times; how, then, can it be decided that they are a sufficient guide . . . ?"

And yet, to quote the Rev. Mr. Lamb, "To the above specious question which has hid underneath it the boldest infidelity and the most wicked deception, it would be an all-sufficient answer to an honest Mormon, to reply as follows: 'The Book of Mormon itself is our proof that not only one verse but in the neighborhood of ten thousand verses in our Bible have escaped pollution, so that they convey the same sense now that they did in the original.' There are probably not less than ten thousand verses from our Bible found in the Book of Mormon and each of these verses is professedly translated by the gift and power of God from ancient Egyptian plates, professedly as pure as God first gave them. And yet each one of these verses is found in the Book of Mormon *precisely as we have them today in our English Bibles.*"

Mormonism and the Bible

Charles A. Shook, a thorough student of Mormonism, reminds us of Shakespeare's words,

MORMONISM

In religion
What damned error but some sober brow
Will bless it and approve it with a text,
Hiding the grossness with fair ornament.

Very true; and eminently applicable to Mormonism. Well I remember a former schoolmate of the Christian School in my home town across the ocean who, with his wife, had been "converted" by two Mormon missionaries. He had swallowed the system, hook, line, and sinker. Both he and his wife defended polygamy ardently. That the Bible predicted the arrival of the Book of Mormon he "proved" from Ezekiel 37:16-19. "Is not the Bible the stick of Judah?" he exclaimed triumphantly. "Then the Book of Mormon must be the stick of Ephraim!" I have since read this astonishing bit of "exegesis" in Talmage's standard book on Mormon doctrine.[16] It is merely another instance showing that everything may be proved from isolated texts.

The Mormons "prove" polygamy from Isaiah 4:1, "And seven women shall take hold of one man in that day, saying, We will eat our own bread, and wear our own apparel [they certainly applied that literally in Utah]: only let us be called by thy name; take thou away our reproach." (Against polygamy, see Matt. 19:4-6; Eph. 5:24-33.)

Matthew 22:30, "For in the resurrection they neither marry, nor are given in marriage," is explained to mean that no new marriages will be made in the hereafter; hence the "sealing" must be done in this life — as if the following words, "but are as angels in heaven," do not exclude this artificial exegesis.

It remains only to point to a few passages of Scripture that seem peculiarly applicable to the system as a whole, with its apostles and revelations and "corrected" Bible passages. Such references we find in:

Matthew 7:15, "Beware of false prophets, who come to you in sheep's clothing, but inwardly are ravening wolves."

---
16. James E. Talmage, *The Articles of Faith*, 5th ed.

II Corinthians 11:13, "For such men are false apostles, deceitful workers, fashioning themselves into apostles of Christ."

II Peter 3:16, "which the ignorant and unstedfast wrest, as they do also the other scriptures, unto their own destruction."

Revelation 2:2, "try them that call themselves apostles, and they are not."

Revelation 22:18, "I testify unto every man that heareth the words of the prophecy of this book, If any man shall add unto them, God shall add unto him the plagues which are written in this book."

We again close our chapter with quotations from accredited Mormon authors on various points of Christian teaching. These will show Mormonism to be a thoroughly antichristian cult.

Angels

"1. There are two kinds of being in heaven—viz., angels who are resurrected personages, having bodies of flesh and bones.

"2. For instance, Jesus said, 'Handle me and see, for a spirit hath not flesh and bones, as ye see me have.'

"3. The spirits of just men made perfect—they who are not resurrected, but inherit the same glory." — JOSEPH SMITH.[17]

Baptism

"Wherefore little children are whole, for they are not capable of committing sin; wherefore the curse of Adam is taken from them in me [Christ], that it hath no power over them; and the law of circumcision is done away in me.... And their little children need no repentance, neither baptism.... Behold, I say unto you, that he that supposeth little children need baptism, is in the gall of bitterness, and in the bonds of iniquity; ... wherefore should he be cut off while in the thought, he must go down to hell."—BOOK OF MORMON.

---

17. *Doctrine and Covenants*, Section CXXXII.

"Millions of earth's sons and daughters have passed out of the body without obeying the law of baptism. Many of them will gladly accept the word and law of the Lord when it is proclaimed to them in the spirit world. But they cannot there attend to ordinances that belong to the sphere which they have left. Can nothing be done in their case? Must they forever be shut out of the kingdom of heaven? Both justice and mercy join in answering 'yes' to the first, 'no' to the last question. What, then, is the way of their deliverance?

"The living may be baptized for the dead. Other essential ordinances may be attended to vicariously. This glorious truth, hid from human knowledge for centuries, has been made known in this greatest of all divine dispensations. . . . It gives men and women the power to become 'Saviours on Mount Zion,' Jesus being the great Captain in the army of redeemers."—C. PENROSE.[18]

The Lord's Supper

"Sitting erect in the pride and dignity of being a human being, each member took a piece of the bread and immediately ate it, without ceremony or genuflection, or kneeling or bowing of any kind.

"The other priest, after the people had eaten, made a plain, short exhortation before passing to the young deacons [about fourteen years old! V.B.] the plate of communion cups filled with pure, clear water. And here, perhaps, is the key to the whole Mormon religion. They live to seek out the purer things of life, as exemplified by the purity of the water. . . .

"The almost startling effect, psychologically, of the ultra-simple communion service was to completely obliterate the feeling of supplication and meekness engendered at such a time in many other churches. A man didn't feel that he drew nigh — 'Unworthy as to so much as gather

---

18. *Mormon Doctrine*, p. 48.

the crumbs from His table' — Not at all! He felt that he sat as an equal and a guest at Jesus' table, and after he had eaten and drunk, he went away with a greater appreciation of his own table, his own body, his own life — all godlike if he would make and keep them so." Thus Joseph Weston describes a Mormon sacramental meeting in his book, *These Amazing Mormons* (p. 21).

Atonement

"It becomes evident that through the great atonement, the expiatory sacrifice of the Son of God, it is made possible that man can be redeemed, restored, resurrected and exalted to the elevated position designed for him in the creation as a Son of God.

"In the first place, according to justice, men could not have been redeemed from temporal death, except through the atonement of Jesus Christ; and in the second place, they could not be redeemed from spiritual death, only through obedience to His law. . . .

"Hence what was lost in Adam was restored in Jesus Christ, so far as all men are concerned in all ages, with some very slight exceptions arising from an abuse of privileges. Transgressions of the law brought death upon all the posterity of Adam, the restoration through the atonement restored all the human family to life . . . . So that whatever was lost by Adam, was restored by Jesus Christ. The penalty of the transgression of the law was the death of the body. The atonement made by Jesus Christ resulted in the resurrection of the human body. Its scope embraced all peoples, nations, and tongues."—JOHN TAYLOR.[19]

"The Church of Jesus Christ of Latter-Day Saints teaches as a doctrine founded on reason, justice, and Scripture, that all children are innocent in the sight of God, and that, until they reach an age of personal responsibility, baptism is not requisite or proper in their behalf; that, in short, they are saved through the atonement of Christ. To a degree,

---

19. *The Mediation and Atonement*, pp. 170, 177, 178.

children are born heirs to the good or evil natures of their parents ... but through Christ's atonement they are all redeemed from the curse of this fallen state; the debt, which comes to them as a legacy, is paid for them, and thus are they left free ....

"*The Special or Individual Effect of the Atonement* makes it possible for any and every soul to obtain absolution from the dread effect of personal sins, through the mediation of Christ; but such saving intercession is to be invoked by individual effort as manifested through faith, repentance, and continued works of righteousness. The laws under which individual salvation is obtainable have been prescribed by Christ. ... Now, that the blessing of redemption from individual sins, while free for all to attain, is nevertheless conditioned on individual effort, is as plainly declared as is the truth of unconditional redemption from the effects of the Fall. ..."—JAMES E. TALMAGE.[20]

The Church

"From the facts already stated, it is evident that the Church was literally driven from the earth; in the first ten centuries immediately following the ministry of Christ, the authority of the priesthood was lost from among men, and no human power could restore it. But the Lord in His mercy provided for the re-establishment of His Church in the last days, and for the last time. ... It has been already shown that this restoration was effected by the Lord through the Prophet Joseph Smith."—JAMES E. TALMAGE.[21]

"The departure from the order, doctrine, ordinances, and spirit of primitive Christianity commenced at a very early period. ... The Church of Christ was gone, without even a shadow of its presence to be seen upon the earth. ... After a time came the reformation. ... Yet there was no direct communication established between them and the heavens. ... There was no inspired prophet, no gifted seer, no appointed revelator through whom the will of God could

---
20. *Op. cit.*, pp. 90, 92.
21. *Op. cit.*, p. 68.

be made known. Therefore, the ordinances of the gospel could not be administered acceptably to God, and all such ceremonies as were established among the various sects were of necessity void and without virtue in heaven. . . . Joseph Smith was the chosen instrument in the hands of God to receive the glad message and direct its promulgation to all the world."—C. PENROSE.[22]

The Fall

"Adam found himself in a position that impelled him to disobey one of the requirements of God. He and his wife had been commanded to multiply and replenish the earth. Adam was still immortal; Eve had come under the penalty of mortality; and in such dissimilar conditions the two could not remain together, and therefore could not fulfil the Divine requirement. On the other hand, Adam would be disobeying another command by yielding to his wife's request. He deliberately and wisely decided to stand by the first and greater commandment; and, therefore, with a full comprehension of the nature of his act, he also partook of the fruit that grew on the tree of knowledge. The fact that Adam acted understandingly in this matter is affirmed by the scriptures. Paul in writing to Timothy, explained that 'Adam was not deceived; but the woman, being deceived, was in the transgression.' The prophet Lehi, in expounding the scriptures to his sons, declared, 'Adam fell that man might be, and men are that they might have joy."—JAMES E. TALMAGE.[23]

Fatherhood of God

"When our father Adam came into the garden of Eden, he came into it with a celestial body, and brought Eve, one of his wives, with him . . . . He is our father and our God, and the only God with whom we have to do."—BRIGHAM YOUNG.[24]

---

22. *Op. cit.*, pp. 33-38.
23. *Op. cit.*, p. 68.
24. *Journal of Discourses*, 1:50.

God's Unity

"The passages are numerous in the inspired writings which indicate a plurality of God."—F. D. RICHARDS.[25]

"And they (the Gods) said: Let there be light and there was light. And they (the Gods) comprehended the light... and they divided the light."—JOSEPH SMITH.[26]

"Each of these Gods, including Jesus Christ and His Father, being in possession of not merely an organized spirit, but a glorious body of flesh and bones, is subject to the laws which govern, of necessity, even the most refined order of physical existence."—PARLEY PRATT.[27]

God's Trinity

"The Father has a body of flesh and bones as tangible as man's; the Son also; but the Holy Ghost has not a body of flesh and bones but is a personage of spirit. ... Were it not so, the Holy Ghost could not dwell in us. A man may receive the Holy Ghost, and it may descend upon him, and not tarry with him."—JOSEPH SMITH.[28]

Good Works

"Abraham received concubines and they bare him children, and it was accounted unto him for righteousness. Go ye therefore and do the works of Abraham, enter ye into my law, and ye shall be saved. But if ye enter not into my law [of polygamy], ye cannot receive the promise of my Father, which he made unto Abraham."—JOSEPH SMITH.[29]

"Now, that the blessing of redemption from individual sins, while free for all to attain, is nevertheless conditioned on individual effort, is as plainly declared as is the truth of unconditional redemption from the effects of the Fall."—JAMES E. TALMAGE.[30]

---

25. *Compendium,* p. 170.
26. *The Pearl of Great Price,* p. 67.
27. *Key to the Science of Theology,* p. 42.
28. *Doctrine and Covenants,* p. 462.
29. *Celestial Marriage,* pars. 12, 14.
30. *Op. cit.,* p. 92.

Inspiration

"Thou fool, that shall say, A Bible, A Bible, we have got a Bible, and we need no more Bible. . . . Wherefore, murmur ye, because that ye shall receive more of my word?"— BOOK OF MORMON.[31]

"And whatsoever they ['those ordained unto the priesthood'] shall speak when moved upon by the Holy Ghost, shall be scripture, shall be the will of the Lord, shall be the mind of the Lord, shall be the word of the Lord, shall be the voice of the Lord, and the power of God unto salvation." —JOSEPH SMITH.[32]

"The written works adopted by the vote of the Church as authoritative guides in faith and doctrine are four — the Bible, the Book of Mormon, the Doctrine and Covenants, and the Pearl of Great Price."—JAMES E. TALMAGE.[33]

"We will first quote from the writings of the Old and New Testaments and, although we are informed by later revelations 'that many parts which are plain and most precious' have been taken away therefrom, yet there is a large amount of testimony left in this valuable and sacred record."—JOHN TAYLOR.[34]

The Holy Scriptures. Translated and Corrected by the Spirit of Revelation, by Joseph Smith, Jr., the Seer. 20th Edition. Lamoni, Iowa. Published by the Reorganized Church of Jesus Christ of Latter Day Saints. 1920.

"Wilfred Woodruff is a prophet, and he has a great many prophets around him, and he can make scriptures as good as those in the Bible."—JOHN TAYLOR.[35]

Justification

"The sectarian dogma of justification by faith alone has exercised an influence for evil since the early days of Christianity."—JAMES E. TALMAGE.[36]

---

31. Section CXXXII, 44.
32. *Doctrine and Covenants*, p. 248.
33. *Op. cit.*, p. 5.
34. *Op. cit.*, p. 11.
35. Cf. Nutting, *Why I Could Never Be a Mormon*, p. 21.
36. *Op. cit.*, p. 120.

Priesthood

"But there are two divisions or grand heads — one is the Melchizedek Priesthood, and the other is the Aaronic, or Levitical priesthood. The office of an elder comes under the Priesthood of Melchizedek. The Melchizedek Priesthood holds the right of Presidency, and has power and authority over all the offices in the church in all ages of the world, to administer in spiritual things."—JOSEPH SMITH.[37]

"The Apostle was so overawed by his presence, that he fell at his feet to worship him; whereas the angel said, 'See that thou do it not; I am thy fellow servant . . .' (Rev. 19: 10). In other words, he had held the holy Priesthood on the earth and had officiated therein; . . . But now the scene was changed; he was officiating in another sphere, and was revealing unto the apostle John. . . . All of these men, having held the everlasting Priesthood on earth, still retain the power and authority conferred upon them, and stand forth as prominent examples of the perpetuity of the everlasting Priesthood, administering on the earth or in the heavens, as the purposes of God . . . or the circumstances require."—JOHN TAYLOR.[38]

Resurrection

"The statement that the heathen dead will have place in the first resurrection is sustained by the word of scripture, and by a consideration of the principles of true justice according to which humanity is to be judged. Man will be accounted blameless or guilty, according to his deeds as interpreted in the light of the law under which he is required to live . . . it is reasonable to believe that the plan of redemption will afford such benighted ones an opportunity of learning the laws of God; and surely, as fast as they so learn, will obedience be required on pain of the penalty."—JAMES E. TALMAGE.[39]

---

37. *Doctrine and Covenants*, p. 384.
38. *Op. cit.*, p. 161.
39. *Op. cit.*, p. 404.

Marriage

"In the case of a man marrying a wife in the everlasting covenant who dies while he continues in the flesh and marries another by the same divine law, each wife will come forth in her order and enter with him into his glory. Is there any reason why this should not be so? Is not each of these wives entitled to her position in eternity, by virtue of the sealing power which made her part of the man? Why should one enter into the exaltation of the celestial world and the other be relegated to singleness and servitude? They all become one in the patriarchal order of family government. And if this be the case in heaven, why should not similar conditions as far as possible exist on earth? Is earth holier than heaven? If there were no law of the land against it and a man received from the Lord more wives than one under the sealing ordinances, where would be the moral wrong? . . . Herein is our Eternal Father glorified and His dominions extended."—C. PENROSE.[40]

"Jesus Christ was a polygamist; Mary and Martha, the sisters of Lazarus, were his plural wives, and Mary Magdalene was another. Also, the bridal feast of Cana of Galilee, where Jesus turned the water into wine, was on the occasion of one of his own marriages."—BRIGHAM YOUNG.[41]

"We say it was Jesus Christ who was married [at Cana, to Martha and Mary], whereby he could see his own seed before he was crucified. The reference is to Isaiah 53:10."—ORSON HYDE.[42]

Virgin Birth

"When the Virgin Mary conceived the child Jesus, the Father had begotten him in his own likeness. He was NOT begotten by the Holy Ghost. And who was the Father? He was the first of the human family. . . . Jesus, our elder brother, was begotten in the flesh by the same character

---
40. *Op. cit.,* p. 66.
41. Quoted in Ann Eliza Young's *Wife No. 19,* Ch. XXXV.
42. Cf. C. A. Shook, *The True Origin of Mormon Polygamy,* p. 207.

MORMONISM 227

that was in the garden of Eden, and who is our Father in Heaven."—BRIGHAM YOUNG.[43]

For Reflection

1. Which books are considered divinely inspired by Mormons?

2. Which of these are considered most important? Does Revelation 22:18 apply here, or are Mormon missionaries right when they say, "That refers only to tampering with the Apocalypse"?

3. What brought on the split between the Utah and the Reorganized branches?

4. On which points do these two groups differ, and on which are they agreed?

5. What good things can you say about Mormonism? Are they also politically dangerous?

6. What do you think now of Dr. Kuizenga's statement that Mormonism has at any rate tried to bring sex under the aspect of religion? Should and can this be done?[44]

7. Explain the Mormon view of the origin of man, of Jesus Christ, of the fall of man, of the atonement by Christ, and of celestial marriage.

8. Is Mormonism a monotheistic religion? Is it Christian? Can one be a Mormon and a Christian at the same time?[45]

9. A minister had a suite of rooms for rent. Two men rang his doorbell and said, "We are Christians. We'd like to rent your rooms." He discovered they were "Latter-Day Saints," and refused them, pointing to II John 10. Was the minister right?

---

43. *Journal of Discourses*, 1:50.
44. Cf. here my chapter, "The Service of Sex" in *Our Christian Heritage* (Grand Rapids: Eerdmans, 1948), pp. 301ff.
45. Dr. Snowden wrote that if the Mormons would abandon their prophet and their book, they might well be accepted among the rest of Christian denominations; and Dr. Braden that "the plan of salvation does not, in its main outlines, differ essentially from the traditional orthodox view." Do you agree with these opinions?

12

SEVENTH-DAY ADVENTISM

William Miller never dreamed that his name would be associated with a movement that denounces all Christians who observe the Sabbath on the first day of the week.

Miller, when he was converted from his deism, studied his Bible and Cruden's Concordance diligently for two years before he began to publish his findings. He was fifty years old when he began to preach, and even then he continued farming for some time. But he found himself led into preaching by divine providence, and yielded as opportunities to "lecture" on the prophecies forced themselves upon him. To the end of his days (Dec. 20, 1849, in the sixty-eighth year of his life), Miller remained a humble and devoted Christian. He and his followers were maligned and ridiculed; they were accused of cashing in on their preaching, and especially those who expected the Lord to return in 1843 and, subsequently, in October, 1844. The sober truth is, however, that Miller spent far more money on spreading his message than he got out of it; that he was as bitterly disappointed as any were when the Lord failed to return at the specified time; and that he remained a Bible-believing Christian who thought to the end that the Lord must come very soon.

Miller's strength lay in the fact that he preached the visible return of Christ to judge the world and to reward the faithful in an age when that cardinal Christian truth threatened to become a forgotten topic. His weakness was that he lacked theological training, and the early ministers who joined him were men of the same caliber.

It is true that a child may find the way of salvation in an emphasized Gospel of John: it is just as true that there are difficult portions in the Bible the interpretation of which a man should no more tackle without a solid theological education than one should begin to practice medicine or law without studying what medical science or jurisprudence has found in former generations.

Seventh-Day Adventists point to the fact that there have been theologians who held to the same views of prophecy which led Miller to his fundamental error, and that Miller was right when he held that anyone can understand the Bible when he studies it earnestly; however, the outcome of Millerism has shown these theologians, together with Miller, to have been in error.

Miller's fundamental mistake was that he took the prophecy in Daniel 8:14 to refer to the end of time, and that he took the days there mentioned to mean years (one would think that "two thousand and three hundred evenings and mornings" is clear enough!). And when Miller found that his chronology had been somewhat off, it was Samuel S. Snow, one of Miller's followers, who changed the date and first suggested the autumn of 1844.

Miller died in the Christian faith and in the hope that he would soon be with the Lord.

It is here the place to remark that the book *The Midnight Cry* undoubtedly proves that most of the rumors about fanaticism in connection with the Miller movement were unfounded. (So was the rumor that the Millerites wore "ascension robes" on Oct. 22, 1844.[1])

It is a pity that Miller's followers failed to read aright the character of their mistake. When both 1843 and October 22, 1844, had gone by without the return of the Lord, they should have drawn the inference that it is wrong to figure from prophecy the time of the coming of Christ. Instead of doing this, however, Hiram Edson, a Millerite in the state of New York, saw a vision on the morning

---

1. This rumor has persisted a hundred years; it was printed even in the 11th edition of the *Encyclopedia Britannica;* also in previous editions of the present volume. Francis D. Nichol's scholarly and sober book, however, disproves these rumors as well as alleged cases of insanity as a result of the Miller movement.

after the "great disappointment." In this vision he saw Christ standing at the altar in heaven, from which he concluded that Miller had been right as to the *time* mentioned by Daniel, but wrong as to the *place*. The words, "Unto two thousand and three hundred evenings and mornings; then shall the sanctuary be cleansed," referred to a cleaning of the heavenly sanctuary.[2]

This teaching was taken over by later S.D.A. whose beginning dates from this new interpretation, according to Nichol.[3] Thus, "they have chosen to emphasize that the 'major mistake' of the Millerites was in their interpretation, not in setting the time. Outsiders may pardonably continue to consider this as somewhat of a quibble."[4]

Elsewhere in this chapter we give what we consider the obvious interpretation of Daniel 8:13, 14. Here we observe that S.D.A., according to its own men, began with this new interpretation of the 2300 days, and that this interpretation rests upon an alleged *vision* of one man.

Equally arbitrary is the choice of the second foundation stone of S.D.A. According to Nichols it was "Father Bates," one of the early converts to Millerism, and a captain at sea, whose "light was the seventh-day Sabbath." Elder James White (the S.D.A. Church had been organized in 1860 and Elder White wrote this in 1868) endorsed the view of Bates and others. To him the three angels mentioned in Revelation 14:6-11 in their "three messages symbolize the three parts of the genuine movement," that is, the genuine advent movement as begun by Miller.

Ellen G. White, who became the "prophetess" of S.D.A., wife of Elder James White, wrote in a similar vein. According to her, Miller and his associates "fulfilled prophecy." They had a clear understanding of the message of the first two angels, but not of the third angel. Mrs. White and others were willing to receive this also, and they did

---
2. Francis D. Nichol, *The Midnight Cry*, 3rd ed. p. 457.
3. *Op. cit.*, p. 457
4. Sidney E. Mead in reviewing Nichol's book in the *Christian Century*, March 7, 1945.

SEVENTH-DAY ADVENTISM   231

receive it; and, says Nichols, "Seventh-Day Adventists believe that the third angel's message, when viewed in positive terms, is a call to men to honor the true Sabbath of God, the 'seventh day' of the Decalogue, that is, the day commonly known as Saturday. The preaching of the seventh-day Sabbath in the prophetic setting of the third angel of Revelation 14 soon became a distinctive part of this newly developing religious movement."[5]

And this conviction also rests, at least in part, upon an alleged "vision" which was "revealed" to Mrs. White,[6] a woman honored by S.D.A. as truly divinely inspired.

Peculiar Doctrines of S.D.A.

S.D.A. deviates from evangelical Christianity in four particulars. For this reason it will not be necessary to append a list of statements by S.D.A. writers on various points of doctrine. When we have considered these four points we have discussed S.D.A.[7]

Moreover, two of the four points have been taken over by Russell and are propagated by Jehovah's Witnesses with added zest. Hence we shall discuss these in our next chapter. They are:

1. The doctrine of the *soul-sleep after death.* "The state to which we are reduced by death is one of silence, inactivity and entire unconsciousness," wrote Spicer; and he added, "Between death and the resurrection the dead sleep." Suffice it here to say that we consider this teaching to be contrary to Luke 16:22-30; Philippians 1:23, 24 and II Corinthians 5:1-8; Psalm 73:24; Revelation 6:9, 10.

2. The doctrine of *annihilation of the wicked.* To quote Spicer again: "The positive teaching of Holy Scripture is that sin and sinners will be blotted out of existence. There

---

5. *Op. cit.,* p. 463.
6. Cf. *The Great Controversy,* by Mrs. White, p. 435. Cf. for other "visions" and "revelations" of Mrs. White, her *Early Writings,* pp. 114, 115.
7. If we leave out of consideration that, like the Mormons, S.D.A. forbids the use of tobacco, liquor, coffee, and tea. Pork and pepper are also frowned upon.

will be a clean universe again when the great controversy between Christ and Satan is ended." In our discussion of Russellism we shall show why we consider this doctrine to be contrary to such passages as Romans 2:6-9 and Revelation 20:10, 13.[8]

The third doctrine which is peculiar to S.D.A. is in reality its foremost and great point of doctrine. It has remained the private property of this sect. I refer to their view of the *atonement*. It is here that S.D.A. deviates most from Scriptural teaching. Before we enter into a discussion of this point we allow ourselves the following remark of a general nature.

It is evident that when we discuss Theosophy, Spiritism, and other cults which do not recognize the Bible as the inspired and final revelation from God, we can do little by citing Scripture. The Book has no authority to the mind of adherents of such cults. However, the matter becomes different when we review S.D.A. and Russellism since these systems claim to be based upon the Bible as the word of God. In such cases, therefore, it is sufficient to show that their teachings are contrary to Scripture, and are in many instances the result of hasty and superficial quoting from the Bible.

It is from their peculiar tenets concerning the atonement that this sect is named *Adventists*. Their deviation is in reference to the second coming or advent of our Lord.

1. Miller had inferred from Daniel 8:14 that Christ must return on October 22, 1844. And Mrs. White desired to vindicate the movement which Miller had inaugurated. Hence her predicament. She found a way out of the difficulty. Miller, so she maintained with a woman's love for the last word, had indeed been correct. If Daniel 8:14 showed that Christ must have returned in 1844, well, then

---

8. One of the most serious attempts to prove the doctrines of soul-sleep and annihilation from Scripture may be found in the two volumes, *Life and Immortality* and *Christ, the Firstfruits*, by Eric Lewis (Boston: Advent Christian Publishing Society, 1949). But see the present writer's review in *The Banner*, Grand Rapids, Mich., March 24, 1950.

He did return in 1844. And if He had not returned to this earth, well, then He had returned somewhere else. In other words, the sanctuary mentioned in Daniel 8:14 — "then shall the sanctuary be cleansed," was not on earth. Where was it then? In heaven, of course.[9]

Heaven, according to Mrs. White, is a counterpart of the typical sanctuary on earth with its two compartments, the holy place and the holy of holies. In the first apartment of

---

9. Both Wm. Miller and Ellen G. White were wrong. Miller's assertion that 2,300 days meant 2,300 years, these being "prophetic days" of one year each, is just as much gratuitous speculation as his statement that these "days" were to be reckoned from Artaxerxes' decree (Ezra's return to Palestine).

Verse 19 states that "the time of the end" refers to "the latter time of the indignation," God's indignation revealed in the Babylonian captivity. The vision therefore begins where the Babylonian captivity ends. Hence verse 20 speaks of the Medo-Persian power, which indeed destroyed the Babylonian empire.

In the vision it is therefore stated, verse 4, that the ram pushed westward and northward, and southward; i.e., the Medo-Persian empire conquered Lydia (north, 564 B.C.), Babylon (west, ca. 554) and Egypt (south, another ten years later).

Then came the strong he-goat, verse 5, who is the king of Greece, verse 21. Greece defeated Persia in 490 and 480 B.C. When Alexander the Great "magnified himself exceedingly," verse 8, he suddenly died at the age of 33. His empire was divided into four parts, and out of one of these divisions came "a little horn," verse 9, "in the latter time of their kingdom," verse 23; that is, when the four divisions of Alexander's empire were going down, one by one, before the power of Rome. This little horn is Antiochus Epiphanes, who marched against "the glorious land" (Palestine, Dan. 11:16,41). He massacred 40,000 Jews in three days, entered the holy of holies of the Jerusalem temple, and offered a large sow on the altar of burnt offering in the temple court. This put a stop to the regular Mosaic burnt offering. Now Daniel 8:14 states that this burnt offering, which was rendered each evening and each morning, was to be omitted 2,300 times, in the evening and morning. That is to say, 1,150 days.

This prophecy was literally fulfilled: the first heathen sacrifice was offered on Dec. 25, 168 B.C. On Dec. 25, 165 B.C. the holy sacrifice was again offered on a newly erected altar. That is to say, the sanctuary was cleansed (I Maccabees 1:59 and 4:53). That makes exactly three years. Three years, however, equal 2,190 evenings and mornings. However, the divinely ordained regular burnt offerings had been ordered stopped some time prior to the offering of the heathen sacrifices in their stead, which accounts for 2,300 evenings and mornings as stated in the text. Cf. the Rev. Wm. Hendriksen in *The Banner*, March 20 and 27, 1942.

the heavenly sanctuary Christ pleaded for eighteen centuries in behalf of penitent sinners. "Yet their sins remained upon the book of records." Christ's atonement had remained unfinished. There was a task yet to be accomplished, to wit, the removal of sins from the sanctuary in heaven.

Now, as upon the great day of atonement the high priest entered into the inner sanctuary to complete, to add to the daily sacrifices for sin offered in the other part of the temple, so Christ began His work of completing His atonement for sin in the inner sanctuary of heaven in 1844. He thereby cleansed the sanctuary from sin.

And how did Christ do this? In 1844 He began His "investigative judgment." He examined all His people and showed the Father those "who, through repentance of sin and faith in Christ, are entitled to the benefits of the atonement."

It remained only to draw the comparison between the earthly and the heavenly holy of holies still further. On the day of atonement there was a scapegoat who was burdened with the sins of the people and then sent into the wilderness. This scapegoat, so Mrs. White taught, typified Satan, the author of sin, "upon whom the sins of the truly penitent will finally be placed."

2. This speculation was duly rounded out with the assertion that when Christ had entered the heavenly sanctuary, *the door was closed.* After that no one could be saved except by receiving the heavenly sanctuary dogma. This, in other words, was a polite way of saying that which many sects have said: "Unless you accept our doctrine, there is no hope for you. We alone have the truth."

Although the foregoing teaching is fundamental to S.D.A., it is not flung into our faces nearly as much as the doctrine from which the system derives the other half of its name. It is not *Adventism* pure and simple. It is *Seventh-Day* Adventism. This is the fourth point on which S.D.A. takes issue with all other Christian churches.

1. In one of her frequent visions Mrs. White saw the ark

in heaven, for surely there must be an ark in heaven's counterpart of the tabernacle. In the ark she saw the two tables of stone which contained the Ten Commandments; and as she looked, behold, the Fourth Commandment stood out above the others, for it was surrounded by a halo of light. With the incontrovertible logic of a woman, Mrs. White concluded that this commandment needed attention above its fellows. It had been neglected more than the other nine. How? It was evident. The Sabbath had not been kept holy. It had, in fact, been destroyed. A nasty Sunday, with wicked New England "blue laws," had been substituted for the Lord's Sabbath.

In her determination that Christians should return to the proper observance of Jehovah's Sabbath, Mrs. White began to look into the history of the Sabbath in the Christian Church. She discovered that one of the popes had caused the change from Saturday to Sunday. Dr. Biederwolf tersely asks between parentheses: which pope? Now it happened that in the days of Mrs. White Christians were pretty well agreed that St. John the Divine spoke rather directly of "the pope." Mrs. White, therefore, duly concluded that Sunday observance is "the mark of the beast." The first beast in Revelation 13, so she added, is the papacy; the second beast is the United States government because this government "in spite of its youthfulness, innocence, and gentleness" speaks "as a dragon" when it makes "Sunday laws." This present writer, who is an obedient subject of the United States Government, not by birth but by his own will and volition, humbly apologizes for this disrespectful reference to Uncle Sam as a beast. He disclaims all responsibility and would not repeat it but for necessity.

Mrs. White identified this beast with the "little horn" in Daniel 7:25 and said that horn meant the papacy (see *The Great Controversy Between Christ and Satan*, pp. 51, 54, 446). In reality the little horn is said by Daniel to appear *after* the other ten horns that come out of the fourth (Roman) empire in the vision, and at the end of history, immediately before the final judgment (7:26, 27). The little horn refers to the man of sin, described in II Thessalonians 2:4, Revelation 11:7; 13:7, cf. 20:7. See for detailed exegesis S. L. Morris, *The Drama of Christianity*, 1928; Charles R. Erdman, *The Revelation of John*, 1936; W. Hendriksen, *More Than Conquerors*, 1939.

2. S.D.A. stresses its view of the Sabbath far above its other peculiar doctrines. We are dealing here with an aggressive system. There is nothing apologetic about these people who call Uncle Sam a beast. They prefer to put the churches on the defensive. They are forever attacking, and their attack is almost invariably upon the wickedness of Sunday worship.

The Atonement

1. The sanctuary doctrine caused S.D.A. to say, "We dissent from the view that the atonement was made upon the cross, as is generally held." Mrs. White's writings on the subject contain a mass of confused ideas. For instance:

"After his ascension, our Saviour was to begin his work as our high priest. . . . The blood of Christ, while it was to release the repentant sinner from the condemnation of the law, was not to cancel sin; it would stand on record in the sanctuary until the final atonement."—*Patriarchs and Prophets* (1908 ed.), p. 357.

"We are now living in the great day of atonement. In the typical service, while the high priest was making the atonement for Israel, all were required to afflict their souls by repentance of sin and humiliation before the Lord, lest they be cut off from among the people. In like manner, all who would have their names retained in the book of life, should now, in the few remaining days of their probation, afflict their souls before God by sorrow for sin and true repentance. . . . Now, while our great High Priest is making the atonement for us, we should seek to become perfect in Christ. . . . It is in this life that we are to separate sin from us, through faith in the atoning blood of Christ. Our precious Saviour invites us to join ourselves to Him, to unite our weakness to His strength, our ignorance to His wisdom, our unworthiness to His merits."—*The Great Controversy* (pp. 489, 623).

These thoughts, scattered through many pages, first of all suggest a dangerous synergism or co-operation between man and Christ in effecting salvation. They are more briefly expressed in these words of the S.D.A. tract, *Fundamental Principles of S. D. Adventists*: "He through the merits of His shed blood, secures the pardon and forgiveness of the sins of all those who penitently come to Him; and as the closing portion of His work as priest, before He takes His throne as king, He will make the great atonement for the sins of all such and their sins will be blotted out."

Another tract, *What Do S. D. Adventists Believe?*, contains this: "That by a life of perfect obedience and by His sacrificial death, He satisfied divine justice, and made *provision for atonement* for the sins of men . . . that in the final day of accounting He will formally blot out the sins of men, and they will be remembered no more for ever."

Regarding its theory of the atonement, Scripture clearly and unequivocally condemns this sect. For,

a. Christ is represented as the *ransom*, the *price for redemption* which pays for the freedom of those He represents. If Mrs. White wishes to point to the sacrifices of the Old Testament, she should have to read the Book of Leviticus. Let the reader refer to Leviticus 1:4; 4:20, 31, 35; 5:10, 16; 6:7; 17:11. It is impossible to distil from these passages anything but what they plainly teach, namely, that the life of the animal is given in exchange for, as a redemption for, the life of the sinner. Thus the animal that is sacrificed atones for the sinner who goes free. Thus Christ is stated in the New Testament to be *lutron*, that is, *price of redemption* for those in Him. The word *lutron* in Matthew 20:28 and Mark 10:45 is the same word which the Septuagint has in Exodus 21:30 where it is clearly the price for freedom, that is, the atonement.

b. Consequently the New Testament is full of this teaching; namely, as the Passover lamb, or some other sin offering, took the place of the sinner, so Christ removes the *guilt*, or the *curse* from His people. For instance, John 1:29, "Behold the Lamb of God, that taketh away the sin of the world." I Corinthians 5:7, "For our passover also hath been sacrificed even Christ." Several chapters of Hebrews compare Christ's sacrifice to atone for sin with the Old Testament sacrifices; see Hebrews 7:27; 9:7, 11, 14.

c. It is therefore stated that sin is removed, forgiven because of the blood of Christ; see Hebrews 9:22-26. The curse is removed by the cross, Galatians 3:13.

d. So complete is this atonement, that not only has the punishment of sin, which is death, been removed by it, but the opposite, that is life, has been gained by this cross; see I Peter 2:24.

e. Hence this atonement is described as, once for all, complete and finished. In Hebrews 9:11, 12 it is pointed out that the atonement of Christ did not need to be repeated because of imperfection, as did the atonement by goats and bullocks. On the contrary, "Christ ... nor yet through the blood of goats and calves, but through his own blood entered in once for all into the holy place, having obtained eternal redemption" (*"lutrosis, liberatio a poenis peccatorum."* Grimm).

The latter passage is not only a sufficient answer to the supposed repetition of the sacrifice of Christ in the Romish mass; it is also a conclusive argument against Mrs. White's "The atonement was not finished on the cross." Compare for the finality of Jesus' sacrifice also Hebrews 1:3; 10:12-14.

2. The teaching that the sins of Christ's people "still remained upon the record" in heaven after Christ's ascension is thus contrary to Scripture. But so is also this other tenet that the sins of the truly penitent will finally be laid upon Satan.

This entire heresy, that Christ did not fully atone for sin by His sacrifice upon the cross, is based upon another error. It may have been born of the "predicament" to interpret the cleansing of the sanctuary as occurring in heaven (contrary to Daniel 8:14, see above); it is bolstered up with a misinterpretation of Leviticus 16.

S.D.A., following Mrs. White, translates Leviticus 16:8, "And Aaron shall cast lots upon the two goats; one lot for Jehovah, and the other lot for Satan (Azazel)."

The later S.D.A. quotes from many encyclopedias and dictionaries and thereby proves that many authorities understand the word "Azazel," which occurs only here in Scripture, to mean Satan or an evil spirit. There is no denying that they are right in this.

It is, however, just as true that other authorities still maintain that the word "Azazel" cannot mean that in Leviticus 16:8 because that translation is contrary to the context. See for example, the *International Standard Bible Encyclopedia* under heading, "Azazel." The matter, then, remains unsettled.

But let us waive this important fact. Let us take for granted that the S.D.A. version of "Azazel" is correct beyond dispute: that does not prove what S.D.A. infers from it, namely, that the scapegoat is "for Satan" because the sins of God's people must be laid upon Satan in the judgment day in order to be removed.

This is first of all contrary to the plain sense of verses 20-22, the only passage that states what is to be done with the scapegoat. After Aaron has made atonement for his own sins and for the sins of Israel, he must lay both his hands upon the living goat and confess over him all the iniquities of the children of Israel; these are laid upon the head of this second goat. This goat is then sent into the wilderness never to return. The obvious meaning is that, since the death of the first goat has made a full atonement for the people's sins (typically, representing Christ), the curse owing to their sins is removed and can never reach them again.

This is in agreemeent with Isaiah 53:6 ". . . and Jehovah hath laid on him the iniquity of us all"; with II Corinthians 5:21, "Him who knew no sin he made to be sin on our behalf"; and with Galatians 3:13, "Christ redeemed us from the curse of the law, having become a curse for us."

To such plain language as these texts contain, S.D.A.'s statements concerning "Azazel" do gross injustice. They detract from Christ's saving work. And even if S.D.A. is correct in feeling irked when it is accused of making Satan a part-saviour (which they do not do), it has given occasion to this misinterpretation by belittling Christ's saving death and by its fantastic and unscriptural reference to the part of Satan.

3. Let S.D.A. cease from wondering when those who believe in Christ's saving work accuse them of splitting up the Christian Church on such flimsy grounds and of parading as "the only orthodox" church with a monopoly on the right interpretation of prophecy.

We now turn to the main plank in the S.D.A. platform, that of observance of the Sabbath on Saturday.

A Wrong Approach to the Sabbath Question

1. Many try to refute S.D.A. by denying the distinction between the *moral* law and the *ceremonial* law as given by Moses. They only know of one law, the law of Moses. This, they assert, belongs to the Old Testament, as it had been given to Israel. We Christians of the New Testament day have nothing to do with Moses' law. We are not under the law, but under grace. Hence the Sabbath has been abrogated. What we now have is the Lord's day, or Sunday, which we observe, not by command, but of our own volition to remember the resurrection of our Lord. It is evident that in this way important ground is yielded to the Seventh-Day Adventists. They can rightly accuse us of having destroyed the Sabbath. Moreover, Sunday observance becomes a matter not so much of duty as of choice. There is no such thing as Sabbath desecration.

2. Over against this erroneous view we hold with the Synod of Dordt of 1618-19 that there is in the Sabbath commandment something ceremonial as well as something ethical, that is, something that was temporary and something permanent. Mrs. White was correct in stating that

the Sabbath, as given by Moses, is the law of God, and no man has the right to change the law. But the form in which the law came contained temporary elements. We have no stranger within our gates, and most of us have no ass.

3. While it is true that Deuteronomy adds this reason for Sabbath observance, "And thou shalt remember that thou wast a servant in the land of Egypt, and Jehovah thy God brought thee out thence by a mighty hand and by an outstretched arm: therefore Jehovah thy God commanded thee to keep the Sabbath day," this additional reason was given when a later generation was in danger of forgetting these things. We find the original form of the Ten Commandments in Exodus 20. And here Sabbath observance is said to be a duty because God kept the Sabbath after six days of labor. Man is to pattern his life after God's manner of working. The Sabbath goes back to creation, and is a perpetual institution.

It is for this reason also that we read of the Sabbath in Exodus 16. Before the law was given on Mt. Sinai, Israel was reminded to "remember" the Sabbath day. Since the Israelites had always had that creation commandment, they were not to gather manna on the seventh day.

It is therefore clear that Noah and Jacob counted time by weeks instead of days, Genesis 8:10-12; 29:27, 28, and that man, created after God's image, lived from Sabbath to Sabbath as did his God.

4. The objection that neither Christ nor Paul ever mentioned the Sabbath day is to no purpose. Jesus quoted from the second table of the law, and He did so at random; see Matthew 19:18, 19 and Mark 10:19. Did that mean that He changed the order, or that He abrogated those commandments He did not happen to quote? We should be careful with such arguments from silence. Certainly when Jesus said, "It is lawful to do good on the Sabbath," and, "My Father worketh until now and I work [namely, on the Sabbath]," He did not annul but recognized the Sabbath. And as to Paul, Dr. Warfield is right: We learn from Ephesians 6:2, first that obedience to parents is right. "The acknowl-

edged authority of the Fifth Commandment is simply taken for granted. Observe, secondly, how the authority of the Fifth Commandment, thus assumed as unquestionable, is extended over the whole Decalogue. For this commandment is not adduced here as an isolated precept; it is brought forward as one of a series, in which it stands on equal ground with the others, differing from them only in being the first of them which has a promise attached to it. . . . Observe, thirdly, how everything in the manner in which the Fifth Commandment is enunciated in the Decalogue that gives it a form and coloring adapting it specifically to the Old Dispensation is quietly set aside and a universalizing mode of statement substituted for it: 'That it may be well with thee, and thou mayest live long on the earth.' "

Paul showed with this quotation that the Ten Commandments were considered binding in the early Church, but the people distinguished between what we have called the moral and the ceremonial, the abiding and the local or temporary aspects of these commandments.

And it is the same with James, as Dr. Warfield reminds us. In the second chapter of James we are informed that the law is a whole: we cannot break one commandment without violating the entire law. "We might as well say, if we have broken the handle or the lip or the pedestal of some beautiful vase, that we have not broken the vase but only the handle or the lip or the pedestal of it, as to say that we have not broken the law when we have broken a single one of its precepts." And this James illustrates from the Ten Commandments. We must not commit adultery, but we must not kill either. For if we keep one or nine of the Ten Commandments and break one, we have transgressed against the law of our God. The Ten Commandments are a unit, and we are to keep them all, including, of course, the Sabbath commandment.

The Right Approach

1. S.D.A. finds it impossible to keep the Sabbath day according to Old Testament specifications. What was possible

in certain regions to which the people of the Lord were limited of old, is not possible today. Thus Mrs. White began by keeping the Sabbath from six o'clock until the following day six P. M. S.D.A. practiced this for ten long years. Then Mrs. White discovered that this should have been from sunset to sunset. Was this change postponed, perhaps, because difficulties were anticipated as a result of the growth of the cult? Certainly it is Biblical to observe the seventh day from sunset to sunset. But how is this possible in lands where the sun sets once in six months? It appears, then, that the unbiblical "from six to six" is better adapted to the universal conditions of the New Testament Dispensation. However, as soon as we grant this, we have departed from the Old Testament, and conceded that a change may be introduced in the manner in which the time of the Sabbath day is determined.

2. Again, S.D.A. does not interpret the Fourth Commandment in the manner in which the "unchangeable law" demands it. On page 409 of *Patriarchs and Prophets* Mrs. White wrote: "One of the people, angry at being excluded from Canaan, and determined to show his defiance of God's law, ventured upon the open transgression of the fourth commandment, by going out to gather sticks upon the Sabbath. During the sojourn in the wilderness, the kindling of fires upon the seventh day had been strictly prohibited. The prohibition was not to extend to the land of Canaan, where the severity of the climate would often render fires a necessity; but in the wilderness fire was not needed for warmth." It is clear that the words in Exodus 35:2, 3, "Six days shall work be done, but on the seventh day . . . . Ye shall kindle no fire throughout your habitations upon the sabbath day," do not refer to the wilderness journey alone, but are also for the time when the Israelites would indeed have habitations, that is, in Canaan. If S.D. A. wants to observe the Fourth Commandment as given in Exodus, let its adherents try it and not tamper with the literal meaning because they consider its plain language

necessary or not. The point is not that sometimes fires might be necessary on the Sabbath Day, and at other times not, but that provision should be made on the sixth day for the eventuality.

3. We have no choice left but to return to the statement that the Fourth Commandment contains something moral and abiding, as well as a ceremonial element which passed away in the transition from the Old into the New Dispensation. "The Sabbath," said Christ, "is for man," not for the Jew. But how much of it?

One might inquire why the New Testament contains no specific commandment as to how much should be kept and how much discarded or changed. The reply is that this was done in no case. The entire ceremonial law passed away; yet there is no series of injunctions as to how much of the Mosaic law may be disregarded. True, Paul fought against the necessity of circumcision in the case of Gentile converts. Circumcision in their case would have meant a denial of Christ's work which made works of the law unnecessary. Yet was there no injunction against circumcision in the case of Jewish converts. It was left to the guidance of the Holy Spirit to lead the Pentecostal church gradually into a consensus as to how much of the Old Testament law was to remain.

Thus, together with other Christians, S.D.A. does not observe the Passover; yet a Jew would have the same right to say to S.D.A., "Show me one text in the New Testament that the Passover has been annulled," as S.D.A. has to say, "Show me one text in the N. T. that says that the seventh day has been done away with."

4. Jesus, referring to what was to happen A. D. 70, evidently assumed that His disciples should at first observe the commandment of the seventh day: "And pray ye that your flight be not . . . on a sabbath" (Matt. 24:20). How could He refer to a future change as a result of that which they, as yet, did not understand, namely His resurrection?

5. It is futile even to attempt to refute the argument that a change slowly came upon the New Testament

SEVENTH-DAY ADVENTISM

Church. There is a gradual, almost imperceptible change from the seventh day to the first day of the week. This begins very early. The disciples are met by Christ on the first day of the week, one week after His resurrection.[10] At Troas Paul met the congregation "upon the first day of the week to break bread" (Acts 20:7). The church at Corinth is advised to lay up their collections for Christian charity on Sunday (I Cor. 16:2). Why on earth should this have been advised if Saturday had been still the official day of worship? Imagine an Adventist laying aside his gifts to the church on Sunday! To John the revelation on Patmos came "on the Lord's Day." By that time the term had firmly embedded itself in the Christian consciousness.[11]

6. *The* text for the change is therefore Colossians 2:16, 17. These verses do not totally abrogate the Sabbath day. They put over against the disappearing, the *shadow,* that which is abiding, *the body.* "The institutions of the law which are referred to in verse 16 as foreshadowing in time

---

10. Seventh-Dayists, holding that Scripture counts the day from sunset to sunset, always, assert that Christ did not meet with the disciples on the first day of the week, therefore, did not sanction that day. He met on the second day of the week, for it was after sunset, they claim. This is clearly contradicted by John 20:19: "When therefore it was evening, on that day, the first day of the week. . . ."
In verse 26 we read, "And after eight days again the disciples were within . . . . Jesus cometh . . . ." Again the Adventists say: "That was one day later, for after eight days is not the same as on the eighth day." But once more they are refuted by Scripture: the Oriental way of counting time is by taking the day of departure as the first day. One week after date, which we would call seven days later, the Oriental calls eight days later. That "after eight days" means the same as "on the eighth day" appears from Mark 8:31. ". . . and after three days rise again," and Mark 9:31, ". . . he shall rise the third day" (A.V.).
It deserves attention, in this connection, that, while the women, still under the O.T. dispensation, counted the day from sunset to sunset, the N.T. immediately begins to count the day from midnight to midnight: Matthew 28:1.
11. The assertion of S.D.A. that "the Lord's Day" means Saturday because Jesus said, "The Son of man is Lord even of the sabbath" (Mark 2:28), refutes itself. Jesus said only this that, as David could do certain things, under certain circumstances, that were contrary to the commandment, so could He as Lord of all things including the Sabbath day.
Already the *Didache* and Ignatius refer to Sunday as "the Lord's Day."

of promise that which was to become real in time of fulfilment, i.e., the present time," says a commentator. So the circumcision of the flesh was a "shadow," of which the circumcision of the heart is the "body," according to the context, verses 11-13. And this same thought is applied to the Sabbath.

7. In accordance with this New Testament teaching and example, S.D.A. has not an atom of evidence for calling the Lord's Day "the pope's day." If some pope finally made Sunday observance the legally recognized thing, this no more proves that before this day the Sabbath was not kept on Sunday than the formulation of the Church's faith at Nicea in 325 proves that the Church did not believe in the true deity of Christ until 325.

8. Consequently, the early writings of Church Fathers contain a large number of references to Sunday as the Sabbath day observed in their time. And these citations, which one may find in many pamphlets dealing with the issue, range all the way from *The Epistle of Barnabas* (A.D. 100) to Eusebius (A.D. 324). And these quotations show that at first the Church observed both days, Saturday and Sunday (just as at first the Jewish church kept circumcision and baptism), but gradually it was realized that the one had come in the place of the other.

9. We confidently return, therefore, to the Synod of Dordt. We are in great danger today of losing the Sabbath which was made for man at the dawn of creation. Sports, joy riding, and frivolity take the place of worship with increasing thousands. Churches stand desolate throughout the country. Should we at such a time endeavor to divide the Christian community even more than it already is divided? As it is, there are only two things which all Christians reverence together, to wit, The Book and The Day. Said the Synod of Dordt:

"There is in the Fourth Commandment of the Divine Law a ceremonial and an ethical element. The ceremonial element was the rest on the Seventh day after Creation, and the strict observance of that day imposed especially upon the Jewish people. The moral element lies in the fact that a certain definite day is appropriated for religion, and that for that purpose, as much rest as is needful for religion and its hallowed contemplation is demanded. The Sabbath of the Jews having been abolished, the Day of the Lord must be solemnly hallowed by the Christians. The day, since the times of the Apostles, has already been observed by the primitive Catholic Church."

Conclusion

S.D.A. has other strange teachings, such as the peculiar view that "during the whole period of the millennium the world is without inhabitants" and Satan will be "confined to a desolate earth for one thousand years." Such queer doctrines, like those of soulsleep and annihilation of the wicked, are arrived at by the simple process of quoting one or two texts without making the slightest effort to view them in the light of other passages; in other words are due to lack of systematic insight. But we prefer to pass by some of these things, and to give, by way of conclusion, an evaluation of S.D.A.

There is much in S.D.A. that is praiseworthy.

(1) Seventh-Day Adventists are doing a great work for the improvement of public health, through their magazine *Life and Health,* their sanatoria, and their medical missions throughout the world.

(2) They maintain free Christian schools in which they educate their children all the way from the kindergarten through college.

(3) They maintain and teach many cardinal Christian doctrines that are foreign to the other cults dealt with in this volume.

(4) They fight successfully for the sanctity of the home, the family, and marriage, and oppose worldliness in theater attendance, dancing, card-playing, and lodge membership.

(5) They put most, if not all, other Christians to shame by their very large per capita financial giving. Not only are they all tithers (even the Mormons here put Christians to

shame), their tithes going toward the support of their own churches, but on top of that they give huge sums of money for missionary work.

It may therefore be asked (as Seventh-Day Adventists ask) why this chapter should be included in a book dealing with isms of a so much more serious nature?

To this the answer is twofold.

First, Seventh-Day Adventists are asking for it. They are not as innocent as they want us to believe when they complain because of our attack. *They* are the ones who began the attack upon all other churches.

Nor are they always consistent in their complaint. Thus it will not do for officials of this church to invite the present writer to forget about Mrs. White and to read current S.D.A. publications, while these same current publications state, "For her emphasis of Bible truth, for her application of specific doctrines, for her simplification of the deep things of God . . . the S.D.A. denomination and the world in general owe a great debt to Ellen G. White."

Moreover: look at the flimsy ground S.D.A. has for following Ellen G. White's hallucination of the Fourth Commandment surrounded by a halo of light, and building upon that a system of theology and a church; compare with that the firm basis for Sabbath observance on the first day which the Church has always found in the New Testament —then turn to the Venden brothers, S.D.A. evangelists, unfolding their banners one after another, and arousing a vast audience into a mob frenzy, repeating: "Is Sunday worship from God?" "No-o-o-o!" "Is it from the pope?" "Yeah!" "Is it of the devil?" "YEAH! !"

Are such methods of "evangelization" Christian? Do they accord with the Godliness these "wonderful people" (H. F. Brown) possess and desire to be credited with?

The methods whereby S.D.A. tries to gain adherents at the expense of churches which hold to all the essentials of Christianity to which S.D.A. confesses plus the ones they deny or distort, are contrary to the many good points S.D.A. reveals.

SEVENTH-DAY ADVENTISM

Secondly: the sin of schism, of causing Christendom to lie divided before a paganizing world, is far from innocent. Until recently the Christian Church has always had two things on which all agreed: the Book and the Day. S.D.A. wants to change all that. By its opposition to Sunday laws, and the like, it not only plays into the hands of the devil; it aids in breaking down the influence of the Church upon the world; it brings into disregard the very Sabbath for which it claims to have a respect that has not been shown these eighteen or nineteen hundred years. Surely, this is a zeal without knowledge. Let, therefore, S.D.A. abandon the rambling writings of a woman who suffered from a serious malady, and return to the voice of Barnabas, of Ignatius, of Augustine, of Luther, Calvin, Bunyan, and all the other great Christians to which Ellen G. White so often refers in her books.

Above all, let them return to the New Testament, which states that:

1. Jesus rose from the dead on the first day of the week (John 20:1).

2. Jesus appeared to ten of His disciples on that first day of the week (John 20:19).

3. Jesus waited one week, and on the next first day of the week appeared to the eleven disciples (John 20:26).

4. The promised coming of the Holy Spirit was fulfilled on the first day of the week—on the day of Pentecost, which by law came on the first day of the week (Lev. 23:16).

5. On that same first day of the week the first gospel sermon on the death and resurrection of Jesus was preached by the apostle Peter (Acts 2:14).

6. On that first day of the week the three thousand converts were united into the first New Testament *ecclesia* (Acts 2:41).

7. On that same first day of the week the rite of Christian baptism into the Name of the Father, Son, and Holy Spirit was administered for the first time (Acts 2:41).

8. At Troas the Christians assembled for worship on the first day of the week (Acts 20:7).

9. At Troas Paul preached to the assembled Christians on the first day of the week (Acts 20:6, 7).

10. Paul instructed the Christians at Corinth to make contributions on the first day of the week (I Cor. 16:2).[12]

11. On the first day of the week Christ came to the apostle John on Patmos (Rev. 1:10).

A Dutch theologian has well expressed this truth as follows:

"Do you desire to know, O man, where the sabbath is, ask where Christ is; you will find him in the midst of Christians on the first day of the week, and not in the midst of Jews on the last. For where Christ is in the midst, there is the sabbath day. And this fact, that Christ is in the midst of His people on the sabbath, makes the day a day of spiritual rejoicing which leaves all the holydays and other days of the week far behind. Here all questions as to what we may do and what we must omit, those painful questions, drop away. Do we not limit ourselves upon a feast day to the most necessary labor? . . . Thus the commandment to rest becomes within us a desire to rest, and an example of the Sabbath of the age to come, a Sabbath that will be without evening."[13]

Finally: the writer regrets to state that a renewed study of the tenets and the methods of S.D.A. has accentuated rather than lessened his conviction that S.D.A. — although its adherents are clearly sincere, and many Christians are among them — as a movement is dangerous.

This conclusion is based upon the following two facts:

1. In its zeal for the seventh day S.D.A. goes far beyond the limits of sound and sober sense. Should, to put the

---

12. Leaflet "Why We Observe the First Day of the Week for Worship." (Lord's Day Alliance of the United States, 156 Fifth Ave., New York, N. Y. 35c per hundred, $1.50 per 500).

It is noteworthy that the word *kuriake*, "Lord's," became the recognized word for Sunday in Christian Greek usage; and it is today, in modern Greek, the word for Sunday. —W. D. Chamberlain in *Presbyterian Life*, Vol. 6, No. 4.

13. J. Van Andel, *Vademecum Pastorale*, p. 175.

matter in reverse, S.D.A. have remained satisfied to hold to its own peculiar view of the sabbath, we as fellow Christians would say, "We regret it, but the Lord will decide the matter. Salvation does not depend upon it." S.D.A., however, in its official periodicals denounces other Christians in language such as the following:

"But what the forces of tyranny really want in this country is religious favoritism and monopoly for a certain group of religionists. They would have their particular brand of religion taught in the public schools, regardless of the rights of other citizens. They would have their particular day of rest enforced upon the nation by state, federal, and municipal laws, instead of leaving the people free to rest in accordance with the dictates of their own consciences. Little by little ecclesiastical combines are bringing pressure to bear upon the powers that be to regulate the religious life of the American people in conformity to the dictates of a so-called religious majority.[14]

"When the American patriots divorced church matters from civil government in this country, they planted the standard of religious freedom upon the solid rock of eternal truth. The majority of the people, in so far as religion is concerned, are not in the right. 'For wide is the gate, and broad is the way, that leadeth to destruction, and many there be which go in thereat: because strait is the gate and narrow the way, which leadeth unto life, and few there be that find it.' Matt. 7:13, 14."[15]

How can we escape the conclusion that these lines imply:

(a) That all who stood and stand for Sunday observance and "hallowing" of the day are tyrants and opponents of religious liberty, including those authors of liberty so much praised in this same paragraph (they certainly enforced Sabbath observance on Sunday);

---

14. "Seventh-day Adventists in Minneapolis have gone on record as 'unalterably opposed' to revival of Sunday closing laws on federal, state, county, or municipal levels" (*Christian Century*, May 6, 1959).

15. *Liberty*. A Magazine of Religious Freedom, Vol. 41, No. 3, third quarter, 1946, p. 16.

(b That as soon as there is a small minority with peculiar views of the Sabbath, the state must abandon all its efforts altogether to make the national life at least outwardly Christian;

(c) That those who observe the Sabbath day on the first day of the week are headed for destruction.

The latter opinion is expressed in many ways in many S.D.A. publications. It is rather preposterous and arrogant.

But this is as nothing when compared with the following.

2. S.D.A., in making salvation dependent upon keeping the law (especially, of course, its own interpretation of the Fourth Commandment), returns to Judaism, not to the pure Old Testament religion, but to that false religion of autosoterism known as Judaism. S.D.A. wants to teach salvation by divine grace apart from added works.[15] Like all evangelical Christians Seventh-Day Adventists state that God's saving grace renews man so as to write the law upon his heart. Well and good. From it follows that the keeping of the law is not necessary unto salvation, but rather is an inevitable result of salvation. It follows also that when two groups of Christians find themselves in disagreement on a minor point of that law, they cannot be lost when they live in accordance with the light that is theirs. But S.D.A. reverses its professed faith in salvation without works when it writes:

> "Sanctification is a definite and all-important part of redemption.... God's true sabbath, the seventh day of the week, is declared to be the sign of sanctification in these words ... Exodus 31:13 and Ezekiel 20:12."[16]
>
> "Yes, the test will come on the question of obedience to the commandments of God.... What we need to remember as we approach the final test is that God will mete out just rewards.... Then if we are faithful to the end, even though we may have to make the supreme sacrifice in order to maintain our loyalty to God, we shall awake to hear His melodious voice saying: 'Well

---

15. See *The Ministry*, Vol. 19, No. 6, May, 1946, pp. 3-6.
16. E. J. Salde, *The Way of Life*, 1929, p. 76.

done... enter thou into the joy of thy Lord.' Such will be the reward of all who successfully pass the final test."[17]

Evangelist D. E. Venden in his mimeographed lectures even refers to refusal to observe the seventh day as "the unpardonable sin," with reference to Matthew 12:32 and Hebrews 6:4.

From this wrong emphasis follow two things:

(a) That S.D.A. requires for baptism a confession that the S.D.A. Church "is the remnant Church" (excluding all others!); and

(b) That S.D.A. falls under the condemnation of Paul to the Galatians: "Behold, I Paul say unto you that, if ye receive circumcision, Christ will profit you nothing." With this last statement, however, we do not condemn individual men (we are not inspired as was Paul), but the system to which they adhere.

And So On, *Ad Infinitum*

Quite a stir was caused in 1956 and 1957 when the Takoma Park men shouted from the housetops that two evangelicals, Donald Grey Barnhouse and W. R. Martin, after prolonged study of, and several days' visit with, S.D.A. leaders and libraries, had reached the conclusion that S.D.A. henceforth should be ranked among the essentially orthodox, that is, evangelical churches. Quotations from writers of a former age who had stated that S.D.A. "rings as true as steel" on all major doctrines, were added to boastful threats that hereafter evangelicals had better beware before condemning any longer these "wonderful people of the Lord."

Rebuttal, however, came quickly and decisively, as one after another of the evangelical defenders of the faith rejected both the Barnhouse and Martin articles in *Eternity* magazine and maintained that S.D.A. has neither (1) denounced its pseudo-prophetess Ellen G. White, nor (2) re-

---

17. *Signs of the Times*, Dec. 24, 1946, p. 12.

canted any of its false doctrines, nor (3) renounced its age-old exclusion from the Kingdom — whether now or ultimately—of all who do not accept its tenets. For a partial list of writers during that time of confusion, see my *Christianity Versus the Cults* (pp. 100-102).

Subsequent publications from Takoma Park have surely corroborated the view of the vast majority of evangelicals. As one major example we may cite the book *Seventh-Day Adventists Answer Questions on Doctrine, an Explanation of Certain Major Aspects of Seventh-Day Adventist Belief* (Review and Herald Publ. Assoc., Washington, D. C., 1957).

This book of 720 pages contains a great deal of double talk, of granting with the one hand and taking back with the other. Like all S.D.A. publications it persistently refuses to reply to evangelical assertions and quotations which prove that the first day was substituted for the seventh day at an early date in the Church's history.

Worse than that, the system's advocates here continue to mix the doctrine of free grace with the claim that some day, no one knows how soon, "The Church of the Remnant" will consist of those who obey the Ten Commandments (emphasis upon the fourth commandment, taken literally) and who adhere to the entire "Health Reform Program" of S.D.A.; and that apart from this there will be no salvation. Witness only the following quotation:

"To your inquiry, then, as to whether Mrs. White maintained that all those who do not see and observe the seventh day as the Sabbath *now* have the 'mark of the beast,' the answer is definitely NO.

"We hold the firm conviction that millions of devout Christians of all faiths throughout all past centuries, as well as those today who sincerely trust in Christ their Saviour for salvation and are following Him according to their best light, are unquestionably saved. . . .

"Seventh-Day Adventists interpret the prophecies relating to the beast, and the reception of his work, as something that will come into sharp focus just before the return of the Lord in glory. It is our understanding that this issue will then become a worldwide test" (pp. 184-185).

It should be at once evident that such a halfhearted admission accounts for much of the two-faced attitude of S.D.A. ministers towards Christians in other denominations.

(1) They admit that others may be Christians, and can be worked with as such (in Ministerial Associations, for example); nevertheless they hold that sooner or later all must be made to see their errors and conform to the S.D.A. program, or be eternally lost.

(2) They believe it is all right to collect money from "other Christians" by house-to-house canvassing, and to advertise later that these gifts came from the Lord's people, that is, S.D.A.

(3) They think it is legitimate, even wise, to refrain from announcing the source of the radio program "The Voice of Prophecy" and the TV broadcast "Faith for Today," since there is, after all, only one true form of Christianity, and all are headed in the direction of S.D.A. That they do not hesitate to camouflage their propaganda may also be seen in the fact that their latest publication, *Seventh-Day Adventists, Faith in Action,* was written by a "non-Adventist" and published by Vantage Press, not by their own enormous publishing facilities.

Finally, a recent convert from S.D.A. to the Baptist Church writes, with ample quotations from authentic S.D.A. sources, that in publications intended for intramural purposes (for S.D.A. workers, etc.), the stress upon the necessity of unanimity in S.D.A. in belief ("We stand with the pioneers. . . . We need no new doctrines") is far more emphatic than in publications intended for purposes of propaganda. This author was himself converted, together with his wife, by an earnest and prayerful reading of the

Bible itself, without "inspired" comments and additions by S. D. A., especially his reading of the Epistle to the Hebrews, chapter 10:12 in particular. He maintains that because of their belief in salvation by grace alone, apart from works of legalism, many prominent S.D.A. adherents have been expelled or have voluntarily withdrawn, and that in his country there are hundreds whose eyes are being opened to the truth and who have turned away from S.D.A.[18]

Aids to Study

1. Where lies the origin of the entire Adventist error?
2. On which four points does S.D.A. differ from the accepted Christian teaching?
3. What is the correct interpretation of Daniel 8:14?
4. Whom did the two goats of Leviticus 16 represent, and how?
5. What is your understanding of the two beasts in Revelation 13? Does it accord with Mrs. White's ideas?
6. Point out the S.D.A. errors concerning the atonement. Reason from Scripture as to the real character of atonement. What do you think of the custom of reading it as "at-one-ment"? What sort of people do this?
7. What do you consider the best approach to the seventh-day position?
8. Does the Sabbath commandment belong to the ceremonial law or to the moral law? Has it been canceled for New Testament times?
9. Is S.D.A. consistent in applying the letter to the Fourth Commandment?
10. What does the New Testament mean by "the Lord's day"?
11. Is S.D.A. in line with other evangelical groups, or is it a divisive force?
12. What is your main objection to the propaganda of this group?

---

18. G. L. Crosbie, "S.D.A. in New Zeeland and Australia" in *The Sunday School Times*, Dec. 20, 1958.

13

THE JEHOVAH'S WITNESSES

The origin of the Russell-Rutherford-Knorr theology, especially of its eschatology, lies in Seventh-day Adventism. This was asserted in *The Chaos of Cults* in 1929, hotly disclaimed by LeRoy E. Froom, and has since been reaffirmed by Lehman Strauss, F. E. Mayer, and E. C. Gruss.

Charles Taze Russell, perturbed by his Scotch-Irish Presbyterian legacy of the doctrine of eternal punishment, was "converted" to the doctrine of the Adventists, and joined them. Afterward differences arose on Biblical interpretation, especially on the manner and object of the Lord's return, although the chronology was left intact. Russell collaborated with the Adventist N. H. Barbour, the two publishing a book together; a year later, in 1878, they parted because they disagreed on the atonement. Russell then launched in 1879 his *Zion's Watchtower and Herald of Christ's Presence*.

Gruss mentions in addition to Adventism the following sources of Russellism: Arius, Socinus, Swedenborg, Unitarianism, Christadelphianism. Similarly some earlier students of Mormonism maintained that this system had borrowed from Christianity, Judaism, Mohammedanism, Fetishism, Buddhism, Manicheism, Communism, etc. The present writer, however, questions whether the early leaders of either Mormonism or Jehovah's Witnesses possessed a sufficient theological background for such plagiarism. He prefers to think that, after all, Satan and his "host of wickedness in the heavenly places" (Eph. 6:12) are of finite, that is, limited inventive genius. Over against the teachings of Scripture the same errors and heresies are bound to recur from time to time.

In the course of their eighty-year history the Witnesses have changed their teachings considerably, and they have accredited this to "progressive revelation," which they understand to be new light on the understanding of the revelation finished in the Bible. The orthodox conception of progressive revelation is that there is progress from Genesis to the Apocalypse: the bud gradually opened into a full-grown flower. Gruss says of such "progressive revelation" of the Witnesses: "Most of such revelation is very subjective."[1] W. J. Schnell reports that "as a progressive light worshipper and Jehovah's Witness in good standing, I had observed the Watchtower magazine change our doctrines between 1917 and 1928, no less than 148 times."[2] Russell himself boldly stated that it would be better to read his six-volume *Studies in the Scriptures* than to read the Bible by itself.[3] Yet, in later years, he called some of his earlier writings "immature."

The early Church, realizing that inspiration ended with the Apocalypse and looking for the illumination of the Holy Spirit, was more patient and deliberate in formulating the doctrines of Scripture; and, once having done so in the great Creeds, it did not alter these afterward.

We may add here that when an infallible and inspired character is ascribed to purely human documents, the invariable result is that such writings supersede and supplant the Scriptures. This has been the case with the Roman Catholic "tradition," the *Book of Mormon,* and *Science and Health with Key to the Scriptures;* and it holds again for the endless stream of Russellite literature that leaves the Witnesses no chance to read the Bible with any sort

---

1. Gruss, *Apostles of Denial*, unpublished dissertation, Talbot Theological Seminary, 1961, p. 55.
2. *Into the Light of Christianity*, p. 13.
3. We need not repeat here our refutation of *The Watchtower's* accusation that the author had made himself guilty of transgressing the ninth commandment with this assertion. See the third edition of *The Chaos of Cults*, 1960, p. 269.

JEHOVAH'S WITNESSES

of independence. For an account of this "brainwashing" see the books of Schnell listed in the Bibliography.

Of late years the history of Russellism has been written so often that this textbook on many cults can afford to be very brief in presenting that history.

The History of the Movement

There is a reciprocity between a man's character and his theology. St. Paul teaches in Romans 9:19, 20 that a bad theology proceeds from a bad heart.

Charles Taze Russell was in frequent clash with the courts, and he did not always come out of these ordeals unscathed. He perjured himself in court, and his wife was given a decree of divorce because the Judge of the High Court of Ontario opined that no woman of ordinary sensibility could live with a man of so much egotism and arrogance. Russell thought nothing of hurling wholesale condemnation at the ministers of "600 warring denominations" in China at a mass meeting in the New York hippodrome, only to admit under duress that he had met none of them during his hurried trip to the Orient. He was charged by *The Brooklyn Eagle* with the practice of fraud. He induced sick people to make over their fortunes to his organizations, while vehemently condemning the clergy for taking up collections in their churches.

So it went continually, until on November 9, 1916, the "pastor" died aboard a transcontinental train. His friend, Mr. Menta Sturgeon, following his request, wrapped him in a bed sheet, which was to resemble "a Roman toga," and and then called the conductor and the porter with the words, "I want you to see how a great man of God can die." But there was nothing in the bed sheet but an elderly man "whose lips did not complain, nor heave a sigh."

This dubious tribute is from the funeral oration by Joseph Franklin Rutherford, who immediately took steps to succeed the deceased. Rutherford, a lawyer and a special judge in the absence of the regular judge of the Eighth Judicial Circuit Court of Boonville, Missouri, prior to 1909, had moved to New York, and was unanimously chosen on January 6, 1917, to succeed Pastor Russell as President of the Watch Tower Bible and Tract Society. This position he held until his death, January 8, 1942, at the age of 72.

Of the period of Rutherford the following features are noteworthy:

(1) The Judge outdid even the Pastor in the volume of his literary output. He wrote a book a year, plus numerous articles for the *Watchtower* and *The Golden Age* (later named *Consolation*, and since 1946, *Awake!*), and successive editions of the *Yearbook of Jehovah's Witnesses*.

(2) The Judge, together with some of his staff, spent nine months in jail because of alleged "unamerican activities" at the beginning of America's entrance into the first world war. This was about as unwarranted as had been the murder of "Joseph Smith and his brother Hyrum, Martyrs." It only resulted in the exoneration of these Bible students, and in an increased hatred on their part of "the devil's organization."

(3) Upon coming out of the penitentiary the Judge found his presidency encumbered by inward dissension and outward persecution. Several splits occurred, the dissenters continuing under various names. It was because of this that on October 9, 1931, at the Annual Convention at Columbus, Ohio, the present name of Jehovah's Witnesses was adopted. Within twenty years this name crowded out every other name for these people.

(4) Rutherford, although a very different personality than Russell — more aloof, outwardly cold, and unapproachable — equaled the founder not only as a writer but also as an organizer and administrator. Wrote Marley Cole, "The greatest triumph of Judge Rutherford's career was to see the organization expand, coalesce, and keep on through

everything, despite the devastating attacks on it of the Fascists, the Nazis, and democratic mobocracies."[4]

Rutherford, six feet four inches tall, was seldom seen in public. When he did appear he was accompanied by two bodyguards, and all were armed with canes to ward off attacks by representatives of the devil's organization.

(5) Admittedly Judge Rutherford and his younger aid, the Texas lawyer Hayden Covington, rendered the cause of religious freedom a major service by winning 46 cases in the U.S. Supreme Court, 150 in State Supreme Courts, plus several in Canada and 22 other countries (up to 1950).[5] At the same time it must be granted that the Witnesses have been to a large extent the cause of their many troubles. They have openly heaped contempt upon a great number of people and institutions in their writings and street meetings, and have attacked with vituperation all who do not agree with them.

Rutherford was at once succeeded by Nathan Homer Knorr as president of the organization. During Knorr's administration the endless books and booklets have appeared under the copyright of the Watchtower Bible and Tract Society, without bearing the name of individual authors. A "committee" is now responsible for the mass of printed matter that leaves the "Central Printing Plant" at Brooklyn, New York.

Besides numerous pamphlets, the standard periodicals are *The Watchtower,* "announcing Jehovah's Kingdom" (3,800,000 copies), and *Awake!* (3,250,000 copies), both semi-monthlies. Their most recent bound books are: *Let God Be True* (1st edition, 10,524,830 copies; 2nd ed., 1952, 6,778,000 copies, printed in fifty languages); *Let Your Name Be Sanctified* (1st ed., 1961, 1,000,000 copies); *Your Will Be Done on Earth* ("based on Daniel's prophecy"); *The New World Translation of the Holy Scriptures* (referred to as "NW" and published in 1955), which does

---
4. Cole, *Jehovah's Witnesses,* 2nd ed., p. 107.
5. Cole, *op. cit.,* Ch. 7.

not only substitute "the torture stake" for the Cross of Christ, but in many other respects reveals its bias and prejudice against terminology reminiscent of the central Christian doctrines.

Organization and Propaganda

Nathan H. Knorr opens his essay on "Jehovah's Witnesses of Modern Times" with the statement, "Jehovah God is the Founder and Organizer of his witnesses on earth."[6] The name is said to be suggested by Isaiah 43:10 (ASV), "Ye are my witnesses, saith Jehovah." The first witnesses were Abel, Enoch, Noah, etc., through John the Baptist. "Christ Jesus was himself the 'faithful and true witness, the beginning of the creation of God,' and takes preeminence among all the Witnesses." "This chief witness designated others to continue Kingdom testimony, saying, 'Ye shall be witnesses unto me . . . unto the uttermost part of the earth.'"

The clear shift from the command to be Jehovah's witnesses to "my witnesses" in Acts 1:8 is ignored because to note this change to "the only name under heaven that is given among men wherein they must be saved," would be to put our Lord Jesus Christ on a footing of equality with Jehovah. All witnesses were and are Jehovah's witnesses, Jesus Christ being only one among many, albeit the chief witness. All witness is in order to vindicate the name of Jehovah.

The modern organization of Jehovah's Witnesses began in 1879, five years after Russell and his associates inaugurated a thorough study of the Bible, particularly the Christ's second coming and millennial reign. In July, 1879, the first issue of *The Watchtower* appeared. Tract distribution played an important role in the early stages, and as the breach between the Witnesses and the orthodox denominations of Christendom became apparent, the 161-page

---

6. *Religion in the Twentieth Century*, edited by Vergilius Ferm, pp. 381-392.

book *Food for Thinking Christians* was published in 1881. In 1884 the society was incorporated as a religious nonprofit organization. The charter name, Zion's Watch Tower Tract Society, continued till 1896, when it was changed to Watchtower Bible and Tract Society. In 1886 the first of Russell's *Studies in the Scriptures, the Divine Plan of the Ages*, appeared; the seventh volume, *The Finished Mystery*, was released in 1917, at the beginning of Rutherford's tenure of office.

Since the beginning of Rutherford's presidency the training of all Witnesses has been stressed. At the Watchtower Bible School of Gilead, South Lansing, N. Y., hundreds of Witnesses are annually trained in courses comprising a few months of study to become ordained ministers, who, as such, claim exemption from military service. The Witnesses resent being called pacifists; they assert that they are conscientious objectors. Their argument is that "when Satan fights Satan" in a war of one political government against another, Jehovah's Witnesses can afford to remain neutral, as they are looking forward to the only vital war that concerns them — the battle of Armageddon, when Jehovah will destroy all His enemies and will lead His Witnesses safely through.

All Witnesses are trained for testimony by means of concerted Bible study in "Kingdom Halls" on Sundays, in "Area book studies" on Fridays, in "District Assemblies" and in the "Divine Will International Assembly of Jehovah's Witnesses." The Assembly of 1958 had an attendance of 253,922 on the final day.

Schnell reports a Seven Step Program of Indoctrination. This begins with getting books into the hands of a prospect, continues through "the back call," book study, attendance at a Kingdom Hall, attending service meetings, and becoming active in publishing (that is, passing out books and tracts), and baptism.

In order to discharge these duties the more effectively

the Witnesses use two 384-page books which give instruction in personal testimony, *Theocratic Aid to Kingdom Publishers* and *Equipped for Every Good Work*. Schnell reports that the Witnesses are under constant duress and in mortal fear lest, by selling an insufficient amount of literature, they shall be relegated to the "evil servant class."

Russell proclaimed himself "the faithful and wise servant" of Luke 12:42. After his death there was substituted for this "the faithful and wise servant class," the "little flock" to total only 144,000. Of this "mystery class," according to Rutherford there were about 50,000 still living on earth in 1926.

These alone will be rewarded "as priests and kings" with Christ in heaven. They alone, therefore, need to be born anew. They will form the body, of which Christ is the head. "For the others, a crowd unlimited by number, belief in the ransom will lead to everlasting life in a righteous, paradise earth — Luke 12:32; Revelation 20:6, John 10:16."[7]

The above leads us to a brief review of the teachings of the Witnesses. Before doing so, however, we add one more word of commendation. It has been stated above that the Witnesses have rendered a valiant service in defending the right of free expression of religious opinion and of assembling together. To this we now add a word of praise for the Witnesses' stand in regard to blood transfusion.

Blood Transfusion

In 1961 The Watchtower Bible and Tract Society published a 63-page booklet under the title *Blood, Medicine and the Law of God*. It is a plea for their position against blood transfusion instead of, or after, surgery. This position has again brought the Witnesses in conflict with the courts, as, earlier in their history, they ran afoul of public opinion in their refusal to render military service, to

---

7. *Awake!*, October 8, 1961, p. 26.

salute the flag (considered by them an act of idolatry,[8]) and in other matters.

We hold the exegetical grounds upon which the Witnesses reject and oppose blood transfusion to be erroneous. The booklet refers to Genesis 9:3, 4; Leviticus 3:17 and 13:14, and 17:10; to Deuteronomy 12:23-25; I Samuel 14:32, 33; and to Acts 15:28, 29.

All of these passages forbid the eating of flesh with the blood, some also with the fat. When we look at them a little closer we soon discover why. The fat was to be burned on the altar as belonging to God. The blood, since it contained *the life* or *the soul* (the translations differ, but this is immaterial, since the life is in the soul which is in the blood), also belonged to Jehovah, not to man. In some cases, this blood was to be poured out upon the ground, as a mere giving back to God the life that was His, as in Deuteronomy 12:24; in other cases the blood was to be poured out upon the altar, in lieu of the sinner's own life, "for it is the blood that maketh atonement by reason of the life [Hebrew *soul*]" (Lev. 17:11, ASV).

The Witnesses, rejecting the Scriptural doctrine of the atonement (see below), have here substituted the fancy that when we donate or receive blood, we give away or accept a portion of the human soul. This, they say, is contrary to the command to love God with all the soul, as it is also in conflict with loving another as ourselves.

That this is untenable appears at once from the fact that we can all do without part of our blood and for a season, without impairing our physical life. A man whose leg has been amputated does not therefore have less of a soul, nor has he lost part of his life. This is completely evident and refutes the exegesis of the booklet.

However, the booklet opens with the statement that the practice of giving blood transfusions has "increased tenfold in the last decade, over fiftyfold since 1938. According to the president of the American Association of

---

8. *Let God Be True*, p. 242.

Blood Banks, in the United States alone there are five million blood transfusions in a year."

There follows such an impressive array of well-documented statements by highly creditable medical authorities pointing to the danger of indiscriminate blood transfusion, that the medical profession will do well to give due attention to this matter. Blood transfusion is a comparatively new phenomenon. The booklet substantiates that it is quite possible that the patient may contact unknown and dangerous maladies from the blood pumped into his veins. It also shows that in many cases some bloodless manner of coping with the disease has proved not only less dangerous but fully successful.

We do not, then, subscribe to the wholesale condemnation of the medical method of transfusing blood, but hold to the contrary that in very many cases it has undoubtedly warded off aggravation of disease and prolonged life without harm to either donors or receivers.

But we agree with the Witnesses that if someone objects to the process, either because he is unwilling to take the physical risk, or because of religious scruples, no human court has the moral right to force him to submit contrary to his own conscientious convictions, or to subject his child to this particular treatment. Education is one thing, force is quite another. Our children belong not to the State, but to their parents.

Doctrine

For all such reasons it is all the more lamentable that the Jehovah's Witnesses continue to propagate, with a zeal worthy of a better cause, their thoroughly unbiblical doctrine, and to disseminate a deadly hatred against all the Christian churches and what they stand for.

The teachings of the Witnesses have been correctly called a system of denials. To prove this will constitute the remaining part of this chapter. However, it should be borne in mind that this is not a book on systematic (or dogmatic) theology; hence our refutation will be brief and incomplete.

Rationalism

The fundamental error of Russellism, which continues to be promulgated by the Jehovah's Witnesses, is its stark rationalism. Schnell may exaggerate when he says that the Witnesses appeal to only 6½ percent of Scripture; it is nevertheless true that they, in spite of their repeated appeal to the Scriptures as the inspired message from God, place their reason above the Bible, and reject whatever is found in Scripture contrary to the human reason. This fault is fundamental, and lies at the root of all their denials.

Wrote Russell: "We have endeavored to uncover enough of the foundation upon which all faith should be built — the Word of God — to give confidence and assurance in its testimony, even to the unbeliever. And we have endeavored to do this in a manner that will appeal to and can be accepted by reason as a foundation. Then we have endeavored to build upon that foundation the teachings of Scripture in such a manner that, as far as possible, purely human judgment may try its squares and angles by the most exacting rules of justice which it can command." — Introduction to the *Studies in the Scriptures*.

Then, after stating that the Bible is a revelation from God, he adds, "Let us examine the character of the writings claimed as inspired, to see whether their teachings correspond with the character we have reasonably interpreted to God."

It should be evident that the very idea of divine revelation to imperfect (sinful) men implies that it contains things that the human mind could not conceive without revelation. The very character of unbelief lies in this that the mind rejects that which it cannot, unaided — reasonably — accept.

The Trinity

The Trinity is denied in virtually all their writings, and in most opprobrious terms. "The plain truth is that this is another of Satan's attempts to keep God-fearing persons from learning the truth of Jehovah and his Son, Christ Jesus. No, there is no trinity."[9]

This cardinal Scriptural doctrine is generally grossly misrepresented and falsely stated by the Witnesses. Although the magazine *Awake!* for October 8, 1961, quotes from the Westminster Confession of Faith: "In the unity of the Godhead there be three persons, of one substance, power and eternity, God the Father, God the Son, and God the Holy Ghost," and from the Augsburg Confession: "There is one divine essence which is called and is God ... yet there are three persons of the same essence and power, who are also co-eternal, the Father, the Son, and the Holy Ghost" — yet most Russellite writings speak far more disparagingly of this precious doctrine. Even *Let God Be True* states on page 100, "The doctrine, in brief, is that there are three gods in one: 'God the Father, God the Son, and God the Holy Ghost,' all three equal in power, substance, and eternity." And, on page 107: "The general thought about the 'Holy Ghost' is that it is a spirit person of the 'Trinity' and equal with God and Christ in power, substance and eternity." Yet these distortions are not nearly as bad as the enormity of one H. E. Pennock of New York City, "regularly assigned to the staff of I.B.S.A. (International Bible Student Association) Lecturers," whose lecture on "Things the Clergy Never Tells" was advertised on a handbill as follows:

"There are some clergymen, no doubt, who are really sincere in thinking that Jesus was his own father, and the Almighty is the son of Himself; and that each of these is a third person who is the same as the other two, and yet different from them."

---

9. *Let God Be True*, 2nd ed., p. 111.

Christ Jesus

When we inquire why the Russellites are so venomously opposed to the doctrine of the Trinity, we need not seek far for an answer. There is not a single Jehovah's Witness who knows himself as a lost sinner in need of a supernatural Savior. Hence this system denies the deity of Christ as vehemently as it does the Trinity.

Pre-existence

"Happily *The New World Translation of the Christian Greek Scriptures* renders John 1:1, 2: 'Originally the Word was, and the Word was with God, and the Word was a god. Thus the Word or Logos came into being long before one of God's later creatures made a devil out of himself. . . .'" — *Let God Be True*, p. 33.

"The chief one of God's creatures under Him is his son who came to earth and took the name Jesus. The Bible shows that this One had lived as a spirit creature in heaven before coming to earth." — *This Good News of the Kingdom*, 1954, p. 6.

This spirit, or archangel, the Word, then, became a man, lived a sinless life, died a ransom for many, was raised a spirit.

Resurrection and Ascension

"Dematerializing his assumed human body and returning to his invisible spirit state, Jesus in his ascension ran no risks to his life such as from radiation belts around the earth or cosmic rays in outer space. While he did not ascend to heaven in the human body that he had sacrificed and that he left forever upon God's altar, he did return to heaven with the merit or value of his human life that he had laid down for dying mankind." — *Let Your Name Be Sanctified*, p. 272.

Second Coming

"Jesus Christ returns, not again as a human, but as a glorious spirit person. He is now the reflection of God's glory, the exact representation of God's very being, and he is seated on the right hand of the Majesty on high. . . . He comes, therefore, not in the likeness of men, but in his heavenly glory." — *Let God Be True*, p. 196.

It should be evident that all this is contrary to the plain statements of Scripture, such as Philippians 2:6, and Acts 1:11.

Lest we become too lengthy, we must here summarize as follows: Christ, according to the Witnesses, returned in 1914, "the time of the end of the Gentiles," and in 1918 came to His "Temple," the 144,000 with whom He forms "The Church," He the head and they the body.

The Ransom

The ransom theory of the Witnesses amounts, briefly stated, to this: The sinless man Jesus gave his life a "ransom," that is, "that which loosens, or releases, providing deliverance." Man was in need of a ransom because he was born sinful, imperfect, and under the sentence of death.

This ransom does not include Adam because he sinned willfully. But it is for all "faithful men," whose "course" determines that they will ultimately receive benefit from the sacrifice of Christ. The willfully wicked do not share in the ransom, but "he that exerciseth faith in the Son has everlasting life." The ransom, therefore, places upon those who want to benefit from it the obligation to "inform themselves of God's mercy through Christ Jesus," and to "abide steadfastly in this confidence."[10]

This autosoteric doctrine runs through all their literature. Russell wrote: "The 'ransom for all' does not give or guarantee everlasting life or blessing to any man; but it does guarantee to every man another opportunity or trial for life everlasting" (*Studies*, II, 128), He also wrote: "They must be recovered from blindness as well

---

10. *Let God Be True*, pp. 112-121 passim.

as from death, that they each for himself, may have a full chance to prove, by obedience or disobedience, their worthiness of life eternal" (*Studies*, I, 158). Rutherford wrote: "This restitution process will continue for a period of a thousand years, viz. the period of the reign of the Messiah, during which time every one of Adam's stock, including Adam himself, will have a fair and impartial trial for life under favorable conditions" (*World Distress*, p. 9). And: "But as he strives to cleanse himself and be obedient to the Lord, he will be helped. There shall be nothing to hinder him, because Satan's influence will be restrained" (*Harp of God*, p. 339) : And the same doctrine appears in a 1954 publication, *This Good News of the Kingdom* (p. 12). In all of this there is not the faintest echo of, "He was wounded for our transgressions," Isaiah 53:5, or of "Christ died for our sins," I Corinthians 15:3.

The Holy Spirit

Denial of the Trinity, of course, involves also the Witnesses in rejection of the divine personality of the Holy Spirit, in spite of the fact that Scripture ascribes to Him the attributes of personality, such as *intelligence* (I Cor. 2:10), *will* (I Cor. 12:11), and describes Him as a divine Person having divine names (I Cor. 3:16, II Cor. 3:17, Matt. 28:19, Acts 5:3), divine works (Ps. 104:30, creating; Ps. 139, omnipresence); divine honor (II Cor. 13:14, Matt. 12:31).

"But the holy spirit has no personal name. The reason for this is that the holy spirit is not an intelligent person. It is the impersonal, invisible active force that finds its source and reservoir in Jehovah God and that he uses to accomplish his will" (*Let Your Name Be Sanctified*, p. 269).

Eschatology

"Christ returned invisibly to the earth in 1914, which marked the end of the Gentile times, and the beginning of the 'time of the end' of Satan's rule, and therefore the time when Christ Jesus the righteous Ruler of the new world received control."[11] In 1918 Christ "came to the spiritual temple as Jehovah's messenger and began to cleanse it . . . . That marked the beginning of the period of judgment and inspection of his spirit-begotten followers."[12] "The dead Christians sleeping in the graves were raised with spirit bodies to join him at the spiritual temple. The living anointed Christians on earth could not precede those who had fallen asleep in death, but they have to keep on maintaining their integrity until their own death. When this remnant on earth die, they do not have to sleep awaiting their Master's return, but receive an immediate change to spirit life."[13] "From the time of Jesus until now the selecting of the members of the heavenly kingdom has gone on, and today, after nineteen centuries of selecting, there is yet a small remnant of the 144,000 on earth."[14]

Meanwhile the testing of the world goes on. The "sheep" are in line for eternal life here on earth. The "goats" are destined for destruction, annihilation. What determines whether we are of the sheep or the goat class? Our attitude toward the remnant of Jehovah's anointed Witnesses and their message of the theocratic government. "The separation now of the people as his 'other sheep' and as 'goats' is part of the composite sign that Christ has returned and is present as King."[15]

In addition to the "heavenly resurrection of the 144,000," there will be "an earthly resurrection." This will be shortly after Armageddon, the great battle in which the Lord will destroy "Satan's organization." "There will be no need for God's servants on earth to take part in the fight. Christ Jesus will lead the heavenly host of Jehovah's angels in the final attack against Satan and his organization, destroying it utterly and delivering obedient man-

---

11. *Let God Be True*, p. 201.
12. *Ibid.*, p. 202.
13. *Ibid.*, p. 203.
14. *This Good News*, 1954, p. 16.
15. *Let God Be True*, p. 204.

kind into a new world of righteousness. Bringing an end to this system of things in this manner is the only way to rid the word of evil and make room for peace and righteousness to flourish. This could be done only by the Almighty God, Jehovah."[16]

At the end of the millennium Satan and his demons are released to test the faith and integrity of those on earth. "His mental attitude unchanged, he will again seek to usurp Jehovah's position of universal sovereignty and endeavor to turn all perfected mankind against God. Some will be misled, . . . those supporting Satan will, with the Devil himself, be cast into the 'lake of fire and sulphur'. . . . They are drowned in everlasting destruction, and for them there is no resurrection."[17]

Then will follow "a world without Adamic death, illness, sorrow, tears, or religious confusion. . . . It will remain, not for a thousand, or a million, or even a thousand-million years, but forever."[18]

Hell, according to this eschatology, consists merely of "everlasting destruction." This non-existence, following upon annihilation, is "eternal punishment." It is minus all suffering, contrary to Jesus' words in Mark 9:47, 48. Gehennah in this system is merely absence of being. There is no "smoke of their torment" as in Revelation 14:11.

Sheol or Hades, which the Authorized Version invariably translated by "hell," is in reality a picturesque word for the state of separation, namely, between the body and the departed soul. Hence Sheol sometimes means *the grave* (e.g., in Gen. 42:38; Eccles. 9:10), at other times the place where the soul is in a *conscious* condition (e.g., Ezek. 32:21). The Russellite assertion that Sheol (New Testament Hades) always means the grave is thus refuted by Scripture.

This error appears also from the story of Dives and

---

16. *This Good News*, p. 25.
17. *Let God Be True*, p. 270.
18. *Ibid.*, p. 271.

Lazarus in Luke 16. The Witnesses say that the rich man in this "parable" represents the Jewish nation which is "in a condition of torment ever since the destruction of Jerusalem." Even if this were true, however, our Lord would not have compared this condition of torment with Hades if Hades were merely a place of unconsciousness or virtual non-existence.

The Witnesses have here further corrupted the Seventh-day Adventist teaching which also denies eternal torment. Mrs. White and her followers have at any rate taught that eternal destruction will be preceded by a period of punishment consciously undergone.[19]

Other heresies that are of minor significance the reader may be spared in this brief treatise. Among these is the error that man *is* a soul; he does not *have* a soul. Thus when he dies, he ceases to exist (no pain or "torment" in the hereafter!) and therefore must be literally *re-created*. It is evident that this runs contrary to all Scripture which teaches that man is a being who *has* both soul and body (see Num. 21:4, "the soul of the people"; Matt. 26:38, "my soul is . . . sorrowful") The conscious state of the soul in the hereafter is clearly taught in Phillippians 1:21, 23.

Finally, to this autosoteric system baptism (by immersion) only signifies "The Witnesses' complete dedication to do the will of Jehovah." It is all man instead of the grace of God. There is nothing in it reminiscent of Romans 6:1-4, or of Galatians 3:27.

What Is Needed

In a following chapter (17) of this book the writer has given a brief example of how he thinks the main errors of the Witnesses should be refuted in personal contact with them. To present a detailed refutation would enlarge this textbook into a complete treatise on systematic theology as well as a more detailed description of all the

---

19. *The Great Controversy*, p. 673.

cults. This would expand the present volume far beyond its intended scope.

There is, however, one thing to be learned from the Russellites. They are diligent Bible students, although they study the Bible with a prejudiced, rationalistic mind. Their frequent references to Scripture passages wrest these out of their context and are all predicated upon preconceived ideas.

If members of evangelical churches wish to stand firm in "the faith which was once for all delivered unto the saints," they must spend good deal more time in systematic Bible study. Ministers would then be troubled far less by people saying, "What must we answer?" The study of such books as the following is to be recommended: *The Lord of Glory*, A Study of the Designation of our Lord in the New Testament with Especial Reference to His Deity, by Benjamin B. Warfield (Zondervan), and *Our Reasonable Faith* by Herman Bavinck (Eerdmans).

For Further Study

1. Jehovah's Witnesses are confessed Arians. When, where, and why was Arius condemned?

2. Show from Scripture what is wrong with the Witnesses' doctrine of (i) the ransom, (ii) man's share in the process of salvation, (iii) annihilation versus judgment (does II Thess. 1:9 teach annihilation?); (iv) conception of hell.

3. Will there merely be a "new society," or is this present world to be renewed after burning up? II Peter 3:12, 13.

4. How do you understand Armageddon?

5. Must the number 144,000 in Revelation 7 be understood literally or symbolically?

6. Prove the NW translation "the word was a god" in John 1:1 to be erroneous from Deuteronomy 6:4, Isaiah 44:6, 45:5; John 17:3, I John 5:20.

7. Prove the deity of Christ from I Peter 3:15 compared with Isaiah 8:13, and from Revelation 1:17 compared with Isaiah 44:6, 48:12.

8. Prove the personality of the Holy Spirit from Acts 13:2 and from Acts 28:25.

9. How does Matthew 22:32 refute the theory of the non-existence of the dead as held by the Witnesses?

10. What is the fundamental fault of all Rationalism?

14

MORAL RE-ARMAMENT

As long ago as 1946 *Newsweek* Magazine called Buchmanism "a cat with nine lives." Many a time the movement has been written off as defunct; but always it has been revived. Indeed, what is perhaps the most exhaustive critique written by an outsider from within, appeared in 1955. It is the book of the English journalist Geoffrey Williamson, *Inside Buchmanism,* An independent inquiry into the Oxford Group Movement and Moral Re-Armament. The book is truly exhaustive, not from a historical point of view, but from a reporter's standpoint who has visited and lived with the Groupers in their Caux, Switzerland, elaborate headquarters, asked questions, and has even submitted his findings to their leading men.

The mountain house at Caux was bought, with all its towers and minarets, after World War II, from the Swiss government for the "bargain price" of 80,000 pounds, less than a French company had offered in the hope of securing the fittings and furniture for resale in France.

One of the abiding mysteries is whence all the money; however, this case is not unlike that of Father Divine, whose devotees give their capital to the cause for the privilege of serving and being provided for from a general fund: there is a sort of communism in these movements that is born of a great love for a cause.

There is no organization, no membership; there is only an organism. Buchmanism is registered in Britain as the Oxford Group (for historical reasons, no doubt), but in Switzerland as Moral Re-Armament (MRA).

The movement is still evangelistic, as it was when it originated around 1910; only its emphasis changes from time to time.

With their highly trained Mackinac singers Buchmanites outdo the standard evangelistic campaigners in creating emotional pitch at the beginning of their meetings. MRA women do not use cosmetics, but good food and elaborate dinners are appreciated at Caux. One marvels at the number of men and women who work without salary. Some throw in their substance, while others donate their time and energy and are rewarded with extravagant living when on tour, because "where God guides He provides."

From the First Century Christian Fellowship, through the Oxford Group, Buchmanism has arrived at *Fondation du Ré-armament Morale,* which held its first international convention, called modestly the First World Assembly, in 1947 at Caux.

The movement is as pretentious as ever: it bids to change effectively the thinking and living of nations and their leaders before it is too late and a third world war destroys us all. And this change it expects to effect by the simple process of changing individual lives by means of its *Four Absolutes*: Absolute Honesty, Absolute Purity, Absolute Self-Sacrifice, Absolute Love.

In the most fundamentalist style the followers of Frank Buchman believe that if we change enough individuals, society and international conditions will change: "Make the man good and the world will be good."

As a result, perhaps, of the tremendous impact of two world wars and the spread of Communism, Buchmanites have changed their emphasis. They now lay stress upon social and economic changes, whereas thirty years ago they planned to change the world by ridding youths of their sex-sins and later South Africa of its racial antagonism. But fundamentally the movement has remained true to itself: change the man by a *washout;* let him confess his sins before his fellow and so rid himself of his hidden obsessions; then let him begin each day with a silent period during which he listens in for divine *guidance,* and his life will be renewed and become an influence to renew the world round about him.

Historical

Frank Daniel Buchman, of German-Swiss Lutheran descent, was born in Pennsburg, Pennsylvania, in 1878. He studied at Muhlenberg College and Mt. Airy Seminary. Ordained to the ministry, he looked for a difficult field, trying to offset the accusation of a friend that he, Frank, suffered from an overdose of personal ambition. At Overbrook, Pennsylvania, Buchman accepted the call of a church in poor condition, and out of his labors there grew a settlement house for boys. "Frank" — as his followers familiarly called him — had a clash with some of the board members, resigned, left, toured Italy, landed in England, and had his first heart-changing experience as a result of an address by a woman whom he heard speak at Keswick on the subject of the Cross.

Having been converted, he at once wrote six letters to as many board members. These were meant as an apology, but remained one and all unacknowledged. Nevertheless, there was a new and complete friendliness when he met the addressees later on.

His mind having been completely healed by a decision to submit his will entirely to the will of God, Buchman decided that religion is not so much a matter of emotion, nor of doctrine, as of the will. His task now became twofold: to be led by God's will, and to induce others to be led by God's will.

Pondering still further the problem of sin, having seen his own sin at the Cross and surrendered his pride, he reached this conclusion: "The degree of our freedom from sin is the degree of our desire to be free." "Further," says Russell, "he believes that wherever possible one should not only hate sin, but confess sin and forsake sin, making restitution to the person sinned against."[1]

"Frank"—for some reason or other the members of the cult all prefer their own and each other's given names—went to Cambridge, where he spent a short time only. At

---

1. A. J. Russell, *For Sinners Only.*

the request of a bishop he went to Oxford, "guided to put his challenging convictions into operation in the intellectual center of England." In untheological language he spoke to university men about changed lives. The following year, which was 1909, he returned to America, where, at the request of Dr. John R. Mott, he cleaned up Pennsylvania State College in three years' time.

In 1915 Buchman went through India, Korea, and Japan. In 1916 we find him teaching in an American theological seminary. From 1917 to 1918 he was again in the Orient, where he became clear as to his convictions, method of work, and so forth.

The first house party was held in Kuling, China, in the summer of 1918, at the summer home of an important lawyer, with one hundred guests attending.

In 1921 Harold Begbie was "changed" at a Cambridge house party. He afterward wrote *Life Changers*, published in America under the title, *More Twice-Born Men*. Buchman continued traveling from one part of the world to another. His movement spread from England to South Africa. In England the leadership of the movement passed into the hands of Louden Hamilton; in the United States into those of New York's Rector of Calvary Church, Samuel M. Shoemaker, Jr.

Shoemaker abandoned the movement in October, 1941, saying: "Be kind and good — the people who do that are Christians. The people who try to act like Jesus and go about doing good — they are the Christians. 'Be like Jesus' that is Christianity. Is that Christianity? Is the poor effort of any man to approach perfection Christianity? Is my attempt to find my way back to God Christianity? . . . I know it is not, and so do you."

"I am sick of all this talk about the Golden Rule. . . . Some of us have never caught original Christianity by the hem. For original Christianity began with the announcement of something that God had done, something that God had given. It was wholly supernatural, not so much in the sense of the miraculous accompaniments of it, but in the sense that it was itself a great miracle, because only God Himself could have created it. Original Christianity, true Christianity for all time, is not a matter of man reaching up to find God, but of God reaching down to find man; not a matter of man trying to live up to a moral code, but of man responding with his whole nature to the mercy and kindness of God."[2]

Buchman himself for many years remained a sort of international supervisor, now in Africa, now in Europe, then in America. From 1946 onward, however, he had his headquarters in London, and his personal abode since the First World Assembly in 1947 at Caux, Switzerland. In 1951 he revisited America, and again in 1958 and 1960 for the World Assembly at Mackinac Island, Michigan. In 1953 he visited India with a "world team." The aged leader then retired to Caux. On August 7, 1961, in Switzerland, Frank Daniel Buchman died, and his body was interred in Pennsylvania.

For the sake of completeness it might be added that the names "Oxford Group" and "Oxford Movement," still in use in Britain for obvious reasons, were first coined in South Africa in 1929, while "Moral Re-Armament" was first used in 1938 in East-Ham when Buchman was 60 years of age.

Appraisal

From the beginning Buchmanism has evoked both favorable and adverse comment, often from similar quarters. When in 1924 President Hibben of Princeton University had banished Buchman from the campus, Dr. Stevenson, President of Princeton Seminary, presided at a house party in New York. Perhaps Ferguson was right when he stated that President Hibben resented Buchman's statement that eighty-five percent of Princeton's students were sex perverts.

Even since that day liberal ministers have condemned Buchmanism for its orthodox theology, while evangelicals

---

2. *Moody Monthly*, Jan., 1942.

have repudiated the movement because of its liberalism and lack of doctrine.³ Buchmanism has no organization and is not interested in denominations; it urges its adherents to improve conditions wherever they are.

(A) *Good Points*

1. Buchmanism is a reaction against mass revivalism gone to seed. Clover C. Loud has been refuted by today's developments (he said that Moody was the last bona fide evangelist in America); yet there is truth in the assertion that increased commercialism, together with a demand for statistics and numbers, has spoiled revivalism in America. Buchman's emphasis upon individual changed lives is a wholesome thing. It is in line with Homrighausen's celebrated small volume written for the Federal Council of Churches in 1943, *Choose Ye This Day*, Philadelphia (The Westminster Press). We need individual conversions, decisions, and commitments rather than mass hysteria and mob psychology.

2. The fact that Buchmanism labors mostly (not exclusively!) among the educated and the rich, should not, in the writer's opinion, be held against it. It is an undeniable fact that generally the Church has greatly neglected the upper classes and has seemed rather afraid of them. It is high time that, beside the many and costly efforts to win "the down and outs," someone should have started something to reach "the up and outs."

3. Buchmanism challenges our dead or lukewarm churches. With its demands for a *testimony* and a *surrendered* life, it throws down the gauntlet to churches whose members have merely "joined a church and sat in a pew," to borrow a witticism of Salvation Army origin, and have brought only their leavings to the collection plate on Sun-

---

3. Because MRA stands for an anti-Christian religious "ideology," the Most Rev. Thos. L. Noa, Bishop of Marquette, has advised Catholics under his jurisdiction that they may not participate in the training courses of MRA on Mackinac Island, in accordance with an instruction from the Holy Office in 1951 (*Our Sunday Visitor*, April 17 to May 8, 1960).

day. Any Buchmanite knows that he may be guided at any time to leave home and to "change" those nearby or far away.

4. There is an element of truth in what the Primate of Denmark said at Berlin, Germany: "We never realized how unintelligible our language was until we heard the Oxford Group . . . . The old language may suit conventional Christians, who probably have been familiar all their lives with the Bible and with Christian phraseology and customs. But we must talk differently to pagans and atheists, skeptics and critics, the wanton, the vicious, the scoffer, and even to those who are in doubt, but are earnestly striving to find the Truth." However, though we admit this need for reaching people by beginning just where they are, and though we confess that the Church has often failed to do this, there remains a difference between dragging the Bible down to the low level of the people and beginning on the low level in order to lift the people to the level of the Bible and the Church. The old terms, such as regeneration, conversion, justification by faith, are not above the capacity of a man with average mentality; and there is a danger lest, in discarding these technical terms, we also lose the ideas they represent.

5. We may wholeheartedly welcome Buchmanism's emphasis upon life as over against dogma accepted by the intellect. It should be added, however, that life without doctrine is just as futile as doctrine apart from life.

6. It may be added that Buchmanism has stressed again something that modern Protestantism had lost. Luther kept the confessional; the Calvinistic branch of Protestantism substituted for it the official family visiting by the elders of the church. Family visitation has the inherent weakness that adolescents in particular hesitate to speak of their sins in the presence of their elders, parents, brothers, and sisters. And thus James 5:16 has gone largely by the board. Buchman has again called attention to the fact that confession is good for the soul: it is that even from a psychological point of view. And truly, many of the Buchmanite "soul-

surgeons" have proved no mean doctors. Some of these men have acquired remarkable skill. When a prospect is reticent, the surgeon begins to take him into his confidence by telling the surgeon's own experience with sin and cleansing. This opens the way to confession, which is to be done in the face of the Four Absolutes: Absolute Honesty, Absolute Purity, Absolute Self-Sacrifice, Absolute Love. This is called sharing. But sharing is also the rehearsal of one's experience in confession and release. This occurs sometimes before one person and at other times before an applauding crowd met for the purpose of exchanges. This then takes the place of the old-fashioned testimonial meeting.

(B) *Weaknesses*

1. The Buchmanites put the cart before the horse when they say that doctrine is based upon experience. My own experience with the Groupers here tallies with that of other evangelical writers. I met with a strange unwillingness to state any doctrinal convictions. "As a Group we do not put theology before experience. If I know anything about the development of theology, it came from the experience of men. It is merely a statement of an experience which has come to men; therefore, you and I have no right to say to people, 'You must believe a set of dogma if you are to be saved.' In the first place, there is nothing magical about a belief, and in the second place, if there is no real genuine experience combined with the belief, it is hollow and unreal. I can say from my own experience that in the five years during which I have lived this life, I have learned more theology than I ever did in my whole seminary career. It is a theology that has grown out of my growing experience of God."

This citation from a letter by one of the leaders presents the dominant view. It is essentially and fundamentally erroneous. It is the view held by all the false mystics. Theology is bound to the inspired Word of God. So is experience. Theology is the formulation of what Scripture tells us about the works of God for us, in us, and through us. Scriptural teaching is to be accepted with the head and the heart; and life is to be based upon it and regulated by it. "To the law and to the testimony! if they speak not according to this word, surely there is no morning for them" (Isa. 8:20).

2. From this fundamental error of Buchmanism follows a neglect of Christian doctrine which makes the entire movement look suspicious. This may be seen from the following facts:

a. A. J. Russell's *For Sinners Only*, one of the chief, older works of the cult, contains no reference to the saving blood of Christ. The same holds true of the "Layman's" *What is the Oxford Group?*

b. There is a general disregard of doctrine. Shoemaker says, "I have not time to align myself with any group who think that by the promulgation of a point of view they are going to save the world." We might well ask if insisting upon Sharing, Surrender, Changing, and Guidance is not a point of view which they promulgate.

c. This undoctrinal and antidoctrinal point of departure results in faulty and totally inadequate definitions. Thus Dr. G. T. Lee, Editor of the *Lutheran Herald*, points out that there is no proper sense of the awfulness of sin. One looks in vain for a statement concerning the *guilt* of sin. Dr. T. T. Shields, who has had considerable experience with the Groups, has never heard them repudiate the most modernistic tenets held by some of the members. Sin, according to Russell, is "anything in my life which keeps me from God and from other people."

Similarly, "Surrender" is described by the "Layman" as "a simple decision put into simple language, spoken aloud to God, in front of a witness, at any time and in any place, that we have decided to forget the past in God and to give our future into His keeping."

d. At times this inadequate respect for wholesome doctrine degenerates into a positive dislike for fundamental doctrines. Thus when a Group convert wrote in *The Church of England Newspaper,* July 29, 1932, "I have lived without God all my life.... I came into touch with the Oxford Group, and life has been transformed for me, I have found a happiness and a peace that I never suspected the existence of. But I feel this difficulty: The Church requires me to stand in the presence of that Baby in the manger and say: 'Lo, there lies God,' and I cannot do it. I feel that He is unique . . . yet, to say straight out, 'There lies God,' is more than I can manage . . . ."

e. In view of such statements, what becomes of Buchman's own conversion which is described as "an experience of the Cross of Christ"? What does it mean? And why did not Shoemaker realize when commenting on Acts 2:42-47, on page 88 of *The Conversion of the Church,* that it is inadequate to say, "Not only was this an experience of fellowship between individuals, but groups in different localities were in touch with groups in other places"? He should have marked the words, "And with great power gave the apostles witness of the resurrection of the Lord Jesus; and great grace was upon them all." Dr. Machen said of Peter's Pentecostal sermon, "There was nothing about Peter's experience, but a great deal about Christ."

(3) In close connection with this is the refusal of Dr. Buchman and others to discuss, or to listen to criticism. There is too much pragmatism. The question, "Does it work?" is insufficient. Changed lives, improved lives, are not necessarily the fruit of regeneration.

4. Rom Landau discovered that the "Sharing" of Buchmanites is not always honest. Stories were repeated and changed from time to time. Moreover, many visitors have remarked that the stories rehashed at the hilarious meetings at house parties were an insult to the majesty of God.

5. To dwell upon sins formerly committed, and to tell them with gusto, as is undoubtedly done at the house parties, often creates the impression of boasting in one's shame. Some critics could not escape the conviction that the Buchmanites enjoyed each other's filth with a vicarious taste of

the sin described. True repentance results in the language of Psalm 51 or Psalm 32. Can we imagine David recounting his sin under applause?

6. "Guidance," with the mind entirely relaxed and surrendered, is dangerous. Such ludicrous and silly suggestions as, "You must eat porridge in the morning," or: "sausage," do not proceed from God as guidance for breakfast or dinner. Buchman's definition that religion is a matter of the will is wrong. When God renews man, He renews his intellect as well as his emotional life and his will. Nor has God given us our intellect to set it aside. The quiet "listening in" must again give way to speaking to God and letting the Bible-saturated mind decide for itself after prayer. Dr. G. H. Stevenson, a Toronto physician, wrote in *The New Outlook*, "The hallucinatory *'voices'* of the mentally ill, the spirit voices of our spiritualist friends, the 'guidance' of the Oxford Group, are as closely related as children of the same parents, and the parents of these three unusual children are a sensitive, emotionally unstable personality in union with the longing for happiness in some other world than the one God has given us."[4]

7. Closely related to this puerile conception of prayer as a one-sided "listening in," with a pad and pencil, are some of the little things wherewith "Frank" amuses his followers. P, R, A, Y, he tells them, means "Powerful Radiograms Always Yours." J, E, S, U, S, means, "Just Exactly Suits Us Sinners."

It is rather interesting to hear Dr. Buchman relate that the totality of Christian experience consists in *The Five C's*: Conviction, Contrition, Confession, Conversion, Continuance. But the terms are insufficiently defined, and there is not enough of Christ according to the Scriptures in them.

8. In regard to "Sharing" in the sense of confession: It may be true that our Protestant reaction against the confessional has gone quite far. It certainly is true that when we become aware of a sin committed against our fellow

---

4. Similarly, Dr. Leslie Weatherhead. Cf. *Religious Digest*, Feb., 1938.

men, we should confess to them as well as to God. It is also laudable that the necessity of restitution is stressed. We are willing to go beyond this. We can agree with Shoemaker's words, "Of course, confession, in the absolute sense, is to God alone: but where there is a human listener, confession is found to be both more difficult and more efficacious. It is, as a matter of fact and experience, a relatively uncostly thing to fall on our knees and confess our sins to God — it should not be, and perhaps would not be if we were closer to God and more sensitive to His will; but it is a very costly thing to say these things out in the presence even of a human being we can trust; and, as a matter of fact, this is extraordinarily effective in making the first break to get away from sins." Dr. Shoemaker points to John Wesley's elaborate rules in 1748 "to meet once a week at the least" to "speak each of us in order, freely and plainly, the true state of our soul, with the faults we have committed in thought, word, or deed: and the temptations we have felt since our last meeting."[5]

But when the same truth is expressed as follows by Mr. Day, "Confession to God alone is often not good enough in that it may cost nothing and may be merely the confession to a subjective picture of God which the person has built up for him or herself. In such a case, what actually happens is that the person does not confess at all — there is no real pain and repentance — It is an easy way of trying to ease one's conscience. Confessing to another person always costs and is thus a test of our honesty in hating sin"; we feel how easily the same truth may be misused and we incline to exclaim with Dr. Shields, "As though man were more real than God!" Surely, if Buchmanites have only a subjective picture of God, the remedy lies not in confessing to men, but in first getting the right conception of this Holy God against whom we have sinned; and this is done by prayerful study of the Word of God and

---

5. *The Conversion of the Church*, pp. 36, 37.

by humble acceptance of the picture of Himself He has revealed to us.

9. Our criticism may return to an earlier remark that the favorite name of "First Century Christian Fellowship" is significant for a proper understanding of Buchmanism. One might subsume one's critique of the movement under this one heading. For:

a. That is an impossibility in the twentieth century. We cannot go back to one o'clock in the morning at eleven o'clock in the evening of the same day. The "guidance" of the Holy Spirit certainly did not begin with Dr. Frank Buchman. Through toil and strife, attacks from within and without, God has guided His Church through nineteen centuries. She has been rent apart by schisms. She has suffered from character faults. Yet she has kept the faith to which all Christians have at all times subscribed. And that faith has been expressed in the great historic creeds of Christendom. To ignore all this, and try to start as though nothing had happened since the first century, is Buchmanism's fundamental mistake. It cannot be done without surrendering vital truths of the Christian religion. It is a denial of the historic *guidance* of the Holy Spirit in the name of spontaneous guidance.

b. And this is all the worse since Buchmanism, as Dr. E. D. Kraan has pointed out, misrepresents first-century Christianity. The early Christians did not form groups for the exchange of experience. In the apostolic age they formed churches. The apostles appointed elders in every church. They laid great stress upon the duty of the pastors to preach and teach, and upon the task of the elders to rule and to discipline.

c. Buchmanism, reading its favorite book of the Bible, The Acts, in this erroneous manner, underestimates the church. This the great reformers of the Church, Martin Luther, John Calvin, John Wesley, did not do.

10. Buchmanism has changed, in practice if not in theory (there is little theory at best, the movement being pragmatic to the core), from evangelism to a wholesale

plea for democracy as the panacea for the nations. Buchman is the recipient of many honors from many governments. However, the endless repetition of such slogans as "Sorry is a magic word," "Families can be fun," and the showing of "films to change the world" and plays of a similar order, such as *The Good Road,* may well be found in the end to be ignored when the international "warmongers" feel the time ripe to strike for world power.

A two-page advertisement in *Time* for January 9, 1956, may serve as proof of this contention. The title of the ad, reads, "An Idea to Win the World: Moral Re-Armament, a Statesmanship that Works." Statesmen from many lands are quoted in favor of the "MRA World Mission," which is said to be "For All Men Everywhere." The means advertised are such plays as *The Vanishing Island.* From London, Beverly Baxter condemns this as an "oversimplification" which "rules out the intellect and appeals purely to the spirit." He further illustrates this with a reference to "a very nice Canadian woman," who said that the town in which she lives has two cinemas; when she wants to decide which motion picture to see, she depends upon "divine guidance." Baxter calls this "the climax of absurdity." He adds that the British press resents the secrecy on the part of Buchmanism as to the source and the expenditure of vast sums of money.[6]

11. Williamson's chapter, "Tears in the Morning," is worth reading. A young girl, amidst the peaceful surroundings of Caux Mountain House, was overheard sobbing as she struggled against the attempts by Buchmanites to make her surrender her own personal convictions to the spirit that brooks no opposition, no criticism of any kind: Buchmanism alone has the key to the solution of the world's problems!

Any movement or group that feels that way in the complicated world situation of today, stands condemned, as suf-

---

6. *Maclean's.* Canada's National Magazine, May 26, 1956.

fering either from an excess of naiveté or of something less excusable.

For You to Ponder

1. Why are such names as *First Century Christian Fellowship* to be condemned?
2. Which principle, overdone by the Church of Rome, neglected by Protestantism, has been re-emphasized by Buchmanism? Has it done justice to this principle?
3. Is it easier to make confession before God or to do so before man? Should both be done? Have you ever confessed your sins to your fellow men? If not, why not? Is it sufficient to confess our sins before God in general terms, without mentioning specific faults?
4. What does Buchman mean by the Four Absolutes? What are the Five C's?
5. What is your main objection to Buchmanism?
6. Why has the original Buchmanism changed its emphasis to Moral Re-Armament?
7. Is it correct to say that a mere listening to the inner voice will reveal God's will to us? Do you know of other Christian groups which are in danger of falling into this error?
8. To what danger do we lay ourselves open when we neglect Scripture at the expense of the "inner voice"?

15

UNITARIANISM-MODERNISM

Perhaps the Modernist would frown at being classified or even discussed together with Spiritism and Unity. There is indeed a marked difference. In fact, there is so much that is good and noble in Modernism that at times it seems rather difficult to classify the movement as antichristian. Are the morals of American youth systematically corrupted by moving pictures portraying the sex- and the crime-life of society? Modernist journals fight tooth and nail the evils of block booking and blind selling. Is the hire of those who labored for the rich kept back? It is the Modernist who openly denounces the greed of the great industrialist and points him to the Golden Rule of Jesus.

Surely, there is much that is good here. In correcting social evils our modernist friends are far more active than many orthodox. The latter fail to realize that condemnation of the world is not sufficient since Christians must let their light so shine before men that they will glorify the Father in heaven. We who are to be the salt and the leaven are not fulfilling our duty when we assign the world to the Devil. Neither may the Church tolerate evil for fear that its revenues will be cut off.[1]

And yet we must condemn Modernism as one more ism. Why? Because of the fundamental difference between the assertion that man in his own strength can do the Father's will, and the Christian doctrine that without the regenerating power of the Holy Spirit "ye can do nothing."

Moral good of a kind is excellent. Civic righteousness exalteth a nation. But of those who deny the necessity of

---

1. Cf. my *Kagawa, the Christian*, pp. 91 ff.

Jesus' death to propitiate for our sins, though we may stand shoulder to shoulder with them in fighting tuberculosis and alcoholism, we must, with the inspired apostle Paul, "tell you even weeping that they are the enemies of the cross of Christ."

Our supreme loyalty must, in the final analysis, be to the Christ of the Scriptures. We need not narrowly condemn those who disagree with us on many points. But when the supernatural character of Jesus Christ and His salvation are questioned and even openly denied, we must draw the line, across which we write, *Non possumus*. Ethics is not necessarily religion, and religion is not the same as Christianity.

The term "Modernism" is used somewhat loosely in our country. "Modernism," said the late Dr. E. E. Aubrey of the Divinity School of the University of Chicago, "is a method, not a creed. Modernists are unified by their approach to theology, not by their theological conclusions." Just like Buchmanism, in other words: a method, not a creed. "The message is the method, and the method is the message." You can believe pretty well whatever you desire, just so you are of a certain mentality. This is why it is difficult to say, "Modernism teaches this or that"; we should rather say, "This Modernist holds to such a view."

For historic reasons, as well as to limit the term Modernism, we speak of Unitarianism-Modernism.

A Hint from History

When the eminent revivalist, Charles G. Finney, arrived in Boston in 1843, Dr. Lyman Beecher said to him, "Mr. Finney, you cannot labor here as you do anywhere else. You have got to pursue a different course of instruction, and begin at the foundation; for Unitarianism is a system of denials, and under its teaching, the foundations of Christianity are fallen away. You cannot take anything for granted; for the Unitarians and the Universalists have destroyed the foundation, and the people are all afloat. The masses have no settled opinions, and every 'lo here,' or 'lo there,' finds a hearing; and almost any conceivable form of error may get a footing." And more than thirty years later Mr. Finney stated, "I have since found this to be true, to a greater extent than in any other field in which I have labored. The mass of people in Boston are more unsettled in their religious convictions than in any other place that I have ever labored in, notwithstanding their intelligence; for they are surely a very intelligent people, on all questions but that of religion. It is extremely difficult to make religious truths lodge in their minds, because the influence of Unitarian teaching has been to lead them to call in question all the principal doctrines of the Bible. Their system is one of denials. Their theology is negative. They deny almost everything, and affirm almost nothing. In such a field, error finds the ears of the people open; and the most irrational views, on religious subjects, come to be held by a great many people."

Such scathing verdicts by men like Beecher, who lived and labored in that hotbed of Unitarianism, and by Finney, who had wide experience in evangelistic work on the Continent, are worthy of attention. But besides, after half a century more of untiring Unitarian propaganda throughout the country, we can corroborate these condemnatory statements ourselves. That "the Unitarians and the Universalists have destroyed the foundations, and the people are all afloat," was meant as the statement of a historical fact in 1843. It has since proved a prophecy. It was Unitarian Boston that became the nursery of Eddyism. Thousands of well-meaning folk have fallen a ready prey to the various antichristian cults of the day, and that without even suspecting that they have abandoned the Christian faith, as the result of the work of Unitarian preachers who had "destroyed the foundations" with their empty denials. Nor is it amazing that this same Boston, at first Puritan, later Unitarian, then nothing in religious convictions, has become the happy hunting ground of that strange and un-American mixture of Christianity, paganism, and corrupt politics that goes by the name of Roman Catholicism.

Unitarianism and Modernism Are One

Denying the fundamentals of the Christian religion is like putting one's feet upon a declining slope. Unitarianism in its beginning was not nearly as radical as it has since become. Gradually, however, it has drifted into a dull pantheism with no hope beyond a universal evolution. The history of the movement in the United States makes sad reading.[2] When we learn of the manner in which Unitarians wrested church buildings and property from orthodox congregations; of how little they spend for missionary work, even after a continued existence of one hundred years, and notwithstanding their great wealth; of the early opposition of most of the Unitarians to the anti-slavery movement; of the Harvard defense of alcoholism; we cannot help but think of the words of Jude, "clouds without water, carried along by winds; autumn trees without fruit, twice dead, plucked up by the roots." One thing they do engage in: they conduct a vigorous propaganda among evangelicals by means of advertising free literature in various periodicals.[3] "Some years a million pamphlets go out from the American Unitarian Association. Local parishes also send them out continually by the thousands."

Of late years Unitarian tactics have changed somewhat. Ministers with Unitarian convictions are now advised to stay in the orthodox churches, and work "from within." This procedure was called "strategic" by Dr. Slaten of the West Side Unitarian Church, New York; it was recom-

---

2. The scope of our work does not allow a comparison between Unitarianism and European Modernism of the last century. The intimate resemblance between them is clearly borne out not merely by their theology, but also by the hateful tactics employed against those who dissented from their views.

3. Of Mormonism, which follows similar tactics, E. L. Mills writes in *The Christian Century*: "It is a parasitic religion, living off Christianity. It does not seek to convert sinners, but to make 'saints' out of church members who already have a fair degree of saintliness."

mended by Dr. Palmer, former editor of the *Harvard Theological Review;* while Dr. J. W. Day, a leading Unitarian minister, wrote, "A good many Unitarians are doing more good where they are than they could do anywhere else. They are undoubtedly capturing strongholds that we could never carry by direct attack. They are the Modernists of Protestantism who are working from within the fold. . . . We want more of them and we want them where they are." Consequently we should not be lulled to sleep when we read that between the years 1916 and 1926 "among the Protestant bodies the two liberal denominations, the Unitarians and the Universalists, suffered a decrease in membership, the former by more than 22,000." Unitarians, after appropriating universities and divinity schools that had been founded and endowed for the express purpose of propagating Calvinism only, now advise "liberal" ministers in evangelical denominations to use the property of their churches in order to undermine those churches "from within," that ultimately "all may be one," when the unnerved denominations shall come over in bulk.

Aversion to Creeds

This, of course, is not saying that all Modernists and all Unitarians think alike on every point of religion. If anything is characteristic of present-day Liberals, it is their profound aversion to fixed doctrine. In this, as also in other points of similarity, they do not yield an inch to the stoutest Ritschlian. "Free-thinkers" is a title these men are proud of. It may perhaps be said that, on the whole, the Unitarian of today is somewhat more outspoken than is the average Modernist in an evangelical church; and denominational "fetters" may well account for the latter's more guarded language. The general feeling on the subject is typically expressed by Dr. C. S. Wicks, for more than twenty-five years minister to the All Souls Unitarian Church, Indianapolis. Says Dr. Wicks, "We have no creed of any kind. Is it because we believe nothing or so little?

No; it is because we believe so much we can find no formula to express our beliefs. To us Truth is infinite and cannot be enclosed in any statement of belief.... Each one of us should have his own creed, the result of his own best thinking, but he has no desire to fix that creed upon any one else. The nearest we have ever come to a creed is the Bond of Union of our former General Conference now merged into the American Unitarian Association, reading, 'These churches accept the religion of Jesus, holding in accordance with his teachings, that practical religion is summed up in love to God and love to man.' "

So much for Unitarianism. What about Modernism? Let Dr. Shailer Mathews, late Dean of the Divinity School, University of Chicago, speak for Modernism. Said the Dean in an interview with Winfred Ernest Garrison: "The modernist's objection to creeds is not that they formulate the intellectual aspects of a religious experience, but that they are made authoritative and final tests of such experience.... Most assuredly I believe that religious thinking must be clearly kept within the limits of what may be called personalism."

It follows that it would be difficult to define the theological system of Unitarian and Modernist preachers in such a manner that they would agree. They have no authoritative or representative statement. Their theology is admittedly the reflection of their religious experience, and the latter varies and changes with time, personality, and the dictates of "science."

Basic Principles

Still, there are some thoughts that may be considered the *communis opinio*. "There is no answer to the question: What do Unitarians believe? I can only say that there are certain things commonly believed among us. So far as I know, all Unitarians affirm:

(1) The divineness of all life.
(2) The oneness of man with the Eternal.

(3) The essential goodness of human nature.
(4) The Rise of Man through a process of evolution.
(5) The universality of Revelation; not to one race or one nation have come glimpses of truth divine.
(6) The reign of Natural Law.
(7) Heaven and Hell not as places but as conditions of the soul.
(8) The primacy of reason in the search for truth.
(9) Character the aim of religion.
(10) There is but one principle in the universe, and that principle makes for good."

This creed (the personal creed of most Unitarians, according to Dr. Wicks) is rather pantheistic, it will be observed. An even smaller number of articles of faith has been kept by some Modernists. Bruce Barton, the celebrated author of *The Man Nobody Knows,* and *The Book Nobody Knows,* offers these "few simple things":

1. *I believe in myself,* i.e., I know that I am.
2. *I know that I am intelligent* . . . . I know that my intelligence (and by *me* I mean, of course, mankind) is the highest and most powerful thing in the natural universe.
3. *Because I am, I believe God is.* A Divine Intelligence is beyond my meager comprehension . . . but I know that men and women are intelligent, and to believe that an unintelligent universe produced something greater than itself . . . this is an absurdity.
4. *He must be* at least as *good* as I am, for He created me, and my intelligence is a tiny fragment of His own.

Methods of Denial

This Unitarian-Modernism with its few articles of faith, when at its worst, simply brushes aside whoever holds that the Christian faith needs more, and more solid, foundations. With Dr. Wicks it says, "Already the Fundamentalists have drawn the line. On one side, all the intelligence, all modern learning; on the other, sincerity, yes, but ignorance and superstition." It sweeps past the serious work of such scholars as Dr. James Orr, Prof. J. G. Machen, Bishop R. J. Cooke, and announces that "everyone who had studied and thought knows that there is not the faintest evidence" of Jesus' virgin birth. Or, it reasons the miraculous element out of the gospel by stating that "the leprosy which Jesus healed was presumably a curable skin-disease"; the words "Peace, be still" were presumably directed to the disciples, "but the wind, as so often happens there, subsided as quickly as it had risen ... the disciples thought that the blowing had ceased in obedience to their master's command."

But when Unitarianism-Modernism is more carefully viewed, the question arises as to how this denying spirit reveals itself. Consider the following. On my desk lies a sermon, entitled "Easter Inevitable," written by Charles Clayton Morrison, former editor of *The Christian Century*.[4] The Introduction dwells upon the thought that Jesus was a true man; not a recluse, but "a man indeed." The first part of the sermon begins by stating, "Our hearts wish to be assured of an event so wonderful as the resurrection of Jesus. Where shall we look for our proof?" It continues by asserting that there are two kinds of evidence, even in a common law court, namely direct and presumptive. Modernistically, the "direct evidence" is disparaged. "If we examine the resurrection narratives we are almost dismayed at their fragmentariness, their doubtful consistency, and the possibilities by which psychology might explain them away." Nevertheless, we are assured, there is plenty of "presumptive evidence." Such a person as Christ could not but have risen. "If there is therefore any guarantee of the resurrection, Christ is himself that guarantee. The more we know of him, the further we enter into his experience of life and sense the power of his personality, the greater miracle we feel would be wrought if he had not risen. His rising from the dead was no miracle but the prevention of a miracle." With enhanced interest we read on. If we regret the

---

4. *The Christian Century*, April 14, 1927.

writer's light esteem for Scriptural evidence, we are glad that, after all, his religious heart forces him to admit that all-important fact of the Christian religion, concerning which Paul wrote: "If Christ hath not been raised, your faith is vain; ye are yet in your sins." But alas, we are immediately robbed of our sense of joy. As soon as the former editor of *The Christian Century* has informed us that Christ must have risen, that it would have been a greater miracle had He not risen, he continues as follows: "I would not divert your thought from the essential faith of Easter to dwell upon the mere physical details of this supreme event. I confess that my own interest in the physical details is so slight that I have hardly so much as a tentative opinion of my own. Whether, for instance, the body of Jesus literally came from the tomb, whether his appearances to his disciples were objective materializations in space and time, whether his ascension from Olivet in which it is said a cloud received him out of the sight was physical — whether these and other such apparent statements of fact are intended to be taken as real statements of fact, or are themselves symbols of an experience impregnated with a vast faith, I leave to those who are interested in such questions to form their own opinions. To me the essential Easter event was not the upstanding of a dead body from the tomb, but the breaking of the fact upon the minds of these disciples that there was something about their Master which death could not touch, which not only survived death, but transcended death and conquered it, and that there was such connection between their world and the world to which death is an open gate that his living presence could still abide with them and guide their thoughts and plans. Stripping off the inconsequent details of the story, we have left this pith of faith which was not alone for the first disciples the great reality, but has been the great reality for those who through all the centuries have worn the name of Christ."

The sermon then continues to expatiate on the thought that it was not possible *for Him* to be holden by death —

the text is Acts 2:24 — since it was a moral demand that He should rise; and it concludes by giving this hope for eternal life that one may and should "accept his human life as your life, his way of thinking about God and man as your way of thinking. To accept Christ is not to believe any doctrine, but to commit yourself to his way of life, to accept his way of life as your way of life, to go with him on the paths of service and self-denial and temptation."

This is a true sample of Modernist preaching. There is no telling what the preacher means by a resurrection without "physical details," and it is perhaps as well for himself that he has not attempted to inform us; there is no telling whether the "essential Easter event" of a living presence that could still abide with the disciples in their world, must be understood after the manner of our friends the Spiritists (what is the difference, just what there is and how it is, as long as you are informed that there is "something"?); and you should not probe the truth of the assertion that this unnamed "something" with or without "the upstanding of a dead body" (?!) has indeed been "the great reality" of Christians "through all the centuries" (they are dead and gone anyhow, and have left only a few worthless doctrinal treatises on the subject!). This, we repeat, is a typical sample. Thus playing with words — akin to the Glossary of *Science and Health,* and born of aversion to doctrine — might be multiplied from sermons by Paul Hutchinson, Alfred Wesley Wishart, and others. But to what end? The sample we gave is by a recognized "liberal" leader. It came after two series of sermons, one by America's twenty-five "Peers of the Pulpit," the other by representative British pulpiteers. Then someone raised the cry, And now, let us see what the editors can do themselves in that line. Dr. Morrison's sermon may be considered to be as good a specimen as Modernism has to offer. Meager Unitarian-Modernism! we are forced to exclaim; and poor people who are thus deluded!

And let us observe right here that, no matter what changes Modernism may have undergone of late years, there is no change as to this loose usage of doctrinal terms, this complete denial of the fundamental doctrines upon which Christianity has been built. When Dr. Morrison continued to write of Christ's resurrection, a Methodist minister, as late as 1946, asked him what he meant by the term, saying, "Do you mean the physical reanimation of Jesus in either his natural or some 'supernatural' body. Or do you mean, as do some theologians, 'the process whereby the Jesus of history becomes the Christ of the Church?' I write because I have nearly a dozen research scientists in my church, devoutly Christian, who would challenge any use of the term at all."

The answer — and this is *The Christian Century* of July 10, 1946 — was as follows:

"I do not pretend to know the precise nature of the resurrection fact, nor am I concerned to know — whether the physical body of Jesus was resuscitated or whether he appeared in some other form. On the whole, I am inclined to stand with Paul, who denied the resuscitation concept and based his argument upon the concept of a 'spiritual body.' Paul's statement is earlier than the date of our earliest Gospel. The manner of the resurrection is not important. But the fact of the resurrection is supremely important. Christianity cannot be understood without it."

One may well ask whatever the meaning might be of a historical fact that eludes all definition and which yet is said to be *sine qua non* of the Christian religion?[5]

Nor is this by any means the only evidence that Modernism is not defunct, and does not change its attitude toward Christ's resurrection. The late Dr. Biederwolf expressed the entire matter in these words, "We are referring, of course, to the resurrection of His body. Who ever heard of a spirit being buried?" But as late as the March, 1952, *Pulpit*, Dr. Morrison wrote, "I have long ago ceased to be concerned about the physical details of the resurrection."

---

5. From a popular apologetic standpoint the physical resurrection of Christ is dealt with in an excellent manner by Dr. A. Pieters in *Facts and Mysteries of the Christian Faith*, Eerdmans, 1933.

And Dr. Robert J. McCracken, Fosdick's successor as minister of the Riverside Church, wrote in *The Christian Century*, April 9, 1952, "In the thought of Greece the keyword is immortality. In the New Testament the keyword is resurrection — not a bare dogma of the survival of some vague and intangible essence, but the re-establishment of personal life on the farther side of the grave, the conviction that the total personality, invested by God's gift with a perfect organism, passes on and encounters God. This is the substance of the Easter faith." How unlike Luke 24:39, 40, and I Corinthians 15:35ff.[6]

Dr. Reinhold Niebuhr, chief exponent upon this continent of dialectical theology, either goes beyond Dr. Morrison, or, perhaps, uses more honest speech. He does not hesitate to call the resurrection "a myth." The creation story in Genesis is also "a myth." God's eternal wrath is "a symbol of the unpredictable possibilities of eternity which may appear in time." Jesus' incarnation, in Niebuhr's opinion, is "an offense to reason." The Chalcedon doctrine of the two natures is the "wooden-headed literalism of orthodoxy." Jesus not only was at times in error, but could not have been tempted had He not first sinned. Jesus is not the Christ, but created the ideal of Christ, an ideal larger than His own possibilities. There was no historic Adam who fell from original righteousness. Every born man is Adam, and the fall of man is an inward conflict "between the *is* and the *ought* of life, between the ideal possibilities to which freedom encourages man and the drive of egoism, which reason sharpens rather than assuages."

Small wonder, then, that Niebuhr does not refer to the atoning blood of Christ, but to "the Cross," which to him is "the defeat of love." The second coming of Christ (the

---

6. See also J. H. Skilton's review of the *Interpreter's Bible*, vol. VII, in the *Westminster Theological Journal*, May, 1952.

To this may be added that Dr. Wilbur M. Smith stated in the *Moody Monthly*, copied in *Action* (N.A.E. organ) for Feb. 1, 1954, that it made his temperature rise when he read in the *Interpreter's Bible* the statement by Dr. J. Edgar Parkes that the demand for an infallible book "is one of the relics of our heathenism."

"ideal") becomes with Niebuhr a mythical symbol. Science teaches that the human body cannot possibly be raised from death. Immortality of the soul is what we now believe in rather than the resurrection of the body.

The power of the Cross lies exclusively in the "conversion" of the sinner, which means a confession of the fact that there is no salvation apart from the intrusion of divine grace into the life with a new power. Repentance and conversion are followed by a sense of relief, as man, who remains imperfect, is judged by God according to "the Christ in us," who is "not a possession but a hope."

And all of this is, of course, the result of Niebuhr's refusal to acknowledge the Bible as containing the objective, God-given, and normative truth.[7]

Nothing New in Modernism

These writers love to refer to "the modern mind" as if it were something altogether novel and superior to the unscientific mind of the barbarous age just concluded. The truth is that their entire system is hoary with age. The *Aufklärung* in the eighteenth century may not have a phraseology as replete with terms borrowed from the dogma of evolution, but its ideas on all points of weight were substantially the same. Ernest Gordon in his chapter *"Modernist Antiques, or The Old and the New Enlightenment"* (*The Lesson of the Sadducees*) has gone to the trouble of putting side by side citations from the eighteenth-century Liberals and from twentieth-century Modernists: the similarity is more than accidental. And Dr. Dowkontt has given page after page of parallel quotations from *The Age of Reason* by the American deist Thomas Paine (1793) and from Harry Emerson Fosdick's *The Modern Use of the Bible* (1924) — and the two are as similar as

---

7. Cf. E. J. Carnell, *The Theology of Reinhold Niebuhr*. Eerdmans, 1951. The author gives numerous citations, some of which (with others) may be found at the close of this chapter. They should fully warrant the conclusions of Van Til, Morrison, and Carnell that "neo-orthodoxy" is in reality "neo-liberalism."

two books by different authors could well be expected to be.[8]
Nor is this all there is to be said. Unitarians, according
to the church historian Prof. Walker, are "of a decidedly
Arian tendency"; and that Modernists are Arians the present writer has shown in another connection.[9] As such they
are related to Russellism as two branches growing out of
the same trunk. Russellism is the type of Arianism that
claims to believe in the inspiration of Scripture, and proceeds to twist its teachings into the opposite; Unitarian is
that form of Arianism that comes out in the open and denies
the inspiration of Scripture.

An Insufficient Change

True, Modernism has changed somewhat during the last
three decades. The superficial optimism which formerly
characterized the movement has given way to a more sober
outlook on life. Two world wars with the amazing bestiality
of man toward men, plus an in-between, world-wide "depression" have sobered even "liberal theologians." Wilhelm
Pauck, H. Richard Niebuhr, Reinhold Niebuhr, H. P. Van
Dusen, and many others have revolted against "the superficial optimism" of the Coolidge era. The hour of repentance
and of realizing the sinfulness of man has arrived. And they
now couch their liberalism-with-alterations in terms largely
borrowed from the old orthodoxy.

"Rousseau's doctrine of man is the curse of the age in
which we live. It has become a curse because it has been
accepted as true, whereas it is palpably false.... The greatest evils which harass the modern world and which threaten
it with destruction are the lineal descendants of the doctrine that man is naturally good. It is that false doctrine
which has made man himself the end-all and be-all of existence and which has filled the world with the cults of

---

8. Dowkontt, *The Deadly Parallel*.
9. See my articles on "The Ritschlians and the Pre-existence of Christ" in *The Princeton Theological Review* of July and October, 1920; and compare my "The Pre-Existence of Christ and (revised) Arianism," in *Religion and Culture*, Grand Rapids, Mich., May and August 1920.

blood and race and nation. And in so far as that doctrine continues to dominate Western thought we may expect the recurring horrors of war and revolution, because it is a doctrine whose logic deprives mankind of a common frame of reverence and in the end sets every man against every other man."

These words of F. P. Miller are paralleled in the same volume by those of H. R. Niebuhr: "Modernism has attempted to interpret religion in all its aspects — philosophical, historical, psychological, doctrinal and practical — from the point of view of anthropology. In spite of all its theoretical and practical knowledge of religion, it has lost God. Hence it is drawn into the conflicts of human life to such a degree that it can no longer speak with that authority or objectivity which ought to be expected of those who believe in God. It is this aspect of Modernism which brings it so dangerously close to the heresy of Humanism."

"From the very start," so Dr. Niebuhr continues, "Modernism has taken Christianity for granted. It has always thought and acted on the basis of the existent church. As a matter of fact, its chief purpose was and is a defense of the church. Modernism is an apologetic movement . . . . But in spite of all this, two questions were very persistently raised: What is Christianity? and, What is the church? The answer which Harnack gave with such scholarly confidence and gentlemanly self-assurance has long been deemed insufficient. But the questions persist. And who among the Modernists can be said to have given them a cogent answer?"

One readily sees from such citations that there is less optimism among Modernists than there was a generation ago. And they are less satisfied with their own achievements than their hopeful outlook would have warranted.

From the evangelical standpoint one can only rejoice at this change. However, when we look somewhat more closely, we are disappointed. The change is not a radical change. It does not go down to the bottom of things. The Modernist outlook is less roseate because men have been disappointed.

The return to God which is advocated is not a return to the God of the Scriptures. The repentance that is spoken of does not go far enough. Modernism still trusts in its own arm. The result is often a pessimism that is as thoroughgoing as the optimism of yesterday. Edward J. Carnell aptly remarks: "Neo-orthodoxy is the construction of the minds of erstwhile liberals. Barth, Brunner and Niebuhr were all schooled as liberals. And the tragic events of history, together with a discovery of Kierkegaard, have forced them from immanence to transcendence. But one of the liberal presuppositions which no member of this school has been able to slough off is the hypothesis that science and higher criticism have forever smashed the doctrine of the plenary inspiration of the Bible."[10]

"The Christian analysis of life," states Reinhold Niebuhr in his *An Interpretation of Christian Ethics*, "leads to conclusions which will seem morbidly pessimistic to moderns, still steeped as they are in their evolutionary optimism."

"Beneath the thin veneer of satisfied self-assurance," according to Dr. Van Dusen, "the man of today is a strangely bewildered, profoundly unhappy mortal .... Today [1935], we confront a generation shorn of self-confidence — disillusioned of its leadership, disillusioned as to the significance of its own achievement, disillusioned of its ability to save the crumbling remnants of its proud domain. The florid optimism of yesterday has evaporated overnight."[11]

But what is the remedy these dissatisfied men offer?

To begin with, they expect to heal the individual through healing the mass. That old cure-all has not been abandoned. "The social gospel" remains the great hope. Thus Van Dusen acclaims first of all that history teaches: *"The ultimate outcome of history is within God's control."* The second thing we are to learn, so he states, is *"the moral determination of history."* God's influence upon society is

---
10. *Op. cit.*, p. 138.
11. For the same vague dissatisfaction with Modernism, see Dr. Fosdick's article, "Beyond Modernism," in *The Christian Century*, Dec. 4, 1935, and Dr. Morrison's "The New Modernism" in the same weekly for March 4, 1936.

continuous, unwearying; and it is for good. Thirdly, we learn that *"God's influence upon society is most easily discerned as judgment and as discipline."* History teaches, even today, that the wages of sin is death. And fourthly, we discover that "the Christian understanding of history declares *the only ways by which social ills can be soundly and permanently rectified.* It dictates the conditions of effective social change, the methods in the social struggle to which Christians can give ready support." In brief, then, this is "The Message in Society's Crisis."

It will be observed that both the disease and the remedy are described as social. Is there no message, then, for the individual? Yes, there are "Gifts of Personal Religion." These are said to be: "1. Vision; 2. Insight; 3. Radicalism; 4. Faith." When it is asked, what is meant by faith, we reply in Dr. Van Dusen's own words: "If one were asked what it is which these times will most urgently need, the answer would be unhesitating — *men and women with sticking power."*

Dr. E. E. Aubrey informs us, "The new social psychology has brought about an important modification of individualism by pointing out that individual personality is a social product. This gives a new setting to any discussion of individualism."

And a few lines further he states, "This serves to explain the interpretation of Christianity in terms of individual worth and the testing of authority and doctrine by individual experience — two emphases in modern preaching." This means that the individual is reached as a unit of society, and so the individual's experience accounts for whatever doctrine he holds. The reason that Buchmanism, with a similar emphasis upon doctrine as the fruit of experience, is severely criticized in modernist circles lies not, of course, in this fundamental concept the two hold in common, but rather in what Modernists term Buchmanism's "pietism": its emphasis upon the personal change at the expense of proper stress on the "social gospel."

UNITARIANISM-MODERNISM

Dr. Wilhelm Pauck, be it observed, has no solution to offer. Writing on "The Crisis of the Church," he concludes, "The considerations of these pages . . . do not offer a solution to the problem to which they are addressed . . . . But they hint at the solution in so far as they contain the observation that an age which has attained more power of world control than any other longs for sanctification by a new sense of God. The spirit of secularism has brought about the crisis of the old and contemporary religion. A new religious sense, built upon a new certainty of God, must bring the spirit of secularism into a crisis. When the event occurs, we shall be saved. Perhaps the time is not far distant when a prophet will arise among us who, fully imbued with the mood and spirit of our era, will speak to us in the name of the living God with such power and authority that all who long for salvation will be compelled to listen. In the meantime, we must learn to be humble in the awareness that it is God, the Lord of all life, who has laid his hand upon us in this crisis. And we must learn to pray: We believe, O Lord, help thou our unbelief. He who will have authority to declare that this prayer has been heard will be the leader of the movement by which the crisis will be overcome."

Very true. But the man with that authority will point back to "the faith which was once for all delivered unto the saints." Jesus Christ came to lay down His life a ransom for many. God did not intend that man should be saved through His blood in the first century, and by an easier, less costly way in the twentieth.

And so the vagueness, rather the absolute lack of doctrinal content of the most modern Modernists, as well as the outspoken aversion to Scriptural and creedal doctrine of the earlier Unitarians, cause us to maintain the verdict of one Modernist as over against that of another.

Dr. Aubrey stated, "The modernist is able to co-operate with any man who is honestly seeking light, be he archconservative or humanist, because they both have the same objective."

That may be true when it comes to closing bars before midnight and fighting prostitution. But when it comes to the service of the "Lord of all life," we remind all Modernists that Dr. Morrison wrote a true word in the January 3, 1924, issue of *The Christian Century*. As a rule Dr. Morrison is far more clear when he writes on sociological matters than when he trespasses upon the field of theology. But in that lucid hour he caused something of a stir with the editorial, *Fundamentalism and Modernism: Two Religions*. " 'Blest be the tie' may be sung until doomsday, but it cannot bind these two worlds together. The God of the fundamentalist is one God; the God of the modernist another. The Christ of the fundamentalist is one Christ; the Christ of modernism is another. The Bible of fundamentalism is one Bible; the Bible of modernism is another. The church, the kingdom, the salvation, the consummation of all things — these are one thing to fundamentalists and another to modernists. Which God is the Christian God, which Christ is the Christian Christ, which Bible is the Christian Bible, which church, which kingdom, which salvation, which consummation are the Christian church, the Christian kingdom, the Christian salvation, the Christian consummation? The future will tell."

We are grateful for the candid admission in the first part of this citation. We cannot agree with the thesis in the latter part. With Dr. Morrison himself stating, "There is a clash here as profound and as grim as that between Christianity and Confucianism," there is no need to wait for the future to tell us which of these two religions is the Christian religion. The Christian religion is as much and as definitely a historical phenomenon as is Confucianism, or Taoism. What the Christian religion is, historical investigation will show undeniably. And such historical investigation will bring to light that the Christian religion has ever held to the God, the Christ, the Bible, and the salvation of supernaturalism, and these are exactly the God, the Christ, the Bible and the salvation that are denied by Modernism. When Dr. Morrison stated editorially that "Christianity according to fundamentalism is another religion," this one time popular modernist should have had the courage of his conviction. He should have changed the title of the magazine from The *Christian* Century to The *Modernist* Century! Like so many men, Dr. Morrison was eager to maintain the name Christian when he admittedly rejected historical, biblical Christianity.

Enter World War II. As long as the United States was not a participant, American Modernism stuck to its position. But when our own nation suddenly became involved by the Japanese attack upon Pearl Harbor on December 7, 1941, the Modernist dream went to pieces. Dr. Morrison, sponsor of "the outlawry of war," frankly abandoned his pacifism and wrote on war as "An Unnecessary Necessity." General Sherman, so he stated, had uttered a far more theological truth than he realized when he defined war as hell.

It was an adroit move. For it took war out of the category of moral good or evil, and made the killing of their fellow men by men who had asserted that under no condition would they again obey the government to the point of killing, an "amoral act."

"Nobody in hell calls hell a sin. By the same token war cannot be called a sin. Nobody imagines that it is his 'duty' to 'renounce' hell, once he is in it. Likewise war can be renounced only before we get into it, that is, while there is peace. No one in hell thinks of 'bearing witness' against hell, by refusing to take part in *some* of its functions. No one in hell thinks it necessary to call certain of its functions 'righteous' in order to engage in them. And certainly no one in hell imagines that he must justify any of his selfish activities by getting the approval of God.

"The only sin against which a soul in hell can bear witness is the sin that brought him there. The only righteousness to which he can bear witness is the righteousness of God's judgment in condemning him to the hell in which he now finds himself. Hell is that realm or condition or situation — call it what you will — where good and evil have lost their distinction, where evil is good and good is evil. This is precisely what war is, and total war answers this description in amazing full details."[12]

So wrote Dr. Morrison. What is wrong with this?

It is not what Dr. Albert Edward Day, former vice-president of the Federal Council of Churches of Christ in America, now renamed as the National Council of the Churches of Christ in the United States of America, alleges against this view. Wrote Dr. Day:

"Hell is not external circumstances. Hell is internal corruption. One is never *in* hell; one *is* hell. Hell is not anything done to a man by events or people; hell is disintegration within a man. It is not something to which God condemns a man. It is separation from God by an atrophy or suicide of the faculties whereby God gets a man or man holds fellowship with God. One repents of *nothing* in hell, neither of hell itself, nor of the sins that have made hell. One has lost all capacity for repentance for he has shut out the God who alone can evoke repentance. One does not have a tormenting conscience. One has only the torment of absence of conscience. One then makes no moral choices of any kind; one has become hell, the paralysis of moral choice. War is not hell."[13]

Thus these rationalists continue to borrow the terminology of Scripture, to pour into it their own conceptions, and, incidentally, to contradict one another.

If they would but turn to the inspired Scriptures, and inquire into the meaning of the words "repentance," "judgment," "hell," they would not have to change their stand so often.

The dramatic book of Revelation, with its returning cycles of sin, judgments and apothesis, presents a clear and different picture.

Take, for instance, the third cycle, that of the seven an-

---
12. *The Christian Century*, Jan. 21, 1942.
13. *The Christian Century*, March 18, 1942.

UNITARIANISM-MODERNISM 313

gels sounding the seven trumpets (Chs. 8 and 9). Here the sins of the apostate nations are visited by judgments in nature: upon the land (8:7), on the sea (8:8,9) and the rivers (8:10, 11), in the heavens (8:12). All of these are in symbolic language, reminding us of the Old Testament calamities in nature with added features to augment their horror.

Then, because there is no return to God as a result of these, an angel announces that another three trumpets will introduce three more judgments which far surpass any divine judgments so far experienced upon the earth (8:13). They are therefore called "woes."

Two of these woes are described in picturesque language. The fifth trumpet inaugurates the increasing influence of demons, let loose to torment men with the removal of all light of righteousness and holiness (9:1-11).

The sixth trumpet introduces a picture of ever larger *wars* as the most terrible of divine judgments upon earth (9:13-19).

Then follows this terrible indictment, "And the rest of mankind, who were not killed with these plagues, repented not of the works of their hands, that they should not worship demons, and the idols of gold and silver, and of brass, and of stone, and of wood; which can neither see, nor hear nor walk: and they repented not of their murders, nor of their sorceries, nor of their fornication, nor of their thefts."

This should logically be followed by the sounding of the seventh trumpet. But the dramatic action is interrupted and a comforting interlude is introduced (10:1 to 11:14).

When the seventh trumpet sounds, we are given a view of eternal bliss *after* the final judgment. The final judgment is not described until the end of the last cycle (20: 11-15). At that point we are told *what hell is*. Hell is the state of final judgment to which all those will be condemned who have not repented as a result of previous divine judgments, which had been so many warnings to seek redemption from the wrath to come in "the blood of the Lamb."

War, therefore, is not hell. Neither is man hell. Hell is

God's final answer to a world that refuses the saving gift of His Son. War is only a warning, a precursor of hell.

Nor was the late war the final calamity prior to the return of Christ. The King of kings and Lord of lords continues to gather "a great multitude, which no man could number, out of every nation and of all tribes and peoples and tongues" which John saw "standing before the throne and the Lamb" (7:9) at the close of an earlier cycle.

In his boyhood years the present writer wondered how destruction could strike against all nations at once. The latest inventions and discoveries of an apostate world have made that clear. Yet even World War II did not strike everywhere at once; large continents, the resources of which have hardly been tapped, are isolated. When, in a future war, bombs will sail through the stratosphere, and one continent will, from its home base, destroy metropolitan areas upon another continent, the words of Christ will be fulfilled, "And except those days had been shortened, no flesh would have been saved: but for the elect's sake those days shall be shortened" (Matt. 24:22).

In those days of the end, false Christs and false prophets will arise, as have already arisen today, and have been described in this volume.

Then, when the humanistic dream of a man-made gospel of tolerance, goodwill, brotherhood, and democracy will have ended in the total collapse of a civilization that owed its rise and development to the light of Christ but used it in the pursuit of sinful and ungodly ends, then, "as the lightning cometh forth from the east, and is seen even unto the west; so shall be the coming of the Son of man" (Matt. 24:27).

Then shall be the final judgment.

Then shall the unrepentant be consigned to "his portion with the hypocrites: there shall be the weeping and the gnashing of teeth" (Matt. 24:51).

"But according to his promise, we look for new heavens and a new earth, wherein dwelleth righteousness" (II Peter 3:13).

It is for us to answer our Lord's question: "Nevertheless, when the Son of man cometh, shall he find faith on the earth?" (Luke 18:8).

Humanism

There are those among the more recent Modernists who resent the name "Humanism" as applied to Modernism, preferring the statement that Modernism is "anthropocentric." But is not this just a different name for the same thing? Dr. Walker has written of the Italian Renaissance, the forerunner of medieval Humanism, "Yet, when all these elements are recognized, it remains true that the Renaissance involved an essentially new outlook on the world, in which emphasis was laid on its present life, beauty, and satisfaction — on man as man — rather than on a future heaven and hell, and on man as an object of salvation or loss. The means by which this transformation was wrought was a reappreciation of the spirit of classical antiquity, especially as manifested in its great literary monuments." Substitute "Unitarianism-Modernism" for "Renaissance," "modern science" for "classical antiquity," "discoveries" for "literary monuments," change all verbs to the present tense, and the statement applies with equal truth to the new Humanism.

This Humanism is observed even in the strictly Unitarian hymns to which we have been treated of late years. Our Modernist friends have at last awakened to the incongruity of closing a service in which the resurrection of Christ is denied with a hymn asserting, "Hallelujah, Christ arose." It was this situation which caused the late Dr. Francis L. Patton to say, with a twinkle in his eye, "Well, they have left us the choir, anyhow." The much advertised and much used volume, *Hymns of the United Church*, with its companion volume, *Hymns for American Youth*, contains a liberal mixture of both orthodox and unorthodox materials. The following "hymn" however, has been advertised most widely as "a typical page from this hymnal":

1. *My Master was a worker,*
   With daily work to do,
   And he who would be like him
   Must be a worker, too;
   Then welcome honest labor,
   And honest labor's fare,
   For where there is a worker,
   The Master's man is there.

2. *My Master was a comrade,*
   A trusty friend and true,
   And he who would be like him
   Must be a comrade, too;
   In happy hours of singing,
   In silent hours of care,
   Where goes a loyal comrade,
   The Master's man is there.

3. *My Master was a helper,*
   The woes of life he knew,
   And he who would be like him
   Must be a helper, too;
   The burden will grow lighter,
   If each will take a share,
   And where there is a helper
   The Master's man is there.

4. *Then, brothers brave and manly*
   Together let us be,
   For he who is our Master,
   The Man of men was he;
   The men who would be like him
   Are wanted ev'rywhere,
   And where they love each other
   The Master's men are there.

The beauty of a product like that lies in the first place in the melody, which is "arranged from Mendelssohn," and further in the almost universal use that may be made of the hymn. If we should ever have to face an audience made up of Spiritists, Theosophists, Freemasons, Russellites, Mormons, and Baha'ists, with a generous sprinkling of Unitarians and Modernists, we could think of no song that might prove more acceptable to that motley crowd than this "typical page from this hymnal." They could all heed our request, "Everybody sing, please." Not only that, but this typical song could also *mutatis mutandis* be recommended to adherents of other religions, provided their prophet had a name not exceeding three syllables. Thus, "Mohammed was a worker, With daily work to do," would not sound bad at all. As a sort of international national anthem this "hymn" could be made to render excellent service with only very slight alterations. Thus the Germans might be asked to sing, "Old Bismarck was a worker, With daily work to do, And where there is a worker, Count Bismark's man is there." Likewise an American can scarcely be expected to object to the paraphrase, "Our Lincoln was a helper, The woes of life he knew, And he who would be like him, Must be a helper, too." The song, then, is indeed of wide usefulness. The only difficulty is to discover why it should be called a hymn. Hymnals usually contain religious songs, while this "typical page" contains no religion, except it be the worship of man.

This chapter would become too long if we tried to take cognizance of the ever shifting opinions with the ranks of a system whose adherents lay more stress upon the method than upon the content of their message, and who write books on such subjects as "One Man's Religion."

Since, however, Dr. Morrison's influence continues to be popular and prevalent among the local churches, we include the following few observations on his provoking series of thirteen articles, *Can Protestantism Win America?*[14] For even if it is impossible to deal exhaustively with the thrust of these articles (which is a plea for an undenominational and nondoctrinal "ecumenicity," that is, a unity of effort under the "Lordship of Christ" over against the Catholic unity of effort under the pope),

---

14. *The Christian Century*, April 3, 1946 to July 5, 1946.

it will be possible to make a few remarks that will cast light upon this latest effort of Modernism.[15]

Our first remark, then, concerns the article, "The Wasted Power of Protestantism." While it remains true and needs to be emphasized more today than ever before that the endless splits from ten to twenty struggling and overlapping churches and Sunday Schools in the average American town of from five to ten thousand population is a "scandal," and a sad waste of money and energy,[16] the solution of the problem can never be found in the method of Dr. Morrison, which fails to reckon with sin as the cause of the present division. "Sin on the one hand and grace on the other account for the distinction between believers and unbelievers and make the universal brotherhood of man, of which the modernists love to speak, an utter impossibility. The difference between the friends and the enemies of the Christ of the Scripture is found not only in the world but in the Church as well. In short, there is truth and error in the Visible Church; there is a true Church but also a false Church. There are synagogues of Satan which call themselves by the name of Christ. There is no recognition of these distinctions, by so much as a syllable, in the series of Dr. Morrison. His entire plea for the union of all Protestant churches is based on the assumption that all Churches, at least those called Protestant, belong to the body of Christ, and that no Church has the right to refuse to fellowship with them as spiritual brethren."[17]

---

15. A good and more detailed criticism has been given by the Rev. H. J. Kuiper, editor of *The Banner*, in the July to Sept. 1946 issues of that weekly.
16. Cf. my *Our Christian Heritage*. (Grand Rapids: Wm. B. Eerdmans Publishing Co., 1948).
17. H. J. Kuiper, *The Banner*, Aug. 30, 1946. That outward union continues to count for more than doctrinal unity or purity is clear from the appraisal of the Graham revival work by the new editor of *The Christian Century*, Harold E. Fey:

"If the effort of Billy Graham succeeds it will make mincemeat of the ecumenical movement, will divide congregations and denominations, will set back Protestant Christianity a half century . . . . Protestants, rightly eager to let every opinion be heard, are letting themselves be identified with a discredited and disavowed version of Christianity. . . ." (*Continued on next page.*)

Our second major objection is against the thesis advocated by Dr. Morrison that ecumenicity should be based upon "the Lordship of Christ." This is not a Christian ecumenicity (though it may be one of high ethical ideas) because it fails to be based upon revealed truth. Evangelicals will never be able to recognize as Christian a conception of the Lordship of Christ that is not based upon an objective, God-given standard, but upon "the dignity of the individual man whose capacity to answer for himself directly to God" is considered apart from the infallible Scriptures.

In close connection with this we list as a third objection to Morrison's plea for an ecumenical Protestantism his gross historical inaccuracy on a basic point. We refer to the fact that Dr. Morrison, in order to clinch his position for a unified Protestantism, asserts in "Protestant Misuse of the Bible" that later Protestantism has erred in viewing the Bible as the inspired Word of God, and the final arbiter and authority of religious opinion. This view is said to have given birth to denominations. For it has substituted a book for a man, but the principle remains the same. "Rome can point to its [Protestantism's] more than 200 denominational *churches* and, looking Protestantism fairly in the eye, can scornfully say: 'These *churches* belie your claim to be ecumenical. Your denominational "churches" are, every one of them, little counterfeit imitations of Rome, resting upon the same kind of basis as that which you say caused you to leave the Roman Catholic Church, namely, an infallible interpretation of an infallible Bible. We have one vice-

---

In the same editorial the entire movement is written off in these scathing terms: "By changing its name to 'evangelical,' yet holding on to its unevangelical creed, fundamentalism unchurches the church. . . . The real tragedy lies in the fact that the churches and their leaders proclaim their own spiritual bankruptcy in pretending, for the sake of an immediate questionable gain, that what was going on [in Madison Square Garden during Graham's New York crusade] helps in any very important way the ceaseless effort of the infinite God to save men by winning them to lasting reconciliation with himself and by helping them to grow in grace in the fellowship of the churches and in service to each other" (Editorial, "Fundamentalist Revival, A Discussion of the Billy Graham Revival in New York City," *The Christian Century*, June 19, 1957).

regent of Christ; you have more than one hundred.' Every word of this indictment would be true; and the scorn with which it was spoken would be fully warranted."

This presentation is palpably inaccurate. In the first place, no Protestant church has ever claimed infallibility for its own interpretation of the Bible. But secondly, and this is more pertinent, Morrison enforces his view with the startling claim that it was Calvin who was to blame for this conception of an authoritative Bible. "Calvin was originally a lawyer, and he interpreted the Bible as if it were a book of law, infallibly and equally authoritative in all its parts and in every word." Of Luther he says that Luther considered not the Bible but Christ as the Word of God.

This view, which discriminates between the Reformers and states that Luther found Christ "where the Book says he is to be found, namely, in the living community of believers from which he has never withdrawn his living presence," and that to Calvin "the Bible was itself the divine revelation," is untenable for two reasons. The first is the historical fact that to all the Reformers Christ was the incarnate Word of God and the Bible the written Word of God, and to the entire Reformation movement the principle of authority was the Bible as distinct from the Church (Rome) or human reason (Modernism).[18] That in this respect Luther was in agreement with Calvin, not with Morrison, see the article, "The Place of the Bible in Protestantism" by Dr. Theodore Graebner in *The Lutheran Witness*, July 2, 1946.[19]

The second reason is that when Dr. Morrison states, "The Protestant mind has not allowed Christ to be the interpreter of the Bible; it has used the Bible as a realistic and literalistic interpreter of Christ," the question immediately arises, Which Christ are you referring to? Do you mean the "resurrection" Christ of Dr. Morrison, or the Christ

---

18. Cf. G. H. Hospers, *The Reformed Principle of Authority*.
19. Dr. Graebner states, "One need only consult the hundreds of references by which the late Dr. M. Reu in his *Luther and the Scriptures* (1944) proves his proposition that the Scripture was Luther's sole authority."

who said, "The scripture cannot be broken" (John 10:35), and, "Till heaven and earth pass away, one jot or one tittle shall in no wise pass away from the law" (Matt. 5:18)?
For the rest, we may remind the reader, to make this brief survey somewhat less incomplete, that the late Prof. L. Berkhof divided the more recent Modernists into two groups, "the social theologians or meliorists," among whom he counted the men then at the Divinity School of Chicago, and the "new theists" among whom he numbered Wobbermin, Hocking, and Fosdick, the Fosdick since *Beyond Modernism*. The latter laid greater emphasis upon the personality of God, and to them He is both transcendent and immanent.

When Barthianism at first took the theological world by storm, it was believed for a while that Modernism had virtually died of old age. Then came Dr. C. Van Til's book *The New Modernism*, in which he placed Barthianism in the camp with Modernism. This was followed by Charles Clayton Morrison's keen analysis, "The Liberalism of Neo-Orthodoxy" in *The Christian Century*, June 7, 14, 21, 1950. And then there was Dr. Wilhelm Pauck's chapter, "A Defense of Liberalism," in his book, *The Heritage of the Reformation* (Boston: Beacon Press, 1950). But with these, one interested in forming a studied opinion should also read *The Triumph of Grace in the Theology of Karl Barth*, by G. C. Berkouwer (Grand Rapids: Wm. B. Eerdmans Publishing Co., 1956).

That the same old Modernism with its denials of the virgin birth, the bodily resurrection of Christ, the inspiration of Scripture, and the like, has by no means abdicated is further evident from such facts as these: In the Netherlands L. Praamsma has argued at some length that the situation has changed but little ("Zijn Er Nog Vrijzinnigen?" in *Gereformeerd Weekblad*, Oct. & Nov., 1950). In China Machen's old book *Christianity and Liberalism* was translated into Chinese in 1950. In the United States Chester A. Tulga argues that the missionaries in Asia are removing from "the gospel" whatever may appear distasteful to the pagan mind (*The Case Against Modernism in Foreign Missions.* Chicago: Conservative Baptist Fellowship, 1950).[20]

The few quotations below from later works, will reveal, we regretfully note, that many men who would seriously object to being classed with Modernism, foster the same attitude toward Scripture as that of the old-time Unitarians and Modernists. The truth of Scripture becomes subjective and dependent upon the reader's reaction to what is written; one does not find in the Scriptures an objective and authoritative statement of truth.

Modernism and Christian Doctrine

That Unitarianism and Modernism are firmly opposed to the essentials of Christianity may be gathered from many of the following quotations which are taken almost at random. As in later Spiritism, so here, we find a swing toward a more suave and less hateful expression. This is not due, it would seem, to greater tolerance, but rather to a larger measure of indifference to all doctrinal teaching, the logical outcome of pragmatism. It will be observed, however, that the cardinal teachings and the great redemptive facts of the Christian religion are often just as decidedly rejected in the latest works.

---

20. It is difficult to refrain from quoting the following apt and eloquent words:

"Does not the modernist know Christ after the flesh, as the man of Galilee? as the beautiful Master, the uncrucified Teacher? Listen to Paul: 'Henceforth know we no man after the flesh: yea, though we have known Christ after the flesh, yet now henceforth know we Him no more' (II Cor. 5:16). These modernists have taken away our crucified Lord and know where they have laid Him; they have smothered Him with flowers. And does not the ritualist have a cross? a gold cross, a white cross, or a brass cross? (A number of years ago it was said there were enough crucifixes in the United States to fence in the state of Kentucky; ere long the whole nation may be fenced in.) The ritualists too have taken away the Crucified; they have buried Him beneath some Christless cross. Both of these extremes are 'after the flesh.' What a relief then to sing:

A Christless cross no refuge were for me;
A crossless Christ my Saviour could not be.
But O Christ crucified, I rest in Thee!"

L. E. Maxwell, *Crowded to Christ* (Grand Rapids: Wm. B. Eerdmans Publishing Co., 1950), p. 203.

The Bible

UNITARIANISM:

"We no longer depend for salvation upon either a man or a book. Men help us; books help us; but back of all stands our divine reason."—CHARLES W. ELIOT (late president of Harvard).[21]

"The Old Testament is a narrative of the early life and thought and struggle of the Jewish people, perhaps the most remarkable and, on the whole, admirable people of whom there is any record. The New Testament is made up of accounts of the life and work of Jesus, accounts given long after His death by persons who had never seen or heard Him, but were profoundly moved by reports concerning Him, reports more or less colored by the fact that they were formulated in a very credulous age by simple and, for the most part, unlettered men. In spite of these drawbacks, the really beautiful and divinely human character of Jesus shines forth, and increasing numbers of men are catching His spirit and following, though afar off and with halting steps, His glorious example." — GRACE JULIAN CLARKE.[22]

MODERNISM:

"Men can get on without the Bible, they can live good and religious lives without it, or without any sacred book. The man who does not know the Bible, or whose acquaintance with it has begun in an unimpressionable age, will probably never know that he is missing anything." — J. B. PRATT.[23]

"The only precious thing in danger is the Church's reputation for honesty and candor. The case of truth can never be advanced by men who dare not face the facts. It is disheartening that even in our day there are men of intelligence and noble purposes who refuse to admit that Paul was mistaken...

---

21. *The Indianapolis Unitarian Bulletin*, pp. 3, 5; 1927.
22. *Ibid.*, pp. 11, 12, 1925.
23. James B. Pratt, "Religion and the Young Generation," *Yale Review*, April, 1923.

"The traditional conception of inspiration must be reconstructed. . . . The image of the inspired and inerrant Apostle, which still hangs in many a mind, is a creation of the pious and uninstructed imagination. . . .

"He [Paul] wrote a letter to the Thessalonians which stirred up so much commotion, that he had to write a second letter to explain what he meant. He wrote a letter to the Corinthians which contained statements so extreme, that it was necessary to write another letter to tone these statements down." — C. E. JEFFERSON.[24]

"So we used to think of inspiration as a procedure which produced a book guaranteed in all its parts against error, and containing from beginning to end a unanimous system of truth. No well-instructed mind, I think, can hold that now." — H. E. FOSDICK.[25]

"We know now that every idea in the Bible started from primitive and childlike origins, and, with however many setbacks and delays, grew in scope and height toward the culmination in Christ's gospel. We know now that the Bible is the record of an amazing spiritual development." —H. E. FOSDICK.[26]

"The Bible, therefore, is not only inspired as all other honest work is inspired, but in the same way. If it reveals a higher measure of inspiration than any other work, it is not because it was given it, but because it has reached it." — BASIL KING.[27]

"For the revelation with which the N. T. is charged is not a fixed dogma, supernaturally conveyed, but a Life generated by the Spirit of Jesus Christ. This Life implies no doubt certain truths or doctrines which have to be retained and from time to time restated. But they are only tenable in and through participation in the Life itself. What enforces them is not any dogma of Church tradition, not any arbitrary hypothesis of verbal inspiration,

---

24. *The Character of Paul,* pp. 37, 154, 155.
25. *The Christian Century,* Sept. 4, 1924.
26. *The Modern Use of the Bible,* p. 11.
27. "The Bible and Common Sense," in *Harper's Magazine,* July-Oct., 1934.

UNITARIANISM-MODERNISM

but the authority with which life speaks to life." — J. MOFFATT.[28]

"The Reformation insistence upon the authority of Scripture, as against the authority of the church, bears within it the perils of a new idolatry. Its Biblicism became, in time, as dangerous to the freedom of the human mind in searching out causes and effects as the old religious authority." — REINHOLD NIEBUHR.[29]

Blood Atonement

MODERNISM:

"He [the primitive beast-like man] lived long before Harvey's discovery of the circulation, but when he slit a throat the blood spurted, and to him that spurting was a manifestation of life in the blood. He came to believe that blood was precious, sacred. It was his habit to divide with his gods whatever good things he gained; he thought the gods liked the flavor and smoke of cooking meat and that above all they liked blood. So bloody sacrifice entered into religions." — BRUCE BARTON.[30]

"Who can look on such a one as he hangs upon the cross and cries, 'It is finished,' and believe that it is indeed finished? Is this all of such a life as that? Are we living in a universe which produces such a man and then so wantonly destroys him? Our soul revolts at the conception. It is *not* finished. We must defend the world against such an indictment." — CHARLES C. MORRISON.[31]

"Christian theology was to find the explanation in the sacrificial system of Judaism; his death [Christ's] was to be the one grand sacrifice that would meet the Divine requirements forever. It is almost certain that Jesus himself did not think so." — W. A. GIFFORD.[32]

"A man's salvation at the cross does not depend upon accepting a certain view of what happened at the death

---

28. Cf., *Princeton Theological Review*, Oct. 1926, p. 608.
29. *The Nature and Destiny of Man*, Vol. II, p. 152.
30. *What Can a Man Believe?*, p. 21.
31. *The Christian Century*, April 14, 1927.
32. *The Story of the Faith*, p. 76.

of Jesus. Beware of the teacher who almost forgets savior and saved in his fascination with the operation, the transaction, the mechanics of the salvation. . . . Instead of getting down to the substantive question of who is saved from what for what, he ties us up in a consideration of how, by what arrangement, by what procedure salvation was effected. Instead of bidding us to the cross, which tells its own story and exhorts its own commitment, he demands subscription to a particular doctrine about what actually happened a long time ago. It is as if we were told that the light switch under our fingers would not turn on the lights until we had initialed the blue prints of a certain special dynamo or turbine. . . .

"The how of the cross remains one of the deep mysteries of the faith, probed only superficially by the best of our metaphors. But the salvation we know there comes from whom we see there and what happens to us there. Some Christians see the Son of God hung there; others see the greatest and truest and best of men crucified. But all see alike who brought this Jesus to this cross . . . *we* brought him there . . . . At the cross we see that God forgives us what we cannot forgive ourselves, that he wants us to be at home with him, not waiting for us to fix ourselves up enough to attract him, but desiring us so much just as we are, in all our confusion and wrongness, that he goes to this incomprehensible length and even — as some of us would say — suffers this ununderstandable agony to tell us that, to show us that, to give us a way back. . . ." — HAROLD E. FEY.[33]

MODERNISM:
The Christian

"The Christian shares with, or is like, other people in very many ways. He is like other people in his instincts, in having friendships, in being loyal to some purpose or some ideal. . . . He has his own distinctive temperament

---

33. Editorial, "What The Cross Certifies" in *The Christian Century*, Mar. 21, 1956.

like other folks. He may be temperamentally jovial or melancholy, active or sluggish. . . . The Christian, however, whatever his original nature, is one who has made up his mind to live his life after the model or pattern of Jesus." — A. W. WISHART.[34]

"It might be subject to question how far one was entitled to call himself a Christian in any complete and adequate sense whose religion is chiefly concerned with his personal salvation in another world, with doctrines, assents to which he therefore calls fundamental." — PROF. LYMAN of Union Theological Seminary.[35]

The Church

UNITARIANISM:

"The Church, according to the Unitarian understanding of things, is a purely human institution . . . . The Church is simply an organization of man's religious interests. The institution, no matter what its traditions and claims and forms, can have no authority above that which proceeds naturally from the intellectual and spiritual attainments of the persons composing it. Like every other institution it has a right to require that those seeking admission shall go through certain forms, but to offer eternal rewards or pronounce eternal doom is wholly beyond its right and power. To belong to a church cannot secure anyone a privileged position after death. The Church is a saving and righteous force in a community when and only to the extent that its members are living examples of purest and noblest character." — CHARLES GRAVES.[36]

MODERNISM:

"We Protestants should today be searching our hearts with this question: Have we given to Jesus Christ the kind of church that he deserves? He is the Head of the church

---

34. *The Christian Life*, etc. Three sermons delivered in the Fountain Street Baptist Church, Grand Rapids, Mich., 1925.
35. *Union Theological Seminary Bulletin*, 1922.
36. *The Indianapolis Unitarian Bulletin*, II, p. 25, 1927.

and as his disciples we are one in him. But we have failed to honor him with a church through which he could manifest himself in the true dignity and power of his redemptive presence. In fact we have not given him a church at all. Instead, we have given him a multiplicity of 'churches.' None of these 'churches' does he recognize as his own. And few if any of us would for a moment tolerate the claim that our denominational church is the Church of Christ. He did not found any of them. They are every one man-made. At their origin his body was broken — 'by schisms rent asunder.' . . . Those who look prayerfully forward to a great spiritual awakening in Protestantism — and who does not long for it? — may be sure that such a revival will not come to pass until we give back to Christ the church which he himself created and which his Lordship deserves. . . ." — CHARLES CLAYTON MORRISON.[37]

Creed

Dr. Charles Edwards Park, late pastor of the First Unitarian Church in Boston, answered the question of why Unitarians do not use the Apostles' Creed in its usual form. "We feel too much respect for it," writes the seventy-three-year-old minister in the July issue of the Unitarian monthly, *The Christian Register*. "Plenty of Christians can still repeat it with perfect honesty. We are not of that number. It does not express our belief." Dr. Park's version:

"I believe in (*a single, eternal, all-inclusive, all-pervading Life Principle whose source and perfect embodiment is God, who finds varying degrees of embodiment in all forms of life, who is the prototype of every grace, power, and nobility found in his creation, and whom I call*) God, the Father Almighty, Maker of heaven and earth; and in Jesus Christ (*not*) his only Son, (*for whose son am I? But*) our Lord (*because he is a more nearly perfect embodiment of the Life Principle than any one I know*) ; who

---

37. Editorial in *The Pulpit*, Feb., 1951.

was (*neither*) conceived by the Holy Ghost, (*nor*) born of the Virgin Mary, (*but was conceived and born exactly as we are all conceived and born; and who*) suffered under Pontius Pilate, was crucified, dead, and buried. He descended into (*no*) hell, (*for as hell is not a spiritual condition, he never saw the outer doormat of hell*). The third day (*the eager women found his tomb empty, and jumped to the conclusion that in the night*) he rose again from the dead; he ascended into (*no*) heaven, (*as heaven is not a place but a spiritual condition, he never left heaven,*) and sitteth on the right hand of God the Father Almighty (*if it is any comfort to you*). From thence he shall come (*if he is not already here*) to judge the quick and the dead. I believe in the Holy Ghost (*whom I call the Holy Spirit: the spirit in which God works;*) the holy catholic Church (*so long as it tries to be holy and catholic;*) the communion of (*what*) saints (*there are;*) the forgiveness of sins; the resurrection of the body (*if body means personality: not, if body means this mortal frame, for I am sick to death of my mortal frame and hope to be rid of it soon*); and the life everlasting (*meaning a chance to finish out the interrupted opportunities of this life*). Amen.[38]

Deity of Christ
UNITARIANISM:

"May I say, as clearly as I can, that I, as a Unitarian, believe in the divinity of Jesus? Then with the next breath say, I believe in the divinity of mankind. I believe, as well, in the divinity of every form of life. The dogma I deny is the exclusive divinity of Jesus. I do not believe the Eternal exhausted himself in one historic manifestation. I do not believe the Infinite can be compressed within the form of one being, even so exalted a personality as the Man of Nazareth. My difference with the Orthodox Church is not that it made Jesus God, but that it stopped there. I see the divine life sweeping on, filling every nook and cranny of the universe. It enters into every man;

---

38. *Newsweek*, July 22, 1946.

appears in every living thing. . . . The difference between the simplest form of life and the highest is not one of kind, but of degree. Jesus differs from other men only in His greater capacity for the one life."—F. S. C. WICKS.[39]

"It is in the face of the necessary admission that disciples of Socrates, Gotama, Confucius, Mohammed, and others could have experienced personal wholeness (salvation) that the Christological expression can be phrased as 'Jesus as a Christ.' Jesus is but one of the Christs of history, and his mediatorship is therefore not uniquely absolute or absolutely unique — even though it is both absolute and unique for those of us who experience it as such." — RONALD M. MAZU.[40]

MODERNISM:

"Perhaps it is sufficient to say that the Jesus of history actually created the Christ of faith in the life of the early church, and that his historic life is related to the transcendent Christ as a final and ultimate symbol of a relation which prophetic religion sees between all life and history and the transcendent." — REINHOLD NIEBUHR.[41]

"Christ is the symbol both of what man ought to be and of what God is beyond man."—REINHOLD NIEBUHR.[42]

Depravity

UNITARIANISM:

"Q. What gospel may we tell to 'the bad'?

"A. It is a gospel that the bad life is not man's true nature. It is a gospel that he can forsake and ought to forsake the evil way and that he will then become like a new creature as soon as he lets the electric touch of goodwill move his soul." — DR. DOYLE.[43]

---

39. *Indianapolis Unitarian Bulletin*, 4, 1, 1927.
40. Ronald M. Mazu, "Unitarians and the Dialogue," in *The Christian Century*, Feb. 15, 1961.
41. *An Interpretation of Christian Ethics*, p. 120, as cited by Carnell, *op. cit.*, p. 162. "Christ is the true mythical symbol of both the possibilities and the limits of the human." *Ibid.*, p. 15.
42. *Beyond Tragedy*, p. 23, as quoted by Carnell, *op. cit.*, p. 144.
43. *Catechism of Liberal Faith*, p. 110.

"Unitarianism is an attitude of the soul towards men. God being our Father, then we are all his children. This is a rather obvious platitude. But its significance is far-reaching. It undermines at once the doctrine of the total depravity of man. . . . That God is our Father means that man is in essence divine. . . . This fundamental thought of Unitarianism has vast practical applications. It modifies all our ideas of education and reform. The modern education is trusting more and more to the natural instincts of the child. Its watchword is not repression, but expression. . . . Character is the final goal of all our efforts." — JOHN H. APPLEBEE.[44]

MODERNISM:

"Christianity has at its heart the promise that no matter how much we may become involved in disobedience, no matter how long our record of deliberate wrongdoing, it is always possible, if we are honest with ourselves and with God, to turn and be changed. We can begin again without thinking of ourselves as under condemnation." — JOHN C. BENNETT.[45]

The Devil

MODERNISM:

"He [Satan] never appeared again in the Old Testament until after Persian influence had begun its work. . . . Having frankly recognized, therefore, the outgrown nature of the category [demons] we need not be troubled by it when we read the Bible." — H. E. FOSDICK.[46]

The Fall

UNITARIANISM:

"The stories of the creation of Adam and Eve, of their primal innocence, and of their fall, have become for us folklore. In it the Fall explained the origin of sin; and a horrible theory of the propagation of sin, reared by Augustine on the basis of the Fall, was accepted by official Catholic theologians. Darwin's triumph has destroyed

---

44. *Unitarianism: What It Is Not, and What It Is.*
45. *Christian Realism,* p. 40.
46. *The Modern Use of the Bible,* pp. 119, 121.

the whole theological scheme." — BISHOP BARNES in St. Paul's Cathedral, London.[47]

"The Real Difference Between Unitarian Christianity and Traditional Orthodoxy. This difference is not about the Trinity. It goes deeper. What Unitarians and many liberals in other churches reject is the Calvinistic doctrine of the Fall of Man and the Depravity of Human Nature. We believe in the age-long Rise of Man, the dignity and divinity of human nature. We seriously, passionately, believe that we are the children of the Highest; that our nature is not ruined but incomplete; that within us a divinely beautiful nature is latent, waiting development. For Calvinistic pessimism we substitute an inspiring faith in human nature, not merely in what it is, but in what it is to be . . . ."[48]

MODERNISM:

"That experience in the old theology has been labeled the 'fall of man,' but if it was a fall it was a fall forward. The man had become like God, knowing good and evil. It was the great upward step." — BRUCE BARTON.[49]

"The metaphysical connotations of the myth of the Fall are, however, less important for our purpose than the psychological and moral ones. It is in its interpretations of the facts of human nature, rather than in its oblique insights into the relation of order and chaos as such, that the myth of the Fall makes its profoundest contribution to moral and religious theory. The most basic and fruitful conception flowing from this ancient myth is the idea that evil lies at the juncture of nature and spirit. Evil is conceived as not simply the consequence of temporality or the fruit of nature's necessities. Sin can be understood neither in terms of the freedom of human reason alone, nor yet in terms of the circumscribed harmonies in which the human body is bound. Sin lies at

---

47. *Indianapolis Unitarian Bulletin*, 11,18, 1927.
48. *Ibid.*, 11, 16, 1928.
49. *What Can a Man Believe?*" p. 22.

the juncture of spirit and nature, in the sense that the peculiar and unique characteristics of human spirituality, in both its good and evil tendencies, can be understood only by analyzing the paradoxical relation of freedom and necessity, of finiteness and the yearning for the eternal in human life." — REINHOLD NIEBUHR.[50]

God

UNITARIANISM:

"Some day we shall be able to treat the myths and legends of the Bible as we do those of other peoples. Then Abraham and Prometheus, Samson and Hercules will appear alike as legendary heroes, while Zeus and Jehovah will be relegated to the dead man-made gods." — F. S. C. WICKS.[51]

MODERNISM:

"As preached in our Protestant churches the Trinity has often been little more than a mathematical formula about three being one and one three. Let it be said to the credit of the early fathers who introduced the church to the philosophical treatment of the Trinity, that they did not deal in such arithmetical absurdity as has characterized our modern pulpits in their identification of one person with three persons. If then, any one is troubled about this formula of the Trinity, the liberal prescription is familiar; translate the formula back into the experience from which it came. The Trinity that matters is the Trinity of experience."—H. E. FOSDICK.[52]

"When, however, the metaphysical presuppositions of Hellenistic thinking are abandoned, the doctrine is regarded as a symbol of Christian faith rather than as a literally exact description. Liberal Protestantism generally takes this position."—GERALD BIRNEY SMITH.[53]

---
50. *An Interpretation of Christian Ethics*, p. 76.
51. *Op. cit.*, 9, 29, 1926.
52. *Op. cit.*, p. 188.
53. G. B. Smith and S. Matthews, *A Dictionary of Religion and Ethics*, article on "Trinity."

"God is the work of human nature, imagination and will." — JOHN DEWEY.[54]

"I do not believe in any God that has ever been devised in any doctrine, that has ever claimed to be revealed, in any scheme of immortality that has ever been expounded. . . . there is no trustworthy evidence as to a God's absolute existence." — CARL VAN DOREN.[55]

"God is neither a Being nor existence of any sort, but rather an order of nature which includes men and all the processes of aspiring social life." — EDWARD SCRIBNER AMES.[56]

"Moses had had an extraordinary religious experience, that led him to enter into an exclusive covenant with Jehovah, or Yahweh, a storm god of Midian.

"It is unlikely that Moses was a monotheist, or even consciously looking towards monotheism." — GIFFORD.[57]

Holy Spirit

"There is simply no gainsaying the fact that the Good News was formulated in terms of a cosmology, a philosophy of history and a psychology, or of several of each of these, which if taken at face value are inadmissible to thinking men today. For example, the Christian is so familiar with the idea of the Holy Spirit as acting upon the believer or upon the sacramental elements that he hardly stops to consider what is implied, namely, a survival of a highly animistic point of view. Invasion of our bodies or selves by a 'spirit' either of God or of Satan is incredible with many today except as a figure of speech, and a Christian apologetics in these terms is under great handicaps."—AMOS N. WILDER.[58]

---

54. *A Common Faith*, New Haven, 1934, p. 71.
55. "Why I Am An Unbeliever," in the *Forum*, Dec., 1926.
56. *Religion*, New York, 1929, p. 177.
57. *The Story of the Faith*, pp. 2, 15.
58. *New Testament Faith for Today*, p. 44.

Judgment

MODERNISM:

"Personally, I do not pretend to know the details of the future life. . . . But I am likewise sure that the old Scriptural framework with its background of a Hebrew Sheol and a Zoroastrian judgment day is not in my mind." — H. E. FOSDICK.[59]

"It is unwise for Christians to claim any knowledge of either the furniture of heaven or the temperature of hell; or to be too certain about any details of the Kingdom of God in which history is consummated. But it is prudent to accept the testimony of the heart, which affirms the fear of judgment." — REINHOLD NIEBUHR.[60]

"The symbol of the last judgment in New Testament eschatology contains three important facets of the Christian conception of life and history. The first is expressed in the idea that it is Christ who will be the judge of history. Christ as judge means that when the historical confronts the eternal it is judged by its own ideal possibility, and not by the contrast between the finite and the eternal character of God." — REINHOLD NIEBUHR.[61]

"This fluidity of conception in the Jewish-Christian mythology is a commonplace of historical study. It should warn us against too literal a reading of the portrayals we find. If we take these pictures literally we do more than the Jews and early Christians did. What was important to them will, however, still be important to us: days of reckoning if not a day of reckoning, and God's governance of men and nations to the end of history."—AMOS N. WILDER.[62]

Man's Nature

UNITARIANISM:

"The difference between the Man of Galilee of the first century and the man of England and America in the

---
59. *Op. cit.*, p. 102.
60. *The Nature and Destiny of Man*, Vol. II, p. 294.
61. *Ibid.*, p. 291.
62. *Op. cit.*, p. 102.

nineteenth century, if I understand my gospels aright, is not in inherent capacity to draw near God, but in the relative degree of realization of a latent power common to humanity. It is this that has created the uniqueness of Jesus."—REV. ANSON PHELPS STOKES.[63]

MODERNISM:

"The incarnation was in man that it might be in men. O child of God, as God lived in his Son, so would he live in his sons and children."—C. S. MACFARLAND, former Secretary of the Federal Council of the Churches of Christ in America.[64]

"Christ is essentially no more divine than we are or than nature is."—A. C. MCGIFFERT.[65]

"Doctrines of human depravity are alleged to enervation and resignation. Not a few Protestant writers have conceived the distinctiveness and finality of Christianity in terms of this doctrine of the sacredness of human personality. This concept which has dominated so much of the Council's [Federal Council of Churches of Christ in America] social thought is clearly and ably expounded in the writings of Dr. F. Ernest Johnson. While his books are in no sense official pronouncements of the Council's position, no one has been in a better position to see and appreciate the real genius of its thought . . . . Let us see what Dr. Johnson has to say about the doctrine of man. Candidly he states, 'If the Christian message is Jesus, its social and ethical character is inescapable, it is the embodiment of deity within the apprehension of the human.' Again, 'The essential truth . . . is that man is under absolute mandate to express divinity in his own life and his whole nature.' Or, 'Little by little though sometimes with a startling suddenness mankind is learning that the essential divinity of man is

---
63. *Indianapolis Unitarian Bulletin*, 3, 25, 1927.
64. *The Spirit Christlike*, p. 68.
65. *The Rise of Modern Religious Ideas*, p. 208.

UNITARIANISM-MODERNISM 337

a first principle, not a derivative.' "—J. A. HUTCHINSON.⁶⁶

"We all, Christians, Buddhists, Shintoists, or whatever other faith, have much to learn from each other and much to contribute to each other. Also we feel that if we spiritual leaders are to accomplish anything constructive for the good of society as a whole we ought first to get together as religionists and come to know each other sympathetically."⁶⁷

Man's Original Righteousness

"Christian theology has found it difficult to refute the rationalistic rejection of the myth of the Fall without falling into the literalistic error of insisting upon the Fall as an historical event. One of the consequences of this literalism which has seriously affected the thought of the church upon the problem of man's essential nature, is the assumption that the perfection from which man fell is to be assigned to a particular historical period, i.e., the paradisaical period before the Fall. This chronological interpretation of a relation which cannot be expressed in terms of time without being falsified must not be attributed to the authority of the Biblical myth alone."—REINHOLD NIEBUHR.⁶⁸

Miracles

MODERNISM:

"Biblical miracles will more and more become unreal ghosts lost in antiquity and, gradually becoming dimmer, will disappear in utter incredulity. . . .

"For this is the principle on which alone can Biblical miracles have a vital part in our faith: Wherever a narrative in Scripture describes an experience in terms of miracle so that we recognize that the same kind of experience is open to us or would be open if we were recep-

---
66. *We Are Not Divided,* p. 303.
67. *Rethinking Missions,* p. 34.
68. *The Nature and Destiny of Man,* Vol. I, p. 267.

tive of God's incoming power, that narrative is fundamentally credible and useful."—H. E. FOSDICK.[69]

"One of the earliest of the prophet-teachers himself used magic to discredit the inferior magic of his opponents, the priests of the Baal. Elijah brought down fire from heaven to consume a water-sodden sacrifice, after making sport of the futile attempts of the Baal-worshipers. A third example of belief in magic can be taken from the regulations given in the book of Leviticus for cleansing a house after a visitation of plague or leprosy. These regulations read like the descriptions of magic one can find in many modern discussions of primitive practices among living peoples, in Africa, Australasia, and the South seas."—HAROLD E. B. SPEIGHT.[70]

Prayer

UNITARIANISM:

"Why pray since we live in a world governed by natural law? Can puny man importuning the Almighty, cause him to change his mind or break his laws to grant our petition? No — men did that in an ignorant, superstitious age, but we have enlarged our idea of God, and now we must revise our idea concerning prayer. We must accustom ourselves to think of prayer, not as supplication, but as co-operation; not as asking God to work for us, but as pledging ourselves to work with God."—AUGUSTUS P. RECCORD.[71]

"We seek to know the way of life that we may walk therein. We seek a revelation which will make known to us the way in which we should go. In vain we lift our eyes to the distant Heavens; in vain we turn to the printed page: for us no revelation from above, no revelation from beyond. And then, turning back in our unavailing search, we turn within and there we find

---

69. *Op. cit.*, pp. 157, 165.
70. "From Magic, through Science, to Faith," in *The Christian Century*, Feb. 4, 1926.
71. *The Indianapolis Unitarian Bulletin*, Feb. 8, 1929.

the light that lighteth every man that cometh onto the earth, the light that illuminates our understanding, the light of conscience and of reason. Finding truth in our minds and justice in our hearts, we have found our lights; and following their leadings, we are in the way of Eternal Life. Amen."—F. S. C. WICKS.[72]

MODERNISM:

"The only prayer which we have a moral right to pray is precisely the prayer which after all we ourselves must answer."—GEORGE BURMAN FOSTER.[73]

Prophecy
MODERNISM:

"That was the message of Jesus — that God is supremely better than anybody had ever dared to believe. Not a petulant Creator, who had lost control of his creation and, in wrath, was determined to destroy it all. Not a stern Judge dispensing impersonal justice. Not a vain King who must be flattered and bribed into concession of mercy. Not a rigid accountant, checking up the sins against the penances and striking a cold hard balance. Not any of these . . . nothing like these . . . but a great Companion, a wonderful Friend, a kindly, indulgent, joy-loving Father . . . ."—BRUCE BARTON.[74]

"It cannot be too strongly insisted upon that predictive prophecy has always been immediately connected with a non-moral theory of inspiration."—KEMPER FULLERTON.[75]

Regeneration
MODERNISM:

"Yet another thing the historic Jesus has done: he has made men believe in the possibility of moral reclama-

---

72. "Words of Aspiration," in "The *Indianapolis Unitarian Bulletin*, July 15, 1927.
73. *The Function of Religion in Man's Struggle for Existence*, p. 184.
74. *The Man Nobody Knows*, p. 86.
75. *Prophecy and Authority*, p. 189.

tion and renewal. He was the great specialist in the conservation of the waste products of humanity — its prodigals and outcasts . . . ."—H. E. FOSDICK.[76]

"Modern interpretation inclines to return to the symbolical use of the conception of Regeneration. Our ethical realities deal with transformed characters. Regeneration expresses thus a radical, vital, ethical change, rather than an absolutely new metaphysical beginning. Regeneration is a vital step in the natural development of the spiritual life, a radical adjustment to the moral processes of life. More commonly a series of ethical renewals is taught. Psychologically, this does not express a miraculous 'new birth,' but new stages of contact with spiritual power."—HERBERT A. YOUTZ.[77]

Resurrection

MODERNISM:

"In the Bible immortality is associated with the resurrection of the body; among us immortality is conceived as escape from the body.

"I believe in the persistence of personality through death, but I do not believe in the resurrection of the flesh."—H. E. FOSDICK.[78]

"The idea of the resurrection of the body is a Biblical symbol in which modern minds take the greatest offense and which has long since been displaced in most modern versions of the Christian faith by the idea of the immortality of the soul. The latter idea is regarded as a more plausible expression of the hope of everlasting life."—REINHOLD NIEBUHR.[79]

"Though men crucified Jesus, the amazing thing," to quote R.L. Smith in his booklet, *The Greatest Question,* "was that when he died he did not lose touch with his followers, but that he entered into a new life which made it

---
76. *Op. cit.,* p. 225.
77. G. B. Smith and S. Matthews, *op. cit.,* article on "Regeneration."
78. *Op. cit,,* pp. 45, 98.
79. *The Nature and Destiny of Man,* p. 294.

possible for him to be always at the Christian's side. He became a living, reachable, spiritual presence, and any man who desired to do so might thereafter live a life which had an entirely new quality. This, John spoke of as 'eternal life,' because it was capable of surviving all experiences, even that of death."—J. W. McKelvey.[80]

Return of Christ
MODERNISM:

"I do not believe in the physical return of Jesus." — H. E. Fosdick.[81]

" 'I go to prepare a place for you. And if I go and prepare a place for you, I will come again, and receive you unto myself; that where I am, there ye may be also.' 'I will come again.' When? Where? Now there are many who interpret this to mean the coming, the so-called Second Coming, when Christ shall come in glory, when the judgment, the division, and the final rounding up of things will take place. To very many that is a very dear doctrine. There are others, however, equally devout and faithful, who think that this refers to the coming of the Spirit of our Lord into the hearts of all who give him room, into our lives, where he comes again and again and again, and tarries with us when we give room to his Spirit. There are still others who think that it refers to his coming to meet us when death has 'kissed down our eyelids still.' Now it seems to me there is room here for a difference of opinion and that the main thing is the promise of companionship, the comradeship of our Lord's Spirit." — Edgar De Witt Jones.[82]

"The time is past when such features of the New Testament could be skirted out of deference to cherished pieties. There are too many today for whom such doctrines are occasions of stumbling if not scandal. We must

---
80. *The Pulpit*, Mar., 1946.
81. *Op. cit.*, p. 104.
82. *The Coming of the Perfect*, p. 186.

frankly concede that no such dramatic return of Christ with the clouds is to be expected in the course of history. He has his own way of coming but not this way. ...

"Clarification of this matter should begin with a double recognition: (1) that the New Testament doctrine of the return of Christ (or Jesus' announcement of the coming of the Son of Man) belongs to the order of symbolic and mytho-poetic statement and was not understood literally in the late Jewish and early Christian religion: and (2) that (as Professor Minear has so well shown in his volume, *The Christian Hope and the Second Coming*) a just understanding of the teaching is only possible in the light of the whole complex of biblical experience." — AMOS N. WILDER.[83]

Sinlessness of Jesus

"Schleiermacher is quite right of course in suggesting that to be tempted means in a sense to have sinned; for temptation is a state of anxiety from which sin flows inevitably." — REINHOLD NIEBUHR.[84]

Substitution

MODERNISM:

"Guilt and merit are personal. They cannot be transferred from one person to another. We tamper with moral truths when we shuffle them about."
— W. RAUSCHENBUSCH.[85]

"Paul's idea of law, of penalty, of expiation, offends the modern sense of justice and contradicts our ethical values at every point of contact. Without caricature it may be compared to ideas that prevail in certain police circles today. A sensational crime is committed; the public is greatly aroused and demands detection and punishment of the criminal. This the police are unable to accomplish, but obviously something must be done to

---

83. *Op. cit.*, pp. 103, 104.
84. *The Nature and Destiny of Man*, Vol. II, p. 73.
85. *A Theology for the Social Gospel*, p. 219.

silence public clamor; so they 'frame up' a case against someone who can plausibly be made the scapegoat. He is convicted by perjury, the public is silenced, the majesty of the law has been vindicated, justice is satisfied. But we are no longer content with that brand of 'justice.' We insist that the guilt of the guilty cannot be expiated, justice cannot be satisfied by the punishment of the innocent. Yet our theology continues to teach that the Almighty could find no better expedient to save men than 'to frame up' a case against His own Son and put to death the innocent for the guilty. And that which fills us with horror when done by man to man, we praise and glorify when done by God to God." — VEDDER.[86]

"In bearing sin for us there is a sense in which we speak of Christ as our substitute. He in His life and on the cross does something for us which we, thanks to Him, are relieved from doing. Those of us who spend our holidays in the mountains know our indebtedness to trailmakers, who blazed paths through the forest and set up cairns on the slopes of the summits above the timber line. . . . In taking on His conscience the sin of the world and in letting men slay Him, our Lord suffered the Righteous for the unrighteous. He offered this sacrifice of Himself once for all. He discovered the path to oneness with God — the path of trust and devotion, the path of love which beareth, believeth, hopeth, endureth all and never faileth. He blazed that trail with His blood. Or (to employ a New Testament metaphor) He opened a new and living way. The trail once found and marked, the way once opened, remains for all time. None can repeat the vicarious sacrifice of Him who gave Himself to discover the route, to be the way. Forever all who attain like oneness with God must come unto the Father through Him. And all will be grateful to Him 'the Pioneer and Perfection of faith,' 'the Author of eternal salvation.' But He is Saviour only to those who obey Him. The path of trust and

---

86. *Fundamentals of Christianity*, p. 191.

devotion must be trod by those who wish to share His life with God. The trail of vicarious love is to be taken and pursued until we, too, bear the sins of men and offer ourselves in service for their redemption." — H. S. COFFIN.[87]

"Thomas Paine remarked truly that no religion can be really divine which has in it any doctrine that offends the sensibilities of a little child. Is there any reader of this page whose childish sensibilities were not shocked when the traditional explanation of the death of Jesus was first poured into his ears? Would any human father, loving his children, have sentenced all to death, and then persuaded to commute the sentence only by the suffering of his best beloved?" — BRUCE BARTON.[88]

The Virgin Birth

UNITARIANISM:

"Among the dogmas held by the Church has been that of the Virgin Birth of Jesus. This has come to be regarded as sacred. Now everyone who has studied and thought knows that there is not the faintest evidence of a fact on which this dogma was built. We know now how it began. It is due to the mistranslation of the Hebrew word, 'Alma,' which means only, a young woman. This word appeared in the Greek translation as 'Parthenos,' virgin. The writer of Matthew, having only the Greek version before him, repeated the mistranslation. Every scholar knows this, but most have been discreet in proclaiming it. . . . I dislike the dogma because it casts a slur on pure womanhood, on your mother and mine. Our birth was as divine as that of Jesus, and the love of our Fathers and Mothers as pure as the love of Mary."—F. S. C. WICKS.[89]

MODERNISM:

"The virgin birth is not to be accepted as an historical fact. To believe in virgin birth as an explanation of great

---
87. *The Meaning of the Cross,* Scribner, p. 101.
88. *The Man Nobody Knows,* p. 59.
89. *Indiana Unitarian Bulletin,* Supplement 3, 8, 1929.

UNITARIANISM-MODERNISM

personality is one of the familiar ways in which the ancient world was accustomed to account for unusual superiority. Especially is this true of the founders of great religions." — H. E. FOSDICK.[90]

"Salvation has come nigh us because we have found God, in Jesus, identified with us. We are to become saviours — which is the fulness of stature set before us in Christ — by becoming identified ourselves with the lives of others. This is the gospel of the incarnation." —PAUL HUTCHINSON.[91]

"Only when it is recognized that humanity is divinity in germ and that divinity is humanity raised to the *nth* power, does a solution become possible. We may disagree with the Creeds of Nicæa and Chalcedon in their methods of explaining the unity of divine and human, but we fully agree with what they were endeavoring to assert — the likeness of Christ to humanity and at one and the same time his difference from it.

"The Virgin Birth is, therefore, in no way connected with the divinity of Jesus unless we regard that divinity as material. We may accept it or may reject it for a more spiritual idea of divinity, and in either case hold fast to the essential underlying truth of the differences, the uniqueness, the majesty, the lordship of Christ, the eternal Son of God. We do not indeed venture to such a length as to say that Christ is God, for this would involve the inconceivable assertion that God Almighty was once born and died." — F. PALMER.[92]

The Wrath of God

MODERNISM:

"Anger is a primitive emotion of resentment associated with the instinct of self preservation. In the history of religions, anger is frequently attributed to God.

---
90. *Shall the Fundamentalists Win?*
91. "Incarnation," a sermon in *The Christian Century*, Dec. 24, 1927.
92. *The Virgin Birth*, p. 28.

Primitive peoples think of their gods as subject to anger and revenge in naive anthropomorphic fashion. The Old Testament writers freely referred to the anger of Yahweh against those who opposed his will. The New Testament writers spoke of the wrath of God coming on those who reject Christ. Christian theology has regularly taught that God experiences anger against sin, but that His anger is not inconsistent with His love."[93]

"To a modern mind such acts of caprice are unthinkable in connection with God. . . . But the writers of J and E [documents] did not hesitate to endow Jahveh with their own passionate natures." — WILLIAM F. BADE.[94]

Goads to Thought

1. Mention some excellent features of modern religious liberalism.

2. In which ways are the evangelical churches to blame that so many upright souls have turned to Modernism?

3. What has Modernism in common with all false religious cults?

4. Was Dr. James Snowden right when he called Luther and similar progressives of their day Modernists?

5. Do Unitarianism and Modernism show a united front (a) as to methods of propagating their views, (b) as to contents of views?

6. Present evidence of the intellectual dishonesty of Modernists, dealing with the doctrinal tenets of historic Christianity (evidence lies spread through the chapter; an incisive indictment on this point may also be found in Machen's review of Fosdick's "Modern Use of the Bible," reprinted in *What Is Christianity?* by Machen).

7. Has Modernism changed essentially either after the first or the second World War?

8. Are Modernism and Fundamentalism the same re-

---

[93]. G. Smith and S. Matthews, *op. cit.*, article on "Anger of God."
[94]. *The Old Testament in the Light of Today*, p. 68.

ligion? Are Fundamentalism and Orthodoxy, that is, historic Christianity, the same religion?

9. To which view of the Apocalypse does the author apparently adhere? What is your own view of the Book of Revelation?

10. What is wrong with "the Lordship of Christ" as a basis for ecumenical unity? And what is wrong with Charles C. Morrison's basis for church unity? Could you possibly agree with Morrison's understanding of the character of the Church?

11. Prove from citations the wide divergence of Modernism from the Scriptural position on fundamental Christian doctrines.

16

THE BOOK AND THE FAITH

The main thought of the present volume has been cogently expressed by Professor Nathaniel Micklem of Mansfield College, Oxford, in these words: "The ultimate scandal of evangelical religion (which in this connection includes both historic Protestantism and the Church of Rome but excludes much of modern Protestantism) lies not in dogma or symbolism but in its intolerable offense to human pride. 'Nothing in my hand I bring; Simply to thy cross I cling' — it is *that* which the man of taste and culture cannot bring himself to say; he feels no need of so utter a salvation; to him therefore it is nonsense or mere mythology that the majesty of God should take a Servant's form.... That is what the Master said: 'the publicans and the harlots go into the kingdom before you'; that is the reason for the aversion of men of taste to evangelical religion."[1]

This has been stressed throughout our discussion: "The great religions," together with the leading isms, object to the supernaturalism of the Christian religion. Yet Christianity, which is the fulfillment of Judaism in its pure form, is not the fruit of evolution, but the gift of revelation. It points man to the divine Source, outside himself, for salvation.

Paul did not deny to the men of Athens that their own poets had said certain good things; but he stated that Christianity is the fulfillment of truth. "The seed of religion" in the human heart needs the fertilization of the Holy Spirit to cause the plant of religion to blossom forth into a fragrant flower, holy and acceptable to God. "Religion" is not enough; man stands in dire need of Christianity; and the

---

1. *Christendom.* A Quarterly Review, Autumn, 1936.

Christian religion, both as a faith and as a life, is the gift of God.

The fundamental error of the anti-Christian cults is their naturalism. They seek, to use Dr. E. Stanley Jones's terminology, syncretism rather than fulfillment. Only a virile, well-defined Christianity can bring fulfillment to the vague longings of the religious heart, not Charles Clayton Morrison's invitation to Judaism to become a universal religion by adding elements of Christianity. "If this position seems paradoxical," says Dr. Morrison, "the paradox will be revealed at once by considering the fact that when two religions meet on the cultured open field of democracy, for free conflict of opinions and comparison of values, the result is not likely to be annihilation or 'liquidation' of either, but the interpretation of both by the enduring values of each."[2]

The editorial from which we quote intimates that the "condemnable cruel injustice" which has been done to the Jews for centuries is, to a large part, due to "the historical fact that the most basic concept of Judaism through the centuries has been that of a covenant race, destined to be the instrument or medium through which God will perform, soon or late, 'some mighty act involving human destiny.'"

It is this that is resented. Judaism, or Christianity, may lay claim to being just another "great religion"! But if, with Dr. Samuel F. Zwemer, we call Christianity "the final religion," we may look for resentment, if not for ultimate persecution, at the hands of the many man-worshippers of one type or another.

We submit, however, that men who place Christianity on a level with the naturalistic, autosoteric religions of paganism have failed to grasp *the* essential of the Christian religion, no matter how greatly we honor them for their valiant fight for social and economic justice. They could never say with Toyohiko Kagawa, "I am grateful for Shinto, for Buddhism, and for Confucianism. I owe much to these

---

2. "Why Is Anti-Semitism?", in *The Christian Century*, July 7, 1937.

faiths. The fact that I was born with a spirit of reverence, that I have an insatiable craving for values which transcend this earthly life, and that I strive to walk the way of the golden mean, I owe entirely to the influence of these ethnic faiths.

"Yet these three faiths utterly failed to minister to my heart's deepest needs. I was a pilgrim journeying upon a long road that had no turning. I was weary. I was footsore. I wandered through a dark and dismal world where tragedies were thick . . . .

"Buddhism teaches great compassion . . . . But since the beginning of time, who has declared, 'this is my blood of the covenant, which is poured out for many unto remission of sins?'"[3]

Christianity differs from other religions. That some other religions come in the name of Christ, or borrow a few symbols, rites, and doctrines from Christianity, only makes them more dangerous.

The question therefore becomes, What is Christianity? To this query the reply of all the evangelical groups has ever been that the inspired Scriptures are the only source of saving knowledge and the determining factor of what is to be believed.

It is therefore an unhealthy sign when the modern man is so mortally afraid of the study of the contents of the Christian faith. Surely the cults are not afraid to parade *their* doctrines nor ashamed to demand that we shall study them. Some forty years ago an American evangelist stated with remarkable clarity, "The common conception of theology is that it is dry, impractical, worthless, whereas it is the sweetest, liveliest, most inspiring of all studies. Christianity has always flourished under the teaching and preaching of a robust theology. And let it also be stated, with a tremendous emphasis, that when men are not sufficiently interested in Christianity to build a Christian theology, then Christianity must languish or perish."[4]

---
3. *Christ and Japan*, pp. 108, 113.
4. G. W. McPherson, *The Crisis in Church and College*, p. 64.

Today, we rejoice to note, some Modernists are again beginning to see this need of theology. Says Dr. H. Richard Niebuhr, "The revolters in the church are learning that without a Christian theory or theology the Christian movement must lose itself in emotions and sentiments or hasten to action which will be premature and futile because it is not based upon a clear analysis of the situation. They have learned from the Communists that years spent in libraries and in study are not necessarily wasted years but that years of activity without knowledge are lost years indeed. They have learned from history that every true work of liberation and reformation was at the same time a work of theology. They understand that the dependence of man upon God and the orientation of man's work by reference to God's work require that theology must take the place of the psychology and sociology which were the proper sciences of a Christianity which was dependent on the spirit in man."[5]

Nor is this conviction and practice limited to the more liberal type of church. The 100,000 ministers' poll of "Great Churches of America" reveals that the same conviction, as might be expected, prevails among evangelical churches. Hollywood's First Presbyterian is a fair example. "Any man who serves as an elder or a deacon in Hollywood gets a three-year course in church history and doctrine. And it is not just a lecture course; each member of session takes home after every meeting a four-page syllabus to encourage and guide him in further study." Moreover, this church has a "thriving College Department" which operates on the principle that "the greater the demands the greater the response." "They are accustomed to hard study in high school and college; give them study just as demanding in Sunday School."[6] Four rural churches made the grade of "great churches" in this poll, namely, the Evangelical and Reformed, New Knoxville, Ohio; Trinity Lutheran (Missouri), Freistatt, Missouri; Washington Prairie Evangel-

---
5. *The Church Against the World*, p. 153.
6. *The Christian Century*, Sept. 20, 1950.

ical Lutheran, Decorah, Iowa; and Olive Chapel Baptist, Apex, North Carolina. It stands to reason that doctrinal instruction would not, alone and by itself, make for a successful church but at the end of a brief study of what makes these churches great, Thomas Alfred Tripp, "a rural social scientist and national director of the town and country department of the Congregational Christian Churches," writes, "The final lesson of *The Christian Century* series is that rural ministers must teach and preach the Word of God. . . . No half-hearted Sunday school can relieve the rural pastor of his duty of teaching his youth the Christian gospel."[7]

Over against the cults and isms which vociferously advertise their own brands of "theology," we must again place a doctrine, a teaching concerning God and man and their interrelationship. We can have no "experience" that hangs in the air; no "life" except it be based upon, and emanates from, certain basal beliefs and convictions concerning God and Christ. "He that cometh to God must believe that he is and that he is a rewarder of them that seek after him." "And they continued stedfastly in the apostles' teaching and fellowship, in the breaking of bread and the prayers." "As a man thinketh in his heart, so is he."

Only one question remains, then, to be answered. It is this: Where is the true doctrine? For all quote Scripture.

This is a momentous question. If practice flows from theory, if life is based upon teaching, it follows that the wrong doctrine will issue in the wrong attitude toward God and Christ, and consequently in warped and twisted Christian life. Whither shall we go to be properly instructed?

To this our answer is of a twofold nature.

First of all and foremost, one should go to the fountainhead. The sacred Scriptures of the Old and New Testament were given by inspiration of God, and they were given for our instruction, that they might make us wise unto salvation. God therefore intended that they should be read and

---

7. *Ibid.*, Jan. 24, 1951.

studied. It did not please the Almighty to present men with "a gospel engraved on a dime." He gave us a gold mine with sixty-six shafts that we might apply our hearts and minds, praying for the illuminating guidance of the Holy Spirit, the primary author of Scripture. Nor is it impossible to seek successfully one's own way through the Scriptures, to find in them the Saviour and the way of salvation. God the Spirit knows how to make His own work understood.

Nevertheless, there is a second consideration. Our blessed Lord who said, "Go and teach, and lo, I am with you always," did not begin to open the minds of men toward Scripture in this present day and age. It is base ingratitude, not to say detestable conceit, and ingratitude not only toward men but toward God, to ignore the results of the sincere and arduous labors of godly and Spirit-filled men of past generations.

We shall therefore consult the findings of the fathers. But where shall we look for the best doctrinal products of the ages? To this paramount question the answer is, *In the great historic creeds of the Church universal.*

True, the foes of the evangelical faith have not wearied to remind us that Protestantism lies prostrate and powerless by reason of its many divisions and subdivisions. There are undoubtedly far too many splits and divisions — groups and denominations innumerable. All of this is a great shame for the Christian world.

However, they who come with a method, not a creed, men who write books under such titles as "One Man's Religion," should not complain because there are those among us who follow Luther, and again those who admire Calvin's doctrine, or that of Arminius. It remains true, in the midst of a difference which is better than indifference, that the divergencies are there not to scare us away from the field. The God who gave us sheep, not woolen clothing; electricity, not refrigerators; air-waves, not radios; also gave us a Bible, not a system of truth.

Which system are we to teach our children and our fellow men? For we must make disciples, teaching them to observe all things whatsoever Christ commanded His disciples.

When we return to the great confessional writings of the fathers, to those shamefully neglected documents that have been composed as a result of days and years of prayerful study of the Church's most eminent and gifted leaders, we make a pleasant discovery. We find that these creeds are charming in their clarity of expression, in their passionate devotion to the great supernatural teachings of the Christian religion, and sound a deeply and warmly spiritual note that pervades them as the breath of God.

What true Bible-lover could not subscribe to these opening words of the *Formula of Concord* of 1576, which happens to be Lutheran?

"We believe, confess and teach that the only rule and norm, according to which all dogmas and all doctors ought to be esteemed and judged, is no other whatever than the prophetic and apostolic writings both of the Old and New Testament, as it is written (Psalm 119:105) : 'Thy word is a lamp unto my feet, and a light unto my path.' And St. Paul saith (Gal. 1:8) : 'Though an angel from heaven preach any other gospel unto you, let him be accursed.'

"But other writings, whether of the fathers or of the moderns, with whatever name they come, are in nowise to be equalled to the Holy Scriptures, but are all to be esteemed inferior to them, so that they be not otherwise received than in the rank of witnesses, to show what doctrine was taught after the Apostles' times also, and in what parts of the world that more sound doctrine of the Prophets and Apostles has been preserved."

And among our persecuted Lutheran brethren in Germany, and even among our Russian brethren who tremble before the deadly hatred of Sovietism, who could not respond with a thrill in the heart to the concluding words of the *Belgic Confession of Faith,* which happens to be a Reformed document, written as a defense before the King of

Spain who had let loose the horrible Inquisition against the innocent citizens of the Lowlands? For these sentences tell of the bodily and visible return of our Lord Jesus Christ to judge the living and the dead, as follows:

"But on the contrary, the faithful and elect shall be crowned with glory and honor; and the Son of God will confess their names before God his Father, and his elect angels; all tears shall be wiped from their eyes; and their cause, which is now condemned by many judges and magistrates as heretical and impious, will then be known to be the cause of the Son of God. And, for a gracious reward, the Lord will cause them to possess such a glory as never entered into the heart of man to conceive. Therefore we expect that great day with a most ardent desire, to the end that we may fully enjoy the promises of God in Christ Jesus our Lord. Amen."

What have Mormonism or Russellism to say in the face of such confessions? What has Mother Mary Baker Eddy to lay alongside of them?

Why should Christians be ashamed of their inheritance?

I conclude this chapter, then, with the following practical observations:

1. We need much prayer for a world-wide revival of true, evangelical religion, increased church attendance, and godly living. But it should be a revival with a strong emphasis upon the intellectual aspects of the Christian religion.

2. We need clearcut, sound, fundamental preaching of the doctrinal, expository, and exegetical type.

3. We must develop a sense of the sinfulness of sin. Our study of a few popular isms has revealed that where the sense of sin is absent there can be no evangelical fervor.

We should do well to restore the pastor's catechetical class in the fundamentals of the Christian religion. This need not consume too much time. There is an age which is particularly approachable, and in that period of time much can be accomplished in one weekly session during school months. The numerous catechetical books by ministers in the Reformed and Christian Reformed Churches, *A Book of*

Instruction by John B. Gardner (Lutheran), *Coming to the Communion* by Charles R. Erdman, and *Preparing to Commune* by George Taylor (Presbyterian) prove that it is not beyond human power to present the main tenets of the Christian faith in a concise and accessible form.

Christian Scientists have their "reading room" with someone in perpetual charge. Bahais, Rosicrucians, Unity School of Christianity not only maintain parlors equipped with libraries but they "conduct classes twice a week to teach divine truth free of charge." The members of the denomination the writer serves may drift as do others; they may join "a church that is not so strict," but they do not fall for pantheism, because since the age of twelve they have been taught the difference between pantheism and the doctrine of the two natures of Christ. A minister who will sit down and study, and afterward stand up and teach, will do more for his people than one who runs from pillar to post and is present at a ceaseless round of "church activities."

5. I am indebted to Dr. Ralph J. White, pastor emeritus of Trinity Evangelical Lutheran Church of Grand Rapids, for the suggestion that it is incumbent upon the ministry in America to help their people in developing "a technique of the Christian life." The strength of today's isms lies partly in this. They have a technique whereby they foster a joyous conviction that their religion is the right thing. Thus, Unity bids its devotees repeat "Healing Thoughts" and "Prosperity Thoughts." So do New Thought and Christian Science, while "Father Divine" accomplished results in Harlem by making his followers exclaim, "Peace, it's wonderful!"

Martin Luther, says Dr. White, prescribed creeds and prayers to be recited by the father for his family. The simple rite for the morning was followed by these words, "And then thou shouldest go with joy to thy work, after perhaps a hymn has been sung, as the Ten Commandments, or what thy devotion may suggest." In a similar manner Luther suggested, "In the evening, when thou goest to bed, thou shalt make the sign of the holy cross, and say: In the name of the Father, and of the Son, and of the Holy Ghost. **Amen.** Then kneeling or standing, thou shalt say the Apostles' Creed and the Lord's Prayer. Then, if thou wilt, thou mayest add this prayer . . . . Then thou shouldest go to sleep immediately and joyfully."

Here is some sort of technique of Christian living. This has been dropped by the Lutherans in the transition from European to American soil. So have the Reformed people dropped the beautiful prayers prescribed, or at least suggested, by their fathers for morning, mealtime, evening, and public worship. The result is that our people have no technique that may aid in fostering a joyful Christianity, and so they fall a ready prey to New Thought and kindred cults.

6. We owe our covenant God untold gratitude for the great heritage He has bestowed upon us as heirs of the British Pilgrims, the Dutch Knickerbockers, the French Huguenots, the Scotch-Irish Presbyterians, the German and Scandinavian Lutherans, the Michigan Dutch. Above all, the fact that we may worship Him freely and unmolested, without interference from, and yet under the protection of, our splendid democratic form of government, should fill us with national pride and Christian humble thankfulness. The times are out of joint. The Christian Church everywhere, for the first time in history, faces an organized atheism, and that from some of the most powerful governments on earth. Moreover, recent German history has taught us that vast and unexpected changes may occur on the religious horizon almost overnight.

We do not know, then, what the morrow may bring. But even if our religious liberties should be taken from us, and even if freedom of worship should give way to religious intolerance in the land of the free and the home of the brave, may there yet be found tens of thousands in America who cannot be shaken in their firm convictions concerning the faith of our fathers which is living still. In the darkest hour of the Church, may we yet be able to sing,

Like a mighty army
  Moves the church of God;
Brothers, we are treading
  Where the saints have trod.
We are not divided,
  All one body we;
One in hope and doctrine,
  One in charity.
Onward, Christian soldiers,
  Marching as to war,
With the cross of Jesus
  Going on before.

Can You Tell?

1. What is the main thought presented in this book (and some closely related thoughts)?

2. Why is a reference to the Bible insufficient for cultists who also claim to believe the Bible "from cover to cover"?

3. What is the relation between Scripture and creeds?

4. Do the great historic creeds reveal any sort of Christian unity? Have you ever read any of them?

17

APPROACHING ADHERENTS OF THE CULTS

Adherents of the cults — and we here use the word, as we have done throughout, in the sense of "any religion regarded as unorthodox or even spurious" (Webster) — are the most difficult people to evangelize. Let us face this fact lest we might grow discouraged after the first or second attempt. This is hard work because:

1. Cultists are not people who have to be aroused to an interest in religion. They are not folks who have drifted away from their moorings but, when duly approached, will grant that a return to "mother's religion" might be a good thing. The average devotee of a cult has left a traditional faith, in which he was more or less reared, and has adopted "something better." Was not Annie Besant the daughter of an English minister and later the wife of another? Did not Frank Buchman start out a Lutheran minister?

2. Not only has the cultist repudiated the orthodox religion you represent, he actually is hostile to it. Remember that every cult is, at bottom, autosoteric. The man who has surrendered God's supernatural plan of salvation for some system of self-salvation cannot but resent the fundamental implications of the gospel that "all our righteousnesses are as a polluted garment" (Isa. 64:6).

3. Inseparable, though distinguishable from this hostility, is therefore a resentment against you as an intruder who ventures to come and lecture him who has found something so vastly superior. If your prospect is a woman, this feeling of ill will may be even more pronounced, as women are led more by intuition and sentiment. Who are you anyway that you deem yourself a teacher? Have you tasted the power of which your cultist boasts?

This resentment against you may assume various forms according to the character of your opponent and the nature of the ism which he represents. It may be haughtiness or even hatred in the case of a Jehovah's Witness, since you represent "Satan, the devil's organization"; it may be a mild contempt for you as an "O. P." (Ordinary Person) with a Theosophist; or it may be a kind indulgence on the part of a Modernist who recognizes you as a fellow Christian for all your mental ballast, and who trusts that some day you will arrive at the realization that his Christianity is just of a somewhat differing conception than your own.

4. Moreover, the well-informed cultist is much alive to the shortcomings of your evangelical Protestant religion. There is first of all the hopeless division into endless varieties of Lutherans, types of Arminians, and shades of Calvinists. (Do not try to defend it: rather point out that your cultist adds just one more group). Take a Baha'i now, or a Spiritist, or a Theosophist: he has reached the heights from which he can scan the whole field of religion and, holding to the underlying foundation of them all, he can work for the unity of a world religion that will be the fulfillment of the Master's prayer that they may all be one. To him you are just behind the unifying spirit of the times with your denominationalism.

Or, take the Mormon. He has the positive revelation of God to Joseph Smith, Jr., the Prophet, or a later revelation; while a Buchmanite is in personal touch with a guiding God. What has your abstract and cold traditionalism to offer in comparison with that?

Make no mistake: the cults as well as the sects (the word "sect" is here taken in the sense of a somewhat odd denomination) owe their rise, in part at least, to the shortcomings of the churches. Should you doubt the truth of that statement, read the excellent article by Dr. Kuizenga.[1]

5. Again, many cultists have made sacrifices. They are a deeply religious type; that is why they went to so much

---

[1] "The Cults: Phenomenon and Challenge," by John E. Kuizenga in *Theology Today*, Vol. 1, No. 1, April, 1944.

investigating. Now that they have finally found peace, and have braved the ridicule of kith and kin, do you think it easy for them to admit that they have erred after all?

6. This hatred, this self-sufficiency, may assume such proportions that it proves altogether a waste of time to deal with many of the cultists. In his book, *The Work of the Pastor*, Dr. Charles R. Erdman has suggested that one should not waste his time on the paid propagandists of the cults. Dr. Kuizenga reminds us that "the cults believe that every member is to be trained as a salesman, and they do it efficiently." The Rev. I. Van Dellen, author of a good book on Mormonism, stated that he had never been able to convince a Mormon. "A man convinced against his will, Is of the same opinion still."

For such reasons as these it is of primary importance that you should assume the right attitude for this particular form of evangelization.

1. You may well postpone approaching adherents of cults until you have gained experience in dealing with human nature and presenting the gospel to others, say, to the large group of those who are just indifferent, of those who think they are "all right," of those who admit that "some day" they should give more attention to religion.

2. When finally you decide to go into the lion's den, if ever you were in need of "guidance," it is now. If ever you should pray for patience, it is here. The cultist you are about to visit is your *opponent*. He may lose his temper, or he may treat you with silken condescension, or again with icy disdain; you are to take it all with unruffled spirit. Bear in mind that in final analysis all his antagonism is not directed against your personality or your past life, but against the message you present.

3. You must be "clothed with humility." Your own church may boast that it has "the true and complete doctrine of salvation," yet your denomination has not gotten beyond Paul who admitted, "Now I know in part." Every race has its peculiarities, and even climate and latitude have left

their mark upon the religion of people. The cold Nordic will never be as emotional as the Negro, and the strict followers of Calvin cannot attain to the "holiness of beauty" of the Church of England, though they may know something of the "beauty of holiness."

Do not take an air of superiority. Your antagonist would soon puncture your self-inflation. Admit whatever he may advance against the peculiarities of the group you represent. You have come to represent Christ, not Christians.

4. Approach the cultist with a sympathetic heart. Hostility does not win. Only love can do that. No matter how much you may hate error, your first approach to an errorist should always be that of seeking love. You must love the sinner while hating the sin in him. There should always be something in you of Christ, who was moved with compassion when He found the multitude as sheep without a shepherd. And yet, how self-satisfied those same multitudes were as the result of faulty leadership!

5. Do not dispute whatever grain of truth or of good there may be in the particular cult you are dealing with. Paul praised the ultrapolytheistic people of Athens because in all things they were very religious, and from that point on he reasoned, saying, "Now therefore, I would tell you of that God you try to worship in your ignorance." If, then, your own orthodox church has failed to emphasize Christ as healer of the body, admit that the Christian Science practitioner has something; and if New Thought, Unity, and the "I Am" cult have "precipitated" wealth, grant that Jesus said He came that men might have life abundantly (John 10:10), and Paul stated that godliness also has the promise of the life which now is (I Tim. 4:8). You should, therefore, become all things to all men, that you may save some (I Cor. 9:22).

6. Above all, never show that you suspect the cultist of dishonesty or mercenary motives. Almost all men's motives are highly complicated, and foreign elements may enter into the devoutness of all. There is also this further con-

sideration that there is a sufficient amount of common grace working in most men for them to resent being suspected of evil. If, therefore, you show a man that you doubt his sincerity, all further efforts to win him are useless. Besides, to do justice to your prospect, the circuitous ramblings of the human mind are so baffling that it is needless to ascribe wrong motives where we are unable to fathom all that has led to a given conviction or course of life.

Though Joseph Smith's biographers do not fail to leave the impression that he was unscrupulous and an impostor, there can be no possible doubt that Brigham Young was sincerely and completely sold on the conviction that Brother Joseph was a prophet of the Lord. The Rev. D. M. Canright, ace exposer of the follies of S.D.A., after many years of personal observation reached the conclusion that Mrs. Ellen G. White came herself to believe in the divine character of her so-called revelations because others looked to her as to a mouthpiece of God.

Or, to approach the matter from a different angle, had your ancestors settled after untold hardships in a certain region and had grasshoppers threatened to eat the entire first year's crop of grain, and if then in the nick of time sea gulls had come and destroyed those myriad grasshoppers, would you not be convinced that the Almighty had approved of this adventure of faith, and that He had at last delivered from "persecution"? That happened to the Mormons in their first year in Utah — and yet, the Mormons are not even monotheists! Would it not be wiser, therefore, to admit that the Mormons have made excellent pioneers, and as such have done much for the cultural development of the West than to deny God's providence in the sea gull episode? And to point out that God may have spared their forefathers that the goodness of God might lead them to repentance (Romans 2:4)?

If 'Abdu'l-Baha said, "I am going to the United States to establish the fundamental principles of our Cause and to proclaim the oneness of the world of humanity and the equality of all men," do not deny the high goal of the ideal (certainly it is far superior to a "Christian" interpretation of Scripture which has misused Noah's curse in order to defend slavery and the colonization of "inferior" races) ; but rather try to point out that this high ideal can only be realized "if ye abide in Me," while apart from Christ all such idealism ends in the deification of man, hence, in the spirit of antichrist.

You are now ready to begin.

1. In general you may remind your prospect that neither "sincerity," nor miracles, nor financial sacrifice are enough to convince of the rightness of a cause. Paul granted that the Jews had a zeal for God, but it was a zeal "not according to knowledge," hence worse than inadequate. Who was ever more zealous than Saul when he persecuted the Church? Yet his sincerity only made him the greatest of sinners. Propaganda and numerical growth are found among all sorts of cults; if they were a mark of the genuine, the Seventh-Day Adventist with his weekly output of a third of a million copies of *Signs of the Times* might as well sell out to Unity with its "battalions of typewriters ... literature of every type to appeal to every taste in tons; telegraph, telephone, radio ... pressed into service" (Ferguson).

What we need to know and to discuss is not the *chronique scandaleuse* of Blavatsky or Aimee MacPherson, is not the apparent statistical or tabulated result of a given cult. It is this: Is there a zeal according to knowledge?

2. Our problem therefore boils down to this question: Whence do we obtain religious knowledge with unerring certainty? As to that question, there are in the nominally Christian world three theories of the source of authority in religion:

a. that the principle of authority lies in the church (Rome) ;

b. that it is vested in man (either rationalism or mysticism). This ultimately casts man back upon his own resources and ends in autosoterism;

APPROACHING ADHERENTS

c. that God has spoken in His Son, the infallible record of which we have in the Bible (according to Heb. 1:2).

True, there are mediating views, such as that the Bible contains the word of God though it is not altogether that, or that the Bible contains a word of God that may mean one thing to one man and another to some one else; but such views finally cast man back upon his own judgment and end in a refined form of rationalism.

3. This should now be very clear: Combating cults is not a dunce's task. To the contrary, this is indeed a specialty of theology, and one that requires accurate knowledge of the fundamentals of other branches of the theological encyclopedia. Needed is a workable knowledge in two fields. First, one must be able to defend the principle of the "Protestant rule of faith" (Hodge); that is to say, one should be able to defend the inspiration, completeness, perspicuity, and sufficiency of Scripture.[2]

4. Secondly: In an argument with an adherent of a different faith you should be able to attack and refute his stand. This can be done in two ways. One way is to refute his principle, the foundation of his system. You must therefore have a clear conception of the fundamental error of your opponent. Do not lose yourself in an argument with a Russellite on whether Luke 23:43 should be read, "Verily I say unto thee, Today shalt thou be with me in paradise," or, "Verily, I say unto thee today, Thou shalt be with me in paradise."[3] Do not argue with a Mormon the question whether the two sticks in Ezekiel 37:15-20 represent the Old Testament and the Book of Mormon; nor if Luke 20:35 means that (plural) marriage must be solemnized in this world in order to be effective in the next. Do not debate with a Seventh-Day Adventist whether the words in Mark 2:28 "that the Son of man is lord even of

---

2. Material may be found in all standard works on Dogmatics (Systematic Theology); also in such a book as H. Rimmer's *Internal Evidence of Inspiration* (Grand Rapids: Wm. B. Eerdmans Publishing Co., 1938).
3. Max Heindel, Rosicrucian, reads it in the same way.

the sabbath" mean that Jesus is Lord of Saturday, and therefore Saturday is "the Lord's day" in the New Testament. For all such exegesis is *a priori* conditioned by an entire theory which they claim to be Scriptural. Destroy the foundation, and the excrescences will disappear; but cut off the growths by dint of a stronger or of one more argument, and you will have gained nothing: the foundation still stands. Deal only with fundamental concepts.

5. There is a second way of dealing with this problem. Your opponent, salesman by the grace of his theological zeal, is by no means a lamb that before its shearers is dumb; he is a mighty warrior, a hunter ready for the kill. He may be in a belligerent mood, in which case he will surely attack, say, your conception of the deity of Christ. If he does not, you are to tackle his. This means that besides debating the fundamental position of the man you intend to convert, you may have to discuss his idea of sundry doctrines of the Christian faith.

Only, let the debate be confined to major issues, such as the Trinity, the two natures of Christ, His bodily resurrection, blood atonement, second coming, the supernaturalness of the work of salvation. Whether the latter is post-, pre-, or nonmillennial should not enter into the discussion: you are endeavoring to convert a man from a non-Christian belief to the Christian faith, not from a less correct to a more correct understanding of the Christian tenets. So you are not to lose yourself in a discussion of adult-only or also infant baptism, nor of the "validity" of "sprinkling." And, frankly, should you convert a Spiritist into a Christian, you would have won the main battle regardless of whether he became a Christian like Luther, Spurgeon, or Moody.

6. It may be said in general that there are two distinct types of cults. Some assert that they believe the Bible. Among these are Jehovah's Witnesses (they write it with a small "w"), Mormons, Christian Scientists, Unity adherents, British Israelites, Swedenborgians ("the Church of the New Jerusalem"). But there are also cults that re-

ject the final authority of the Bible. In this class are they that lean heavily upon the Orient, and also Spiritism, Freemasonry, Rosicrucianism, and numerous smaller fry.

Hence, not all the foregoing applies to all isms.

In dealing with the first named group it is sufficient to prove the completeness and sufficiency of the divine revelation in Scripture, plus the fact that the clear and historically accepted meaning of the Bible's main teachings is not what these cults distill from it. Difficult? As stated before, trying to convert those who are firmly rooted in and posted concerning an erroneous religious ism is no task for babes in the woods. It is more than time that some easygoing "personal workers" discover that not all classes of men can be gained for Christ with a superficial, "Come under the blood, brother!" Nor are people to be neglected because gaining them entails earnest mental labor.

7. If it be any comfort to you, there is more to follow.

With the second group, who do not admit that the Bible is the end of contradiction, you will have to pursue a different tactic. Here you must be at home, in the fundamentals at any rate, of yet another theological study. This is the field of comparative religion, also called Christian Evidences. You should be able to speak of the reasonableness of monotheism over against both polytheism and dualism, of the superiority of theism to pantheism and deism. You should know that religion results from revelation, not from evolution.[4] You must know that in spite of the too numerous divergencies, there is such a thing as Christian belief and a Christian view of life, and that it is superior to all pagan views; that Christianity is the only religion that has a universal appeal; that it alone offers a divine salvation and thus delivers man from "broken cisterns that can hold no water." You will reason that Christianity, although it has never been tried upon a national scale, is yet the only religion that has raised nations from savagery

---

4. Cf. S. M. Zwemer, *The Origin of Religion*.

to a high cultural level; that it alone has given mankind freedom from want and fear, freedom of speech and of religion; and that it is the sole religion which for the life to come has offered something that is superior to the life we now have.

Yet this should not prove too arduous a task. When the Baha'i asks you to observe that "all these things we have today, wars and labor troubles, etc., have been predicted in the ancient writings," and hands you a copy of *The Wisdom of 'Abdu'l-Baha*, what a far cry that is from the eschatological address of Jesus, and from the apostles John and Paul! Only, bear in mind that when you set out to convince men like that, you cannot do it by leaving a tract: it will take hours and days of reasoning together. Converting the cultists will often prove a hopeless task because you cannot find a common ground upon which to stand, a mutual point of departure; in other cases it will demand much knowledge, skill, and endless patience.

If, however, "by their fruits ye shall know them," why should the Theosophist and the devotee of the swamis and yogis return to the wisdom of the East which has left women enslaved, children despised, nations illiterate and wallowing in filth?

You may point to the sinlessness of Jesus as an evidence of Christianity, or you may refer to His miracles and His resurrection as indisputable evidence of His deity.[5]

You may have heard the anecdote of the colored preacher who was asked by a committee from the church to resign his pastorate. "What's the matter, brethren?" inquired the astonished man. "Don't I splanify to suit yuh? Don't I argify to suit yuh?" "Yessuh, pastor Jones," was the reply, "yuh-all splanify to suit us and yuh argify to suit us; but yuh dohn tell us wherein." The colored brethren wanted a practical application!

Lest I be accused with the dusky minister, I shall en-

---

5. Quite helpful is Dr. A. Pieters' *Facts and Mysteries of the Christian Faith* (Grand Rapids: Wm. B. Eerdmans Publishing Co., 1933).

deavor to give an example or two of how I conceive of your task. And this will be done the more gladly if it may appear that the work is not as forbidding as it seems when we refer to the theory of it (no work ever is!).

1. No one can ever know too much, and the more thorough our knowledge, the more easily we can use it for practical purposes. At the same time, a few facts that we have truly mastered are of far greater use to us than many facts of which we have a general idea but which we cannot defend against subtle attack. The school boy's retort, "I know it but I can't say it," deceives only the school boy. If you cannot answer the argument of a cultist, it is only because you have not mastered the facts. It is your inadequate knowledge that makes you leave the field defeated and that leaves your Lord dishonored.

2. Before entering upon this discussion, however, let us make sure of our ground. We have fallen upon days in which the "proof-text method" is repudiated as something of the dark ages. Now it is true that everything can be "proved" (or distilled) from the Bible by taking isolated texts from their context, or by substituting a period for a comma. Nonetheless, the proof-text method is legitimate and even mandatory, provided it be used rightly. The Bible authors were not men who expressed themselves in indistinct and ambiguous speech. It is possible to quote them so that others perceive what they meant.

In using the proof-text method you must be absolutely fair and honest, and at the same time on your guard. Never quote a text apart from its connection unless you are firmly convinced that the context is not needed to make its implication clear or that you use it in a sense that is compatible with the context. Never allow yourself to build upon a word at the expense of another word that must be ignored in order to press your preferred interpretation of the first text. Always compare Scripture with Scripture.

But if you will bear these few simple rules in mind, here is a note of encouragement. You and I are not the first ones to tread this path. There are a number of charts, folders, and booklets dealing with these (and other) cults and sects, and some carry Scriptural and erroneous statements in parallel columns.[6]

3. Coming now to our concrete example, we may well begin with the doctrine of the two natures in Christ. Did not the apostle John state that a correct Christology is the earmark of orthodoxy (I John 4:1-3)? And did not the oldest and the most numerous errors in the early Church center around the person of Christ?

Yet, no one can speak scripturally concerning the Person of Christ who has not first a true conception of (a) the personality of God, and (b) the trinity in the unity of God. We may leave the discussion of polytheism versus monotheism, and that of deism out of the present phase of our argument; for it is evident that we must begin somewhere. We desire to direct attention now to the *deity* of Christ.

Christian Science says: "God is incorporeal, divine, supreme, infinite Mind, Spirit, Soul, Principle, Life, Truth, Love."

Unity states: "God is a mind Principle whose foundation is ideas.... It does not matter what you call this fundamental Principle.... God is, therefore, not a person, but omnipresent mind, principle, and law."

Theosophy asserts: "God is Universal Life, the Limitless Consciousness, the Eternal Love, the very source and heart of all that is."

Rosicrucianism maintains: "God is an expression of the positive pole of the Universal spirit (matter is the negative pole)."

Spiritism teaches: "We abrogate the idea of a personal God."

These are just a few samples, taken at random. Of all

---

6. Special mention should here be made of an organization called in existence in August, 1946, for the specific purpose of combating false religious cults and sects. This organization publishes and lists a voluminous literature, and also a bi-monthly paper, *The Discerner*. Address, *Religion Analysis Service, Inc.*, 902 Hennepin Ave., Minneapolis 3, Minnesota.

such pantheism Dr. Charles Hodge remarked (after discussing some nine theories of pantheism) that it is evidently a hypothesis, something which in the nature of the case cannot be proved. And also that it is impossible in any of its forms to reconcile it with what the Bible teaches concerning God. He further states that it does not only contradict the laws of belief which God has impressed upon our nature, but also subverts the very foundation of religion, and of morality, and that it involves even the deification of sin.[7]

You must, then, be able to show from Scripture that the Bible certainly does speak of God as personal, and as transcendent (for example, in Acts 17:24), and that this transcendence eliminates an immanence after the pantheism of the above named cults.

What interests us right now, however, is to show that when the Bible refers to our Lord Jesus Christ as divine, it speaks of a deity such as could not be attributed to any other man or to mankind as a whole. The Unitarian-Modernist theory that Jesus' deity ("divinity" they prefer to call it: why?) differs only in degree from that of our own deity must be disproved. If that can be done, you see, you will have defeated every pantheistic cult in such an important point that there can be little left.

Various cults would agree to Dr. Fosdick's statement, "In our theology no longer are the divine and human like oil and water that cannot mix," and with the saying of a prominent Ritschlian, "What He was in this world we hope to be in the next"; namely, sons of God whose "sonship is not disturbed by sin."

You may discover to your surprise that some adherents of the pantheistic cults are not even aware of their divergence from orthodox belief. Point out, therefore, that the Church universal has always held that the sonship of Christ differs in essence from that of other men. The Jews, who

---

7. The last point has been demonstrated in our chapters on Spiritism, Theosophy, and Christian Science.

had been raised on the conviction that God is One and that He is far above the creature, realized full well that Jesus asserted His deity in a metaphysical sense, and they wanted to stone Him "because thou, being a man, makest thyself God" (John 10:33).

The entire Fourth Gospel was written for the purpose of proving first of all the deity of Christ (20:30-31), and it is made clear at the beginning that this deity put Him on an equality with God (1:1), and makes His Sonship to differ from that of others (1:12). What man would even today, after various pantheistic theories have been dinned into our ears, dare say with Jesus, "Before Abraham was born I am" (John 8:58)?[8]

Both Paul and James call Jesus "the Lord of glory" (I Cor. 2:8; Jas. 2:1) and both men were Jews, thoroughly sold on the idea that the Lord of Glory is Jehovah of the shekinah. Paul calls Christ a Jew, or Israelite, according to His human nature, but "God over all" according to His other side (Rom. 9:5). John states of Him, "This is the true God, and eternal life" (I John 5:20).

You will probably find, by probing the beliefs of your opponents, that their difficulty is more one of the heart than of the head (in speaking of Rom. 9:19, 20 Dr. Warfield remarked one day in class, "You see, gentlemen, that Paul lays down the rule that a bad theology comes from a bad heart"). What the sinner refuses to admit is the awful guilt of sin, so great indeed that we actually are *enslaved* by Satan, the originator of sin, and hence can only be redeemed, that is, bought back to freedom (or to God, which is the same) by the ransom of Christ's blood (Matt. 20:28; I Peter 1:19). Hence this Jesus becomes Lord, that is, owner, master, proprietor. For "Lord" is *Kurios*, which is the Greek equivalent throughout the Septuagint of the Hebrew

---

8. Rosicrucian Max Heindel saw in these words proof for reincarnation: both Jesus and Abraham were reincarnations of an older Ego; hence the Jews were not Abraham's seed. But the evolutionistic theory of rebirth, and deliverance through it, runs contrary to all of Jesus' teachings. Certainly, His hearers did not understand Him in that way (John 8:59, 10:33).

Jahweh. So while the Pharisees rejected Jesus because they wanted a Messiah who was David's Lord (Matt. 22: 41-46), Paul gladly called Him "Jesus Christ our Lord," and himself the bondservant, slave, *doulos*, of this divine master. And Thomas exclaimed, "My Lord and my God!"

4. However, even so you may not yet have reached the end of contradiction. You may encounter a Russellite (Jehovah's Witness). Ask him if he believes that Jesus is God. He cannot, of course, for he holds that Jesus was the archangel Michael changed into a man. Press him for his beliefs, and he will admit the deity of Jesus in a Socinian sense: the man Jesus did not arise from the tomb as a man, but a spirit, and this spirit was raised to the divine dignity because of his perfect righteousness and his sacrificial death while he was a man. Your Russellite will say, "He is not Jehovah-God." For there are few things these people hate worse than they do the doctrine of the Trinity. In dealing with such a man, then, you cannot suffice with quoting, say, Hebrews 1:3, 4. The Witness will interpret this as meaning that Jesus Christ, because of the perfect obedience rendered in the flesh, has been raised to the dignity of God. You cannot refer to John 1:1, for the Witness has grown smart: Whereas formerly he would refer you to your concordance, of late he has graduated from that and will ask you to "look into your polyglot Bible." If you inform him you thought only great libraries own such works, he will shake his head and inform you that if only you owned a polyglot Bible you might have known that John says, "the word was a God." And this he will explain in an Arian fashion, as something neither fully god nor fully a lower creature, as he will also do in the case of Romans 9:5b.

You will, then, have to show from Scripture that Jesus is indeed the Jehovah of the Old Testament. If you succeed in that, either the Witness will have to surrender, or he must flatly contradict the Bible. Well then, Isaiah said that he saw the glory of Jehovah (ch. 6:1-3), while John states that Isaiah saw the glory of Jesus (John 12:41). Isaiah says, "Jehovah of hosts, him shall ye sanctify (Isa. 8:13), and Peter substitutes, "But sanctify Christ in your hearts as Lord," (I Peter 3:15). When Malachi states that the messenger shall prepare the way before the Lord (3:1), Mark says that this prophecy is fulfilled in the coming of John the Baptist before Jesus Christ (1:4), and so says Luke (3:3-6, 15-17). What is more, Jeremiah calls the name of the "branch of David" (i.e., a son of David, hence a man, namely, Jesus) Jehovah: "And this is his name whereby he shall be called: Jehovah our righteousness," (23:6). For that matter, John himself has cut off the translation, "The word was a god" when he stated in 17:3 that there is but one true God.

At this point you might inquire of your Russellite friend why it is that his organization leaves upon people's doorsteps folders that bear at the top a citation of Isaiah 9:6, stopping short of the words, "Wonderful, Counselor." Do they not know that the same verse calls the same *Child* "Mighty God, Everlasting Father"?

You now have him cornered.[9] If he refuses to admit the evidence (he most likely will), do not get angry, which might be construed as a sign of weakness in argument, or as a lack of saintliness (though there is a holy anger); but let him go, and turn to another prospect. You cannot convince a man against his will. Tell him frankly that you and he have come to the parting of the way. You might ask him if he is willing to have a word of prayer with you before you leave him, and inform him that prayer is going to be a petition that the Lord may speak to the mind of him who is in error. If he refuses, let him go; but impress clearly upon his mind this one cardinal point because of which you leave

---

9. On January 18, 1952, two earnest and courteous Russellites walked a considerable distance to my home in 20 degrees below zero. We had a two-and-a-half-hour discussion of the doctrines of the Trinity and the Deity of Christ. When I confronted them with this question, one of them, who stated that he is "a barber, but also a minister of the gospel," replied that Christ may be called "Mighty God," but that does not identify Him with Jehovah, for the latter is "Almighty God" (!) But what of "Everlasting Father," and the fact that "the mighty God" is used of Jehovah in Isaiah 10:21?

him. You two have argued a good deal; but you quit because he claims to believe the Bible, yet he cuts off words that do not appeal to him. That is the point. This he must remember. This should continue to ring in his ears.

If, however, he should grant your proposition, your next step might well be to show him that in yielding on this point he has wandered far away from Russellism which, like all rationalism, denies the Trinity. Make clear to him that the Church does not mean with the word "trinity" the horrible distortion that Russell-Rutherford have made of it ("that Jesus was his own father"); or, that "the trinity is accepted and upheld by Christendom and heathendom" (Leaflet on public address by A. Nichol).[10]

5. Christ's humanity is as vital as His deity. Christian Science denies the reality of the human nature. Its pantheism, its one-sided stress upon the spiritual and divine, led to this. But Scripture teaches that Jesus suffered in the *body*, which was nailed to the Cross, and that He was sorrowful in His *soul*. It is reprehensible from a psychological viewpoint to deny some of life's manifestations because of others (the muscles suffer though pain may be ultimately mental or spiritual). Logically, it is nonsense to say that the bodily pain was "an erroneous mental concept," while at the same time affirming that the mind is divine and cannot err. And it is morally indefensible to substitute meanings for words in the Bible that were never in a dictionary; for example, to read, "As in Adam (Error) all die, so in Christ (Truth) shall all be made alive."

6. And so it goes all along the line. Never lose yourself in a discussion of minor points. Always stay with the cardinal doctrines of the Christian religion. When you deal with a Mormon, you might perhaps grant with Dr. Kuizenga, "Mormonism has at least the merit of trying to bring sex life within the pale of religion"; but do not try to refute

---

10. Additional excellent material regarding this point may be found in W. J. Schnell's *Into the Light of Christianity*, and in Bruce M. Metzger's *The Jehovah's Witnesses and Jesus Christ*.

them on this point by referring to the sexual exploits of Joseph Smith as reported by his enemies (even if you think their documents well authenticated). Rather show that polygamy is contrary to Genesis 2, to Matthew 19:6, to Ephesians 5:24-33 and to I Corinthians 7:2. For as to the first named passages, it is apparent that if *the two* (God created one wife for the one man) are to be one flesh, three, that is one man and two women cannot be one flesh, nor can the one man be one flesh with the one woman while his body does not belong to her in the same sense that hers belongs to him because it is partly some other woman's. As to Ephesians 5 it is evident that marriage is taken as an illustration of Christ's union with His Church. This can only be if the husband has one wife as Christ has one Church which is His entirely. The third passage, I Corinthians 7:2, teaches that every man should have his own wife in order to prevent fornication, and each woman her own husband. This prevents a sharing of one partner with two of the other sex. Hence Paul, in the midst of a polygamous world, directed that no one could occupy a position of leadership in the Church if he were the husband in a polygamous marriage (Titus 1:5, 6; I Tim. 3:2).

And here you are touching upon an error in Mormonism which is even more foundational than polygamy: the God with whom we are dealing was at one time the man Adam, a polygamous man, and Jesus was married to many women.

7. There remains but one more point. You may meet with people who adhere to a cult or sect that stresses several fundamentally Christian doctrines; such as S.D.A. or British Israelism. They will wonder why you debate with them. Tell them it is they who do the attacking. Inform them that a body is known not by what it holds in common with all others but by what it defends in distinction from every other group. Seventh-Day Adventists decry every group of Christians as bearing the mark of the beast; British-Israelites lead Americans to the humanism of believing that they will save the world from war and distress merely by

being the chosen children of promise by the sole virtue of having been born in the United States.

If now the foregoing pages should have convinced the reader that approaching the adherents of cults is a work fraught with difficulty, there is neither the desire nor the attempt on the part of the writer to deny this.

And what of it? Evangelization has been altogether too much undertaken by well-meaning but ill-equipped witnesses. While the winning of one who has been part of a zealous, proselytizing group is worth more in its indirect results than the winning of one who may have been a lost sheep but never was one of a pack of detrimental wolves.

Above all: America's need of Christ is so great! In 1912 American women kissed the hands of 'Abdu'l-Baha, and one enthusiast said that she "had seen God." In Harlem a little man has been hailed as God for years by thousands of whites and blacks, and all because he supplied them with sixty-course, three-hour banquets. "Peace! It's wonderful."

Yes, it is. And it is sad beyond words.

Almost anything, perhaps positively everything, will sweep some people off their feet, and fill them with fake religious ecstasy.

Our country needs Jesus Christ, Him of the sacred Scriptures. And it needs to be told just what that means, and what it does not mean.

Recapitulation

1. How many reasons can you give why it is particularly difficult to convince a cultist of the error of his way? The text mentions six.

2. Can you state seven requisites in a personal worker who wants to attempt this hard task?

3. Mention from the text of this chapter instances of good principles emphasized by adherents of false religious systems. Do you remember additional ones from previous chapters?

4. Why is some knowledge of so-called Evidences of Christianity valuable in coping with the cults? What other names are given to this study?

5. Do all cults recognize the Bible as the final religious authority? Which do not?

6. Is it possible from the Christian standpoint to answer every argument of the cults?

7. Can sectarian opinions be silenced by quoting texts from Scripture? If so, what conditions must such citing measure up to?

8. How would you meet pantheistic assertions concerning Jesus' deity?

9. What is your answer to the Russellite assertion that the Logos was "a god" according to John 1:1?

10. Is Jesus' true manhood important? Who deny it?

11. How will you meet Mormon references to Scripture in favor of polygamy?

12. What does America and what does the war stricken, sin-cursed world need most of all?

18

THE CHRISTIAN RELIGION

Surely there are too many denominations in the United States of America. In the thinly populated state of Washington I came upon a town of 2,400 in which twenty-eight churches are represented. People mockingly call it "the holy city."

Individualism, inability to co-operate, refusal to see eye-to-eye — these pronounced American weaknesses, rather than firm conviction, have, in all too many cases, given rise to disruption and schism.

Someday, perhaps, God will cleanse us by means of persecution from the filth of our disobedience to Christ's will that Christians should be one "that the world may believe that thou didst send me" (John 17:21). For if there were no atheists in foxholes, there can be little display of denominationalism in concentration camps.

A candid appraisal of facts, however, will lead to the frank admission that the Church's divided existence is not the sole reason why entire towns lie asleep when on Sunday mornings a few straggly worshipers answer the call to prayer. There are things that are worse than either radical or minor difference of opinion in matters religious. Among these is a total indifference to all religious conviction.

Moreover, if those who sneer at the Church would take the trouble to examine the credentials of the various Christian churches, they might discover a remarkable unity and agreement on fundamentals far beyond their expectation.

Our troubles lie far deeper. The great heritage of the Christian Church, so painstakingly arrived at, so profoundly thought through and so zealously guarded again and again at the cost of blood and tears, has been brushed aside by multitudes who have come to the loose belief that a varnish of outward morality will do as a substitute for Christianity. We have come to the point where a none too pessimistic religious weekly has stated editorially: "An honest appraisal requires the acknowledgment that American Protestantism is spiritually weaker today than at any time in its history."[1] And again: "It is no exaggeration to say that, since the time when the invention of printing gave the Bible to the common people . . . there has been no generation of Christians so religiously illiterate as our own."[2]

There are those among us who are convinced that the Christian religion has been God's greatest boon to mankind; that it has removed barbarism and illiteracy; that it has promoted the more abundant life of art and science, of high moral standards to be found nowhere outside the pale of Christendom.

They hold that when these by-products of Christianity are relished while their fountainhead is trodden under foot, God calls the Christianized nations back by turning their boasted civilization against them, lest a worse evil befall them.

Such a time is upon us even now.

Are we heeding the divine voice that calls us back to the Father? Or are we seeking oblivion in alcohol and fornication, in wholesale denunciation of other nations as evil and indiscriminate praise of our own American goodness?

It should not be an impossible task to determine what is the essence of the Christian religion.

This cannot be done by obliterating all differences of interpretation. No thing on earth can mean one thing and its opposite at the same time. That popular student and teacher of comparative religion of our day, Dr. Marcus Bach, recently wrote that "Mormonism and Christian Science have long since become denominations in every sense of the word, and their emergence from a modern cult or a

---

1. Chas. C. Morrison, "Protestant Reorientation," in *The Christian Century*, Oct. 27, 1943.
2. Morrison, in *The Christian Century*, Dec. 1, 1943.

minority religious group is total and complete." But he could so recognize these un-Christian cults only by referring in almost the same breath to our historic Christian faith in these words, "The old symbolisms, the clichés, the ancient shibboleths out of which the meaning has gone, are irrelevant."³

Surely, there is a better way of determining what constitutes Christianity than this method of embracing everything half-Christian and non-Christian together with the tenets of the Christian faith.

If God is infinite and man finite, man can but know God because He has made Himself known.

It is equally certain that when God wants to be known, He can reveal Himself in such a manner that man may respond to His self-revelation. And His unveiling of Himself must needs be consistent throughout: there may have been progress but there can be no contradiction.

Ever since its beginning Christianity has believed that God has spoken to man in the Bible and, at the same time, that the Holy Spirit must guide the human mind that it may both understand the divine revelation in Scripture and love it.

For man is not only finite; he is also depraved. Sin has affected all men, at all times and in all places, so as to make them inclined to follow error instead of truth, to drift toward evil rather than to excel in goodness.

Above all, man is so sinful that he puts his own interests far ahead of God's honor and the promotion of His cause on earth: many men and women will dismiss the suggestion that they are sinful with the reply that they "have never done anything out of the way, and they fail to realize that their great sin is that "God is not in all their thoughts."

"All have sinned, and fall short of the glory of God," is the fundamental Biblical statement concerning man. This is written in Romans 3:23, but the same thought runs

---

3. In a review of C. S. Braden's *These Also Believe* in *The Christian Century*, July 6, 1949.

through all the Scriptures. "For we are all become as one that is unclean," said the greatest of the Old Testament prophets, "and all our righteousnesses are as a polluted garment: and we all do fade as a leaf; and our iniquities, like the wind, take us away" (Isa. 64:6). "You are," said Jesus, to those Jews who gloried in being Abraham's seed, "of your father the devil, and the lusts of your father it is your will to do" (John 8:44). Neither did Jesus distinguish between bad men and good men as though the latter were to be congratulated because there was so little of imperfection left in them; but, "Every one that committeth sin is the bondservant of sin" (John 8:34).

Isaiah's statement that our iniquities, like the wind, carry us away is but the poetic phrasing of the common scriptural teaching that "the wages of sin is death" (Rom. 6:23); "that God cannot be tempted with evil, and he himself tempteth no man: but each man is tempted when he is drawn away by his own lust and enticed. Then the lust, when it hath conceived, beareth sin; and the sin, when it is full grown, bringeth forth death" (Jas. 1:13-15).

According to Scripture neither sin nor death can possibly be the result of evolution; they are the fruits of a fall. Sin, therefore, is not a disaster, or a weakness to which man is heir as a result of his brute ancestry; quite to the contrary, it is the effect of willful, uncalled-for rebellion against a good God who had created man able to know the will of his Creator and to recognize it as only good, wise, and beneficial.

Thus the Christian religion, the only religion which offers a gospel worthy of the name, begins with condemning man and holding him solely responsible for the evil condition that has him in its iron grip. The Bible is not like a charlatan who puts some salve on a sore spot and calls it whole while underneath a deadly gangrene does its vicious work. It is rather like a surgeon who cuts deeply, but his cutting is an act of kindness because he removes the source of evil.

The very first requisite, therefore, in order to get rid of

evil in its every form is the humble acknowledgment of one's lost condition. "Only acknowledge thine iniquity, that thou hast transgressed against Jehovah thy God" (Jer. 3:13). Salvation begins with David's confession, "Against thee, thee only, have I sinned, and done that which is evil in thy sight; that thou mayest be justified when thou speakest, and be clear when thou judgest" (Psa. 51:4).

When man has arrived at the point where he blames neither God nor his fellow, ill luck nor circumstances, but only himself for his transgressions, he is ready to benefit by the gospel. "For the sacrifices of God are a broken spirit: a broken and contrite heart, O God, thou wilt not despise" (Ps. 51:17).

For only the gospel, in contrast with every so-called "great religion" and every false cult, begins with casting man down in his pride and continues with holding before him the unfathomed, infinite love of God, who being offended, mended the breach in His own Person and at infinite cost.

It has become quite fashionable to refer to the devil, that archenemy of mankind, as to a mythical boomerang, and to speak of hell as a fictitious place to which we lightheartedly consign the enemy.

Back of this lies the hatred of the natural, that is, the sinful heart against divine truth. Ignoring the righteousness of God which cannot tolerate evil, this spirit steps lightly (Christian Science, Modernism) or roughly (Russellism) over Jesus' words, "There shall be the weeping and the gnashing of teeth" (Matt. 8:12). For it ignores or minimizes the Old Testament verdict, so clearly corroborated by the world in which we live today: "The heart is deceitful above all things, and it is exceedingly corrupt: who can know it? I, Jehovah, search the mind, I try the heart, even to give every man ... according to the fruit of his doings" (Jer. 17:9-10). And the New Testament words, "It is appointed unto men once to die, and after this cometh judgment" (Heb. 9:27).

Since this cardinal truth has been tampered with and toned down, Christianity has been gradually diluted to a wishy-washy, help-yourself religiousness, in which Jesus Christ has become the pattern of clean living, just a few steps ahead of the rest of us in moral evolution.

The denial of the deadly character of sin is serious not only because it belittles God's holiness and righteousness; it also detracts from the love of God. Had sin been less enormous, God might have paid a smaller price for the redemption of mankind; but now it was only in the Cross of Christ that "righteousness and peace have kissed each other." The love of God, concerning which we thoughtlessly quote the most famous Bible verse (John 3:16), is so incomparably great: *First,* because it was for sinners that God gave His Son, though God is too pure to have a share in iniquity and can experience only revulsion against sin; *secondly,* because with His only begotten Son God gave His divine all to the point of entering into the sinful human race; and *thirdly,* because God "gave up" the Son "who is in the bosom of the Father" (John 1:18) to the point where He "was made sin on our behalf" (II Cor. 5:21) and "become a curse for us" (Gal. 3:13).

Refusal to accept this gift of infinite love therefore constitutes the greatest sin, whether it be done in blasphemous insolence or in politely passing by the supreme sacrifice. "Is it nothing to you, all ye that pass by? Behold, and see if there be any sorrow like unto my sorrow which is brought upon me, Wherewith Jehovah hath afflicted me in the day of his fierce anger" (Lam. 1:12), "All we like sheep have gone astray; we have turned every one to his own way; and Jehovah hath laid on him the iniquity of us all" (Isa. 53:6). But our Bible is nothing if it is not consistent. God forsooth does not teach that "out of the heart come forth evil thoughts, murders, adulteries, fornications thefts, false witnesses, railings" (Matt. 15:19), only to state in the same breath that man may at any time change his Ethiopian's skin or his leopard's spots and "accept Jesus," as a good proposition which he considers worth his while to look into. Man must be "born anew, born of the Holy Spirit," says the Saviour (John 3:3,5).

Being born again, however, is as much a thing to undergo as is being born of a woman: the beginning of salvation is of God and of Him alone.

> *I sought the Lord, and afterward I knew*
> *He moved my soul to seek Him, seeking me;*
> *It was not I that found, O Saviour true;*
> *No, I was found of Thee.*

Thus the Bible deals with the sinner in true pedagogical style. Having laid the responsibility at man's door, it guards against indifference and false passivity; then, having reminded man that he cannot even begin to save himself, it casts him back upon the Lord as the sole author of his salvation.

This done, the Scriptures give the penitent sinner full encouragement in the words of Jesus: "No man can come to me, except the Father that sent me draw him"; consequently: "and him that cometh to me I will in no wise cast out" (John 6:37, 44). For the Father and the Son cannot but work together.

Let him, therefore, who has seen his sin and dreaded its result rejoice: Jesus Christ is "able to save to the uttermost them that draw near unto God through him" (Heb. 7:25). God is more willing than man is, "not wishing that any should perish, but that all should come to repentance" (II Peter 3:9). The thirst for salvation at His once pierced hands is itself unmistakable evidence of the saving process of the Father, by means of the Son, and applied by the Holy Spirit: "... he that is athirst, let him come: he that will, let him take the water of life freely," is the Bible's final word (Rev. 22:17).

There is another point at which full salvation halts in the case of many who call themselves Christian, yet fail to let their light shine before men.

The word of God does not teach that "the Son of man came to give his life a ransom for many" (Matt. 20:28), only to stop there.

God removes sin as well as its consequence. "If we confess our sins, he is faithful and righteous to forgive us our sins, and to cleanse us from all unrighteousness" (I John 1:9), and "the blood of Jesus his Son cleanseth us from all sin" (1:7).

Today the world is in a worse plight than it has ever been, not because Christianity has failed, but because it has never been seriously put to the test.

For where Christ holds undisputed sway He comes with His law of love, which is the only thing that can destroy hatred; and hate has bred all the world's woe.

Then the Golden Rule is put into practice as well as admired; to do unto men as we would have them do unto us because God requires it results in true altruism, an altruism of individual toward fellow man, of class toward class, of race toward race, of nation toward nation. Had there been a more universal and earnest endeavor to love God with all the heart and had we loved our neighbor as we should love ourselves — in other words, had there been more true Christianity — wars would have been abolished long ago, class hatred would have been a thing of the past, racial antagonism would have disappeared; the Christian nations, rather than exploit the backward races, would have raised them to their own level of abundance for all; the "four freedoms" would have been an accomplished fact after more than nineteen centuries of the Christian religion; religious intolerance among Christians would have been an unknown quantity.

The Scriptures, however, do not promise a gradual and total Christianization, of the world in this age. To the contrary, they warn us that unbelief, selfishness, and greed will wax worse. *"But know this, that in the last days grievous times shall come. For men shall be lovers of self, lovers of money, boastful, haughty, railers, disobedient to parents, unthankful, unholy, without natural affection, implacable, slanderers, without self-control, fierce, no lovers of good, traitors, headstrong, puffed up, lovers of pleasure rather than lovers of God; holding a form of godliness, but having denied the power thereof: from these also turn away"* (II Tim. 3:1-5). (Here is the reason why this book has been written.)

But the Scriptures do promise the visible return of the Son of man in great power and majesty, to judge the living and the dead. Then shall all wrongs be righted. Then shall the righteous shine as the firmament. A new heaven and a new earth will appear out of the conflagration of this old, sin-stricken universe (II Peter 3:10). Then will the Son of man own His disciples, in spite of all the imperfection, and they shall enter with Him into the glory of eternal life (Matt. 10:32; 25:46; I John 3:2). Wars shall be no more (Isa. 2:4) nor tears (Rev. 21:4) " . . . And there shall be no curse any more" (Rev. 22:3). "For Christ, having been once offered to bear the sins of many, shall appear a second time, apart from sin, to them that wait for him, unto salvation" (Heb. 9:28).

Thus our Lord Jesus Christ, Son of God and born of a woman, once slain, now exalted above all, is the center of the Christian religion. It is He who leads us to the Father (John 1:12). It is He who is the Christian's object of loyal service and adoration. And He is Christ Jesus our hope (I Tim. 1:1).

Like Paul, every Christian is a bondservant, that is, a slave, of Christ. But this bondage is true freedom: "If therefore the Son shall make you free, ye shall be free indeed" (John 8:36). For He delivers us from the bondage of Satan and restores us "into the liberty of the glory of the children of God" (Rom. 8:21). This is the true freedom from want and freedom from fear. No evil can touch the Father's children, beloved in Christ. He may chasten, but He will never punish them. He cares for them to the point of having numbered their very hairs (Matt. 10:30), and whatever seems to be to their hurt, He makes to work together to their ultimate gain (Rom. 8:28).

Harassing times are upon us. The present unrest is beyond human ken, and its dire aftermath may well prove past all previous human experience. Today's problems are staggering, and they raise questions of such gigantic proportions that it will call for the accumulated wisdom of the best heads in all lands to bring order out of chaos.

Yet there is one question that is of paramount importance.

More weighty it is than questions of post-war reconstruction.

More pertinent is this question than all the world's quest after peace, goodwill, and mundane happiness.

It is the question that must be answered by every soul in the privacy of the inner chamber.

This question was answered wrongly by him who first asked it; answered wrongly for political reasons; answered wrongly to his everlasting sorrow.

It is the question of the Roman procurator Pontius Pilate.

This question must now be faced by every one who has read through these pages:

"*What shall I do then with Jesus which is called Christ?*" (Matthew 27:22).

> *Will you evade Him as Pilate tried:*
> *Or will you choose Him whate'er betide*
> *What will you do with Jesus?*
> *Neutral you cannot be;*
> *Some day your heart will be asking,*
> *What will He do with me?*

For the Classroom

1. Try to face sincerely the Roman Catholic accusation that Protestantism, by its many splits, has definitely shown that it is the rebellious daughter of the one holy Catholic Church.

2. Do you think the World Council of Churches is the

THE CHRISTIAN RELIGION 389

right answer to the divided condition among the churches? If not, what are your objections to this movement?

3. Do you think it possible (a) over against the many cults, (b) in spite of the hopeless division and confusion of Christendom, to present the true Christian religion in its main tenets, in such a manner that all born-again Christians will assent to the presentation?

4. Has the author, in your opinion, succeeded in doing so in this chapter?

5. Have you personally considered the implications of the final question?

19

THE UNPAID BILLS OF THE CHURCH

There is an old saying to the effect that "the cults are the unpaid bills of the church." This saying contains more than a grain of truth. Elements of truth that have been neglected by the various Christian denominations have not seldom occasioned the rise of cults that unduly stressed such ignored or belittled truths to the point of creating a lopsided religion.

We should here bear in mind the statement of J. Stafford Wright: "The essence of deception is to speak 90 per cent truth and 10 per cent error. If I were a demon, trying to deceive a decent-minded person, I should employ the tactics of 'Lord Haw-Haw' in the Second World War. By speaking a great amount of truth, I should hope to receive acceptance of vital errors. Thus I should propagate good advice and philanthropy, but omit those unique pillars upon which the Christian faith stands, the Deity and Atoning Death of the Lord Jesus Christ, and salvation through faith in Him."[1]

Carl F. H. Henry has pointed to gaps in our evangelical position in his book on *The Uneasy Conscience of Modern Fundamentalism* (1947). We have "not applied the genius of our position constructively to those problems which press most for solution in a social way." We must learn to "press redemptive Christianity as the obvious solution of world problems." If we fail to do this, we can only expect to "continue for a generation or two, even as a vital missionary force, here and there snatching brands

---

1. *Man in the Process of Time*, p. 111.

from the burning"; but we shall forget that we are not only pilgrims, but ambassadors also. So writes Dr. Henry.

Causes of One-Sidedness

There are, no doubt, a number of contributing factors to the one-sidedness of American evangelical Christianity. In the first place, the attacks upon the fundamentals of the Christian faith have been so numerous, so universal, and so subtle, that it is small wonder that, to stem the onrush of an infidelity parading under the guise of an advanced Christianity, the emphasis was laid upon the great, basic, doctrinal truths of the Christian religion. Secondly, the Christian religion upon our continent has been largely influenced by an Anglo-Saxon emphasis upon the practical which has all too often led to a measure of pragmatism. And as a third cause we may perhaps state that intermarriage between people of different national and religious backgrounds and the desire to save all through the Church and for the Church, has in many cases led to the inclination to stress only such doctrinal truths as are held by all and offensive to none. Thus we have developed a type of smallest common-denominator faith that has left little to be believed and less to be taught. Elements of the Christian faith that should have been taught — for Christianity is a way of life based upon a view of life as much as are Communism or Islam — have been sorely belittled. These elements have then been avidly seized upon and lifted upon a pedestal by the cults.

Enter the Cults

We may take the case of Jehovah's Witnesses by way of example. Surely these deluded and fanatic followers of Russell-Rutherford-Knorr distort the teachings of Scripture in a hideous manner. The long-time "Watchtower slave," W. J. Schnell, has stated that the hold which the Watchtower hierarchy has upon its victims is due to the fact that the leaders make it virtually impossible for the followers to read anything but Watchtower distortions of the Bible. These distortions consist of comment upon a few Scriptural teachings wrested from their contexts.

But in spite of that, the fact that the Bible is so continually held up as the sole source of Russellite teaching is a powerful weapon in gaining access to those who look for divine authority. All too many persons have lost all certainty as a result of a widespread teaching and preaching that casts seeking souls back upon a Bible that cannot be trusted because no two scholars are in agreement as to how much is true and how much is mythology or outdated scientific error. Thus from Jehovah's Witnesses we may learn with shame the power of pointing men to the infallibly inspired Scriptures.

Again, dread of the "social gospel" that was widely acclaimed a generation or two ago has perhaps also contributed considerably to the fear of passing off the Christian religion as a "this-world" affair. An extreme Dispensationalism with its times and seasons has taken over and left the impression that "this old world" is tottering near the brink of destruction, and all we are expected to do is to snatch what little may be saved from the imminent universal conflagration.

Christianity, however, has the promise of the life which now is and of that which is to come (I Tim. 4:8), and our Lord has said that He came that men might have life and have it abundantly (John 10:10). The glory of the nations must be carried into the next world (Rev. 21:24).

Brotherly love is a duty for Christianized nations as well as for individuals. John Calvin knew this and therefore sought to impregnate all of Genevan life with the ethical principles of the Bible. John Knox tried to do the same in Scotland. And a generation or two ago Abraham Kuyper with a measure of success related Christianity to the national life and thought in the Netherlands. Toyohiko

UNPAID BILLS OF THE CHURCH

Kagawa in Japan stated as his ideal: "Even though the nations of the West turn their backs on Christ, I stake my all on the adventure to realize Christ's redemptive love in the total life of my land." When Kagawa came to America to advocate Christ's redemptive love as the one possible source of international peace, he was received almost exclusively by Liberals only. American evangelical Christianity must bear the shame of this fact.

That God is "the Lord thy healer," of the body as well as of the soul, is taught clearly both in the Old and the New Testaments. Neglect of this truth is to a large extent responsible for the rise of the many mind- and faith-healing cults that now thrive among us.

Similarly, the ultimate salvation of the soul for and in the next world has been so one-sidedly overemphasized that such an extremely important aspect of human life as the sex-urge has been all but ignored under the influence of a prudish Victorianism. This has left tens of thousands of well-meaning Christians totally unprepared for understanding the Scriptural data regarding marriage and the married life as a symbol of the relationship between Christ and His Church.

The Mormons, on the other hand, in spite of their mistaken notions on polygamy, celestial marriage, and continued procreation in the next life, have made a serious effort to view sex as a God-given talent. They have encouraged dancing as a religious exercise under the prayerful guidance and supervision of bishops and elders. Moreover, the very high standard of Mormon family life has given way to divorce only where intermarriage with those of other faiths has increased.

The practical results of Mormonism in this respect have been superior to those of a pietism that has merely condemned dancing and theater attendance, and has all too often left adolescents to their own devices, such as petting and necking on the side of the road in some youngster's "jalopy."[2]

Again, the Scriptural injunction that it is not sufficient to bid a brother who suffers from want to "go in peace, be ye warmed and filled" (Jas. 2:16) has moved the Mormons to build a co-operative society that is completely self-sufficient and self-supporting, one in which those temporarily in need, rather than being thrown upon the public welfare, are receiving that to which they are entitled by virtue of the time and services they have rendered to "The Church." This action leaves the dole handed out by many diaconates and trustees far behind in effectiveness and value.

In this connection it must be admitted that the movement known as "the social gospel," although undoubtedly one-sided to the point of omitting the doctrinal foundation of the gospel, was in a large measure a reaction against one-sided preaching of theology. What is known as "the order of salvation" has, all too often, been dwelt upon to the exclusion of the ethical, social, and economic implications of the gospel.

And thus we might continue in citing reasons for the rise of cults. We might point to the notorious superficiality of thousands of American pulpits, and to the Liberal ministers who announce a Biblical text and then ignore it by preaching on their own text, never referring again to the "Scripture lesson." We might refer to the Liberals who assert that preaching must be done in the language of the man in the street rather than in the language of the Bible, which abounds in such words as "God's elect," "justification," "sanctification," "regeneration," "redemption," "atonement," "reconciliation," and other theological terms.

---

2. We should be grateful for the fact that the book, *Sex Without Fear*, a publication of Medical Research Press, 136 West 52nd St., New York 19, N. Y., is currently being distributed in quantities by ministers in many denominations.

Or we might mention with equal right the Fundamentalist preachers who seek their strength in activity rather than in thorough study of the Scriptures; who think that they can win men to Christ by a bland repetition of the cry, "Come under the blood, brother!" Is it surprising if well-educated and thinking people shy away from so much superficiality and conclude that the evangelical position is good only for such as are controlled by their emotions?

In the face of such facts as these, is it strange when those who fancy themselves intellectuals, but are religiously without a solid background, fall a prey to the spurious profundity of Christian Science, Rosicrucianism, Theosophy, and its cognate, Zen Buddhism?

And so we might go on to show that the cults are the unpaid bills of the churches. Indeed, this truth may be extended to include those movements and beliefs which are either to the left or to the right of the cults as commonly defined.

To the left, we may cite Marxian Communism. It should not prove difficult to convince sincere Christians that there would have been no Marxian Communism but for the centuries of failure in social morality by the Church. Have not serfdom and slavery, together with all sorts of gross economic injustices, been condoned, if not openly defended, by the Church? Has not all of this had something to do with Marx's *Das Kapital?* Did not, in our own land, orthodox ministers defend the institution of slavery with the Bible in hand? When the Church hides behind the slogan that only "ecclesiastical" matters and disciplinary supervision belong to her realm and when church members of various "social ranks" meet only at the Lord's Table, then is there not some excuse for the term "opiate of the people" and the sarcastic ditty that the Church promises the poor of this world, "Pie in the sky, by and by"?

On the other side, to the right of the cults, we may cite Pentecostalism. This movement embraces various denominations and has enjoyed a phenomenal growth during the last half century.[3]

The Pentecostal movement must not be listed with the unchristian cults, as has sometimes been done, for the core of Pentecostalism is Christian and evangelical. There are certain excrescences on the fringe of Pentecostalism that approach the character of cultism quite closely, but it should be noted that such an overemphasis upon and copying of certain, onetime, temporary workings of the Holy Spirit are directly traceable to the Church's sad neglect of the Person and the work of the Holy Spirit. Despite the truth that the application of Christ's objectively completed work is the immediate result of the Pentecost described in the second chapter of the book of Acts of the Apostles, many churches have for years failed to observe this event, although they have diligently marked Christmas, Holy Week, and Easter on the Church calendar. The objective facts both of Pentecost and of the Return of Christ—the one historical, the other as yet to be enacted—should have been, and ought to be today, annually observed by all genuinely Christian churches.

The Church's Unfinished Task

Time and again movements to combat glaring evils rampant throughout the Christianized nations, such as slavery, prostitution, child labor, racial discrimination, underpayment of employees, sweatshops, and war, have originated in, and received their chief impetus from, the world rather than the Church and church members. The latter have frequently been satisfied with "saving souls," to the sad neglect of the economic and social implications and applications of the Gospel. For hundreds of years the orthodox churches have stressed too one-sidedly the "other-

---

3. Cf. any such work as the *Yearbook of the Churches*, or Frank S. Mead, *Handbook of Denominations in the United States*, or F. E. Maier, *The Religious Bodies of America*.

world" outlook of the Christian religion — contrary to the Old Testament prophets and the New Testament apostles!

It lies, of course, beyond the scope of this book to present suggestions or to submit a program for the application of the social principles revealed by the Word of God.

It should, however, not be deemed out of place for these pages to conclude with the reminder that a full-orbed Christianity must be both purely taught and earnestly practiced. Regarding the teaching, not only must the doctrines of forgiveness of sin and eternal life be taught, but fully as much the principles of holy living, especially as these latter principles bear upon the many ramifications of our highly complex life. And, surely, there is much material in the teaching of our Lord and His apostles.

Regarding the practice, we must remember that Christianity is not only a theory, but also a life. It is now, as it was in the early New Testament days, *The Way* — a way of living that is based upon the revelation concerning God and man in their mutual relationship, a relationship once pure, long since disturbed by sin, but redeemable by the grace that is in Christ Jesus our Lord. Since our Lord has clearly stated that it is not for us to know the times and seasons that will precede His return, we must fight courageously for the recognition of Christian principles in every walk of life. The Christian Church, *whether as an organism or as an organization* (let the distinction be marked!), must, as the corruption-staying salt of the earth, by the impact of Christianity upon a world now sadly torn apart, work for the postponement of the final debacle.

The God who welcomed even the halfhearted repentance of the Ninevites and postponed the destruction of their vast city, who informed Hezekiah that because of his personal godliness the judgment would not fall upon Judah during his lifetime, will also approve our feeble efforts to establish the righteousness that exalts a nation. It is for Him to decide whether these efforts shall prove to the erring nations a savor from death unto death, or a savor from life unto life (II Cor. 2:16).

Above all we should bear in mind that humility and modesty are of the very essence of the Christian religion. No denomination may pride itself upon its orthodoxy and point to the shortcomings of other Christian groups. Even the most conscientious exponent of the gospel of full and free grace may well think twice before he preaches a farewell sermon on the text, "For I did not shrink from declaring to you the whole counsel of God" (Acts 20:27). Every preacher and every denomination suffers, more or less, from personal, racial, and historical bias and limitations.

Yet even the beginner in the faith need not become discouraged in the face of increasing and most subtle attacks upon the Christian religion. The apostle Paul, who reminded Timothy, "Let no man despise thy youth" (I Tim. 4:12), confessed of himself: "Not that we are sufficient of ourselves, to account anything as from ourselves; but our sufficiency is from God; who also made us sufficient as ministers of a new covenant" (II Cor. 3:5, 6).

Thus also, and in this manner only, may God's rule be extended on earth by His loyal servants, and His sovereign dominion exalted to the honor of Him unto whom all power has been given in heaven and on earth, and whom God has appointed King of kings, and Lord of lords.

Bibliography

SELECTED BIBLIOGRAPHY

The following bibliography is a rather complete list of works consulted by the author; it is not meant to be an exhaustive list of references for a study of the cults. The card index of the public libraries in large cities may give some of the titles which are not found here. An asterisk (*) indicates that the source is a pamphlet.

Chapter 1 — The Issue Defined
Atkins, G. G., *Modern Religious Cults and Movements* (New York, 1923).
Burrell, D. J.,*The Religions of the World* (Philadelphia, 1922).
Jones, J. P., *India, Its Life and Thought* (New York, 1911).
Lowman, I., *Non-Christian Religions. A Comparative Study* (Wheaton, Ill.)
Radhakrishnan. *Comparative Studies in Philosophy*. Presented in Honor of His Sixtieth Birthday (New York, 1950).
Thomas, W., *Hinduism Invades America*.
Warfield, B. B., *The Plan of Salvation* (Philadelphia, 1915; Grand Rapids, 1946).
Wright, J. Stafford, *Man in the Process of Time* (Eerdmans, 1956).
Adams, Evangeline, *Astrology, Your Place in the Sun* (1931).

Chapter 2 — Astrology
Adams, Evangeline, *Astrology, Your Place in the Sun* (1931).
———, *Astrology, Your Place Among the Stars* (1937).
Edersheim, Alfred, *Life and Times of Jesus the Messiah*, I, 202-216.
Ramm, Bernard, *The Christian View of Science and Scripture*, (1955), pp. 163-168.
Richter, Carroll, *Astrology and You* (1958).
Rogers, Clement F., *Astrology and Prediction in the Light of History, Science, and Religion* (1948).
Sepharial's Astrology (Philadelphia).
Unger, M. F., *Biblical Demonology* (1952).
Your Personal Astrology Magazine, published quarterly by Star Guidance, Inc., New York.
Articles in the following reference works have been found helpful:
  Christelijke Encyclopedie; Dictionary of the Bible, ed. by J. Hastings, I, 140-149; *Dictionary of the Bible*, ed. by Smith, II, "Magi"; *Encyclopedia Britannica*, 11th ed., "Astrology"; *Encyclopedia of Religion and Ethics*, ed. by J. Hastings, "Sun, Moon, and Stars"; *International Standard Bible Encyclopedia*, ed. by J. Hastings, "Babylon," "Star of the Magi"; *Twentieth Century Encyclopedia of Religious Knowledge*, "Astrology."

Chapter 3 — Spiritism

Colville, W. J., *Universal Spiritualism. Spirit-Communion in All Ages Among All Nations.* (New York, 1906).
Doyle, A. Conan, *The New Revelation* (New York, 1918).
———, *The History of Spiritualism*, 2 vols.
Fox, John, "Spiritist Theologians" in *Princeton Theological Review* (1920).
Hanson, T. F., *Demonology, Or Spiritualism, Ancient and Modern* (Belfast, Me., 1884).
Jones, R. B., *Spiritism in Bible Light* (London, 1921).
Lodge, Sir Oliver, *Raymond; or Life and Death with Examples of the Evidence for the Survival of Memory and Affection After Death* (New York, 1916).
Mind and Matter; The Banner of Light; and other spiritist periodicals.
Panton, D. M., the following pamphlets: *Gnosticism: the Coming Apostasy; The Medium and the Witch; Spiritualism: Its Origin and Character.*
Proskauer, Julien, *The Dead Do Not Talk* (New York, 1946).
Schofield, A. T., M. D., *Modern Spiritism, Its Science and Religion* (Philadelphia, 1920).
Stoddart, Jane T., *The Case Against Spiritualism* (New York, 1909).

Chapter 4 — Theosophy

Besant Annie, *The Changing World* (Chicago, 1910).
———, *Esoteric Christianity; or, The Lesser Mysteries* (Adyar, 1914).
———, *Man's Life in Three Worlds** (Adyar, 1919).
Blavatsky, Helena Petrovna, *The Secret Doctrine*, 3 vols.
Bouwman, H., *Boedhisme en Christendom* (Kampen, 1906).
Cooper, I. S., *Theosophy Simplified** (Krotona, 1919).
De Heer, J., *Anti-Christelijke Stroomingen* (Zeist, 1925).
De Korne, John C., *Chinese Altars to the Unknown God* (Grand Rapids, 1926).
De Purucker, G., *Messages to Conventions and Other Writings on the Poliuis, Work and Purposes of the T. S.* (Covina, Calif., 1943).
Judge, William Q., *The Ocean of Theosophy* (Pasadena, Calif. 1948).
Krishnamurti, *Commentaries on Living*, Vol. I (1956), Vol. II (1958).
Landau, Rom, *God Is My Adventure* (New York, 1936).
Rogers, L. W., *What Theosophy Is** (Chicago).
Sheldon, H. C., *Theosophy and New Thought* (New York, 1916).
Sinnett, A. P. *Nature's Mysteries and How Theosophy Illuminates Them* (Krotona, 1918).
Sloan, Mersene Elon, *Modern Theosophy; An Exposition and a Refutation with Corrective Bible Teaching* (Rome, Ga., 1922).
Williams, Gertrude Marvin, *The Passionate Pilgrim: A Life of Annie Besant* (1931).
———, *Priestess of the Occult: Madame Blavatsky* (New York, 1946).

BIBLIOGRAPHY

A complete list of theosophical publications may be had by addressing the Chicago Theosophical Book Concern for their catalog.
Literature on the Liberal Catholic Church may be ordered from 2041 N. Argyle Ave., Los Angeles, Calif.

Chapter 5 — Christian Science

Beasley, Norman, *The Cross and the Crown in the History of Christian Science* (1952).
———, *The Continuing Spirit* (1956).
"Christian Science," in *20th Century Encyclopedia of Religious Knowledge* (Grand Rapids, 1955).
Eddy, Mary Baker, *Science and Health with Key to the Scriptures.*
———, *Miscellaneous Writings.*
Orcutt, Wm. Dana, *Mary Baker Eddy and Her Books* (Christian Science Publishing Society, 1951).

BIOGRAPHIES OF MRS. EDDY:
Bates, E. J. Sutherland, Ernest, and Dittemore, John V., *Mary Baker Eddy, The Truth and the Tradition* (New York, 1932).
Dakin, E. F., *Mrs. Eddy, The Biography of a Virginal Mind,* published by Scribner's with a pamphlet entitled *The Blight That Failed,* which tells of the attempt to suppress its publication by intimidation on the part of the Christian Scientists.
Eddy, Mary Baker, *Retrospection and Introspection.* An autobiographical sketch by Mrs. Eddy.
Milmine, Georgine, *The Life of Mary Baker Eddy and the History of Christian Science* (1909). This work was bought up and suppressed. The plates were destroyed by arrangement with the publisher.
Powell, Lyman, *Mary Baker Eddy* (1930). Supposed to be an answer to Dakin.
Wilbur, Sibyl, *Life of Mary Baker Eddy.* This is the biography officially approved by the Scientist Church.

REFUTATIONS OF EDDYISM: These are too numerous to mention. Among them are:
Bates, E. S., and Dittemore, John V., *Mary Baker Eddy* (New York, 1932).
Haldeman, I. M., *Christian Science in the Light of Holy Scripture.*
Marsten, F. E., *The Mask of Christian Science* (New York, 1909).
Martin, W. R., and Klann, N. H., *The Christian Science Myth* (Grand Rapids, 1954).
Snowden, J. H., *The Truth About Christian Science.*
Swain, R. L., *The Real Key to Christian Science; a Surprising Discovery* (New Rork, 1917).
Warfield, B. B., *Miracles Yesterday and Today* (Eerdmans, 1954).
Wyckoff, A. C., *The Non-Sense of Christian Science* (New York, 1922).

There is further an endless stream of pamphlets against Christian Science by A. E. Bell, R. E. Neighbor, Wm. Evans, Wm. E. Biederwolf, I. M. Haldeman, J. Ritchie, G. H. Cooper, and others. These may be ordered for propaganda purposes from the Bible Institutes, such as Moody, Los Angeles, Swengel, Pa. Excellent is *The Religio-Medical Masquerade, A Complete Exposure of Christian Science* by F. W. Peabody, LL.B. of the Boston Bar (New New York, 1910, 1915).

Chapter 6 — Rosicrucianism

The literature used in the chapter is from *The Rosicrucian Fellowship* as stated in the text. A rival group is A.M.O.R.C., i.e., *The Ancient and Mystic Order Rosae Crucis* with the "Supreme Temple for North and South America" at Rosicrucian Park, San Jose, Calif. Cecil A. Poole is "Supreme Secretary." They are "neither a religion, nor a creed, nor a church"; just a friendly organization, apparently, to help men gain control of their destiny, and to give every woman "an unseen guide." They number 35,000 members. For a statement of sincerity of purpose, a declaration that you believe in God, or a Divine Mind, or an Architect of the Universe, and that you are "of good moral repute," you may become an aspirant to the Grand Lodge, and receive the monthly *Rosicrucian Digest* and the bi-monthly *Rosicrucian Forum*. There are numerous get-acquainted folders and pamphlets, in attractive form and well illustrated; also such intriguing books (to those on the West Coast, at any rate) as *Lemuria, The Lost Continent of the Pacific*, telling about the first races of man in America, the magic dwellers of Mt. Shasta, etc.

Chapter 7 — Unity

Atkins, Gaius Glenn, *Modern Religious Cults and Movements* (1923).
Dresser, Horatio W., *The Quimby Manuscripts* (1921).
Ferguson, Charles W., *The Confusion of Tongues* (New York, 1929).
Fillmore, Charles, *Christian Healing*.
———, *Talks on Truth*.
Numerous other propaganda books are advertised in *Unity*; propaganda literature is sent upon request from Unity School of Christianity, Kansas City, Mo.
Marden, Orison S., *Peace, Power, and Plenty; Every Man a King*; and numerous other books.
Putnam, C. E., *The Unity School of Christianity and What Its Teachings Reveal** (Chicago, 1921).
Sheldon, Henry C., *Theosophy and New Thought* (1916).
Van Baalen, J. K., "Unity" in *The Challenge of the Cults*, a symposium (Zondervan, 1961).
Zweig, Stefan, *Mental Healers: Mesmer, Eddy, Freud* (1932).

Chapter 8 — Baha'ism

"Baha'ism" in *Encyclopedia of Religion and Ethics*.
"Baha'ism" in *20th Century Encyclopedia of Religious Knowledge* (Grand Rapids, 1955).
Baha'u'llah, *The Book of Assurance* (1924).
Esselmont, J. F., *Baha'u'llah and His Message**
Ferraby, *All Things Made New*, a Comprehensive Outline of the Baha'i Faith (1958).
Miller, Wm. *Baha'ism: Its Origin, History, and Teachings*. Intr. by R. E. Speer (New York, 1931).
Miller, Wm., "The Baha'i Cause Today," in *The Moslem World*, Oct. 1940.
"My Experience in the Baha'i Movement," in *The Sunday School Times*, Aug. 25 - Sept. 15, 1923.

Remey, Charles Mason, *The Baha'i Movement*. A Series of Nineteen Papers Upon the Baha'i Movement (1912).
———, *Observations of a Baha'i Traveler* (1909).
The Baha'i World. A Biennial International Record. Vol. V. 1932-1934 (New York).
The Wisdom of 'Abdu'l Baha. From Addresses Delivered in Paris (1910 - 1911).
White, Ruth, *Baha'i Leads out of the Labyrinth* (1944).
Wilson, S. G., *"Baha'ism and Its Claims* (New York, 1915).
———, "Is Baha'ism Anti-Christian?" in *Bible Magazine*, Aug., 1915.

Chapter 9 — Destiny of America

There is a voluminous literature published in various places.
PRO: Chiefly publications from Destiny Publishers, Haverhill, Mass.; 313 Sherbourne St., Toronto, Ontario, Canada. Also Teggler Bldg., Edmonton, Alberta, Canada. Many pamphlets are issued by The British-Israel Association of Greater Vancouver, 163 W. Hastings St.
Dobbs, F. S., *Israel in the New Testament.**
Goard, Wm. Pascoe, LL.D., F.R.G.S., *The Second Coming of Our Lord.**
Haberman, Frederick, *Tracing Our Ancestors* (St. Petersburg, Fla.).
———, *The Seven Times of Prophecy and the Seventy Weeks of Daniel.*
Harris, Reader, *The Lost Tribes of Israel.**
Houghton, Henry D., *The Marks of Israel.**
Rand, Howard B., *Who Shall Possess Palestine?**
Williams, R. Llewelyn, *God's Great Plan a Guide to the Bible.*
Destiny — The Magazine of National Life, Haverhill, Mass., and *The Interpreter*, a Journal for promulgating the Kingdom of God on Earth. Conrad Gaard, editor, Ruth Gaard, assoc. editor. P.O. Box 619, Tacoma, Wash.; and the radio broadcast *Destiny in America* from Tacoma; *British-Israelism* broadcasts on Sunday noons from Edmonton, Alberta.
CONTRA: A host of brochures and folders, many by the followers of the Scofield Reference Bible, but also by others.
Gispen, W. H., *Het Pyramide Geloof* (Kampen, 1953).
Moyer, Robert, *The British-Israel Delusion** (Minneapolis).
Pollock, A. J., *The British-Israel Theory Briefly Tested by Scripture* (London).
Roadhouse, Rev. W. F., *The Incredibility and Delusion of Anglo-Israelism as Shown by Scholarship and Scripture.*
———, *Puncturing the Pyramid Prophecies** (Toronto).
Smith, William Henry, *The Ten Tribes of Israel Never Lost*. An Answer to the British-Israel Theory. Here also a broad literature on certain phases of our problem may be found. Reference, among others, is made to Dr. Abraham Pieters' *The Ten Tribes in History and Prophecy*. This is perhaps the most scholarly and exhaustive work against the movement by a Vancouver, B. C., professor of theology.

Chapter 10 — Swedenborgianism

The principal works of Swedenborg are these:
Arcana Coelestia
Conjugial Love
Heaven and Hell
Miscellaneous Theological Works
The Divine Love and Wisdom
The Divine Providence
The Four Chief Doctrines
The True Christian Religion

An exhaustive study which mentions many sources is:
Sigstedt, Cyriel Odhner, *The Swedenborg Epic. The Life and Works of Emmanuel Swendenborg* (New York, 1952).

A popular presentation is:
The True Christian Religion.* A digest of Swedenborg's larger work by the same name, prepared originally as a talking book for the blind by Rev. Arthur Wilde, now printed for general distribution by Swedenborg Foundation, Inc., 51 East 42nd St., New York 17, N. Y., 1952.

Chapter 11 — Mormonism

Anderson, N. *Desert Saints.* The Mormon Frontier in Utah. Written by a Mormon "by conversion, not by heredity" (Chicago).

Arbaugh, George, *Revelation in Mormonism* (Chicago, 1932). A good source book in the study of Mormonism, incorporating in its pages the findings of Shook, Lamb, Linn, and others.

Bales, James D., *Apostles or Apostates.* Have the Latter-Day Saints Perverted the New Testament Teaching Concerning Apostles of Christ? (Searcy, Ark., 1944).

Brodie, Fawn M., *No Man Knows My History.* The Life of Joseph Smith, the Mormon Prophet (New York, 1946). Said by reviewer in *The Christian Century,* June 5, 1946, to be "as unprejudiced and honest a study of a baffling character as we are likely to get."

Davis, Inez Smith, *The Story of the Church.* Mormon source, giving special attention to the rift which occurred after the murder of Joseph Smith. 3rd ed. (Independence, Mo.).

Evans, John Henry, *Joseph Smith.* An American Prophet (New York, 1936).

Evans, Bishop R. C., *Forty Years in the Mormon Church. Why I Left It!* (Toronto, Canada, 1920).

Gates, Susan Young, and Widtroe, Leah, *The Life Story of Brigham Young* (1930).

Hall, Thomas Cuming, *The Religious Background of American Culture* (Boston, 1930).

Lamb, M. T., *The Mormons and Their Bible* (Philadelphia, 1903).

Larson, Gustave O., *Prelude to the Kingdom, Mormon Desert Conquest.* A Chapter in American Cooperative Enterprise (Francestown, N. H.). A history of the Mormon movement by a Mormon, centering attention upon the economic and administrative aspects of the great migration to the Salt Lake region, the planting of prosperous communities, and the bringing of 85,000 converts from Europe in the years 1840-87.

Penrose, Charles, *"Mormon" Doctrine Plain and Simple;* or, *Leaves from the Tree of Life* (1897).
Pratt, Parley, *Key to the Science of Theology* (7th ed., Salt Lake City, 1925).
Pryor, Elinor, *And Never Yield.* A novel dealing with the Missouri and Nauvoo phases of the enterprise. Written by a devotee of the cult (New York).
Richards, F. D., *A Compendium of the Doctrines of the Gospel*, 1924 ed.
Shook, Charles A., *American Anthropology Disproving the Book of Mormon* (1916). This is a resumé of Shook's larger work, *Cumorah Revisited.*
———, *The True Origin of the Book of Mormon* (Cincinnati, 1914).
Smith, Joseph, etc., *The Pearl of Great Price.* A selection from their Revelations, Translations, and Narratives (1913).
Snowden, James H., *The Truth about Mormonism* (New York, 1926).
Sorenson, Virginia, *A Little Lower than the Angels* (New York, 1942). A novel by a descendant of early Mormons, describing life in Nauvoo under Joseph Smith, his death, growing friction between Mormons and "Gentiles," and the departure of the former from Illinois. With particular stress on the beginnings of polygamy and its effect upon Mormon family life.
Talmage, James E., *The Articles of Faith* (5th ed., Salt Lake City, 1909).
Taylor, John, *The Mediation and Atonement of Our Lord and Saviour Jesus Christ* (Salt Lake City, 1892).
The Book of Mormon (7th ed., Independence, Mo.).
The Doctrine and Covenants of the Church of Jesus Christ of Latter Day Saints, Containing the Revelations Given to Joseph Smith, Jr., the Prophet, for the Building Up of the Kingdom of God in the Last Days.
Werner, M. R., *Brigham Young* (1925).
Weston, Joseph H., *These Amazing Mormons.* Large size, double-column book, published and republished by the Desert News Co., Salt Lake City. Written by a recent convert to Mormonism, it is very revealing of "how they do it."
Whitmer, David, *An Address to All Believers in Christ.* By a Witness to the Divine Authenticity of the Book of Mormon (Richmond, Mo., 1887; reprinted by Bales Bookstore, Searcy, Ark.,1960).
Young, Ann Eliza (Brigham Young's apostate wife), *Wife No. 19,* or, *A Life in Bondage*, Being a Complete Exposé of Mormonism (1876). This book is bought up by Mormon missionaries and shipped to Utah. It is difficult to obtain and is becoming valuable.
Young, Kimball, *Isn't One Wife Enough?* (New York, 1954). Written by a grandson of Brigham Young. "This scholarly book," writes *Newsweek* magazine, "is filled with astonishing little-known facts."
Numerous pamphlets against Mormonism may be ordered from the American Desert Mission, Inc., P.O. Box 1743, Phoenix, Arizona.

Chapter 12 — Seventh-Day Adventism

Berry, David Anderson, *Seventh-Day Adventism* (Glasgow).
Canright, D. M., *Seventh-Day Adventism Renounced* After an Experience of Twenty-eight Years (Chicago, 1889).
Carson, Gerald, *Cornflake Crusade* (Rinehart, 1957).
Clark, Elmer T., *The Small Sects in America* (Nashville, 1937).
De Korne, J. C., *The Bible and Seventh-Day Adventism*.* The best pamphlet for distribution against S.D.A. (Faith, Prayer, and Tract League, Muskegon Heights, Mich.).
Easton, W., *Seventh-Day Adventists and the Sabbath** (Swengel, Pa.).
Haynes, Carlyle B., *Our Lord's Return*.
———, *What Is Coming*.
and other booklets.
Health. A Doctor's Magazine for Everybody (Mountain View, Calif.).
Hodge, Charles, *Systematic Theology*, Vol. III, pp. 321-348.
Kuyper, Abraham, *Tractaat van den Sabbath* (Amsterdam, 1890).
Leaves of Autumn (Takoma Park).
Liberty. A Magazine of Religious Freedom.
Mauro, Philip, *Concerning the Sabbath*.*
The Ministry. Official Organ of the Ministerial Association of Seventh-Day Adventists. Review and Herald Publ. Assoc.
O'Hair, J. C., *The Sabbath or First Day of Week; Which for the Christian?**
The Present Truth, a semi-monthly by the Review and Herald Publ. Assoc. (Takoma Park).
Putnam, C. E., *Legalism and the Seventh-Day Question** (Chicago).
Signs of the Times, The World's Prophetic Weekly, Pacific Press Publ. Assoc., Mountain View, Calif.
Spicer, W. A., *Our Day in the Light of Prophecy*.
Tait, Asa Oscar, *Heralds of the Morning*.
Warfield, Benjamin B., *The Foundations of the Sabbath in the World of God** (Glasgow, 1918).
The Watchman Magazine (Nashville, Tenn.).
White, Elder, *The Life of William Miller*.
White, Ellen G., *The Ministry of Healing*.
———, *The Great Controversy between Christ and Satan*.
———, *Patriarchs and Prophets*.
and other books.
Literature against several cults may be ordered from Religion Analysis Service, Inc., 902 Hennepin Avenue, Minneapolis, "a specialized False-Isms-Exposing, Soul-Saving Ministry, Evangelical, Denominationally Unrelated." They sell a reprint of Canright's standard work, *S.D.A. Renounced.*, Conradi's *The Founders of the S.D.A. Denomination*, and their own periodical, *The Discerner*.

Mr. Henry Francis Brown, secretary of the Home Missions Department, Michigan Conference of Seventh-Day Adventists, writes: Mr. van Baalen should have read:
Andross, *Story of the Advent Movement* (Review and Herald, 1926).
Dick, Rev. and H., *Founders of the Message* (Review and Herald).

BIBLIOGRAPHY

Froom, Le Roy Edwin, *The Prophetic Faith of Our Fathers* (4 vols., Review and Herald).
Howell, Emma E., *Great Advent Movement* (Review and Herald, 1935).
Loughborough, *Great Second Advent Movement* (Review and Herald, 1892).
Nichol, Francis, D., *The Midnight Cry*: A Defense of William Miller and the Millerites (Review and Herald, 1944).
Olsen, *Origin and Progress* (Review and Herald, 1925).
The Seventh-Day Adventist Bible Commentary, edited by Francis D. Nichol. Vol. I: Pentateuch, 1120 pp. First major effort of S.D.A., to deal with the whole Bible systematically. Six more vols. to follow. (Review and Herald, 1955).
White, Mrs. E. G., *Desire of Ages* (Pacific Press, 1898).
———, *Life Sketches* (Pacific Press, 1915).
White, J. E., *Life Incidents* (1868).
"The Voice of Prophecy" is the name of the "International Radio Broadcast" sponsored by S.D.A. In Canada S.D.A. publications are the work of Signs of the Times Publishing Association, Oshawa, Ontario.

Chapter 13 — Jehovah's Witnesses

The latest work on Jehovah's Witnesses is *Apostles of Denial*, A Thorough Examination of the History, Doctrines, and Claims of the Jehovah's Witnesses, by Edmond Charles Gruss. This work is an unpublished thesis presented to the Department of Systematic Theology at Talbot Theological Seminary, June 1961. This work presents an excellent and up-to-date bibliography.
Sources consulted by the present author include:
PRO: Russell, Charles Taze, *Studies in the Scriptures* (7 vols., Brooklyn, New York).
The Watchtower. Semi-monthly of the Watchtower Bible and Tract Society.
Awake! (successor to the *Golden Age* and *Consolation*).
Cole, Marley, *Jehovah's Witnesses.* The New World Society. (New York, 1955).
Rutherford, J. F., *The Harp of God. Deliverance. Creation. Comfort for the Jews. World Distress.* (Brooklyn, N. Y.)
The New World Translation of the Holy Scriptures, 1955.
Let God Be True, 2nd edition.
Let Your Name Be Sanctified.
CONTRA (Pamphlets): Burridge, J. H., *Pastor Russell's Position and Credentials and His Methods of Interpretation* (New York).
———, *"Pastor" Russell's Date System and Teachings on the Person of Christ, the Atonement, etc.* (New York).
Ross, J. J., *Some Facts and More Facts about the Self-Styled "Pastor" Russell* (Philadelphia).
Gray, James M., *The Errors of Millennial Dawnism* (1920).
———, *Milllennial Dawnism,* or the Blasphemous Religion Which Teaches the Annihilation of Jesus Christ.
Pollock, A. J., *How "Pastor" Russell Died.*
Reid, R. J., *How Russellism Subverts the Faith* (New York).
Metzger, Bruce M., *The Jehovah's Witnesses and Jesus Christ* (Princeton, New Jersey, 1953).

CONTRA (Books):
Haldeman, I. M., *A Great Counterfeit, or, The False and Blasphemous Religion Called Russellism and Millennial Dawnism* (New York).
Mayer, F. E., *Jehovah's Witnesses. An examination of the Religious Tenets*, etc. (St. Louis, 1943).
———, *The Religious Bodies of America* (St. Louis, 1954).
Pike, Royston, *Jehovah's Witnesses. Who They Are. What They Do. What They Teach*, (New York, 1954).
Martin, W. R. and N. H. Klann, *Jehovah of the Watchtower*. This book shows conclusively the continuity between Russell's and Rutherford's teachings. Gives a good bibliography. (Grand Rapids, Mich., 1953).
Schnell, W. J., *Thirty Years a Watch Tower Slave. The Confessions of a Converted Jehovah's Witness* (Grand Rapids, Mich., 1956).
———, *Into the Light of Christianity.* The Basic Doctrines of the Jehovah's Witnesses in the Light of Scripture. Has an excellent chapter on how to convince the Witnesses on the Deity of Christ. (Grand Rapids, Mich., 1959).

Chapter 14 — Moral Re-Armament

Begbie, Harold, *Life Changers*.
Brown, J. C., *The Oxford Group Movement. Is It of God or of Satan?** (Glasgow).
Brunner, Emil, *Meine Begegnung mit der Oxforder Gruppenbewegung* (Basel, 1933).
Clark, Walter Houston, *The Oxford Group, Its History and Significance* (New York, 1951).
Day, Sherwood Sunderland, *The Principles of the Group*.
Howard, Peter, *Ideas Have Legs*.
———, *Innocent Men*.
———, *Fighters Ever*.
———, *Men on Trial*.
Kraan, E. D., *De Buchman-Beweging* (Kampen, 1935).
Landau, Rom, "The Man Whose God Was a Millionaire" in *God Is My Adventure* (New York, 1936).
Layman with a Notebook, *What Is the Oxford Group?* (1933).
Russell, A. J., *For Sinners Only* (New York).
Shields, T. T., *The Oxford Group Movement Analyzed** (Toronto).
Shoemaker, Samuel M. Jr., "House-Parties Across the Continent," article in "Buchmanism Pro and Con" (*The Christian Century*, Aug. 23, 1933).
———, *The Conversion of the Church* (New York, 1932).
———, *Children of the Second Birth* (New York, 1927).
Williamson, Geoffrey, *Inside Buchmanism*. An Independent Inquiry into the Oxford Group Movement and Moral Re-Armament, (New York, 1955).

Additional literature and information on the Movement may be found in:
Christianity Today, Jan., 1934.
New World News. Issued monthly. Published by the Oxford Group — Moral Re-armament — MRA, Inc., Box 1516, Washington, D. C.

Rising Tide, a Buchmanite publication, 61 Gramercy Park, New York City, 1937.
The Banner, Feb. 10, 1934.
The Religious Digest, Oct., 1935, Mar., 1936.

Chapter 15 — Unitarianism-Modernism

Aubrey, Edwin E., *Present Theological Tendencies* (New York, 1936).
Babson, Roger, and Zuver, Dudley, *Can These Bones Live?* (New York, 1945).
Baillie, J., *What Is Christian Civilization?* (New York, 1945).
Barton, Bruce, *The Man Nobody Knows: A Discovery of the Real Jesus* (1925).
Bennett, John C., *Christian Realism* (New York, 1942).
Brown, Wm. Adams, *Pathways to Certainty* (New York, 1930).
Coffin, H. S., *The Meaning of the Cross* (New York, 1931).
Fosdick, Harry Emerson, *The Modern Use of the Bible* (1924).
On Being Fit to Live With ("His final book of sermons") (New York, 1946).
Gifford, William Alva, *The Story of the Faith*: a Survey of Christian History for the Undogmatic (New York, 1946).
Hutchinson, John A., *We Are Not Divided*. A Critical and Historical Study of the Federal Council of Churches, etc. (New York, 1941).
Inge, W. R., *Christian Ethics and Modern Problems* (New York, 1930).
Jefferson, Charles E., *The Character of Paul* (New York, 1924).
Jones, Edgar DeWitt, *The Coming of the Perfect* and 16 other sermons (New York, 1946).
Knight, F. H., and Merriam, T. W., *The Economic Order and Religion* (New York, 1945).
Knox, John, *The Man Christ Jesus* (New York, 1942).
———, *Christ the Lord* (New York, 1945).
MacFarland, Chas. S., *The Spirit Christlike* (1904).
———, *Spiritual Culture and Social Service* (1912).
———, *Across the Years* (1936).
Mathews, Shailer, and Smith, Gerald B., *A Dictionary of Religion and Ethics* (1923).
Niebuhr, Pauck, and Miller, *The Church Against the World* (New York, 1935).
Niebuhr, Reinhold, *The Nature and Destiny of Man* (2 vols., New York, 1941, 1943).
Ogburn, Wm. Fielding, editor, *American Society in Wartime* (Chicago, 1943).
Palmer, Frederic, *The Virgin Birth* (New York, 1924).
Park, Wm. E., *Narrow Is the Way*. Addresses to Students by the President of Northfield Schools (New York, 1945).
Scott, Ernest T., *Man and Society in the N. T.* (New York, 1946).
Sweezey, Geo. S., *The Keeper of the Door*. Sermons (New York, 1946).
Van Dusen, Henry P., *God in These Times* (New York, 1935).
———, Editor, *The Christian Answer* (New York, 1946).
Wishart, A. W., *Evolution and Religion: God in Jesus*; and other sermons (Grand Rapids).

The Christian Century, published weekly. *The Pulpit*, published monthly.

Further, an endless stream of books published without let-up and advertised from week to week. From the other side, either orthodox or at least critical of the liberal position, are:

Barth, Karl, *The Resurrection of the Dead* (New York, 1933).
Bergen, J. T., *Evidences of Christianity* (1916).
Berkhof, L., *Recent Trends in Theology* (Grand Rapids, 1946).
Gordon, Ernest, *The Leaven of the Sadducees* (Chicago, 1926).
Graebner, Theodore, *God and the Cosmos* (3rd ed., Grand Rapids, 1946).
Haas, John A. W., *The Unity of Faith and Knowledge* (New York, 1926).
Henry, Carl F. H., *Remaking the Modern Mind* (Grand Rapids, 1946).
———, *Fifty Years of Protestant Theology* (New York).
Horsch, John, *Modern Religious Liberalism* (Scottdale, Pa., 1921).
Hospers, G. H., *The Reformed Principle of Authority* (Grand Rapids, 1924).
Keyser, Leander S., *The Doctrine of Modernism* (Chicago, 1925).
Knox, John, *Chapters in a Life of Paul* (Nashville, Tenn., 1950). See the review by Dr. N. B. Stonehouse in *Westminster Theological Review*, Nov., 1950.
Kretzmann, P. E., "Modern News About Inspiration" in *The Princeton Theological Review*, April 1929.
Macartney, Clarence, *Twelve Great Questions About Christ* (New York, 1923).
McPherson, G. W., *The Crisis in Church and College* (Yonkers, N. Y., 1919).
———, *The Modern Conflict Over the Bible* (1919).
Mullins, E. Y., *Christianity at the Cross Roads* (New York, 1924).
Nash, Arnold, *The University and the Modern World* (New York, 1944).
Patton, Francis L., *Fundamental Christianity* (New York, 1926).
Ramm, Bernard, *The Christian View of Science and Scripture* (Eerdmans, 1955).
Rimmer, Harry, *Internal Evidence of Inspiration* (Grand Rapids, 1938).
———, *Dead Men Tell Tales* (Berne, Indiana, 1939).
———, *Crying Stones* (Grand Rapids, 1941).
———, *The Magnificence of Jesus* (Grand Rapids, 1943).
———, *That Lawsuit Against the Bible* (Grand Rapids, 1940).
Schaff, Philip, *The Creeds of Christendom* (New York, 1877).
Trueblood, Elton, *The Predicament of Modern Man* (New York, 1945).
———, *Foundations for Reconstruction* (New York, 1946).
Tulga, Chester E., *The Case Against Neo-Orthodoxy* (Chicago, 1951).
Warfield, B. B., *The Lord of Glory* (New York, 1907).
———, *Revelation and Inspiration* (New York, 1929).
Wilson, R. D., *A Scientific Investigation of the Old Testament* (Philadelphia, 1926).
Wood, H. G., *Christianity and Civilization* (New York, 1943).
Zwemer, Samuel M., *The Origin of Religion* (New York, 1935).

General

Anderson, J. N. D., *The World's Religions*. A new handbook presenting a factual survey of Animism, Judaism, Islam, Hinduism, Buddhism, Shintoism, and Confucianism. The author is a lecturer at the University of London, and one of the world's foremost authorities on Islam (Grand Rapids, 1950).

Bach, Marcus, *They Have Found a Faith* (New York, 1946). This book deals with Jehovah's Witnesses; The Four-square Gospel; Spiritualism; Oxford Group-MRA; The Kingdoms of Father Divine; The Baha'i Faith; Unity; Psychiana.

A sequel to this book is: *Faith and My Friends* (New York, 1951). It describes: The Trappist; The Vedantist; The Hutterite; the Penitente; The Swedenborgian. The first and last chapters are called, characteristically: I. "The Right to Believe"; VIII, "Something to Live By."

Braden, Charles Samuel, *These Also Believe* (New York, 1949). The author discusses: The Peace Mission Movement of Father Divine; Psychiana; New Thought; Unity School of Christianity; Christian Science; Theosophy; The I Am Movement; The Liberal Catholic Church; Spiritualism; Jehovah's Witnesses; Anglo-Israel; The Oxford Group Movement; Mormonism.

Bach's book is brilliant and speaks of these movements from the standpoint of one who has spent time with them and reports his findings. Braden's is scholarly and reveals much knowledge of literary sources.

Henry, Carl F. H., *Re-making the Modern Mind* (Grand Rapids, 1946).

Kellogg, S. A., *A Handbook of Comparative Religion*. An authoritative guide to the chief concepts of the world's great religions. Contrasts in their positions on sin, salvation, moral conduct, immortality, etc., with the Christian view (Grand Rapids, 1951, reprint).

Machen, J. G., *Christianity and Liberalism* (Grand Rapids, 1956, reprint).

———, *What Is Faith?* (Grand Rapids, 1956, reprint).

———, *The Christian View of Man* (Grand Rapids, 1947, reprint).

———, *The Christian Faith in the Modern World* (Grand Rapids, 1947, reprint).

———, *The Origin of Paul's Religion* (Grand Rapids, 1947, reprint).

———, *God Transcendent* (Grand Rapids, 1949, reprint).

———, *What Is Christianity?* (Grand Rapids, 1951, reprint).

Dr. Machen's books are among the clearest and best against Modernism.

Martin, Walter R., *The Rise of the Cults* (Grand Rapids, 1955).

Mayer, F. E., *The Religious Bodies of America* (2nd ed., St. Louis, 1955).

Mead, Frank S., *Handbook of Denominations in the United States* (Nashville, 1951). The author is a Methodist and former editor of *The Christian Herald*.

Religion in the Twentieth Century, edited by Vergilius Ferm (New York, 1948). Contains 28 chapters on oriental and occidental religions. Each chapter is written by an outstanding representative of the cult described.

Smith, Wilbur M., *Therefore Stand*. A Plea for a Vigorous Apologetic in the Present Crisis of Evangelical Christianity (Grand Rapids, 1945).

20*th Century Encyclopedia of Religious Knowledge*. It contains articles on "Social Gospel"; "World Council of Churches" (Grand Rapids, 1955).